John Brown

Apostolical Succession in the Light of History and Fact

John Brown

Apostolical Succession in the Light of History and Fact

ISBN/EAN: 9783337254032

Printed in Europe, USA, Canada, Australia, Japan

Cover: Foto ©Lupo / pixelio.de

More available books at **www.hansebooks.com**

APOSTOLICAL SUCCESSION

IN THE

LIGHT OF HISTORY AND FACT

THE CONGREGATIONAL UNION LECTURE FOR 1897

BY

JOHN BROWN, B.A., D.D.,

Minister of the Bunyan Church, Bedford.

LONDON:

Congregational Union of England and Wales

MEMORIAL HALL, FARRINGDON STREET, E.C.

1898.

ADVERTISEMENT

By the Committee of the Congregational Union of England and Wales.

THE Congregational Union Lecture has been established with a view to the promotion of Biblical Science, and Theological and Ecclesiastical Literature.

It is intended that each Lecture shall consist of a course of Prelections delivered at the Memorial Hall, but when the convenience of the Lecturer shall so require, the oral delivery will be dispensed with.

The Committee hope that the Lecture will be maintained in an Annual Series; but they promise to continue it only so long as it seems to be efficiently serving the end for which it was established, or as they have the necessary funds at their disposal.

For the opinions advanced in any of the Lectures, the Lecturer alone will be responsible.

Congregational Memorial Hall,
Farringdon Street, London.

PREFACE

THESE Lectures were prepared at the request of the Committee of the Congregational Union of England and Wales; and portions of them were delivered in the Memorial Hall, Farringdon Street, during the months of November and December, 1897.

The volumes of the Congregational Union Lecture fall into two Series, one commencing in 1833 and continuing on to 1860, the other extending at intervals down to the present time. It is now fifty years since Dr. Samuel Davidson delivered the Lectures in the First Series on "The Ecclesiastical Polity of the New Testament;" and twenty-one years since Dr. Enoch Mellor delivered the Lectures in the Second Series on "Priesthood in the Light of the New Testament." The Lectures here presented, though cognate in subject, proceed upon somewhat different lines, and are intended to deal with the question mainly after the historical manner and from the altered point of view necessitated by the researches and inquiries of the last twenty years.

Those most conversant with the region of inquiry traversed in these pages will best know how extensive yet how intricate it is, and will be most lenient in their judgement of a work which, with all its defects, may yet claim to be the result of prolonged and careful thought; and may plead also that it has had to be carried out amidst the inevitable demands and interruptions of active ministerial life.

I was led to the choice of subject by a growing conviction of the serious evils inflicted upon the religion of Christ by priestly assumption and exclusiveness; and by seeing how great a hindrance these present to that wider Christian brotherhood in this land, which so many good men desire to see.

I have endeavoured in fitting place, as I went along, to acknowledge my obligations to other workers in the same field of service. It is possible, however, that after years of reading and research I am more deeply indebted than I am aware of; I can therefore only express regret beforehand if I should be found unmindful of help, where help may at any time have been received.

I cannot, more than others, claim that I have been able to divest myself altogether of biasing influences arising from private predilection or denominational association. I think I may claim, however, that I have honestly sought to be fair in my treatment of opponents and loyal to the claims of truth. I have endeavoured to serve in such way as I was able the good cause of my Lord and Master, and I humbly commend to His gracious blessing the work I have desired to do for Him and for that Church "which is His Body, the fulness of Him that filleth all in all."

BEDFORD, *January* 3, 1898.

TABLE OF CONTENTS

LECTURE I.

INTRODUCTORY.

	PAGE
The historical investigation of Church Organisation a present question	3
i. Influences favourable to such investigation :—	
The consensus of opinion as to a primitive standard	8
The increase of materials for determining primitive usage	11
The new and better methods of historical inquiry ...	15
ii. The position and authority of the bishop the crucial question...	18
Episcopal claims were challenged from the first ...	21
The discussions on the question at the Council of Trent	23
Further discussion in the 17th century and later ...	26
iii. Apostolical Succession as set forth—	
In the Papal Encyclical of June, 1896...	27
In Canon Gore's *Ministry of the Christian Church* ...	31
One universal Church Organisation hitherto unattained and unattainable	34

LECTURE II.

APOSTOLICAL SUCCESSION — ITS GRAVE UNCERTAINTIES.

Canon Gore's definition tested by the practice of the Church of Alexandria	39

While devolution of authority is declared to be essential—
  i. There is no certainty as to the time and fact of devolution ... 43
  ii. There is no agreement as to the essentials of valid ordination ... 53

LECTURE III.
FURTHER UNCERTAINTIES AND OBJECTIONS.

iii. There is no certainty as to the line of transmission ... 81
iv. As a fact supernatural grace has not been restricted to official lines ... 89
v. The assumptions of the clergy have superseded the self-governing and mutually edifying functions of the Church itself ... 100
vi. Estrangement, exclusiveness, and intolerance have been engendered by clerical pretensions ... 111

LECTURE IV.
EARLIEST FORMS OF CHURCH LIFE.

The question started by Baur and the Tubingen School ... 122
The Discovery of *The Teaching of the Twelve* and its importance ... 124
The twofold division of Church Leaders ... 128
  i. The Universal or Spiritually-endowed ... 129
    Apostles other than the Twelve ... 131
    Prophets the honoured of the Churches ... 133
    Teachers or systematic instructors ... 137
  ii. The local officers of administration ... 139
    Important distinction between the Churches of Judea and the Churches of the Gentiles ... 140
    In the Jewish Churches the officers were presbyters or elders ... 141
    In the Churches of the Gentiles, bishops and deacons 151
As "leaders" was the generic term for apostles, prophets, and teachers, so "presbyters" or "rulers" was the generic term for bishops and deacons when spoken of together ... 153
This shown by the following facts :—
  Where presbyters are spoken of there is no mention of bishops or deacons ... 154
  Where bishops and deacons are mentioned elders are not ... *ib.*
  The general terms are not confused with the particular ... 155

Elders are mentioned in one place and bishops and deacons in another in such a way as to show they mean the same thing ... ... *ib.*
The differentiation of local administrative officers into bishops and deacons as described by Justin Martyr, Tertullian, and the Apostolical Constitutions 157

LECTURE V.

THE IGNATIAN EPISTLES.

The bishop as described by Ignatius 166
  i. The various recensions of the Epistles 169
    The person of the Writer 171
    The question of the Date 179
    The Epistle of Polycarp and its bearing 180
  ii. Granting that the Epistles are genuine what follows?—
    They furnish evidence of the early existence of forms of Church Organisation other than episcopal ... 184
    The bishop as described by Ignatius was not diocesan in character, but simply the pastor of a separate community 187
    There is no trace of the later idea of Apostolical Succession 189
    Neither is there any tinge of sacerdotal language ... 190

LECTURE VI.

THE TRANSITION FROM PROPHET TO PASTOR.

Church Organisation as found in leading cities at the beginning of the second century 199
The process of transition from elders to bishops and deacons in the Jerusalem Church 201
Flight to Pella and settlement in a region where episcopos was the prevailing title of municipal functionaries 203
I. Process of transition as seen in the Church at Corinth:—
  i. In the year 53 the First Epistle to the Corinthians shows the existence of charismatic gifts among the whole body of believers 204
  ii. In the year 95 the Epistle of Clement shows that the Church has come to be organised under the rule of presbyters or elders 209
  iii. From about 150 A.D. we find a presiding bishop in the person first of Primus, and next of Dionysius; the

Epistles of Dionysius showing the same arrangement to obtain in many Churches 211

II. The process by which there came to be a presiding bishop in each Church :—
  i. Dr. Hatch's theory based upon financial considerations —Objections to this view as stated by Loening, Kühl, and Foucart 214
  ii. Professor Ramsay's view basing the pre-eminence of the episcopos on the necessity for intercommunication among the Churches 216
  iii. Both these views defective as taking insufficient note of the internal life and worship of the Church ... 218
  iv. Influences at work tending to place the conduct of teaching and worship in the hands of local leaders :—
    The cessation of charismatic gifts among the general body of believers... 219
    Similar cessation in the case of itinerant apostles, prophets, and teachers ... ... *ib.*
    The increasing spread and prominent influence of the New Testament writings 220
    The germ of the prophet's function already present in the office of presbyter 221
  The Christian bishop or pastor thus succeeded to the function of the New Testament prophet as he had previously succeeded to that of the prophet in Israel 223
  The importance of the prophetic or preaching function in the Christian Church 224

LECTURE VII.

HIERARCHICAL DEVELOPMENTS IN THE CHURCH.

Causes of transition from simple Church life to ecclesiasticism :—
  i. The change of emphasis from spiritual life to orthodox creed as the qualification for admission to the Church 233
  ii. The consequent development of clerical claims inasmuch as the Order of Succession was supposed to guarantee not only the priority of truth over the lateness of falsehood, but also a *certum veritatis charisma* 241
  iii. The ascendancy of the clergy leading to a gradual transition from self-government to centralisation ... 248
Cyprian and the Unity of the Episcopate 249
Positions laid down in his *De Unitate Ecclesiæ* 252

Contents xiii

PAGE

Archbishop Benson's statement of Cyprian's "Theory" ... 254
Abatements of the "Theory" as stated by Cyprian :—
   He held that the bishop derives his authority from the
   people 257
   Also that no one bishop may have authority over another *ib.*
   The facts of Church life never corresponded to the
   "Theory," since there were always orthodox communities
   outside the Catholic Church 258
The self-governing power of the Churches lost in the
centralised power of the bishops, the centralisation being
accelerated by the action of Church Councils 261

LECTURE VIII.

THE IMPERIAL CHURCH.

i. The effect on the development of the priestly idea pro-
   duced by the Union of the Church with the Empire ... 268
   The Church came to be organised on the lines of the
      Empire; the Churches in the chief cities acquiring
      ascendancy over others 272
   The granting of civil immunities to the clergy led to
      their becoming a separate caste; and to the intro-
      duction of unspiritual men into their ranks 274
   The laity fell into a subordinate place 276
   The State repressed by force all opinions and teach-
      ings contrary to the priestly pretensions of the pre-
      vailing Church 278
   The Theodosian Code in its effect on separate Church
      communities in Africa and on the Montanists ... 280
   Later persecutions of Priscillianists and Paulicians ... 283
ii. The effect of contact with Paganism on one side and
   Gnosticism on the other in the development of priestly
   ideas 286
   (1) Heathenism still lingered and heathen men and
      women were forced into the Church by the
      Theodosian Code, bringing their superstitions
      with them 291
      Well-meaning but dangerous concessions were
      made by Church leaders for the purpose of con-
      ciliating the heathen thus forced into the
      Churches ... ... *ib.*
   (2) The influence exerted by the Greek Mysteries
      coming through Gnosticism 294

	PAGE
The connexion between the Mysteries and Gnosticism as seen in the treatise *Pistis Sophia*	296
The superstitious significance which thus came to be attached to Baptism and the Eucharist	297

LECTURE IX.

THE DEVELOPMENT OF THE PAPACY.

Importance of the bishop of Rome to the theory of Apostolical Succession 305
Examination of his claim to supremacy :—
   The bishop at the outset derived his importance from the Church, not the Church from the bishop 306
   The claim to personal authority when first made by Victor was resented by Irenæus and Polycrates 309
   Cyprian's theory of the Unity of the Episcopate prepared the way for the claim of Rome to be regarded as the *Ecclesia principalis* as being the throne of Peter ... 310
   The process by which the lesser Churches became subject to the greater and the greater to the authority of Rome 311
   The growth of spiritual ambition during the forty years' cessation from persecution 312
   The action of the Council of Nicæa by which custom was changed into law 315
   The sixth Canon of Nicæa and its bearing on the existing Patriarchates 316
   The letter of Julius I. as the next landmark in the history of Papal development 319
   The canons of the Council of Sardica 320
   The victory of the Athanasian party over the Arian as a decisive step in development 324
   The formal assertion of universal authority first made by the Roman Decretals commenced by Siricius 325
   The heightening of the power of the Pope by the fall of the Western Empire 327
   The beginning of the Temporal Power of the papacy under Gregory the Great 331
   The claim of Rome to spiritual supremacy contested by the Patriarch of Constantinople 332
Considerations which further diminish the strength of the claim :—
   i. Rome has allowed that claim to be supported by means of frauds and forgeries such as the so-called

Donation of Constantine and the false Decretals of Isidore ... 334
ii. If we accept the claim of the Pope to Apostolic Succession, we must also accept, as authoritative, teachings distinctly opposed to those set forth by the apostles themselves ... 339
iii. The claim of the papacy to Unity and Sanctity cannot be sustained at the bar of History ... 342

LECTURE X.

THE ANGLICAN CHURCH IN TUDOR TIMES.

The continuity of the Anglican Church before and after the Reformation ... 354
The Anglican claim to Apostolical Succession since the separation from Rome is recent and modern, as shown— 358
i. By the formularies of the Church, especially the Prayer Book of 1552, the Ordinal, and the Articles of 1553 360
ii. By the Erastian character of the Establishment, especially as reconstituted under Elizabeth ... 370
iii. By the known opinions of the Elizabethan divines ... 378
iv. By the policy adopted towards the foreign Protestants, and the Presbyterian Churches in the Channel Islands ... 386

LECTURE XI.

THE ANGLICAN CHURCH FROM 1603–1833.

The claim to Apostolical Succession first urged as a counter-claim to that of Presbyterianism ... 399
Bancroft's Sermon at St. Paul's Cross ... 401
Bilson's *Perpetual Government of Christ's Church* ... 402
Apostolical Succession not accepted by Churchmen themselves ... 404
The position of Richard Hooker on the question ... 405
Archbishop Abbot, Richard Field, and Bishop Andrewes ... 408
Foreign Presbyterians instituted to English benefices ... 410
Laud as the reviver of the Apostolical claim ... 412
His censorship of Hall s *Episcopacy Asserted* ... 414
The "ever-memorable John Hales of Eton" ... 417
The overthrow of Episcopacy by the Long Parliament ... 419
The Restoration and the Savoy Conference ... 421
Bishop Cosin and Edward Stillingfleet... 422

	PAGE
The Revolution of 1688 and the Commission on Comprehension	426
Archbishop Wake's Correspondence with foreign Churches	429
The Nonjurors and Apostolical Succession	430
Reform and the "Tracts for the Times"	431
Apostolical Succession as a harbour of refuge...	435
The grounds on which Newman rested the claim	436
His abandonment of Anglicanism for Rome	439
The ultimate seat of authority	440
The Oxford Movement as a reaction from Erastianism	441
The future of Sacerdotalism and of the Free Churches	442
APPENDIX—"A Vindication of the Bull 'Apostolicæ Curæ,' a Letter on Anglican Orders, by the Cardinal Archbishop and Bishops of the Province of Westminster"	447

LECTURE I

INTRODUCTORY

LECTURE I

INTRODUCTORY

"THE historical investigation of the *Origines* of Christianity is a study scarcely second in importance to a philosophical arrangement of its doctrines." These suggestive words of Mark Pattison are true not only of investigations into those facts of our Lord's life, death, and resurrection, which form the foundation of historical Christianity, but also of such inquiries as may be made into the manner in which the Christian Church, as a Divine society, first took its place in history, and in organised form became one of the permanent institutions of human life.

Events in recent years have invested this question of Church organisation with increased interest and importance. The present century had not gone far on its way when, in the Oxford Movement, the Anglican Church took a new departure, and, in a way she had not done before since the Reformation, accentuated her claim to Apostolical Succession. As we might expect, this movement has profoundly affected both the internal condition and the external relations of the National Church. And this in apparently contrary ways. For while on the one hand the ecclesiastical temper has been growing keener, and the line of separation between episcopal and non-episcopal Churches more sharply defined, on the other hand, in certain quarters, there has been a stronger feeling in the direction of Home Reunion than has been known since the days of Archbishop Tillotson and the Comprehension Bill of 1689. And, so far as the foreign relations of the Anglican Church are concerned, there have been more distinct approaches towards friendly feeling with both the Russian and Greek branches of the Eastern Church, and also with the Roman Church, than there have been since the correspondence in 1718 between Archbishop Wake and Dr. Dupin on some form of union between the English and Gallican Churches.

In 1889 the Lambeth Conference of Bishops addressed an Encyclical Letter to the Free Churches suggesting Reunion on certain bases which were set forth. But as the acceptance of the Historic Episcopate was from the outset declared to be indispensable, the Nonconformists felt at once that further consideration must necessarily prove fruitless. While recording their satisfaction at every movement in the direction of catholicity of feeling and conduct, they respectfully replied that they could not thus lightly surrender their own most cherished and sacred convictions or so stultify the struggles and sufferings of their fathers. To those who were best acquainted with the inner life and feeling of the Free Churches it was manifest from the first that the Lambeth overtures were foredoomed to failure.

These events taking place at home were followed by movements of some significance among the Churches abroad. In June, 1894, on the occasion of his Episcopal Jubilee, the Pope addressed an Encyclical Letter to the princes and peoples of the world on the unity of the Church, especially making proposals of Reunion to the Eastern Church on the basis of their acknowledgment of his position as supreme pontiff, highest spiritual and temporal ruler of the Universal Church, sole representative of Christ upon earth, and dispenser of grace. It was not till the autumn of the following year that the Patriarch of Constantinople, with twelve other prelates of the Eastern Church, made reply. The Orthodox Church of the East, they said, is, as always, ready to accept proposals of Union if only the Bishop of Rome will shake off, once for all, the whole series of anti-Evangelical novelties which have been privily brought into his Church. The innovations they point out as objectionable are: the introduction of the "Filioque" into the Creed, the use of unleavened bread, communion in one kind, sprinkling in place of trine immersion; the doctrines of supererogation, of purgatorial fire, and of the Immaculate Conception. As for the claim of primacy, they remind the Pope that it was first made in the pseudo-Clementine writings and supported by the forged decretals of Isidore; and though these documents are now admitted to be spurious even by the Roman Church herself, she has never withdrawn the claim to absolute authority first built upon them. As to infallibility, beyond the Son and Word of God ineffably made man, the Orthodox Eastern Church knows no one as infallible upon earth. Even Peter himself, whose successor the Pope presumes himself to be, thrice denied the Lord, and was twice rebuked by the Apostle Paul. They further remind Leo XIII. how many of the Popes, his predecessors, have been guilty of grievous defection from the Orthodox Faith—how Liberius in the fourth century subscribed an Arian Confession ; how Zosimus in the fifth century approved an heretical confession denying original sin ; how Vigilius in the sixth century was condemned by the Fifth Great Council for false opinions ; and how Honorius, having fallen into heresy, was, in the seventh century, condemned by the Sixth Œcumenical Council.[1] From this reply there was evidently but scant hope of Eastern and Western Churches coming together again. Just as little hope was there of Anglican and Roman becoming one ; for though not a few Anglicans were sighing for recognition on the part of the Pope, the Papal Encyclical of June, 1896, *Satis cognitum*, was followed in September by the Papal Bull, *Apostolicæ Curæ*, formally declaring the Orders of the Anglican clergy to be absolutely null and utterly void.

While in this way the three great hierarchies have been refuting each other's exclusive pretensions, and so justifying the continuous protest of the Free Churches against an unscriptural ecclesiasticism, these Free Churches themselves have been making significant movement in the direction of closer federation and conjoint action. Thus, what with movement and countermovement, advancement of claim and repudiation of claim, the coming nearer together of some Churches and the flying further apart of others, it is not wonderful that people begin to ask more searchingly what is the meaning of it all, and what are the real facts concerned. A shrewd suspicion has come over the minds of not a few that the more closely these facts are investigated the less

---

[1] *Answer of the Great Church of Constantinople to the Papal Encyclical on Union*, edited by the Very Rev. Archimandrite Eustathius Metallinos. Manchester, 1896.

they will be found to bear the construction ecclesiastics seek to put upon them. Questioning and research lead to doubt and unrest, and there is a vague presentiment of impending change. Even so conservative a thinker as Dr. Döllinger came to the conclusion that "signs are not wanting which portend wide and comprehensive changes in the great Churches of the present day. On the one hand the exclusive spirit seeks by every device to widen and deepen the gulf of separation. On the other there is at work in the religious world a growing desire for peace and mutual understanding which is moving bodies, hitherto at variance, if not to unite, at least to live side by side in brotherly love." [1]

It has been said—perhaps it is not too much to say—that the problem which the providence of God and the course of history present to the modern Church for solution is that of the true theory of Church polity; that the great central doctrines of God, of the Trinity and the Person of Christ; of sin in man and grace in God, and of the justification of man by faith—these have received investigation in past ages, and such expression as was possible in œcumenical symbols. And now, while there is a growing feeling after Unity, which is surely a movement from the Spirit of God, it seems as if the time has arrived when a renewed study of the Organisation of the Primitive Church should be of peculiar interest. For if we could only clearly grasp the principles which underlay apostolic methods, by which the narrowness of the Jew and the latitudinarianism of the Gentile were harmonised, and by which, amidst all the national and local diversities of the ancient world, an elastic yet powerful federation

[1] *Addresses on Historical and Literary Subjects*, p. 71.

of Churches was created, it might do much towards helping us to that greater Christian unity after which many are earnestly seeking.

In entering upon this inquiry two facts are in our favour: first, there is a general agreement that the practice of the earliest time, the primitive usage of the Christian Church, should, so far as essential principles are concerned, determine the practice of the Church in subsequent ages. We say, so far as essential principles are concerned, for the details and precise historical conditions of the Primitive Church can no more be reproduced in our own time than the surroundings of the Saxon age can be reproduced in our modern English life. A man cannot unlive his life and go back to the limitations of his childhood, neither can the Church go back in imitative Chinese literalness to the apostolic age. Even if it were possible it would be calamitous. It would show that eighteen centuries of stormy and vigorous life had done nothing for us; had contributed nothing to the deeper knowledge and further unfolding of that infinite truth which the first century gave us. But while this is so, there is a backward look which is a forward note of progress. Professor Freeman contended that in our history as a nation every step in advance has been at the same time a step backwards; that our latest constitution is, amidst all external differences, essentially the same as our earliest; and that every struggle for right and freedom, from the thirteenth century onwards, has simply been a struggle for recovering something old.[1] In like manner, if we study the apostolic age in the true historic spirit, it is not that we may reproduce that

[1] *Historical Essays*, iv. 253.

age in exact mechanical detail. It is that we may learn from its Divine Founder, and from its genesis in the world, what Christianity really is, and what are the eternal principles which constitute its essence—principles which through all vicissitudes of human life and history must ever remain unchanged in their purity and freedom.

With this preliminary understanding as to what we mean by the appeal to apostolic precedent and usage, we may note that it began to be made in very early times, began, indeed, as early as the close of the second century, when the Montanists raised their protest against the changes in the direction of ecclesiasticism then beginning to be introduced. Tertullian, who became a Montanist himself, pleading for the simplicity and spirituality of an earlier time, maintained that that is true in Christianity which was from the beginning, and that that is spurious which was brought in after the beginning. Centuries later this was also the contention of Wickliff, Huss, and the later Reformers. Luther maintained that his was no new doctrine but simply a return to the faith of apostolic times as he could show from Scripture; and when Charles V. entreated the Protestant princes of the Empire not to set up a new religion in the world which had never been heard of before, their reply was that really theirs was the old religion and popery the new. This position was elaborately sustained by Matthias Frankowitsch, the greatest of the Lutheran historians and founder of the Magdeburg Centuries, who in his *Catalogue of Witnesses to the Truth*, preserved the memory of a long line of faithful men who through the ages of darkness had maintained the testimony of the earlier days of light.

The same ground was taken by the Puritans of the sixteenth century and the Nonconformists of the seventeenth; also, which is a fact to be noted, by the leading men of the Anglican Church. Bishop Ken, it will be remembered, declared with pious fervour at the close of life that he died in the faith of the Church before the separation of East and West; an appeal from present to past in which he was followed by his fellow non-jurors. The leaders of the Oxford Movement from the first declared their intention to return to the arrangements of primitive antiquity. In this they were joined by men of the older High Church school, and also, though for different reasons, by Evangelical members of the Church of England. It was a representative of the latter section who urged that, "after the long and varying ages through which Christianity has passed, we should from time to time correct our own impressions and review our own ideas by going back to the clear and indisputable evidence of those early days when light still shone clear and bright from the Divine rays of apostolic truth, and the tones had hardly died away that fell from apostolic lips."

While appeal has thus been made, and is still being made, to primitive life and usage, by representative men of various schools of thought in the National Church, it is significant that similar appeal is also persistently made by those religious communities outside that Church who decline to accept the episcopal system and refuse to concede the priestly claims of its clergy. The Nonconformists of to-day, while in the main following in the steps of those of the sixteenth and seventeenth centuries, distinctly affirm that they do not regard these men as the founders of their system, but trace their ecclesiastical lineage back to apostolic men and primitive times. So that, turn to what period we will or to what point of the ecclesiastical compass we may, there seems to be some sort of agreement on one subject at least. Men of all Churches appear to be in accordance with men of no Church, like Renan, who regarded the story of early Christianity as the most heroic episode in the history of humanity, and who went so far as to say that "never will man display more self-devotion, or a larger love of the ideal than in the hundred and fifty years which rolled away between the sweet Galilean vision under Tiberius and the death of Marcus Aurelius; never was the religious consciousness more eminently creative; never did it lay down with more absolute authority the law of the future."[1]

Another point in our favour is that while there has been growing unanimity in the opinion that the earliest time should be the standard of appeal, the materials for an enlightened judgement as to what that earliest time really was have been increasing on our hands in most surprising and unexpected manner. Niebuhr laid it down that Providence furnishes every generation with the necessary means of arriving at the truth it most needs to know, and for the solution of the doubts it most keenly feels. The question of Church organisation seems to be a case in point. For we are now in possession of new and better manuscripts of important Patristic works of which the text was either corrupt or defective than we were sixty years ago; and what is more important still, entirely new and hitherto unknown primitive Christian writings have come to light which have important bearing on the controversies in which

[1] *Hibbert Lecture*, p. 8.

we are engaged. Perhaps a brief enumeration of the principal gains of the last few years may be of interest, and may help us to realise the improved position we have now attained.

In 1842 the French Minister of Public Instruction, M. Villemain, commissioned Mynoides Mynas, a Greek scholar, to make a collection of such Greek MSS. as might be obtainable from the East. Among those he brought from the monasteries of Mount Athos, and which were deposited in the National Library in Paris, was one which did not receive any special attention at the time. Afterwards, however, it was discovered to be a lost work of Hippolytus in ten books, entitled *The Refutation of all Heresies*. In the interval between the discovery of this MS. and its publication by the Clarendon Press in 1851, Canon Cureton, first in 1845, and more fully in 1849, issued an ancient Syriac Version of the Ignatian Epistles which had been found in the Libyan Desert; and in 1849 also the Armenian Version of these Epistles was for the first time made available by the appearance of Petermann's edition. Then in 1853 the lost ending of the Clementine Homilies was recovered and given to the world by Dressel, who also, in 1857, contributed large additional materials for the Greek and Latin text of the Apostolic Fathers. The Æthiopic version of Hermas, edited by A. d'Abbadie, followed in 1860, and two years later came the memorable publication by Tischendorf of the *Codex Sinaiticus*, which not only gave us an additional early MS. of the New Testament, but also nearly the whole of the "Shepherd" of Hermas and the beginning of the Epistle of Barnabas in the original Greek. In 1875 Bryennios published a complete text of the so-called Epistles of Clement, portions of which had previously been missing ; and there also came to light a complete Syriac version of these Epistles, of which Dr. Lightfoot gave the first full account in 1877. The previous year great interest was excited by the publication of what proved to be the main part of the text of Tatian's Diatessaron, or Harmony of the Four Gospels, of which we had some previous knowledge from Eusebius and other ancient writers. In the second volume of a Collection of Armenian translations of the works of St. Ephraem the Syrian, published by the Mechitarist monks of Venice in 1836, was a work purporting to be an Exposition by St. Ephraem of a Harmony of the Gospels. In 1841 this was translated into Latin by J. P. Aucher, one of the fathers of the Order, but not published. The work still, therefore, remained the exclusive possession of those acquainted with Armenian language and literature, till in 1876 Professor Mösinger, of Salzburg, published a revised edition of Aucher's translation. This commentary, by means of its quotations, puts us largely in possession of Tatian's text and gives positive evidence as to the position the Gospels occupied in his time and as to the text then current.

It was in 1883, however, and in Constantinople, that the most important discovery of all was made—that of the " Didaché or the Teaching of the Twelve Apostles." Of this, from its special bearing on the question of Early Church organisation, more will have to be said hereafter. Later in the same decade, in the winter of 1886-7, as the result of excavations carried on amongst the Christian tombs at Akhmim in Upper Egypt, by the French Archæological Mission, several interesting

Greek documents were found. At the end of the ninth volume of the series of studies in Egyptology and associated matters, published by the Mission, there are portions of no less than three lost Christian works—the Book of Enoch, the Gospel of Peter, and the Apocalypse of Peter. Then in the spring of 1889 a Syriac translation of the whole, or substantially the whole, of the missing Apology of Aristides was discovered by Professor J. Rendel Harris in a volume of Syriac extracts preserved in the library of the Convent of St. Catherine on Mount Sinai; and shortly after Professor J. Armitage Robinson, turning over Latin Passionals at Vienna, came upon a clue which led to the discovery of the greater part of the original Greek text of this Apology, which had been imbedded in the "Life of Barlaam and Josaphat," a religious romance connected with the name of John of Damascus. Finally, in the Library of the Holy Sepulchre at Jerusalem, Professor Rendel Harris made the surprising discovery of the Greek version of the "Acts of the Martyrdom of Perpetua and Felicitas," which he subsequently gave to the world in 1890. The Canons of Hippolytus (c. 218 A.D.) cannot be said to be recent discoveries, seeing they were first mentioned by Wansleben in 1677, but they were not published till 1870, and it was not till Dr. Hans Achelis gave a revised Latin translation of the Arabic text in the series of *Texte und Untersuchungen* that they became really available for scholars. Whether further discoveries are in store for us or not, it is certainly remarkable that within the short space of half a century, and after centuries of oblivion, light should spring upon us from quarters so diverse and so unexpected—from Mount Athos and Mount Sinai; from the monasteries of the Libyan Desert and the Christian tombs at Akhmim; from Mechitarist Fathers in Venice; and from Greek and Armenian monasteries in Jerusalem and the city of Constantine.[1]

Further, it is to be noted that this new material has been accumulating upon our hands at a time when new methods of historical inquiry have begun to prevail, and when the history of the Christian Church is being more closely investigated in its relations to and connexion with the civil and social life of the ancient world. And, while we have thus grown "rich in historical points of view," perhaps it is not too much to say that in our methods of inquiry the controversial spirit has more and more begun to make room for the scientific; and we have the authority of Lord Acton for saying that in the second quarter of this century a new era began for historians, which has made history a very different thing from what it was to the survivors of last century.[2] Not that there is anything specially novel or startling in the newer historical methods. It is simply that the range of vision is widened; that original documents are more relied upon and more critically estimated as to their genuineness and authenticity; that stricter attention is paid to historical sequence and the law of continuity; and that it is required of us in estimating the Past we shall not be unduly influenced by the associations of the Present. This detachment from the current

[1] *Texts and Studies*, edited by J. Armitage Robinson, M.A., vol. i. No. 1.
Urkundenfunde zur Geschichte des christliche Alterthums, G. V. Lechler. Leipzig, 1886.
Present State of Research in Early Church History, Adolf Harnack, 1886.
Tatian's Diatessaron, Henry Wace, M.A., *Expositor*, 2nd ser. vol. ii.
[2] *The Study of History*, a Lecture delivered at Cambridge.

ideas of our own time, in estimating the facts of history, important as it is, is not so easy as it seems. Too often terms are used as if they meant precisely the same thing in the second century they have come to mean in the nineteenth. The term "bishop," for example, has a very different connotation from what it had in the New Testament or even in the Epistles of Ignatius; and it is misleading, to say the least, to speak as some Church writers do of the *See* of Antioch, or the *See* of any other city in the first or second century. For what is so described was simply a single congregation presided over by its own pastor. Even great scholars have not been altogether free from blame in this matter. Dr. Lightfoot, for example, tells us that when Polycarp went to Rome he "might have fallen in with Eleutherus, at this time, or soon after, acting as deacon under bishop Anicetus—the earliest recorded instance of an archdeacon, but destined himself to ascend the papal throne the next but one in succession."[1] As we read this we remember that Lightfoot himself has fixed the probable date of Polycarp's death as early as 154 A.D., and we naturally feel that to speak of an archdeacon and a papal throne at that early date is to introduce modern terms and ideas in a way historically untrue. So, again, when he describes Xystus as "the earliest of those Roman prelates," of whom Irenæus writes to Victor, even the authority of so great a master fails to make us willing to accept the term "prelates" as a satisfactory equivalent for "presbyters," which, according to Eusebius, was the word Irenæus actually used. In this way, without intending to mislead, but simply from the influence of life-long personal associations, subtle

[1] *Apostolic Fathers*, Part ii. vol. i. 435.

suggestions of present modes of thought, and of present institutions which have only come to be what they are through the changes of many centuries, are carried back into a past which these institutions have long since left behind them.

If, as has been suggested, we are on the eve of the next great readjustment of Church life to the circumstances of the time, that readjustment will be greatly facilitated by a more careful investigation of the facts of the past. For to explode error, on whichever side it lies, is to ensure progress. Ideas which in religion and in politics are truths, in history are forces; and we have been reminded that "the greatest changes of which we have had experience as yet are due to our increasing knowledge of history and nature."[1] Institutions and systems based upon unreal foundations may seem for a while to be impregnable; but sooner or later the scientific appeal to history and fact, with its ever-growing influence upon the intelligence of mankind, acts as a powerful solvent upon whatever is unable to stand the test of truth. Unexpected changes come silently, and sometimes even swiftly over institutions which once seemed august, impressive, and all-enduring. Vested interests, social prestige, the long usage of centuries have all to appear and justify themselves before that tribunal of enlightened judgement which is the ultimate court of human appeal. Dr. Döllinger, referring to the familiar symbol of the Church as a ship tossed upon stormy waves, remarks significantly that the ship which will glide peacefully and safely over the billows of the ocean will be that which is not too deeply laden with the burdens of the

[1] Jowett, *Plato* i. 414.

past; and that amongst the reefs and rocks upon which even a three-masted vessel may make shipwreck is the rock of history. Changing the figure from the sailing of a ship to the march of an army, we may recall the eloquent words of one we still sorely miss from among us: "We may hear if we will the solemn tramp of the science of history marching slowly, but marching always to conquest. It is marching in our day almost for the first time into the domain of Christian history. It marches, as the physical sciences have marched, with the firm tread of certainty. In front of it, as in front of the physical sciences, is chaos, behind it is order. We may march in its progress, not only with the confidence of scientific certainty, but also with the confidence of Christian faith. It may show some things to be derived which we thought to be original; and some things to be phantoms which we thought to be realities. But it will add a new chapter to Christian apologetics; it will confirm the divinity of Christianity by showing it to be in harmony with all else we believe to be Divine; its results will take their place among those truths which burn in the souls of men with a fire that cannot be quenched, and light up the darkness of the stormy sea with a light that is never dim."[1]

In all discussions on Church organisation the central point, the stronghold around which the storm of battle has raged, and must continue to rage, is the position and office of the bishop in the Church. The claim he makes for himself, and which is persistently made for him by many of his adherents, is that he is specially commissioned from Heaven to confer some Divine authority, to impart some supernatural power no other

[1] Dr. Hatch's *Hibbert Lecture*, p. 24.

man not duly consecrated can confer or impart; and that in consequence the men he ordains are separated from all other ministers of religion by sharp dividing lines, and placed upon a vantage ground of privilege recognised and accorded by the great Powers of the spiritual universe. The point at issue, therefore, is not a mere question of ecclesiastical jurisdiction or Church arrangement, but of supernatural grace. More than sixty years ago Hurrell Froude asserted that those who separate themselves from the Anglican Communion "separate themselves not only from a decent, orderly, useful society, but from the only Church in this realm which has the right to be quite sure that she has the Lord's body to give to the people."[1] This claim, which has always been challenged, and has never been substantiated, is still repeated. It is still declared that "the English Church offers the supernatural to all who choose to come." It is admitted that Nonconformists hold and affirm the doctrines of the Trinity, the Incarnation, and the Atonement; of sin, redemption, and grace. It is admitted, authoritatively admitted, that they have a valid baptism, and as the Anglican by baptism means regeneration, the creation of spiritual life, an admission is made on the one side which the Nonconformist would shrink with awe from claiming on the other.[2] It is admitted that Nonconformists

[1] Tract No. 4, *Ad populum*. Oxford, September 21, 1833.
[2] Canon Liddon says plainly: "If the non-episcopal bodies have no true Orders they have unquestionably a true baptism, supposing the matter and words of that true sacrament to be truly administered; since lay baptism is of undoubted validity" (*A Father in Christ*, 3rd ed., p. xxxix.). But there is authoritative deliverance as well as individual opinion on this point. In 1809 an action was brought in the Court of Arches against the Rev. J. W. Wickes, rector of Wardley-cum-Belton, for refusing to bury a child which had been baptized by a Congregational minister, when judge-

have a most real religious experience, an experience which no one has a right to question or gainsay—they have all these things which, according to that Divine Revelation which is our only source of knowledge as to the unseen world, constitute the very essence and substance of the supernatural, yet is there an indefinite supernatural something still beyond which the great Lord of all men has specially reserved to one Church by virtue of her episcopal organisation, and which she alone is empowered to offer to all who choose to come. Is she entitled to say this? Is it fact or is it fiction?

It will be seen at once this is no mere academical question devoid of practical issue, but one which vitally affects the relations of the various branches of the Church of Christ to each other. Sacred feelings are wounded and conscientious convictions trampled on by the action taken on a mere question of organisation nowhere insisted on in Scripture. When unfounded assumptions of superiority on the one hand are met by resentment on the other, the brotherliness of Christian life is embittered at its fountains. Priestly pretension has done more than anything else to rend

---

ment was given against the defendant by Sir John Nicholl [Judgement in Kemp *v.* Wickes, pp, 5, 6]. In 1841 a similar suit was brought in the same Court against the Rev. T. S. Escott, vicar of Gedney. No stress was laid by counsel on any supposed clerical claims on the part of the minister baptizing, and therefore the question turned almost entirely on the validity of lay baptism. Sir Herbert Jenner (afterwards Jenner-Fust) gave judgment against Mr. Escott chiefly on the ground that lay baptism was admittedly acknowledged in the Church of England up to 1604, and that the later rubrics had not formally rescinded its acceptance. An appeal was made to the Judicial Committee of the Privy Council, and Lord Brougham gave judgement, July 2, 1842, sustaining the decision of the Arches Court. There, legally, the question still remains. Cf. *Church Quarterly Review*, October, 1887—" Lay Baptism."

the body of Christ. It creates the schism it professes to deprecate. If the question involved were merely one of worldly privilege or social prestige, it might well be passed by for what it is worth. But it is more than that. It is a question as to whether the Christian ministry is a vocation from God, or the work of an official caste like that of the Brahmins; whether religion is a spiritual and inward thing, a life of love and service to God and man, or something mechanical, external, sacramental, dependent upon certain technical qualifications in the person who officiates. It is scarcely too much to say that it is a question on which very largely depends the religious future of the nation, determining whether it shall advance to a broader and more enlightened spiritual life, or whether, as some fear, we shall under priestly influences go back to the ages of superstition, and be, as Milton expresses it, "re-involved in that pitchy cloud of darkness in which we shall never more see the sun of Divine truth again, never hope for cheerful dawn, never more hear the bird of morning sing."

As the whole question of priestly claims turns avowedly on the position held by the bishop in the Church, that position will be the subject of extended critical inquiry hereafter. Meanwhile it is worthy of note that almost as soon as that position was assumed it was challenged, and has since been challenged again and again. The challenge began even as early as the time of Jerome, who taught that originally presbyter and bishop were one and the same, but that afterwards, to prevent divisions and for the sake of order, one was chosen as president and to that extent placed above the other. But it was the Reformation that raised the discussion to practical significance. Even before that great movement became an accomplished fact the question was seething in men's minds. As early as the middle of the fifteenth century John of Goch, the founder of a priory in Mechlin, contended that the presbyter as a sacrificing priest was even higher than the bishop, for his is the highest place who is nearest to Christ, and this the priest is as the leader and dispenser of spiritual benefits to the people. Whatever privileges belonged to the bishop which the priest had not, such as the power to confirm and to confer orders, were either the offspring of custom or of the appointment of the Church; that if bishops alone are said to be successors of the apostles it is so only in respect of custom and enactment, not of Divine appointment. John of Wesel went a step beyond this, inasmuch as he recognised the universal priesthood of all Christians in opposition to that of a separate priestly class. "All Christians," he says, "are anointed by the Holy Spirit. If, therefore, originally all Christians are priests, the clergy do not constitute a special rank as mediators between God and man. The Church does not exist for the sake of the clergy, but the clergy for the sake of the Church."[1] But it was, as we have said, after the Reformation that the controversy about bishops and priests entered upon a more acute phase. Both by the Lutheran and Calvinistic leaders on the Continent the claim of bishops to succeed to the office of the apostles was assailed with vigour. The Calvinists went a step beyond the Lutherans in maintaining that only government by presbyters was in conformity with Scriptural teaching.

[1] *De Dignitate et Potestate Ecclesiastica*, Opp., pp. 748 *sqq.*

So strongly did the discussion take hold of the public mind that the Church of Rome felt it could not remain silent while the very foundations of its system were being overturned, and the question came urgently forward in the deliberations of the Council of Trent. There was, however, far from being unanimity even there among priests and bishops themselves. Paolo Sarpi tells us, some contended that above priesthood there was nothing but jurisdiction on the part of the bishop. Some held that the bishop's function consisted in Order only, some in Jurisdiction only, and some in the union of both. Eventually this third opinion came forth, and was generally approved. This point being reached there was further disputation on the Fifth Article as to whether the Holy Ghost was given in ordination in His proper Person, or only His grace. They disputed much on both sides, but those especially who affirmed grace. Concerning the degree of bishops the question was revived, and the controversy was greater as to whether it was one of Orders merely. Sarpi tells us that many of the Council were weary with hearing so many difficulties started, and "did willingly give ear to those who said they ought to pass them by and speak only in general terms." But the friars protested, and were angry to see in them "a disposition to define Articles and pronounce Anathemas, not understanding the points and abhorring those who would enlighten them."

In a subsequent Congregation of the Council (October 1, 1562) on the discussion as to whether bishops were superior to priests, Michael Oroncuspi, a Spanish divine, said they must distinguish as to whether the bishops were superior *de facto* or *de jure*. Evidently they were *de facto*, for the history of past ages showed the bishops exercising authority and the priests obedience, therefore it was only necessary to discuss the point *de jure*. But it was not clear whether *de jure* meant *jure Pontificio* or *divino*. John Fonseca contended for the latter, affirming that bishops are instituted by Christ, and by His Divine ordination are superior to priests. This superiority he proved to be *jure divino* by authority of many Fathers who say that the bishops do succeed the apostles, and the priests the seventy disciples. After him, Antonius Grossetus, a Dominican friar, argued from the passage in the Acts (xx. 28) that the bishops were bishops by the Holy Ghost, therefore they do not receive their commission from men. No mention is made of their ordainer, but all is attributed to the Holy Ghost. Antonius saw from the faces of his superiors that he had gone too far. "Perceiving that he displeased the Legates by this kind of talk, and some more besides, and fearing some bad encounter, as had happened on other occasions, he excused himself on the ground that he had spoken without premeditation, being carried along by consequence of words and heat of discourse, not remembering that that point was forbidden to be spoken of." Father Laynez maintained that the apostles themselves were ordained bishops not by Christ, but by St. Peter, receiving jurisdiction from him only; and that the bishops were not the successors of the apostles, except that they are in their place, as one bishop succeeds to another, not because they have been ordained by them. The more the infallible Council argued, the less it seemed likely to come to agreement. The Legates protested that they would assist no more in Congregation or Session, and met separately to declare that the institution and superiority of bishops was of right divine. Then came twenty Italian prelates to argue with the Legates. Feeling ran higher and higher, and the tumult proceeded so far that there was fear of grave scandal. Eventually, finding it easier to propound dogmas than to explain them, and to fulminate anathemas than to produce conviction, the Council of Trent, in its twenty-third session, gave forth the Decree of Faith, to which was appended eight anathemas, the seventh of which ran thus : " If any one shall say that Bishops are not superior to Priests, or have not power to confirm and ordain, or that Priests also have the same power . . . let him be anathema." Clearly, if there is an inquiring mind anywhere, anxious to know what the grace is which is conferred by the bishop through ordination, or along what line the bishop himself gets the grace he is supposed to give, he need not look for much light from the deliberations and decisions of the far-famed Council of Trent. Thus in 1563 there was on the one side an authoritative deliverance of the Roman Catholic Church, in Council assembled, declaring to be anathema all and sundry who maintained that a bishop was not superior to a priest ; while on the other side there was one of the Articles of the previous Smalkaldic League of German Protestant Princes of 1537 which laid it down that the difference between presbyter and prelate was not one of Divine institution, but of human arrangement. In the same direction, but going further, was the declaration of the Reformed Churches of Switzerland, France, and the Netherlands to the effect that the Presbyterian system alone is in accordance with the Word of God.

Here the matter rested till the following century,

when another phase of the question was entered upon in the controversy which arose between the Anglican Church on one side, and the English Puritans and the French Reformers on the other. Of all the Protestant Churches the Anglican alone has retained the episcopate in the sense of the Catholic Church, regarding the bishop as the true successor of the apostles, and tracing back his office and his authority in unbroken succession to them. In this contest the question of the genuineness or otherwise of the Ignatian Epistles played an important part. On the one side appeared the Anglican bishops and theologians, Hall (1639), Ussher (1644), Hammond (1651), Pearson (1672), Dodwell (1684), and Bingham (1708); and on the other John Milton (*Of Prelatical Episcopacy*, 1641), Salmasius (1645), Blondel (1646), Daillé (1666), and Vitringa (1694). Out of this controversy grew that of the seventeenth and eighteenth centuries, canonists and Church historians of the Roman Church, such as Natalis Alexander, Thomassinus, Mamachi, and others, using the weapons forged for them by Anglican writers; while in Germany J. H. Böhmer, M. Pfaff, Pertsch, Mosheim, Zieglew, and others, drew their arguments from Salmasius, Blondel, and Daillé. This brings us to the nineteenth century and to the more recent views on Church organisation, associated with such names as those of F. C. Baur, Rothe, Bunsen, Ritschl, Lightfoot, Renan, Hatch, Harnack, Loening, and others, with which we shall be more closely concerned hereafter.[1]

In proceeding to the discussion of present-day aspects of the question of Apostolical Succession, and of the

---

[1] *Die Gemeindeverfassung des Urchristenthums*, Dr. Edgar Loening. Halle, 1888.

previous question of the original foundation of the Church, on which that of Apostolical Succession really rests, perhaps the most satisfactory way of proceeding will be to let some duly qualified exponents of Church theories first speak for themselves. On behalf of the Church of Rome we have such utterances as may be fairly accepted in that Papal Encyclical of June, 1896, to which reference has already been made. This serves our purpose all the better in that while it is meant to be authoritative, it does not rest upon authority alone, but makes its appeal openly to Scripture, reason, primitive usage, and the teachings of the Fathers. The Pope thus steps down, so to speak, from that *Cathedra Petri* on which he sits alone, and enters the intellectual arena open to all men. His end and purpose is, he says, to describe the lineaments of the Church, and he begins by affirming what all will assent to, that in the spiritual world as in the natural God wills to help man by means of man, and that inward blessings are conveyed by external means. Therefore the apostles received a mission to teach by audible and visible signs, for faith cometh by hearing, and hearing by the Word of God. His next step is not so easy to follow, inasmuch as he assumes the one thing which requires to be proved when he says that while heavenly grace is internal the means of obtaining grace are external—that is, the sacraments administered by men specially chosen for that purpose by means of certain ordinances. Christ, he contends, did actually transmit to the Church, that is, to His apostles and their successors, the same mission and the same mandate He Himself had received from the Father : " As the Father hath sent Me, I also send you " ; the Church, therefore, is bound to communicate without stint to all men, and to transmit through all ages, the salvation effected by Jesus Christ and the blessings flowing therefrom.

There is here that subtle confusion between salvation and the message of salvation inherent in all hierarchical systems and the quiet assumption that men are to come into the Church to be saved, instead of their being added to the Church because they are saved. There is also introduced fatal confusion between the spiritual body of Christ and mere external organisation when Leo XIII. affirms that the members of scattered and separated communities cannot possibly cohere with the Head so as to make one body; separated from the Head they must of necessity die. The Church of Christ is one and the same for ever : those who leave it depart from the will and command of Christ the Lord ; leaving the path of salvation they enter on that of perdition. In other words, we are asked to believe that if a man should leave a given form of Church organisation, which has changed and, in his opinion, grown corrupt, for one which seems more spiritual and more in accordance with the mind of Christ, it is all the same as if he had cut himself off from Christ Himself.

There must be one organisation under one visible head, says the Pope ; and in order to the unity of the Body there must be unity of Faith. But unity of Faith there cannot be if Faith is left to the human intellect, for then there will be various and contradictory interpretations. Therefore Christ commanded that the teaching of the apostles should be religiously accepted and piously kept as if it were His own. Then as these apostles, like all other men, were under the universal law of dissolution by death, it was provided of God that the *magisterium* (or teaching authority) should be perpetuated by being delivered from hand to hand. For the apostles consecrated bishops, and each one appointed those who were to succeed them immediately in the ministry of the Word. Wherefore Christ instituted in the Church a *living, authoritative,* and *permanent magisterium,* and willed and ordered under the gravest penalties that its teachings should be received as if they were His own. Whatever is declared on this authority to be contained in the deposit of Divine Revelation must be believed by every one as true. No one can reject any one of such truths without by the very fact falling into heresy, separating himself from Christ, and repudiating in one sweeping act the whole of Christian teaching. As to the sanctifying and saving of mankind, faith alone cannot compass so great, excellent, and important an end. There must needs be also the fitting and devout worship of God, which is to be found chiefly in the Divine Sacrifice and in the dispensation of the Sacraments, as well as salutary laws and discipline. All these must be found in the Church. The power of performing and administering these Divine mysteries, together with the authority of ruling and governing, was not bestowed by God on all Christians indiscriminately, but on certain chosen persons. For to the apostles and their legitimate successors alone these words were spoken: "Going into the whole world, preach the Gospel"; "baptizing them"; "do this in commemoration of Me"; "whose sins you shall forgive, they are forgiven them."

Up to this point we may assume that Roman and Anglican are well agreed. A bishop of the English

Church, who was also chairman of the Church Historical Society, described "the earlier parts of the Encyclical as an admirable exposition of the foundation of the Church on Jesus Christ and of the devolution of power upon the apostles generally, and from them to their successors in due course." The Pope is admirable, he thinks, when he denounces non-episcopal churches, not so admirable when he asserts the primacy of Peter, and shows that the Anglican Church has gone as far wrong as Presbyterians and Congregationalists. You must have a visible head, says Leo; no perfect human society can be conceived of without it. Since Christ willed that His kingdom should be visible, He was obliged (*sic*) when He ascended into heaven to designate a vicegerent on earth. Thus ignoring important aspects of Scripture truth, the Pope arrives at the universal jurisdiction of Peter and Peter's successors with all the unfounded assumptions and unhistorical assertions therein involved. Having reached this point in this far from satisfactory manner, he concludes by disavowing the validity of all ministerial Orders not sanctioned by his own Church. "It must be clearly understood," he says, "that bishops are deprived of the right and power of ruling if they deliberately secede from Peter and his successors; because by this secession they are separated from the foundation on which the whole edifice must rest. They are, therefore, outside the edifice itself. . . . The Episcopal Order is rightly judged to be in communion with Peter, otherwise it necessarily becomes a lawless and disorderly crowd (*multitudo confusa ac perturbata*)".

Such is the Roman position as stated by the highest authority of that Church; let us now see what are the views held by the clergy of the more advanced section of the Anglican Church. Of these Canon Gore's work on *The Ministry of the Christian Church* may be taken as fairly representative. In the opening chapter on the "Foundation of the Church," he sets forth with the question, Did Christ found a Church in the sense of a visible society? All will agree with him as he proceeds to show that the Divine Founder of Christianity instituted a society, a brotherhood into which His disciples should be incorporated; that the early Christians themselves believed that Christ had founded such a society or brotherhood; and that the outside heathen world regarded the Christians as belonging to such a community. For this conception pervades the New Testament. Everywhere, writ large, is the thought of that kingdom of God, which "is the Church expressed in the terms and mind and person of its Founder; and of that Church of God which is the kingdom done into living souls and the society they constitute."[1]

We not only concede this to Canon Gore, we earnestly maintain it, but quite as earnestly we maintain that our Lord has nowhere authoritatively prescribed one definite organisation for the Church He instituted. The one cardinal, vitiating error of Canon Gore, as it is that of the school he represents, is that he persists in confounding a spiritual community, which became a society by virtue of a Divine life, with one definite form of organisation, which as a simple matter of history came into existence generations after the time of the apostles, and is the product of a variety of forces and of a succession of important changes. So far as we know our

[1] Fairbairn's *Christ in Modern Theology*, p. 529.

Lord said almost nothing on the subject. He prescribed an organisation for His Church in the sense in which it may be said that God prescribed the erection of cities, by planting in the heart of man the need of association with his fellow-man.

As this may possibly be looked upon merely as an *ex parte* judgement, it may be well to sustain it by the opinion of one of the ablest New Testament scholars of Canon Gore's own Church. Dr. Hort is very explicit on the point: " In the apostolic age," he says, "the offices instituted in the Ecclesia were the creation of successive experiences and changes of circumstances, involving at the same time a partial adoption first of Jewish precedents by the Ecclesia of Judea, and then apparently of Judean Christian precedents by the Ecclesiæ of the Dispersion and the Gentiles. There is no trace in the New Testament that any ordinances on this subject were prescribed by the Lord, or that any such ordinances were set up as permanently binding by the Twelve or by St. Paul, or by the Ecclesia at large. Their faith in the Holy Spirit and His perpetual guidance was too much of a reality to make that possible." [1]

When Pentecost had completed the gift of the Divine Son by the gift of the Divine Spirit, the disciples consorted together, not because their Lord had prescribed a definite constitution, forms of government, official persons and order of worship. Still less did they form a society merely because the spirit of association was in the air, and clubs and guilds were a secular feature of

---

[1] *The Christian Ecclesia*, a Course of Lectures, by F. J. A. Hort, D.D., Lady Margaret's Reader in Divinity in the University of Cambridge, 1897, p. 230.

the time. They came together and were of one heart and soul because of the deep necessities of the new life created within them by the Spirit of God—a life drawn from the common fountain of life which is in Christ. They shared the same joy of forgiveness, the same dignity of sonship as children of God ; they were heirs together of the same heavenly inheritance, and comrades side by side in the same great crusade for Christ. With so many spiritual influences all working in the same direction, the marvel would have been had they kept apart. The uniting force was vital, not institutional. Life came first and, as elsewhere, organism grew out of life. Life and freedom, not officialism and ecclesiasticism, were the notes of the new brotherhood. By a new birth of the Spirit through a living faith in Christ, they became an elect race, a royal priesthood, a holy nation, a people for God's own possession, and they became all this that they might show forth the excellences of Him who called them out of darkness into His marvellous light.

While arguing strenuously for one definite form of Church organisation, Canon Gore seems all at once to be haunted by a misgiving that he is proving too much —that while he is arguing against Free Church communities he is giving away his own Church to the Romanist, who can very easily turn his arguments against himself. Recalling himself, therefore, and turning round, he contends truly, but inconsistently enough, that when under the influence of the papacy "the primary conception of the Unity of the Church became that of *Unity of Government*, the sort of unity which most readily submits itself to secular tests, the dominant idea became that of authority," and, as a consequence, "the idea of the Church became in a measure secularised."

He might have gone further than this. When the primary conception of the Unity of the Church is merely that of Unity of Government, not only is the Church idea secularised, it is also narrowed intolerably. The idea of the Church as found in the New Testament is truly sublime. It is that of a great spiritual community composed of men from all lands and nationalities and from all the ages of time. To accept either the Roman or Anglican organisation as being exclusively the body of Christ is to do the true Church of God a serious wrong, "itself being so majestical." And of the two the Anglican conception of the Church is poorer and smaller than that of the Roman, and carries with it the incurable taint of its connexion with the State. For it is stamped with the narrow insularity of our national feeling, a feeling as self-contained and almost as exclusive as that which marked even the Jewish people in the days of old. On the other hand the mediæval idea of the Unity of the Church, though impracticable, was yet a noble and beautiful vision. It was the idea of a Church co-extensive with the Christian name, ruled by a power which was supposed to rest its rights and draw its influence from a sphere beyond this world. But even then the organisation never comprehended the whole of Christendom or approached the grandeur of the Scriptural and spiritual idea. The Church was never one organised society in any natural sense, never as a complete whole acted together with unity of effort or of will. There was no such thing as a Council strictly œcumenical or a creed strictly Catholic. Even when the so-called Catholic Church was at the height of its grandeur and power the great Eastern Church was outside its borders. Twice over, the idea of a vast external unity rose as a dazzling vision before the mind of the West. The coronation of Charles the Great by the Pope, and the setting up thus of the Holy Roman Empire, more than a thousand years ago, had root in the ideal aspirations of men's hearts, in the yearning for universal brotherhood which Christianity had taught mankind. It has been described as an attempt to express in the form of outward organisation the belief in the unity of Christendom, and to set up by the side of a Catholic Church which was to care for the souls of all Christian people, a universal Empire which was to rule their bodies. But it did not succeed. When the strong hand of Charles was withdrawn the national feeling of the various peoples rose against the tendency to centralisation, and the unity embodied in the Empire broke up into separate States. This having failed, the idea of a Holy Roman Empire gave place to the idea of a Holy Roman Church, to an attempt to combine these States once more into a theocracy under the rule of the Pope. In the days of Hildebrand the attempt was made to bring back the brightest age of the Church. It was a splendid dream, but it was only a dream. The Papacy became a great political institution, as every Church must which enters into alliance with the State; and its spiritual significance became merged in its worldly importance. Becoming thus secularised, the Church had to face the growing feeling of nationality, which was the rising enemy of the mediæval system; and the attempt to weld the nations into one great confederacy over which the Pope should preside only brought to light how great a gulf had been slowly widening between the aims of the Papacy and the aspirations of Europe. The development of national life among the nations of the West overthrew the project of one great religious organisation which should embrace all the peoples of Christendom. Pretensions on the one side provoked resistance on the other. Pope excommunicated king and king made a prisoner of the Pope. "The drama of Anagni is to be set against the drama of Canossa."[1] The Great Schism which followed and the seventy years' captivity of Avignon were the beginning of the end. The dream was dreamed out, and the vision of a united Christendom under a visible Vicar of Christ vanished for ever!

Creighton's *History of the Papacy*, i. 28.

LECTURE II

APOSTOLICAL SUCCESSION — ITS GRAVE UNCERTAINTIES

LECTURE II

APOSTOLICAL SUCCESSION—ITS GRAVE
UNCERTAINTIES

AFTER giving his conception of the Church as an organised society, Canon Gore, in a chapter on Apostolic Succession, next sets forth his theory of the ministry of the Church. Adopting the deductive method and proceeding by way of hypothesis, he deals largely in suppositions. Let it be supposed, he says, that Christ in founding His Church founded also a ministry in the Church in the persons of His apostles. These apostles must be supposed to have had a temporary function in their capacity as founders under Christ. But underlying this function was another—a pastorate of souls, a stewardship of Divine mysteries. This office instituted in their persons was intended to become perpetual, and that by being transmitted from its first depositaries. It was thus intended that there should be in every Church and in each generation an authoritative stewardship of the grace and truth which came by Jesus Christ, and a recognised power to transmit it, derived from above by apostolic descent. Those to whom this stewardship was transmitted might indeed fitly be elected by those to whom they were to minister, and so their ministry would express the representative principle: "but their authority to minister in whatever capacity, their qualifying consecration, was to come from above, in such sense that no ministerial act could be regarded as *valid*—that is, as having the security of the Divine covenant about it—unless it was performed under the shelter of a commission received by transmission of the original pastoral authority which had been delegated by Christ Himself to His apostles" (p. 71). "This," he adds, "is what is understood by the apostolic succession of the ministry."

He introduces, however, this qualifying expression: " It is a matter of very great importance—as will appear farther on—to exalt the principle of the apostolic succession above the question of the exact form of the ministry in which the principle has expressed itself" (p. 72). He speaks thus cautiously because " farther on " he is confronted with what is for him the perplexing case of the Church of Alexandria, where not only is the " exact form of the ministry " for which he contends not to be found till the beginning of the fourth century, but where on the hard rock of fact, so far at least as that Church is concerned, "the *principle* of the Apostolic Succession," as well as the " exact form of the ministry " for which he contends, is seriously wrecked. A few explanatory words will suffice to set this matter clearly before us.

Eutychius, who was himself Patriarch of Alexandria in the tenth century, states that " there were no bishops in the whole of provincial Egypt until the time of the Patriarch Demetrius "—that is, until 188 A.D. He also tells us that at Alexandria " Mark the Evangelist constituted twelve presbyters, to remain together with the patriarch in such wise that when the patriarchate became vacant they might choose one of the twelve presbyters, upon whose head the remaining eleven might lay their hands, bless him and create him patriarch; and should after this choose some other man to supply the place of the promoted presbyter, so that the presbytery should always consist of twelve. This constitution concerning the presbyters, namely, that they should create the patriarch from among themselves, remained in force till the time of the patriarch Alexander, who was of the 318"—that is, one of those present at the first great Council of Nicæa. To the same effect and quite as decisively Jerome, writing (c. 412 A.D.) to Evangelus, says: "For even at Alexandria, from the time of Mark the Evangelist until the episcopate of Heraklas and Dionysius, the presbyters always named as bishop one of their own number chosen by themselves, and set him in a more exalted position, just as an army elects a general, or as deacons appoint one of themselves, whom they know to be diligent, and call him archdeacon" (*Ep.* lxvi.). Jerome uses the term "bishop" instead of "patriarch" because by the fifth century this term had become general; otherwise his testimony is in complete accord with that of Eutychius. Here, then, in the case of one of the most important Churches of the Early Christian world, and for nearly three hundred years after Pentecost, there was no bishop but only a body of twelve presbyters. Further, these presbyters were accustomed to choose a president from among themselves, whom they designated patriarch, upon whom they laid hands and blessed him, and so created him patriarch. There was, therefore, no devolution of authority from above, but delegation from below, and in this important case the whole theory of Apostolical Succession falls hopelessly to pieces.

The passage from Eutychius was first published by Selden with a commentary. An attempt was made to refute him, first by Abraham Echellensis, and afterwards by Renaudot and Le Quien. Still the awkward fact remains. By way of explanation Canon Gore quotes Dr. Lightfoot, who says that the succession at Alexandria was not a succession of bishops but of the heads of the Catechetical School; but it may be replied that a succession of that kind is no more Apostolical Succession in the ecclesiastical sense than would be the succession of a series of heads of colleges. As to the most perplexing fact of all, that the presbyters ordained the patriarch and not the patriarch the presbyters, Canon Gore has a theory which may be satisfactory to himself but can scarcely be so to his readers. He thinks these presbyters themselves must have been ordained, *ex hypothesi*, "on the understanding that under certain circumstances they might be called, by simple election, to execute the bishop's office. They were not only presbyters with the ordinary commission of the presbyter, but also bishops *in posse*. Elsewhere there were two distinct ordinations, one making a man a bishop and another a presbyter; at Alexandria there was only one ordination which made a man a presbyter and potential bishop" (p. 143). This scarcely rises above the character of ingenious guess-work, and may be described as an attempted accommodation of fact to theory which, if permissible, would no doubt clear many difficulties out of the way.

Leaving the case of Alexandria, however, Canon Gore maintains that the vital point is that ordination is conferred, and that episcopal powers are not assumed by the individual for himself, but conveyed to him by the Church: "for this is the Church principle, that no ministry is valid which is assumed, which the man takes upon himself, or which is merely delegated to him from below. That ministerial act alone is valid which is covered by a ministerial commission received from above by succession from the apostles. This is part of the great principle of tradition" (p. 74).

Thus, then, the main thing being devolution of authority from above, manifestly the *starting-point* of devolution is all-important. *When* was it begun? *By* whom, and *to* whom was it first given?

I.

It must be noticed at the outset that while everything is made to depend upon devolution, *there is no agreement or certainty as to when or how it began.* Sarpi tells us that one of the divines at the Council of Trent maintained that power and commission were first delegated by Christ at the celebration of the Supper before His Crucifixion. "Having consecrated the bread," he says, "He gave it to His disciples who then were laics, and represented the whole people, commanding that they should all eat of it; afterwards He ordained them priests in these words: 'Do this in remembrance of Me'; and in the end He consecrated the cup and gave it to them now consecrated priests." This suggestion, however, met with not much acceptance: "The wiser sort," says Sarpi, "did lightly pass over this kind of argument." Morinus traces the matter much further back. "The Most High," he says, "came down on Mount Sinai and consecrated Moses; Moses laid hands upon Aaron;

Aaron upon his sons; his sons' successors upon those that followed them until John the Baptist; John laid his hands upon our Saviour; our Saviour upon His apostles; His apostles on the bishops that succeeded them; and they ever since on those who are admitted into Holy Orders."[1] Bishop Beveridge was of opinion that the actual power was conferred at the precise moment when, as John tells us (xx. 22, 23), Jesus appeared in the midst of the disciples and said: "Peace be unto you: as the Father hath sent Me, even so send I you. And when He had said this, He breathed on them, and saith unto them, Receive ye the Holy Ghost: whose soever sins ye forgive, they are forgiven unto them; whose soever sins ye retain, they are retained." Beveridge adds: "Now were the keys of the kingdom of heaven, according to His promise, given to the apostles. All sacerdotal power was now conferred upon the apostles, even whatever is necessary to the government and edification of the Church unto the world's end." Archer Butler accepts this view and gives it philosophic explanation as follows: "As 'breathing the breath' of natural life into the first man God gave him by a single act a power thenceforward physically transmissive through the whole immense series of the human race, so (with evident allusion to that act) breathing on the apostles the Holy Ghost, He conferred once for all a spiritual power, analogously transmissive to innumerable spiritual successors." The present Pope, on the other hand, in his recent Encyclical, lays more stress on the sending referred to than on the breathing: "What did

---

[1] *De Ordinationibus Maronitarum.* Quoted by Prebendary F. C. Harrington, *Apostolical Succession*, 1847, p. 34; and described by him as "a very beautiful and curious remark."

Christ the Lord ask? What did He wish in regard to the Church founded, or about to be founded? This: to transmit to it the same mission and the same mandate which He had received from the Father, that they should be perpetuated. This He clearly resolved to do; this He actually did. 'As the Father hath sent Me, I also send you' (John xx. 21); 'as Thou hast sent Me into the world, I also have sent them into the world' (John xvii. 18)." The ground thus taken by Leo XIII. is taken also by the advocates of Apostolic Succession in the Anglican Church. Mr. Haddan says: "The doctrine as held by the Church is that a supernatural work should need supernatural sanctions; and that which is rightly held to be the grace of Orders, and not a merely outward appointment, should be transmitted by those only who have themselves, in succession, received that grace, and the authority to transmit it from its one original source. The doctrine so stated rests upon the commission given by our Lord to the apostles: "As My Father hath sent Me, I also send you;' and again, ' Receive ye the Holy Ghost.'" Canon Gore also says there was a ministerial commission given apparently on this occasion, recorded by St. John. The opening words, 'As My Father hath sent Me, even so send I you," contain a manifest reference to the apostolate, and the subsequent act of breathing, with the words accompanying, seems to be the actual bestowal in power and spirit of " the keys of the kingdom." " What is bestowed is a judicial power with a supernatural sanction—the power, in pursuance of Christ's redemptive mission, to admit men into the new covenant of absolution, and to exclude them from it according to considerations of their moral fitness."

In the main, then, it is agreed that it is to this recorded

appearance of Christ to His disciples we are to look as the fountain and source of that devolved authority and grace claimed in Apostolic Succession. Let us, therefore, examine this a little more closely. The first thing to be noted is that our Lord used two different verbs in describing the sending forth of Himself and His disciples: "As the Father hath sent [ἀπέσταλκέ] Me, I also send [πέμπω] you." On this Dr. Westcott remarks: "The contrast between the verbs (ἀποστέλλω, πέμπω) in the two clauses is obviously significant. Both verbs are used of the mission of the Son and of the mission of believers, but with distinct meanings. The former (ἀποστέλλω) corresponds with the idea of our own words 'despatch' and 'envoy,' and conveys the accessory notions of a special commission, and so far of a delegated authority in the person sent. The simple verb, πέμπω" (the word used of the disciples), "marks nothing more than the immediate relation of the sender to the sent." After tracing the varied use of the words, Dr. Westcott says that the general result of the examination "seems to be that in this charge the Lord presents His own mission as the one abiding mission of the Father; *this He fulfils through His Church.* His disciples receive no new commission, but carry out His."[1]

So far, then, as the mere words are concerned, they do not necessarily imply the bestowal of supernatural grace or exclusive authority upon a priestly caste. The conviction that they do not is strengthened when we pass from the words themselves to the occasion on which, and the people to whom, they were spoken. The facts seem to show they were not spoken exclusively to the Twelve, but to the general body of the disciples. It

[1] *Gospel of St. John*, Additional Note on chap. xx. 21, p. 298.

will be admitted that the appearance of our Lord to
His disciples described by Luke (xxiv. 36 *sq.*) is the same
as that recorded by John in the passage under consideration (xx. 19 *sq.*). They both took place on the evening
of the day of our Lord's resurrection ; they were alike
in the suddenness of the appearance of Jesus in the
midst of the disciples, and in the mode of His salutation.
Luke tells us that when Cleopas and his companion
returned from Emmaus to Jerusalem they found the
Eleven gathered together, *and them that were with
them ;* and that while they were relating what had
happened at Emmaus Jesus Himself stood in the
midst of them. John says the doors were shut where
the disciples—not merely the apostles—were gathered
for fear of the Jews. It is evident, therefore, that while
Thomas was not there, Cleopas, who was not one of the
Twelve, was ; as we have seen, Luke tells us that when
he arrived he found others besides the apostles in the
company within locked doors. Further, it is to be
noted that Luke says nothing about any special commission of supernatural sort to be sent on by devolution from the apostles to their successors. Surely such
omission is strange and inexplicable, if, as is assumed,
the whole Church life of the future was to depend upon
unbroken succession and absolutely certain devolution of
supernatural authority and grace. Luke tells us that
our Lord on that memorable occasion opened the mind
of the disciples, showed them how His sufferings, death,
and resurrection fulfilled the Scriptures, and charged
them that repentance and remission of sins should be
preached in His name unto all the nations, beginning
from Jerusalem. But beyond saying, " Ye are witnesses
of these things," there is not one word about any special

commission such as that which is claimed on the Succession theory. It is true He said He would send forth the promise of the Father upon them, and that they were to tarry in the city until they were clothed with power from on high. But this promise referred to the descent of the Spirit at Pentecost, and was certainly not fulfilled in the case of the Eleven alone, but for the hundred and twenty who were all together in one place. If our Lord did say anything about a special commission and devolution of power along a given line, we are inclined to ask, How is it that Luke did not think it important enough to record? Was it not to the last degree vital to the welfare of the Church?

Then, again, as to the fact which John relates, that Jesus breathed on the company assembled, "and saith unto them, Receive ye the Holy Ghost: whose soever sins ye forgive, they are forgiven unto them; whose soever sins ye retain, they are retained," Dr. Westcott points out that "the act is described as one ($\dot{\epsilon}\nu\epsilon\phi\acute{u}\sigma\eta\sigma\epsilon$) and not repeated. The gift was once for all, not to the individuals, but to the abiding body." Also that in the power granted of remitting or retaining sins, the pronouns are unemphatic, and "the main thought which the words convey is that of the reality of the power of absolution from sin granted to the Church and not to the particular organisation through which the power is administered." The Bishop adds these weighty and significant words: "There is nothing in the context to show that the gift was confined to any particular group (as the apostles) among the whole company present. The commission, therefore, must be regarded properly as the commission of the Christian Society, and not as that of the Christian Ministry." He subsequently adds that "the promise, as being made not to one but to *the Society*, carries with it, of necessity, though this is not distinctly expressed, the character of perpetuity: *the Society never dies*."[1]

The truth is, if we seek from the Scriptures the *essentia* of the apostolic office, the special and distinctive function of the apostles, differentiating them from all other preachers of the Gospel, then and since, we shall find that it consisted in bearing witness to the facts of our Lord's life, and especially of His death and resurrection. Christianity, as a historic religion, simply rests on these facts. If we are not sure of them we are sure of nothing in relation to the Christian redemption. It is, therefore, of the first importance to have perfectly reliable witnesses and absolutely trustworthy testimony. This we have in the case of the apostles, and this primary work of theirs is invariably kept well in the foreground. On the very evening of the day of His resurrection, when our Lord appeared in the midst of the disciples, He said to them, "Ye are witnesses of these things" (Luke xxiv. 48). Also on the day of His ascension, as He parted from them, He said again, "Ye shall be My witnesses, both in Jerusalem, and in all Judea, and Samaria, and unto the uttermost parts of the earth" (Acts i. 8). It is further recorded that when their Lord had left them, the apostles, rightly or wrongly, proceeded to fill up the vacancy in the apostolate caused by the death

[1] Commenting on this explanation of Dr. Westcott's, his friend, Dr. Hort, remarks: "In such a matter the mere fact that doubt is possible is a striking one. It is in truth difficult to separate these cases from the frequent omission of the Evangelists to distinguish the Twelve from other disciples; a manner of language which explains itself at once when we recognise how large a part discipleship played in the function of the Twelve" (*The Christian Ecclesia*, p. 33).

of Judas. The account of that election is important as emphasising what they regarded as the special function of an apostle. The time of election to an office is the time to define its duties. When thus defining the apostles laid no special stress on intellectual qualities or direct commission. They set forth the necessary qualifications of an apostle as follows : " Of the men who have companied with us all the time that the Lord Jesus went in and out among us, beginning from the baptism of John, unto the day that He was received up from us, of these must one become a witness with us of His resurrection." It appears that Matthias had these qualifications; on this ground and no other he was elected, and was "numbered with the eleven apostles" (Acts i. 21 *sq*.). So, again, if we follow these men in their after-ministry, we find that, whenever they have to speak of themselves, it is always in the character of witnesses to fact. On the great day of Pentecost, as our Lord had done on Easter Sunday and Ascension Day, Peter described his own principal function and that of the rest of the apostles : " This Jesus did God raise up, whereof we all are witnesses " ; to the people in Solomon's porch he said : " Ye killed the Prince of Life, whom God raised from the dead ; whereof we are witnesses" (Acts iii. 15). After their appearance before the Council "with great power gave the apostles witness of the resurrection of the Lord Jesus" (Acts iv. 33). Again, when brought a second time before the Council, to these leaders of the nation they declared : We cannot be silent ; " we must obey God rather than men. The God of our fathers raised up Jesus, whom ye slew. . . . And we are witnesses of these things" (Acts v. 30–32). On another occasion

Peter declared that their witness extended to the whole of our Lord's ministry as well as to the facts of His death and resurrection, and that for this work of witness-bearing they were specially chosen of God beforehand. To the company gathered in the house of Cornelius at Cæsarea, speaking of Jesus, he said : " And we are witnesses of all things which He did both in the country of the Jews, and in Jerusalem ; whom also they slew, hanging Him on a tree. Him God raised up the third day, and gave Him to be made manifest, not to all the people, *but unto witnesses that were chosen before of God*, even to us, who did eat and drink with Him after He rose from the dead " (Acts x. 39-41).

It is plain from these passages, all spoken on special and typical occasions, that the central idea, the very essence of the apostolic office as distinguished from that of the ordinary preacher of the Gospel, was the work of bearing witness to that series of supernatural facts on which the whole structure of Christianity rests. If so, as witnesses to fact, from the very nature of the case they can have no successors. If it is not so, if their one distinctive function was, as the theory of Apostolic Succession assumes, the mechanical transmission from hand to hand of special commission and supernatural grace, how is it that this is not so much as indicated? If this transmission is so absolutely vital and indispensable to the very existence of the Church, surely the occasions referred to were the time to say so. But this was not said, nor anything like it, and we are therefore justified in saying that the apostles were specially chosen as being plain, honest men, without any theories or philosophies of their own, who would simply tell other men what they themselves had seen. This testimony was vital to the existence of the Church, and for it they were chosen of God beforehand. " That which was from the beginning," said they, " that which we have heard, that which we have seen with our eyes, that which we beheld, and our hands handled, concerning the Word of life (and the life was manifested, and we have seen, and bear witness, and declare unto you the life, the eternal life, which was with the Father, and was manifested unto us); that which we have seen and heard declare we unto you, that ye also may have fellowship with us" (1 John i. 1–3).

If anything were needed to confirm this position, it is to be found in the fact that, in the development of the Church and in the preparation of the Scriptures, men not apostles were more prominent than some who were. It is to Mark, an ordinary disciple, we owe the second Gospel ; and to Luke, probably one of the Christians of Antioch, we owe the third, and also that extension of the Gospels imperfectly described as the Acts of the Apostles. And while in the later story we read of the important work done by Stephen, Philip, and Barnabas, who were not of the Twelve, of the greater part of those who were we hear nothing at all. It was a certain disciple at Damascus, named Ananias, a layman of whom we had never heard before, who was sent to Saul of Tarsus, as he lay stricken and blinded, and who, laying his hands on him, said, " Brother Saul, the Lord, even Jesus, who appeared unto thee in the way which thou camest, hath sent me that thou mayest receive thy sight and be filled with the Holy Ghost." So in the case of the all-important Church at Antioch. Among the branches this was the leader of the tree. The disciples were first called Christians at Antioch. It was from this Church the first body of missionaries went forth to the Gentiles. This was the gate through which the Gospel passed to the great Western world. Yet this Church was founded not by apostles but by laymen, whose names even have not been preserved to us. Of those "that were scattered abroad upon the tribulation that arose about Stephen there were some of them men of Cyprus and Cyrene, who when they were come to Antioch spake unto the Greeks also, preaching the Lord Jesus." While even Peter was defending himself in a half-apologetic tone before those of the circumcision for having gone to the house of Cornelius, these men leaped the fence of Jewish narrowness and were out in the great world doing the needed work. "The hand of the Lord was with them, and a great number believed and turned unto the Lord." And when tidings of all this came to the ears of the Church in Jerusalem, they, that is, the Church, sent forth the Cypriote Barnabas, who was not one of the Twelve, to inspect and report.

II.

While thus, as we have seen, the starting-point of the supposed devolution of apostolic authority is all uncertain, *so also is the act by which it is supposed to be transmitted.* In other words, *there is no certainty as to what are the essentials of what is called a valid ordination.* It is not without significance that the original terms employed to describe ordination were derived from civil functions. "*Ordo,*" the origin of the word "Orders," is not found in the New Testament. It occurs for the first time in the writings of Tertullian (*De exhort. Cast.*

c. 7), and was transferred from Roman civil life where it was the well-known name of the municipal senates of the Empire. Even as late as the end of the sixth century Gregory the Great uses "*ordo*" of the civil authorities of Ariminum and "*clerus*" of the ecclesiastical. So, too, with the word (χειροτονεῖν, χειροτονία) used in the New Testament for ordination, or setting apart, and which is also used in the same sense in the Clementines, the Apostolic Constitutions, and the Apostolic Canons. Its original meaning was "to elect"; and even in classical Greek it came afterwards to mean simply "to appoint to office," without indicating any particular mode of appointment. The same thing is true of that other word (καθιστάνειν, κατάστασις), first used by Clement of Rome (i. 42), and which afterwards was the word most commonly employed when speaking of ordination. It was simply the ordinary classical and Hellenistic word for appointment to any office. The Latin word "*ordinatio*," from which "ordination" comes, was never used by the Romans except for civil appointments.

Noting this by the way, we pass now to call attention to the extreme uncertainty there is, both in the Roman and Anglican Churches, as to what is supposed to constitute a valid ordination. So far as Rome is concerned, while she has recently declared what orders are not valid, she has never defined the essentials of orders that are valid. In the Council of Trent care was taken to avoid anything like definition. Very varied forms were in use, all of which seem to have been allowed. The Abbé Boudinhon, Professor of Canon Law in the Catholic University of Paris, has printed a collection of some of the principal forms of ordination, giving eight for the priesthood and eight for the episcopate. For the priesthood, omitting the oldest Roman form, that contained in the recently available Canons of Hippolytus, he gives the following: the old Roman, as found in the Leonine Sacramentary, the old Gallican, the Greek, the Coptic, the Maronite, the Nestorian, the Armenian, and, lastly, the form given in the Apostolical Constitutions.[1] Varying as these do, they have all been used and all authorised.

On the other hand, because of alleged serious divergence, Anglican Orders have recently, on the highest authority, been declared to be invalid. As the result of appeals from certain quarters in the Church of England, privately made, the Pope instituted a Commission to inquire into the subject. It included the Abbé Duchesne, Monsignor Gasparri, Father Scannell, and the Padre de Augustinis, a professor of the Roman College, all of whom were regarded as favourable to the claims of the Anglican Church, and two of whom had, indeed, published opinions in that direction. The Commission, presided over by Cardinal Mazella, consisted of twelve persons, who were first to state the grounds of their judgement in writing to the Cardinals of the Holy Office, these again in their turn to discuss the whole subject in the Pope's presence, each giving his opinion. The final outcome is that, in the Bull *Apostolicæ Curæ*, of September, 1896, the Pope has "pronounced and declared that ordinations carried out according to the Anglican rite have been and are absolutely null and utterly void." He has not only declared judgement but has given reasons for that judgement. The Anglican mode of ordination, he says, is defective both in *matter*

[1] *De la Validité des Ordinations Anglicanes*, pp. 27-45.

and form. In the language of the Schools the thing done is called the *matter*, and the words used are called the *form*. The Pope lays the stress of his judgement on the latter. He says the *matter*, that is the imposition of hands, " by itself signifies nothing definite, and is equally used for several Orders and for Confirmation. But the words which until recently were commonly held by Anglicans to constitute the proper form of priestly Ordination—namely, ' *Receive the Holy Ghost*'—certainly do not in the least definitely express the Sacred Order of Priesthood, or its grace and power, which is chiefly the power ' of *consecrating and of offering the true body and blood of the Lord.*'" From all the prayers used in the Anglican Ordinal " has been deliberately removed whatever sets forth the dignity and office of the priesthood in the Catholic rite. That form, consequently, cannot be considered apt or sufficient for the Sacrament which omits what it ought essentially to signify." The same holds good, he says, of the consecration of the bishop as well as the ordination of the priest: the prayer of the preface, "*Almighty God,*" has been stripped of the words which denote the *summum sacerdotium :* " hence the sacerdotium is in no wise conferred truly and validly in the episcopal consecration of the same rite; for the like reason, therefore, the episcopate can in no wise be truly and validly conferred by it; and this the more so, because among the first duties of the episcopate is that of ordaining ministers for the Holy Eucharist and sacrifice."

Inasmuch, then, as the right form of expression has not been retained in the Edwardine Ordinal, and there has been, further, defect of *intention* as well as of *matter* and *form*, all consecrations of bishops and all ordinations of priests in the Church of England for the last three hundred years, are by the Church of Rome, declared to have been absolutely null and void. Yet it turns out upon investigation that till the tenth century the prayer by which priests were ordained in the Roman Church itself had precisely the same defect, that is, it said absolutely nothing about "the power of consecrating and of offering the true body and blood of the Lord." Through all those centuries the bishop in ordaining priests simply prayed that God would grant to them the dignity of the presbytery; that He would renew in their hearts the spirit of holiness; that they might obtain the gift of the sacred rank received from God, and recommend a true life by their conversation; that they might be serviceable and prudent fellow-workers with their bishop, and let the pattern of complete righteousness shine out in them, so that they may give a good account of the stewardship committed to them.[1] It is to be specially noted that there was nothing said about the power of consecrating the elements till after Paschasius Radbert, in the ninth century, boldly asserted the doctrine that in the Holy Eucharist the substance of the bread and wine is changed into the substance of the body and blood of Christ *by virtue of the priestly consecration.* This new doctrine at once divided the theological leaders of the time into two opposite camps. On the side of Radbert were Hincmar of Rheims and Ratherius of Verona; on the other side was Rabanus Maurus, a scholar of Alcuin, and who is described as perhaps the most distinguished theologian of his time; along with him were, speaking generally, the Caro-

---

[1] The prayer is quoted by the Abbé Boudinhon, *De la Validité des Ordinations Anglicanes*, p. 50.

lingian divines, and, most memorable of all, Ratramnus. These and others with them, leading men within the Church of Rome itself, denounced this teaching of Paschasius, denounced it as novel and erroneous, as a violent outrage upon the intellect, and a reduction of the spiritual under the laws of the senses. Unhappily their protest was in vain. The two centuries which intervened between Paschasius and Berengar of Tours were, among the dark ages, two of the darkest; and when in 1050 A.D. Berengar had come to the conviction that the teaching of Paschasius, which by this time had become general in the Church, was wholly without foundation, he was condemned at a Council held in Rome, without a hearing, without even a summons. There the matter has remained ever since, and the significant thing is that the Pope has just declared Anglican Orders invalid for lack of teaching which was unknown in his own Church for eight hundred years, and which was only formulated after discussion and conflict through two centuries more.

Then there have been other variations. In the fifteenth century Pope Eugenius IV. defined ordinations to be valid where there had been no imposition of hands at all, if there had been what is called the *porrection of the instruments* or *tradition of instruments* accompanied with the formula. That is to say, the handing the chalice with wine and the paten with a host to a priest on ordination came to be regarded as the "matter" of the sacrament, while the "form" was the words: " Receive power to offer sacrifice to God, and to celebrate Mass as well for the living as for the dead." The Pope referred to having, as he supposed, succeeded in reconciling the Greeks to the Roman Church, and

in the hope of further completing the reunion of
Christendom, received deputies of the Armenians, the
Copts, the Iberians, the Maronites and Jacobites of
Syria, the Chaldean Nestorians, and the Ethiopians.
In the case of these various Christians, as in that of
the Greeks, the reconciliation proved unsubstantial;
but as a matter of fact Eugenius IV., by the famous
Bull *Exultate Deo*, promulgated at the Council of
Florence of 1443, "the Holy Council approving,"
recognised the very various orders of these Churches
as valid. Defining what in each case was its matter
and form, in regard to ordination to the priesthood
he ruled that the *matter* consisted in the porrection
of the instruments and the *form* in the words already
given, but made no requirement of the imposition of
hands. As this had been the custom for a few
centuries, the Pope concluded, as Thomas Aquinas
and others of the Schoolmen had concluded before
him, that it had always been the custom. But by
and by appeared Morinus with his learned work on
the Ordinations of the Church, from which, after long
and careful investigation, it appeared that for the first
thousand years in the history of the Western Church
there had been no such custom as the handing of the
chalice and the paten, and that it never had been the
custom in the Eastern Church at all. If, therefore,
additions or omissions in the form employed in ordination affect its validity, then there is no certainty of
validity. One ancient pontifical prescribes the usual
prayer for a blessing upon the ordinand; the Mainz
Pontifical directs that the bishop shall say: "The Holy
Ghost shall come upon thee, and may the power of the
Highest keep thee without sin"; the later English

Ordinals, on the contrary, direct that the bishop shall say nothing ; while, according to a Toulouse Pontifical of uncertain date, quoted by Morinus, in some Churches the bishop said, " Receive the Holy Ghost, whose soever sins ye forgive, they are forgiven unto them ; whose soever sins ye retain they are retained." These words are not, nor ever have been, used to describe the consecration of bishops or archbishops. It is certain that for the first twelve centuries they were never used in any ordination. It is equally certain that in the whole Eastern Church they are never used at all for this purpose. They were added in the Exeter, Bangor, and Sarum Pontificals as a separate rite immediately before the post-communion. But there is no mention of the rite in the earlier English Ordinals or in any Ordinal earlier than the twelfth century, that is, not till the time when materialistic theories of sacraments and extravagant sacerdotal pretensions were at their height. They are not found in any of the great liturgical writers of the Middle Ages, and there was no canonical authority for them till the Council of Trent. They were first introduced into the later Ordinals of the Latin Church, and from thence, at the Reformation, retained in the Ordination Service of the English Church and the Lutheran Church of Germany. Then again, for the first twelve centuries the words used in the consecration or the ordination of a priest were, as we have seen, in the form of a prayer, but subsequently the opinion gained ground that these words should be not precatory, but imperative ; therefore formulæ couched in the imperative were introduced into the Ordination Services of the Western Church, and, as Morinus. tells us, Nuñez went so far as to make this change an essential of faith, to maintain the contrary of which was manifest heresy.

Thus, on a matter supposed to be of the most vital moment to the very existence of the ministry, and to the maintenance of the spiritual life of the Church, on the strength of which, indeed, impassable walls of separation have been built between Church and Church, there has been no uniformity of procedure, and to this day there is absolutely no certainty. Heaven is supposed to restrict supernatural grace to ministers ordained by one particular form, yet the men who maintain this are at direct issue with each other as to what that form should be. The recent Papal Bull declaring Anglican Orders to be null and void, on the ground of change and defect, has brought this fact into unmistakeable prominence. The Anglican bishops and clergy have thus been put upon their defence in a manner which they evidently very keenly feel. The two Archbishops, under date February 19, 1897, made formal reply to the Pope's letter, addressing that reply "to the whole body of Bishops of the Catholic Church," in which they speak of that letter as aiming to overthrow the whole position of the English Church. " It has, therefore," they say, " seemed good to us, the Archbishops and Primates of England, that this answer should be written, in order that the truth on this matter might be made known. . . . The duty, indeed, is a serious one—one which cannot be discharged without a certain deep and strong emotion." In Clause III. of this answer they say : " There was an old controversy with respect to the form and matter of holy orders which has arisen from the nature of the case, inasmuch as it is impossible to find any tradition on the subject coming from our Lord or His apostles, except the well-known example of prayer with laying-on of hands. But little is to be found bearing on this matter in the decrees of Provincial Councils, and nothing certain or decisive in those of Œcumenical and General Assemblies." Referring further to various Roman documents—the letter of Innocent III. on the necessity of supplying unction, the Decree of Eugenius IV. for the Armenians, certain historical documents of the sixteenth century, various decisions of later Popes, Clement XI. and Benedict XIV., and the Roman Pontifical as reformed from time to time—of all of them they say: " From these documents, so obviously discordant and indefinite, no one, however wise, could extract with certainty what was considered by the Roman Pontiffs to be truly essential and necessary to holy orders."

So much for the grave uncertainties of the case. The Archbishops, by way of defending the status of their own Church against the Pope's serious charges, maintain that the earliest forms of ordination were very simple indeed : " In the most ancient Roman formulary used, as it seems at the beginning of the third century after Christ, nothing whatever is said about 'high priesthood' or 'priesthood,' nor about the sacrifice of the Body and Blood of Christ. . . . Again, in the old Roman Sacramentary, which may perhaps be assigned to the sixth century, only three prayers are employed for the ordination of presbyters. Two are short collects, and a third longer, which is the real Benediction, and was in former times attached to the laying-on of hands. These prayers from the sixth to the ninth century, and perhaps later, made up the whole rite for ordaining a presbyter in the Church of Rome, with no other ceremonies whatever." So say Canterbury and York.

Even before this authoritative reply from the Archbishops, the Bishop of Stepney, now Bishop of Bristol, had been still more explicit. At a meeting convened to consider the question of the Papal Bull, he is reported to have said that "in the apostles' times there were two essentials, and only two, for valid ordination—special prayer (the words of which are in no case recorded) and the imposition of hands. It was now allowed, he believed, on all hands, that these are the only essentials."[1] Later on in his speech he "read the operative words in the essential prayer from the various rites whose validity has not been questioned from the third century onwards—the Canons of Hippolytus, the Apostolic Constitutions, the Ancient (Leonine) Roman Use, the Ancient Gallican, the Greek, the Coptic, Maronite, Nestorian—and showed how exceedingly simple the essential part was, not more than this: 'Look upon this man whom Thou hast called to the presbyterate, and give him grace to perform duly the duties of that office.'"

If these officials are right, if there are only two essentials to a valid ordination, and this simple prayer is one of them, then the ordination of Congregational ministers, in this respect at least, is not wanting in validity—not that they are greatly concerned on this

---

[1] Speech at the Church House meeting on *Anglican Orders*, October 15, 1896. Similarly, Canon Gore, in an address at St. Paul's Schoolroom, November 16, 1896: "That, and that only, which has been common to the whole Church, and which had belonged to the Roman Church all the way down through all these centuries, namely . . . the laying-on of hands with some accompanying words of prayer ; whether the words are in the form 'receive,' or in the form of a prayer that God would give, it has been the laying-on of hands with an accompanying form, or a prayer of that kind. This is all that can be admitted to be necessary for the form of ordination, and that has been admitted by the Roman Church."

point. "Valid Orders" is a mere ecclesiastical phrase, for which there is not the slightest warrant in Scripture. No ordination is valid—in other words, worth anything—by whomsoever performed, if the man ordained has received no inward call from God, has no qualifications spiritual or intellectual for the work of the ministry, and has never commended himself to spiritual men as a true servant of Christ. Not all the bishops in the world, or all the forms ever invented, can give valid ordination to a man in whom these conditions are wanting. On the other hand, if these conditions are present any form of ordination is valid, provided it is reverent and fitted to the solemnity of an occasion when a man is being set apart as an ambassador on behalf of Christ. If living, earnest prayer be one of the essentials of validity the ministry of the Free Churches is not wanting in that. The part of the Ordination Service on which the most devout and earnest stress is laid is that of the Ordination Prayer. Indeed it may well be doubted whether the prayers preserved in any of the Ordinals, Roman or Anglican, have in them more of spiritual fervour, or more prevailing power with Heaven than those offered on such occasions by venerable men, who, with sacred emotion and mingled memories of their own ministry, its toils and pleasures, its joys and sorrows, have solemnly commended to God in the presence of His Church some younger brother who was thus entering upon a work they knew to be so responsible yet so honourable, so arduous yet so glorious.

But perhaps it will be said, the vital thing in the transmission of supernatural grace is not the prayer at the ordination, but the laying-on of hands by the bishop. Let us therefore examine more closely also into this. The practice of laying-on of hands, it need scarcely be said, goes back to very early times, as early indeed as the time when Jacob stretched out his hands and laying them on the heads of Joseph's sons invoked the God of his fathers to bless the lads. Along the course of revelation we meet with the practice again and again, and examining the instances given we find two fundamental ideas involved—the invoking of blessing and the dedication to some course of service. Now the one idea is prominent, now the other, and frequently both. The case of Jacob and his grandsons in the Old Testament is one of blessing, and that also of our Lord in the New when He took little children in His arms "and blessed them," literally brought blessings *down* (κατηυλόγει), "laying His hands upon them." This idea of blessing, again, may take varied form according to the requirements of the case. It may mean the general prosperity of the whole course of life, as it did mean with Jacob and with our Saviour, or it may mean gifts for service, equipment for the serious work of life. In the latter form of blessing we may place the gifts bestowed upon the Samaritan converts when Peter and John going down "prayed for them that they might receive the Holy Ghost. . . . Then laid they their hands on them, and they received the Holy Ghost" (Acts viii. 14–20). The thing to be noted here is that the endowment of the Spirit thus bestowed, like the charismata bestowed upon the Corinthian Church, took such manifest form that Simon Magus could see the result, and offered money to be able to do the like, took the form therefore of "miracles (or miraculous powers), gifts of healings, helps, governments, divers kinds of tongues," and the like. And again, as in the case of the Corinthian Church, these gifts were bestowed not upon officials only, but upon the whole body of believers. As is plain on the face of the narrative, these Samaritans upon whom Peter and John laid their hands were entirely new converts, the fruit of Philip's recent mission in Samaria.

Neither from this case, therefore, nor from that of the members of the Church of Corinth, can anything be inferred as to a distinct order of ministry and its supernatural endowment, inasmuch as the persons concerned were simply private believers. The case of Timothy is more to the purpose, and demands fuller consideration. The passages relating to it are these: " Till I come, give heed to reading, to exhortation, to teaching. Neglect not the gift that is in thee, which was given thee by prophecy, with the laying on of the hands of the presbytery" (1 Tim. iv. 13, 14); "stir up the gift of God which is in thee through the laying on of my hands " (2 Tim. i. 6). The expression, "which was given thee *by prophecy*," has light thrown upon its meaning by a previous passage (1 Tim. i. 18) in which the apostle says, " This charge I commit unto thee, my child Timothy, according to *the prophecies which went before on thee*." The Revisers give this translation of the intransitive participial form (προαγούσας) in preference to the one they place in the margin—"led the way to thee." This preference is justified by the fact that in every other case where the intransitive form of this verb is employed it refers to that which precedes, is prior in place or time, previous (Matt. xxi. 9, 31; Mark ii. 9; Luke xviii. 39; 1 Tim. v. 24; Heb. vii. 18).

What, then, are we to understand by "*prophecies which went before on thee*," or *by* or *through prophecy*? It will be remembered that among the specially endowed " God set some in the Church, first apostles, secondly prophets, thirdly teachers." The prophets were men gifted with the fulness of the Spirit in such manner as to be able to express the mind of the Spirit in reference to different persons or various courses of action. It would seem, then, there had been such expression beforehand of the mind of the Spirit concerning Timothy and the work he was to do. Thus the "prophecy" or "prophecies" really amounted to a call from God. This was the vital thing, and this came first; the laying-on of hands, or the setting apart, came afterwards. When, therefore, the apostle says, "Neglect not the gift which is in thee which was given thee by or through [διὰ] prophecy," he virtually says: Be not unmindful of that solemn call from God which came to thee through the voice of His prophets in the Church. To modernise Chrysostom's interpretation of the words: "We laid our hands upon you, but it was God who elected you, God who gave you your commission, and with it the power to fulfil it. Do not therefore dishonour His appointment, or neglect or abuse His gift."

Thus, then, taking all these passages together, we arrive at these results: (1) The call of God to Timothy came through the prophets beforehand; (2) he was then set apart to service by the act of laying-on of hands in which the apostle and elders of the Church were associated; and (3) the gifts bestowed were to be exercised in (*a*) public reading of the Scriptures; (*b*) public exhortation, dealing with the activities of life; and (*c*) public teaching concerning itself with the doctrines of the faith, "Till I come, give heed to reading, to exhortation, to teaching, neglect not the gift that is in thee. Be diligent in these things: give thyself wholly to them, that thy progress may be manifest unto all. Take heed to thyself, and to thy teaching. Continue in these things; for in doing this thou shalt save both thyself and them that hear thee."

It might seem as if special endowment would scarcely be requisite for the mere public reading of the Scriptures. But the office of Reader in the Early Church was regarded as of great importance. He had often to translate the sacred writings into the language of the people before whom he was standing. It was virtually a gift of tongues. Like the Readers in Nehemiah's time, who had to make God's law plain to a people who during a long captivity had lost the language of their fathers, the Christian Reader had to read in the book distinctly, that is, with an interpretation, and give the sense, and cause the people to understand the reading. It was an arduous duty, requiring both intellectual and spiritual qualifications. In the directions given for selecting a man for this post, as we find them in that early document the Apostolic Canons, it is said: "For Reader one should be appointed after he has been carefully proved; no babbler nor drunkard nor jester; of good morals, submissive, of benevolent intentions, first in the assembly at the meetings on the Lord's Day, of a plain utterance and capable of clearly expounding, mindful that he rules in the place of an evangelist: for whoever fills the ear of the ignorant will be accounted as having his name written with God." In the later Apostolic Constitutions it is thus enjoined: "Ordain a

Reader by laying hands upon him, and pray unto God and say, 'O Eternal God ... look down upon Thy servant who is to be entrusted to read Thy holy Scriptures to Thy people, and give him Thy holy Spirit, the prophetic spirit.'" Justin Martyr, also describing the worship of the Christians in the second half of the second century, tells us that "the memoirs of the apostles or the writings of the prophets are read as long as time permits; then when the Reader has ceased the President" commences his function. All this points to the importance of one part of the work to which Timothy was called, the other part being exhortation and teaching. There is nothing said anywhere about a commission to transmit supernatural grace by ordination. The things which he has heard from Paul among many witnesses he is to commit to faithful men, who shall be able to teach others also; but the things which have been heard, the historic facts and truths of the Christian faith, are now handed on by the Scriptures and by the whole body of Christian men, and cannot be made to mean supernatural grace passed on from man to man in strict line of apostolic succession. This idea is not brought out of the Scriptures, it is a later ecclesiastical invention thrust into them.

The first suggestion, then, to be found in the act of laying-on of hands is that of a prayer for blessing and for such gifts and qualifications as shall equip a man for the work of his life. The next thing it signifies is solemn and formal dedication to the office or service for which gifts and qualifications are being sought in prayer. Take the case of Moses and Joshua: "And Moses spake unto the Lord, saying, Let the Lord, the God of the spirits of all flesh, appoint a man over the congregation, which may go out before them, and which may come in before them, and which may lead them out, and which may bring them in; that the congregation of the Lord be not as sheep which have no shepherd. And the Lord said unto Moses, Take thee Joshua the son of Nun, a man in whom is the Spirit, and *lay thine hand upon him;* and set him before Eleazar the priest, and all the congregation; and give him a charge in their sight" (Numb. xxvii. 15–19). In this case Joshua was already possessed of the Spirit, and the laying-on of hands was the public designation of him to his lifework. So with the Seven in the Acts of the Apostles chosen to serve tables. They were chosen as being full of the Spirit and of wisdom, and being so were simply "set before the apostles, and when they had prayed they laid their hands on them." Sometimes the act of designation to office was done by the people themselves. The Levites as a tribe were to be wholly given unto the Lord to do the service of the Lord. Their consecration to this service was to be by definite and solemn act in the presence of the whole congregation: "Thou shalt present the Levites before the tent of meeting, and thou shalt assemble the whole congregation of the children of Israel: and thou shalt present the Levites before the Lord, *and the children of Israel shall lay their hands upon the Levites*" (Numb. viii. 9, 10). This may have been done by the princes of the tribes in the name of the tribes, but whichever way it was done it was to all intents and purposes the act of the people. The devolution of office and service was from them.

Turning from the Old Testament to the New, we meet with the case of the Church at Antioch consecrating Paul and Barnabas to missionary service (Acts xiii. 1–3). Professor Ramsay has called attention to the fact that it was the Church itself, not the prophets and teachers previously mentioned, who laid their hands on the two brethren who were set apart. The community at Antioch was no longer a mere "congregation," but a fully organised Church, having its own prophets and teachers to whom the grace of God was given, so that there was no lack in that respect. The occasion, too, was one of special significance, for a great step in the development of the Church was being taken, nothing less than "the opening of a door to the Gentiles." " As they ministered to the Lord and fasted the Holy Ghost said, Separate me Barnabas and Saul for the work whereunto I have called them. Then" (to give Professor Ramsay's translation) "they" (*i.e.*, *the Church*) "held a special fast, and prayed and laid their hands upon them and gave them leave to depart." The persons meant by "they" in this verse, he contends, cannot be the five prophets and teachers just mentioned, the officials of the community, because they cannot be said to lay their hands on two of themselves, and the simplest interpretation is that the Church as a whole held a special service for the solemn purpose. It seemed to the author, he suggests, so obvious that such action was performed by universal consent, that he did not feel any need to express the nominative. Such a way of thinking was possible only at a very early time. Professor Ramsay also points out that *Codex Bezæ* makes all clear by inserting the nominative "all" (πάντες), because in the second century the action of officials began to supersede that of the whole congregation in such matters, and "the Bezan Reviser belonged to the period when the change had begun and the need of expressing the nominative was felt; but he lived before the time when official action had regularly superseded that of the congregation, for in that case he would have taken the officials in this case to be the agents (as many modern commentators understand the passage).[1]

Taking, then, all the instances to be found in Scripture, of the laying-on of hands—that of Timothy and the kind of gifts conferred on him; that of the Samaritans who were private Christians, not officials of the Church; and that of the Church at Antioch, the members of which designated even an apostle and his colleague in this way for missionary service—it may be safely affirmed that there is no foundation in the Word of God for the idea of supernatural transmission involved in Apostolical Succession. If this idea came in after the Canon of Scripture was complete we may well ask by what right it came in. Even in sub-apostolic times we find a distinction drawn between ordination and the laying-on of hands, as though there were no necessary connexion between them. The Apostolical Constitutions, which probably took their latest form before the Council of Nicæa (325 A.D.), lay it down that a bishop blesseth, lays on hands and ordains; and that a

[1] *St. Paul the Traveller and the Roman Citizen*, by W. M. Ramsay, D.C.L., LL.D., pp. 64-66. The position here taken is sustained by the high authority of Dr. Hort. He says: "On careful consideration it is difficult to doubt that the mouthpieces of the Divine command should be distinguished from those who have to execute it. In other words, the members of the Ecclesia itself are bidden to set Barnabas and Saul apart; and it is the members of the Ecclesia itself that dismiss them with fast and prayer and laying-on of hands, whether the last act was performed by all of them, or only by representatives of the whole body, official or other. So also on their return they gather the Ecclesia together (xiv. 27) and report what has befallen them" (*The Christian Ecclesia*, 1897, p. 64).

presbyter "lays on hands but *does not ordain*" (viii. c. 28). The essentials of the ordination of a bishop (that is, of a pastor of a church) are also laid down in detail (viii. c. 4). He is to be chosen by the people; then on a Lord's day all are to be assembled and the people are to be asked if this is the man they desire; this answered in the affirmative, it is asked whether he has a good testimony in the outside world, whether his family is well ordered, whether he is unblameable in the course of his life. Three times the question is to be asked as to whether he be truly worthy of this ministry. "And if they agree the third time that he is worthy, let them all be demanded their vote." This being done and silence being made, one of the bishops present offers prayer, during which the deacons "hold the Divine Gospels open upon the head of him that is to be ordained." While all these minute directions are given, not a word is said about imposition of hands; if, therefore, this be an essential to the transmission of the "sacred Order," the sacred Order was not transmitted in these early ordinations.

Then, again, in the case of the Meletian Schism, the synodical letter of the Egyptian bishops provides that if any of the ministers ordained by Meletius are received into the Catholic Church they are not to be re-ordained, but "it is necessary to lay hands upon them again that they may afterwards be admitted to communion with the Church, to give them their work and to restore to them the honours which are their due." That no supernatural gift was thereby implied is clear from the words of Augustine: "If the laying-on of hands were not applied to one coming from heresy, he would be as it were judged to be wholly blameless; but for the unity of love, which is the greatest gift of the Holy Spirit, hands are laid on heretics when they are brought to a knowledge of the truth" (*De Bapt.* c. Donat., bk. v., xxiii. 33). In the same work also Augustine, referring to the laying-on of hands, asks : " What is it more than a prayer offered over a man ? " (iii. 16). On the point of the reception of the clergy who had been ordained by Meletius, Hefele (*Hist. of the Councils*, i. 352) maintains that Gratian is in opposition to the text of the Egyptian synodical letter and also to the practice of the ancient Church in supposing that the Eighth Canon of Nicæa prescribes their reordination. If so, then ordination and laying on of hands are separate things. Indeed, the present Pope in his recent decision on Anglican Orders plainly says so : " The imposition of hands by itself," he says, " signifies nothing definite, and is equally used for several Orders and for Confirmation." This is true even from early times. In the Apostolic Constitutions laying-on of hands is prescribed in the case of a deaconess, of a sub-deacon, and of a reader, where apostolic succession is certainly not implied. It is also ordered that at a certain point both of Morning and Evening Prayer the deacon shall say to all the people : " Bow down for the laying-on of hands!"[1] Thus, then, it is clear that on other occasions when the Orders of the clergy were certainly not being conferred there was the laying-on of hands, and contrariwise it has not always and everywhere been the uniform custom when only the clergy were receiving ordination. We have seen that the Apostolic Constitutions enjoin the holding of the open Gospels over the head of the ordinand and say nothing about the laying-on of hands ;

[1] *Apostolic Constitutions*, bk. viii. cc. 19, 21, 22, 37, 38.

Pope Eugenius IV. authoritatively declared the tradition of the instruments to be sufficient without anything further beyond the words of the prayer; the Armenian Church ordained its clergy by the dead hand of Gregory the Illuminator, the Alexandrian Church also at times by the dead hand of a predecessor; in the Alexandrian and Abyssinian Churches it was and still is by breathing, while the Eastern Church simply lifts up the hands in the ancient oriental attitude of benediction instead of laying them on the head of the person to be ordained; and finally the early Celtic Church conferred ordination by the transmission of certain relics or a pastoral staff. In the face of all these uncertainties, contradictions, and variations we are asked to believe that only one class of men, ordained in one particular way, have power to perform ministerial acts which can be regarded as *valid*, that is, as having the security of the Divine covenant. Can there be a greater demand on credulity or a nearer approach to unreasoning superstition?

Let us come close home and ask what is really meant by a valid ministerial act? Is it meant that Christ's Gospel brings no peace to a burdened soul, Christ's promises no consolation to a troubled heart, unless proclaimed by official lips? If that is what is meant thousands of undoubted facts in human experience declare this to be untrue. It cannot mean that baptism has no significance unless administered by clerical hands, for the Anglican Church, as we have seen, has officially acknowledged the validity of lay baptism. The vital thing in a valid ministry in the eyes of churchmen is the power to work some mysterious change in the sacramental elements. The recent Papal Bull declares the grace and power of the priesthood is chiefly the power " of consecrating and of offering the true body and blood of the Lord." Without putting it quite so plainly, Canon Gore says that "one of the richest and holiest parts of the priest's ministry is that of celebrating the Holy Eucharist, and that the Holy Eucharist is a sacrifice." Contrasted with such language as this one cannot fail to notice how little stress is laid in Scripture on any officiating person at the Communion Service. Judging from the account given in the Gospels, and in the classical passage on the subject in the Epistles, neither our Lord nor the Apostle Paul said anything about indispensable qualifications on the part of the "celebrant," as he has come to be called. He is not even mentioned. With the apostle a " valid eucharist " seems to depend upon there being valid communicants. If those who come to the table eat and drink the cup of the Lord unworthily, they are guilty of the body and blood of the Lord ; if they do not prove themselves, if they discern not the Lord's body, they receive no blessing—they eat and drink judgement unto themselves. We find the same spirit in the little Church manual of half a century later. The Didaché lays stress on the element of thanksgiving, which is all that the word Eucharist means, as being the offering of the people themselves: "Concerning the Eucharist, thus give *ye* thanks : First, as regards the cup: We give Thee thanks, O our Father, for the holy wine of Thy Son David which Thou madest known unto us through Thy Son Jesus ; . . . And after ye are satisfied thus give *ye* thanks: We give Thee thanks, Holy Father, for Thy holy name which Thou hast made to tabernacle in our hearts, and for the knowledge and faith and immortality which Thou has made known unto us through Thy Son Jesus." It is further said, in addition to these thanksgivings on the part of the people, they are to "permit the prophets to offer thanksgiving as much as they desire" (cc. ix., x). So, again, if we pass on another half-century, and come to the time of Justin Martyr, we still find thanksgiving, not consecration, the prevailing idea. Describing the custom of the Christians (c. 151, A.D.), he tells us that at a certain point in their worship, bread and wine are brought "to the president of the brethren," or, as the words may be translated, "to that one of the brethren who was presiding ($\tau\tilde{\wp}$ προεστῷτι τῶν 'ἀδελφῶν), and he, taking them, gives praise and glory to the Father of the universe, through the name of the Son and of the Holy Ghost, and offers thanks at considerable length for our being counted worthy to receive these things at His hands." Evidently this act of thanksgiving was regarded as that of the people themselves, for it is further said: "When he," the presiding brother, "has concluded the prayers and thanksgivings, all the people present express their assent by saying, Amen" (*Apology* i. 65).

Thus for something like a hundred and twenty years after our Lord instituted the Supper in remembrance of Himself, to show forth His death till He come, there was no stress laid upon a duly commissioned "celebrant," or on the power of consecrating and offering the true body and blood of the Lord. This kind of teaching came in later, and we may surely ask by what right it came in? Priests and prelates may bring in superstitions to exalt themselves, but they cannot alter the spiritual facts of the universe or change the eternal laws of God. These remain sublimely unaffected by clerical inventions and by all that Councils or Convocations may decree. " Thus saith the Lord of hosts, Hearken not unto the words of the prophets that prophesy unto you ; they teach you vanity : they speak a vision of their own heart, and not out of the mouth of the Lord. The prophet that hath a dream let him tell a dream ; and he that hath My word let him speak My word faithfully. What is the chaff to the wheat ? saith the Lord."

LECTURE III

FURTHER UNCERTAINTIES AND OBJECTIONS

LECTURE III

FURTHER UNCERTAINTIES AND OBJECTIONS

III.

IN our investigations thus far we have found two uncertainties gravely affecting the theory of Apostolical Succession, one relating to the starting-point of the commission, the other to the ceremony of ordination by which it is supposed to be transmitted. We now come upon a yet further uncertainty, *that, namely, which relates to the line of transmission* along which the supernatural commission is said to come.

Since the one Church parted into the two streams of East and West, the Churches of the West trace their line of descent through the Church of Rome. It is thus, of course, the Anglican Church derives such Orders as she claims to possess. The validity of these Orders, if there be anything in the ecclesiastical theory, depends, therefore, upon the validity of the succession from the apostles as preserved by the Church of Rome. Uncertainty here must necessarily involve uncertainty all along the line. Yet we find it was not till far on in the second century that this Church acquired precedence among the Churches of the time, and even then precedence was due to the civil greatness of the city rather than to any ecclesiastical or prescriptive right. As far on in the century as the time when Irenæus wrote (c. 180 A.D.), Jerusalem, not Rome, was still looked up to as the Mother Church of the Christians. Referring to the answer of Peter and John to the Sanhedrin, while admitting elsewhere the influence of the Church in Rome, Irenæus says of that in Jerusalem: "These are the voices of the Church from which every Church had its origin; these are the voices of the metropolis of the citizens of the New Covenant; these are the voices of the apostles; these are the voices of the disciples of the Lord, the truly perfect" (*Adv. Hæres.* iii. 12. 5). Now, so far as the apostles are concerned, the connexion between the Church in Rome with that in Jerusalem was not closer than that of the Church in Antioch or Alexandria or the Churches of Asia Minor or Macedonia. The Church in Rome was not founded by any of the apostles, for it was in existence before any of them had passed beyond the bounds of Syria. As we gather from the Epistle of Clement, there were in the year 95 A.D. old men who had been members of that Church from youth to old age (c. 63). It had long been in existence when Paul wrote his Epistle to the Romans; and up to that time, as he tells us, he had not been there himself; while the probability is that Peter never saw the city till he was taken there for martyrdom. We may almost certainly say that the Church in Rome was founded by Christian laymen, by those "sojourners from Rome, both Jews and proselytes," who were among the three thousand converted in Jerusalem on the day of Pentecost, and who carried back the glad tidings to the city from which they came. As late as the year referred to (95 A.D.)

there is no mention of a bishop in the Epistle of Clement; the letter being written in the name of the Church. And what is more striking still, while Ignatius, or the Pseudo-Ignatius, is ever bent on glorifying the bishop's office, in his Epistle to the Romans he passes by the bishop altogether, as though the Church had no such officer. He speaks of the Church in Rome as "beloved and enlightened," as "having the presidency in the country and region of the Romans," the precedence being one "of love, of walking in the law of Christ, and bearing the Father's name"—all this about the Church, but not one word about the bishop of the Church, upon whom, as a connecting link, the welfare of Christendom is now, by many, supposed to depend. Dr. Lightfoot, who held to the genuineness of the Ignatian Epistles, frankly admits that if Ignatius had not incidentally mentioned that he was "the bishop of" or "from Syria," his Epistle to the Romans would have contained no indication of the existence of the episcopal office. He says: "With all the importance attributed to the Roman Church it is the more remarkable that not a word is said about the Roman bishop. Indeed there is not the faintest hint that a bishop of Rome existed at this time. Yet, startling as the omission is, it entirely accords with the information derived from other trustworthy sources. All the ancient notices point to the mature development of episcopacy in Asia Minor at this time. On the other hand, all the earliest notices of the Church in Rome point in the opposite direction."[1] In other words, the only way Dr. Lightfoot could account for the absence of all mention of a bishop in Rome in the letter of Ignatius to the Romans is by

---

[1] *Apostolic Fathers*, Part i. vol. i. p. 383.

supposing that while episcopacy had received development in Asia Minor, at the date he fixes for the Ignatian Epistles (c. 118 A.D.), there was no episcopacy in Rome. Yet by this time all the apostles had been dead for years, Peter and Paul for more than half a century, so that the bishop of Rome, when he did come, was, on this hypothesis, certainly not in succession from the apostles. So, again, with the other document of the period, the "Shepherd" of Hermas, which had its origin in Rome. If we had no other information we should be unable to say what was the form of church government in Rome when this work was written. Dr. Lightfoot says that "the internal history of the Church in Rome is shrouded in thick darkness from the end of the first century to the beginning of the third, from the age of Clement to the age of Hippolytus—scarcely a ray here and there penetrating the dense cloud."[1] There must, therefore, be great uncertainty as to the Roman succession. The earliest computation we have is that of Irenæus (175-190 A.D.), and he leaves Peter out of the catalogue (*Adv. Hæres.*, iii. 3. 3). If we are right in supposing that it is the list of Hegesippus which Epiphanius has preserved (*Hær.* xxvii. 6)—both Irenæus and Hegesippus make Linus the first bishop, Anencletus the second, and Clement the third. Jerome, on the other hand, at the beginning of the fifth century, makes Peter to be the first bishop, as do other early authorities. The Armenian version of the Chronicon of Eusebius, and also the Syriac Catalogue, make him to be bishop of Rome for twenty years; and the Chronicon, as translated by Jerome, for twenty-five years; one later list gives twenty-two years, and another twenty-eight. The Liberian

---

[1] *Apostolic Fathers*, Part i. vol. ii. p. 317.

Catalogue affects to be very precise, setting down the length of Peter's bishopric as twenty-five years, one month, and nine days (30-55 A.D.). It places Clement next after Linus, and treats the name of Cletus or Anacletus as that of two distinct persons, each with a separate term of office. In the early editions of the "Liber Pontificalis" (c. 687 A.D.) an explanatory paragraph inserted in the biography of Peter states that both Linus and Cletus were appointed during Peter's lifetime to act as suffragans, and relieve him from routine business (*Ed. Duchesne*, p. 118). It represents the apostle also as ordaining Clement to be his immediate successor. In the life of Clement, in the same work, he is said to have undertaken the pontificate on the charge of Peter; and this though Clement is made to be bishop nine years and to have died in the third year of Trajan (101 A.D.), while Peter was martyred in the reign of Nero, about 64 A.D. The tradition that Peter was twenty-five years bishop of Rome, was, so far as we know, first started by Jerome, 390–415 (*De Vir. illus.* c. 1), that is, not till more than 300 years after the death of Peter. The further assumption that Peter came to Rome in the reign of Claudius (41–54 A.D.) contradicts all we know of him from authentic sources. Paul tells us distinctly (Gal. ii. 7–9) it was arranged that while he himself went to the Gentiles, Peter should be the apostle of the circumcision, confining his labours to the Jews, an arrangement which was amicably carried out. In 44 A.D. we know he was in Jerusalem (Acts xii. 3), and also in 51 A.D. (Acts xv.); a little later he was in Antioch (Gal. ii. 11). Then, as we learn from his first Epistle, in some part of his life he laboured in various provinces of Asia Minor, and almost certainly as far east as Babylon. He could not have been in Rome when Paul wrote his Epistle to the Romans (57 or 58 A.D.), for no mention is made of him among the greetings with which the Epistle concludes; nor can he have been there when Paul wrote from Rome during his captivity (61 or 62-63 or 64 A.D.). In fact we come upon no early trace of his being in Rome at all until we get to the probably well-founded tradition that he met his death there. In that case he would be likely to reach the city in the early summer of 64 A.D., and suffer martyrdom shortly after. It is therefore upon this extremely slender foundation that the Popes of Rome base their claim to be the successors of Peter. So far as the trustworthiness of the Roman succession is concerned, Dr. Döllinger, ever a candid historian, tells us that the list of the Popes drawn up under Liberius from the death of Christ till his own time (352–369 A.D.) is *the oldest* there is, and the source of the later ones; and that while the second part is reliable and historic, the first part, up to 230 A.D., contains serious errors, and the contemporary consulates and emperors are given in a random and very incorrect way. This is not much to say for a record from which all later Roman lists and records were derived.

Thus for more than two hundred years we have, in our search for certainty, to cross a region of shifting sand, and we naturally ask what is the security of an edifice that has no better foundation than this? If succession be vital, not to the well-being merely, but to the actual existence of the Church of Christ, we might reasonably expect something more reliable than we find here. There was succession in the Jewish priesthood, but it was a succession which could be verified at any moment. The sole qualification of the priest was that he must belong to the family of Aaron, and the genealogical tables of that family were all carefully and publicly preserved. The credentials of any given priest could therefore be produced at any given moment, and for centuries doubt seems never to have arisen. When after the seventy years' captivity in a foreign country doubt did arise, those priests who could not find their register among those that were reckoned among the genealogy "were deemed polluted, and put from the priesthood. And the Tirshatha said unto them that they should not eat of the most holy things till there stood up a priest with Urim and Thummim," that is with a Divine oracle which should compensate for the chasm in the register of the genealogy (Ezra ii. 62 ; Neh. vii. 64). No hope, it seems, can be looked for of such supernatural intervention in the case of Apostolical Succession. No "priest with Urim and Thummim" may be expected to bridge over the awful chasm. Mr. Haddan, a strenuous advocate of the Succession theory, contends that unless the gift of Orders descend in unbroken line from those who first had it, namely, the apostles, "nothing short of a new revelation, or a new commission from God can create afresh the gift which Christ gave once for all at the beginning." [1] In like manner Bishop Sage exclaims : " If such a succession is once interrupted, how shall it begin again? How shall commissions be had? Who is authorised to give them? There is a *necessity* of having them, and they are not to be expected immediately from heaven."[2] It appears, however, that in such contingencies and dire

---

[1] *Apostolical Succession in the Church of England*, by Arthur W. Haddan, B. D.
[2] *Reasonableness of Toleration*, p. 208.

possibilities when ecclesiastical comfort fails, mathematical consolation is near at hand. Lord Macaulay, in his own trenchant fashion, puts the case thus : " Whether a given clergyman be really a successor of the apostles depends on an immense number of such contingencies as these : whether, under King Ethelwolf, a stupid priest might not, while baptizing several scores of Danish prisoners who had just made their option between the font and the gallows, inadvertently omit to perform the rite on one of these graceless proselytes ; whether in the seventh century an impostor, who had never received consecration, might not have passed himself off as a bishop on a rude tribe of Scots ; whether a lad of twelve did really, by a ceremony huddled over when he was too drunk to know what he was about, convey the episcopal character to a lad of ten." [1] Canon Gore replies to this that invalidating irregularities in episcopal ordinations would not have the effect supposed, because succession comes of interlacing lines, each bishop having, as a rule, been consecrated by three of his order ; and that it has been mathematically argued [2] that even if we make the supposition of one consecrator in twenty not being validly consecrated, the chances will be 8,000 to one against all three consecrators in any given case being in a like position. To this argument it was long since replied that though mathematical in form it yields but a probable conclusion, while *certainty* is what is required ; and that even for that probability the data are all to be *assumed*. What is wanted is a criterion which shall distinguish the *genuine* Orders from the *spurious*. No man knows but *he* may be the unhappy 8,000th, and

---

[1] Essay on *Gladstone on Church and State*.
[2] By Mr. Gladstone, *Church Principles*, pp. 235, 236.

therefore on this mathematical theory no minister in the Church of England has a right to say that he is a duly ordained priest, but only that he has $\frac{7999}{8000}$ parts of certainty that he is.[1] Of course this is said by way of showing that one absurdity can only be met by confronting it with another. For questions of this kind are not to be settled by the doctrine of chances mathematically computed, or by traditionary catalogues of the occupants of particular sees for centuries. The theory is not only weakest where it needs to be strongest—that is, at the starting-point—what is more to the purpose is that it is entirely foreign to the spiritual genius and character of Christian faith and life. It has been truly observed that on such invisible evidence as is produced in this case, nothing can be believed, or if anything, everything.

IV.

The theory of Apostolical Succession, further, assumes, what is contrary to the plainest and most obvious facts, *that supernatural grace and spiritual power are restricted to official lines.* It is contended by the advocates of this theory that a commission in order to be valid must come from above, not *from below*, *from Church authority*, that is, from the bishop, not from the people. It should be as distinctly understood as it is possible to make it that in the opinion of non-episcopalians a valid commission comes neither from the bishop nor the people, but from God Himself. Commission from a bishop is not high enough for them. They hold, and hold strenuously, that, as the apostle said, it is God who "set

[1] *Essays* by Henry Rogers, iii. 21.

in the Church first apostles, secondly prophets, thirdly teachers" (1 Cor. xii. 28), or, as he puts it in another Epistle, Christ Himself "gave some apostles and some prophets and some evangelists, and some pastors and teachers" (Eph. iv. 11). The true preacher of Christ's evangel receives his commission direct from heaven. He has heard the voice of the Lord saying, "Whom shall I send and who will go for us?" and in moments of life, sacred and never to be forgotten, he has humbly given back response, "Here am I, send me!" From profoundest experience he knows what the ancient prophet meant when he said, "There is in mine heart, as it were, a burning fire shut up in my bones, and I am weary with forbearing and I cannot contain!" If a man has received a call from God like that all that either bishop or people can do is to recognise it and give it free play in the Church. If the man has it not, neither bishop nor people can give it or in any way make up for its absence. If the commission comes not from heaven it is not in the power of officials to confer it, if it does they are not within their right to forbid it. Then, so far as man is concerned, whether bishop or people, it is a simple question of recognition on their part of call and gifts already bestowed on God's part. Whether the bishop is more fitted to recognise the gifts and call of a man than a body of spiritual men whose hearts have responded to the exercise of those gifts, is a point on which there may be difference of opinion. Not a few are strongly convinced that a body of prayerful, spiritually minded men are quite as capable as any bishop of judging whether a man has really been sent of God, and indeed more capable than many bishops of whom we have heard. A Church recognising a man's gifts from God as qualifying him to teach and lead them, and inviting neighbouring presbyters to join them in setting him apart, are well within their Scripture rights, and certainly have primitive usage in their favour. In the ancient document known as the Apostolic Canons it is provided that "if there are few men and not twelve persons competent to vote at the election of a bishop, neighbouring Churches should be written to, in order that three selected men may come thence and examine carefully if he is worthy." An assembly so constituted might fitly recognise the Divine gift in a man and solemnly set him apart to the service of God and His Church. A bishop can do no more. At all events, if an ordination so conducted was valid in the second century it may very well be equally valid in the nineteenth.

The call from God, then, is the vital element, and this is restricted to no one form of organisation. Disregarding all official lines, it comes to some men now as it came to Amos of old, who said to Amaziah, "I was no prophet, neither was I a prophet's son; but I was a herdman and a dresser of sycamore trees: and the Lord took me from following the flock, and the Lord said unto me, Go, prophesy unto My people Israel!" Though belonging to no privileged caste, qualified by no official initiation, he was yet commissioned of heaven to receive and give forth the message of the Eternal. What was true of the ancient prophet is true also of the prophet of New Testament times. There is not a line to show that our Lord ever set up a priestly caste in His Church. Neither He Himself, nor, so far as we know, any of His apostles came of a priestly line; and while Scripture, as a revelation from God is in all its essentials professedly complete, there is nothing in it to prescribe or sanction one exclusive form of organisation. The very fact that the primitive office-bearers were popularly elected, of itself, made a priestly caste impossible, and in no single instance is the term " priest " (ἱερεύς) applied to an office-bearer of the Church. From their youth the apostles had been familiar with the hereditary priesthood of the Jewish temple, but they never thought of introducing it into the Christian Church. The only High Priest they knew of under the new dispensation was Christ Himself; the only human priesthood they recognised was the universal body of believers which was constituted a holy priesthood to offer up spiritual sacrifices, acceptable to God through Jesus Christ. It was not till the Jewish temple was literally razed to the ground, the city destroyed, and its very name changed to Ælia Capitolina that the idea began to be suggested that the Christian teacher had taken the place of the Jewish priest. Once suggested, it was strengthened by the life-long associations with heathen priests and temples which many of the new converts brought with them. But the Old Dispensation was never meant to be the final law for Christian men. Christ is the mediator of a better covenant, and He ever lives to make that better covenant a living reality. To create vicars of Christ on earth, mediating human priests between God and the soul, is to disparage the abiding Presence and all-pervading action of Him who has said, " Behold I am alive for evermore "; " Lo I am with you alway, even unto the end of the world." It was a bishop of the Church, and one learned in Christian antiquity above all the bishops of his time, who has said that the kingdom of Christ " has no sacred days or seasons ; no special sanctuaries, because every time and place alike are holy. Above all it has no sacerdotal system. It interposes no sacrificial tribe or class between God and man, by whose intervention alone God is reconciled and man forgiven. Each individual member holds personal communion with the Divine Head. To Him immediately he is responsible, and from Him directly he obtains pardon and draws strength."[1] In support of the views he holds Canon Gore uses an illustration which might, one would have thought, have made him aware of the fallacy of his position. The priesthood of the Church, he says, follows analogies elsewhere: there is a priesthood of science ministering the mysteries of nature; a priesthood of art ministering and interpreting beauty to men; a priesthood of political influence, organised and made authoritative in offices of state; and in like manner a natural priesthood of spiritual influence belonging to men of spiritual power. This argument would be deserving of consideration if it could be shown that the men whom God calls to be high priests of literature, of art, of science, of political life derived their genius, influence, and authority always and only along an official line and within the prescribed limits of a rigidly defined and exclusive organisation. It need hardly be said that nothing of the kind can be shown. Certainly it was not under such conditions that Dante, and Shakespeare, and Milton illumined the world; that Michael Angelo, and Titian, and Raffaelle glorified Art; or that Faraday, Darwin, and Huxley enlarged the boundaries of Science and opened up new worlds of possibility to human life.

So much stress being laid upon Apostolical Succes-

[1] Dr. Lightfoot, *The Christian Ministry*, p. 179.

sion, it may be worth while to trace the expression to its source and find out, if we can, what it really meant in the lips of those who first used it. It occurs in the very first line of the preface to the Ecclesiastical History of Eusebius. Stating the purpose of this history, which he says is to place upon record "the successions of the Holy Apostles" (τὰς τῶν ἱερῶν ἀποστόλων διαδοχὰς), he explains that he regards as successors of the apostles all witnesses to the truth who have ensured the continuous connexion of the Church of Christ with its original source, and guaranteed the faithful preservation of the teaching of the Church. For him the episcopate is only one element in the succession of the apostles. That succession, according to him, included the martyrs and the continuous line of teachers who, either by spoken word or by their writings, have contributed to the furtherance of Christ's Gospel in the world. The one thing with which Eusebius is concerned is the propagation of the all-important truth, the Divine Word, not with the development of Church institutions, and therefore not primarily with the position of the hierarchy. He makes it clear that the succession of teachers—Apologists like Quadratus, Aristides and Justin, who were not bishops, "all who in each generation, with or without writings, proclaimed the Divine Word" (*pref.*); indeed, all the many nameless evangelists of the reign of Trajan who were transmitters of the tradition were really in the first rank of the succession of the apostles, inasmuch as being holy disciples of such men they built up the Churches the apostles had founded (*H. E.*, iii. 37). Here, as Harnack says, it is especially clear that the conception of succession is by no means to be understood as hierarchic-clerical; and Heinrici refers to the fact that Eusebius has restored the expression of Josephus—"an exact succession of prophets" (*H. E.*, iii. 10. 4), using it in such a way as to show that he did not connect the succession only with bishops. With Eusebius the first succession of the apostles is not the episcopal succession, but the first generation after the apostles. Having given the names of leading teachers under the reigns of the different emperors, he says in the preface to his eighth book that he has already " related the successions of the apostles in all his Seven Books," the application being obvious. Clement of Alexandria also speaks of himself as coming under the influence of various eminent teachers during the formative period of his life. "The last of these," he says, " who was first in power, gathering the spoil of the flowers of the prophetic and apostolic fields, engendered in the souls of his hearers a deathless element of knowledge " (*Strom.*, i. 1). Eusebius says this passage refers to Clement's teacher Pantænus, who was head of the Catechetical School of Alexandria : " This same man also Clement seems to me to refer to in the first book of his Stromata when he points out the most distinguished of the Apostolic Succession " (ἀποστολικῆς διαδοχῆς). It is obvious from this that Eusebius regarded Pantænus, though he was not a bishop, as not only in the apostolic succession, but as one of the most distinguished in that succession.[1] It is clear also that he regards the succession of the other teachers whom Clement names along with Pantænus as forming part of the Apostolic Succession. With Eusebius, as with Hegesippus before him, the fragments of whose writings

---

[1] Harnack, *Die Chronologie der altchristlichen Litteratur*, 1897, pp. 64-67.

he has preserved for us, the master-idea of the succession was the handing on of apostolic teaching, not the transmission of a special commission or of supernatural grace. Hegesippus, who wrote nearly a century and a half before Eusebius (c. 180 A.D.), seems to have been the first to draw up a list of the various pastors or bishops. While at Rome, he says, "I drew up the list of the succession as far as Anicetus," but the great point with him was that "in every succession and in every city they adhered to the teaching of the Law and the Prophets and the Lord." He conversed with most of the bishops as he travelled to Rome, and "he received the same teaching from all" (*H. E.*, iv. 22).

Not only in those first ages of the Church of which Eusebius wrote, but in all ages, the great religious teachers of mankind have never been confined to the official circles of the priestly systems. A writer of our own time has reminded us that, by the highest rank of the whole profession of the clergy—the Pontificate of Rome—the key of knowledge has been perhaps wielded less than by any other great institution in Christendom; that of the 257 prelates who have been Popes of Rome only about four have done anything by their writings to enlarge the boundaries of knowledge and to raise the moral perceptions of mankind, and that the services of these were in the form of occasional acts of toleration towards the Jews, the rectification of the calendar, and a few similar examples of enlightenment. He contends also that if one-half of mediæval Christendom was influenced in its desires after goodness by the clerical work of Thomas à Kempis, the other half was no less elevated by the lay work of the divine poem of Dante; that if the religion of England has been fed in large part by Hooker, by Butler, by Wesley, and by Arnold, it has also been fed, perhaps in a yet larger part, by Milton, by Bunyan, by Addison, by Cowper, and by Walter Scott ; and, finally, that the almost uniform law by which the sins and superstitions of Christendom have been bound or loosed, has been that some one conscience or some few consciences, more enlightened or more Christlike than their fellows, have struck a new light or opened some new door into truth ; and then the light has been caught up and the opening widened by the gradual advance of wisdom and knowledge in the mass.[1]

Such services as have been rendered by the clergy of the Church to the great cause of spiritual enlightenment and progress—and they have been many and great—have come from their possession of a Divine influence which they shared in common with the rest of their brethren in Christ rather than from any special grace received from episcopal consecration. The qualities displayed and the services rendered were Catholic only because they were Christian. Any other theory of the Christian ministry than this of personal gifts and spiritual fitness is sure to act disastrously. In order to establish the theory of Apostolical Succession and the validity of sacraments as dependent upon the presence and acts of an officiating priest, it has been found necessary to show that the acts are valid irrespective altogether of the character of the man who performs them. It is a sound instinct, which surely comes from God and commends itself to every sensible man, that raises the searching question, How is it conceivable that men of evil or utterly unspiritual lives, such as too many of the clergy

[1] Stanley's *Christian Institutions*, pp. 138–9.

have been, can be God's instruments to impart His spiritual gifts to others? Dire indeed must be the exigency which led a man like Leighton to reply: " God can convey grace by those to whom He has given none; He can cause them to carry this treasure and have no share in it ; carry the letter and not know what is in it." Canon Gore maintains that the objection to unspiritual men performing spiritual functions is one that rather admits of being strongly felt than consistently argued, forgetting that that which is strongly felt is often truer than that which is consistently argued. The unworthiness of the minister, he says, hinders not the grace of the sacrament, because the Holy Spirit, and not the minister, is the giver of the grace ; that even our Lord recognised the official authority of the Scribes and Pharisees who sat in Moses' seat ; and that in a visible society in which good and bad are mingled together there is really no more difficulty in believing that bad men can share the functions of the ministerial priesthood than that bad men share the priesthood which belongs to all Christians. Apart from the fact that it has yet to be shown that bad men *do* share the priesthood which belongs to all Christians, we feel instinctively that this kind of argument is confusing to one's moral sense, and would never have been used except under the stress of direst emergency, and for the purpose of bolstering up, by a perversion of Scripture, an ecclesiastical system foreign to the Scriptural idea. The power of God is not conveyed by physical contact, but by the reception of a spirit. God in His spiritual realm works not through the hands of a man, but through his soul, and thus working love begets love, and faith generates faith. The mind of Christ, as set forth in the minds of His servants, acts on other minds, whether by ideas or character, and so produces likeness to itself. On the mechanical theory of transmission one is shocked to find that no amount of wickedness can invalidate Holy Orders, though, strange to say, a mere technical informality at ordination may. The Pope has definitely and formally decided that the absence of certain words in ordination has completely invalidated clerical Orders in the Church of England for three centuries and more. On the other hand, the Orders of the Holy Father Rodrigo Borgia, and his son Cæsar, the cardinal, were not invalidated, though the record of their lives presents a picture of flagitiousness, treachery, rapine, and murder unsurpassed in the records of guilt. Of the Papal Court at Avignon we have in Petrarch's Letters the report of an eye-witness, who calls it the third Babylon, the shameless abode of cruelty, avarice, and lust, where honour, innocence, and piety are of no avail against gold; and heaven and Christ themselves are put up to sale. The men who did these things were in Holy Orders; violations of the most sacred human obligations were committed on the steps or from the very seat of the Papal throne, still these Orders were not invalidated. Straightforward, single-minded men, uncorrupted by ecclesiastical systems, refuse to bewilder their moral sense by these outrages upon Scripture; and since sanctity is an attribute which belongs to the indivisible will or personality, refuse to draw a distinction between private character and official functions. What would He have said who in other days, with stern severity and holy scorn, drove out worldliness from the temple of God? He did say, by their fruits ye shall know them.

V.

In addition to the objections already urged against the theory of Apostolical Succession, there is one of constitutional sort not to be lightly set aside : it is that *the undue stress laid upon official authority in the Church has had the effect of superseding the self-governing and mutually edifying functions of the Church itself.* The Christian Churches of the earliest time were communities gathered from the outside world, and when thus gathered each community was complete in itself and self-governing. They were communities existing within the greater community of the national life. They regarded themselves as sojourners (πάροικοι), dwellers by the side of others. As to their heavenly citizenship, they were no more strangers and sojourners (πάροικοι), but as dwellers in the cities of this world they were sojourners ever. In the Greek version of the Old Testament scriptures the Hebrew captives in the cities of Babylon were so described, and those who returned after the seventy years were known as "the sons of the sojourning" (παροικίας). The word passed over to the Christians because they felt that they lived in a world of their own, and in a real sense separate from their neighbours. The letter known as the Epistle of Clement bears the superscription : " The Church of God which sojourneth in Rome to the Church of God which sojourneth [παροικούσῃ] in Corinth." They were transitory dwellers (πάροικοι) as contrasted with those who made their home in this world, and were permanent residents in the secular sphere (κάτοικοι). The feeling is finely expressed in the Epistle to Diognetus (c. 5.) : " Christians," says this writer, "are not distinguished from the rest of mankind either in locality, or in speech, or in customs. For they dwell not somewhere in cities of their own, . . . but while they dwell in cities of Greeks or barbarians, as the lot of each is cast, and follow the native customs in dress and food and the other arrangements of life, their own citizenship is quite of other sort. They dwell in their own countries, but only as sojourners; they bear their share in all things as citizens, and they endure all hardships as strangers. Every foreign country is fatherland to them, and every fatherland is foreign."

This feeling of separateness from the outside unspiritual world drove them quite naturally the closer to each other. United by the most powerful of bonds, that of common religious sympathies and aspirations, they came together under a feeling of common brotherhood and received that kind of stimulus which men always get from association with those animated by like aims and hopes. Spiritual brotherhoods thus constituted, and dwelling in the midst of unsympathetic surroundings, were almost of necessity autonomous communities, and all the facts which have come to our knowledge show that they actually were. For example, from the earliest time, and for long after, they elected their own officers. They even took prominent part in choosing an apostle to fill the place left vacant by Judas. It was among the hundred and twenty disciples that Peter made the proposition that the vacancy should be filled, and they, that is, the whole company, put forward two men to be decided on as the lot should direct. Again, at a later time, when the apostles needed help in the administration of affairs, they called the multitude of the disciples unto them and said: "Look *ye* out, brethren, from among you seven men of good report." The saying pleased the whole multitude, and *they* chose Stephen and others to be set apart by the apostles. As we learn from the Epistle of Clement, the Church in Corinth not only elected its presbyters but also dismissed them. It is true their brethren in Rome remonstrated with them for doing it, but not because they had no right to dismiss their officers, but only because they had exercised their power in the case of men who did not deserve to be dismissed, who had "ministered unblameably to the flock of Christ in lowliness of mind," and who had been appointed "with the consent of the whole Church." We gather that Polycarp approved of the action of the Church at Philippi in setting aside an unworthy presbyter in the person of Valens (*Ep.*, c. 11). The Didaché of about the same date charges the Churches to appoint for themselves bishops and deacons, worthy of the Lord, men true and approved. The Apostolic Canons, as we have just seen, in the case of a Church so small that "there are not twelve persons who are competent to vote at the election of a bishop," urges them to send for three persons from some neighbouring Church to assist them in making their choice. The Apostolic Constitutions also enjoin that the bishop shall be "chosen by the whole people, who, when he is named and approved, let the people assemble with the presbytery and bishops that are present on the Lord's Day and let them give their consent" (viii. 4). Up to and even after the conversion of the Empire under Constantine bishops and presbyters were chosen by the whole body of the people by show of hands ($\chi\epsilon\iota\rho o\tau o\nu i\alpha$); and Eusebius tells us (*H. E.*, vi. 29) that when Fabianus was chosen successor to Anterôs, all the brethren were met for the purpose, and the whole body with all eagerness and with one voice, as if moved by the one Spirit of God, proclaimed him worthy, and without delay placed him in the bishop's seat. Other elections, such as that of Damasus at Rome, of Gregory at Constantinople, of Ambrose at Milan, and of Chrysostom at Constantinople, prove conclusively that the right of popular election continued in the Church for centuries, and that too after great constitutional changes in other important respects had been brought about. Even Cyprian, with all his strongly pronounced ecclesiastical proclivities, charged the people to separate themselves from an unworthy minister, especially since they themselves have the power either of choosing worthy ministers or of rejecting unworthy ones. He speaks also of his colleague Sabinus as having had a pastorate conferred on him "by the suffrage of the whole brotherhood"; and he regards it as a thing of Divine authority that a minister be chosen in the presence of all the people, under the eyes of all, and be approved worthy and suitable by public judgement and testimony.

Returning to early apostolic times, we find that the Churches not only elected their own permanent officers, but also chose their representatives for special occasions and purposes. They sent forth Paul and Barnabas as missionaries to the heathen (Acts xiii.); and the Churches afterwards received the accounts of the work of God which were brought back by such missionaries. When tidings of the work at Antioch "came to the ears of the Church which was in Jerusalem, *they* sent forth Barnabas as far as Antioch" (Acts xi. 22). When Paul and Barnabas returned "they gathered the Church together, and rehearsed all things that God had done with them." When the question arose at Antioch as to the Gentile converts being required to conform to the Jewish custom of circumcision, it was the brethren there who appointed Paul and Barnabas and certain others to go up to Jerusalem and hold consultation with the apostles and elders on the question ; when these delegates set forth they were " brought on their way by the Church," and when they reached Jerusalem " they were received of the Church " as well as of the apostles and elders. It is said that the apostles and the elders were gathered together to consider of the matter, but it is clear from what follows that it was really a conference of the whole Church, for we read that when Peter spoke "all the multitude kept silence; and they hearkened unto Barnabas and Paul rehearsing what signs and wonders God had wrought among the Gentiles by them." Then when a decision in favour of liberty had been arrived at, "it seemed good to the apostles and elders *with the whole Church* to choose men out of their company and send them to Antioch along with Paul and Barnabas." The document containing the decision arrived at in Jerusalem ran in the name of the apostles and elder brethren and was addressed "unto the brethren which are of the Gentiles in Antioch and Syria and Cilicia, greeting." The delegates thus appointed when they were dismissed came down to Antioch, and having gathered the multitude together, they delivered the epistle. "And when they " (*i.e.*, the multitude) "had read it they rejoiced for the exhortation " (or declared decision). These brethren having spent some time in Jerusalem "were dismissed in peace *from the brethren* unto those that had sent them forth " (Acts xv.). In another instance we find Paul saying that along with

Titus he was sending to Corinth "the brother whose praise in the Gospel is spread through all the Churches," but he straightway adds that this very brother whom he is sending had really been elected by the Churches to assist the apostle in the matter in hand (χειροτονηθεὶς ὑπὸ τῶν ἐκκλησιῶν). Thus special commissioners as well as ordinary officers were elected by the Church, as the word seems to indicate, by show of hands. Then, too, each Church controlled its own expenditure and exercised discipline within its own borders. The Church, as a Church, as a primary assembly, passed judgement upon erring brethren in their fellowship. Paul, referring to the action of the whole body, enjoins upon the Galatians to restore a lapsed brother in a spirit of meekness; and he calls upon the Church at Corinth to deal firmly with a case of grave immorality which had occurred among them. They "being gathered together" are to exercise discipline upon the man who has dishonoured the Christian name. They have the right, and duty is involved in the right: "Do not ye judge them that are within, whereas them that are without God judgeth? Put away the wicked man from among yourselves." [1]

This autonomy of the several Churches is further recognised in the fact that it was to the Churches themselves and not to their officers that the apostle addressed his various Epistles. This was universally the case. These Epistles were addressed to the Church in Rome, "beloved of God," to the Church in Corinth,

---

[1] "Nothing, perhaps, has been more prominent in our examination of the Ecclesiæ of the apostolic age than the fact that the Ecclesia itself, *i.e.*, apparently the sum of all its male adult members, is the primary body, and, it would seem, even the primary authority" (Hort's *Christian Ecclesia*, p. 229).

"called to be saints," to "the Churches of Galatia," to "the saints which are in Ephesus," to "the saints and faithful brethren in Christ which are at Colossæ," and to "the Church of the Thessalonians in God the Father and the Lord Jesus Christ." The one exceptional instance of an opening salutation where reference is made to the officers of the Church is that in the Epistle to the Philippians, but even here the people take precedence, and the letter is addressed "to all the saints in Christ Jesus which are at Philippi, with the bishops and deacons."

On the other side it may be alleged that Paul reminded Titus that he had left him in Crete to set in order the things that were wanting, and appoint elders in every Church. But, if we may judge by analogy elsewhere, even in Crete the people would choose their own elders, and the function of Titus would be confined to seeing the arrangements carried out and setting those apart whom the Churches had chosen. We have no reason to suppose he exercised any kind of surveillance over these Churches afterwards. No doubt in the case of converts newly gathered and communities newly formed the missionary who introduced the Gospel among them would have more than ordinary influence for a while. But the normal condition was that of self-government. So again when Paul says that there pressed upon him daily "anxiety for all the Churches," we have no reason to suppose that this implied formal or authoritative supervision of their affairs, but only brotherly care for the great enterprise which lay so near his heart. We may be reminded, too, of the letter of Clement to the Church at Corinth, in which he seems to exercise a sort of episcopal authority over the brethren there. But this letter proves too much. For when we look more carefully into it we find it is from a Church, to a Church, not from a bishop to a Church. It is, as we have seen already, a letter from "the Church of God which sojourneth in Rome to the Church of God which sojourneth in Corinth, to them which are called and sanctified by the will of God through our Lord Jesus Christ." Dr. Lightfoot is emphatic enough on the point: "There is every reason," he says, "to believe the early tradition which points to St. Clement as its author, and yet he is not once named. The first person plural is maintained throughout: '*We* consider,' '*we* have sent.' Accordingly the writers of the second century speak of it as a letter from the community, not from the individual. Thus Dionysius of Corinth, writing to the Romans, (c. 170, A.D.) refers to it as the Epistle 'you wrote us by Clement' (Euseb., *H.E.*, iv. 23). Irenæus says, 'the Church in Rome sent a very adequate letter to the Corinthians urging them to peace.' Later still Clement of Alexandria calls it the Epistle of the Romans to the Corinthians.... Now that we possess the work complete we see that the existence of Clement is not once hinted at from beginning to end. The name and personality of Clement are absorbed in the Church of which he is the spokesman."[1] Whatever changes after years may have brought, there was at first no diocesan episcopate, no authority exercised by one Church over another.[2] The members of one Church

---

[1] *Apostolic Fathers*, Part i. vol. i. 69.
[2] "Of officers higher than elders we find [in the New Testament] nothing that points to an institution or system, nothing like the episcopal system of later times" (Dr. Hort's *Christian Ecclesia*, p. 232).

received the members of other Churches to hospitality, letters of commendation were given and received, apostles, prophets, and teachers moved to and fro among the various Churches, tarrying and teaching here and there, and so begetting a kind of corporate congregational unity among the many brotherhoods scattered abroad. But anything like authoritative control from without came much later. Even Councils when they first began were simply brotherly conferences without power of legislation. There is a significant passage in Tertullian (*De Jejuniis*, c. xiii.) in which he says that "throughout the provinces of Greece (*per Græcias*) there are held in definite localities those Councils gathered out of the universal Churches, by whose means not only all the deeper questions are handled for the common benefit, but the actual representation of the whole Christian name is celebrated with great veneration. And how worthy a thing is this, that under the auspices of faith men should congregate from all quarters to Christ! 'See how good and how enjoyable for brethren to dwell in unity!' This psalm you know not well how to sing except when supping in a goodly company!" From these words we gather that up to the time of Tertullian Church Councils were confined to the nations bearing the name of Greeks, and had not been adopted either in Africa or in the Latin Church, or among the Churches along the Nile; that they were mere convenient human arrangements and not Divine institutions; that they did not interfere with the internal government of the several Churches, but conferred in brotherly manner on spiritual matters of general interest and importance; and finally that the bishops or pastors present at these Councils were there as representatives of their respective Churches, and not in their private and individual capacity.

The general history of the period, so far as known to us, bears out this statement of Tertullian. There is no reference to any ecclesiastical Council prior to the second century. The Conference recorded in the fifteenth chapter of the Acts was not really a Council proper. A Council in the technical sense means an assembly of several associated Churches, or a congregation of delegates representing a number of Churches met to consult on the common welfare. The gathering on the occasion referred to was merely a meeting of the members of one individual Church consisting of the apostles, elders, and people. Ecclesiastical Councils properly so called came much later, and, as Tertullian says, were at first confined to Greece, from which towards the close of the second century they passed into Palestine and Syria. Mosheim, whose keen insight into early Church history has not been surpassed by more recent writers, said long since that while in the first age of Christianity the Churches were united in one common bond of faith and love, "yet with regard to government and internal economy, every individual Church considered itself an independent community. Neither in the New Testament nor in any ancient document whatever do we find anything recorded from which it might be inferred that any of the minor Churches were at all dependent on, or looked up for direction to, those of greater magnitude or consequence; on the contrary, several things occur therein which put it out of all doubt that every one of them enjoyed the same rights, and was considered as being on a footing of the most perfect equality with the rest."[1]

This equality of the Churches among themselves was the natural outcome of the equality of all the brethren in each separate Church. They were all sons of God through faith in Christ, and therefore all entitled to participation in their common affairs. All differences of gifts or vocation were outweighed by the common dignity. Self-government was the logical outcome of sonship, and ecclesiastical office could only represent the rendering of service. These early communities were fully empowered to exercise the most important rights. They, as we have seen, elected and dismissed their own officers; chose representatives for special service; sent out missionaries and received reports of their work; exercised discipline, controlled finance, and

[1] *Commentaries on the Affairs of the Christians before the Time of Constantine*, i. 263, Vidal's ed., 1813. Dr. Hort is quite explicit on this point in his *Christian Ecclesia*. Speaking of Paul's Epistles he says, "Connected with this carefulness to keep individual membership in sight is the total absence of territorial language (so to speak) in the designations of local Ecclesiæ" (p. 114). "Plural designations of a plurality of Ecclesia are designated by a genitive of the region: the Ecclesiæ of Judæa (Gal. i. 22), of Galatia (1 Cor. xvi. 1), of Macedonia (2 Cor. viii. 1), of the nations or Gentiles (Rom. xvi. 4). We find no instance of such a form as the Ecclesiæ of Ephesus (a city) or the Ecclesiæ of Galatia" (a region), p. 115. "It is important to notice that not a word in the Epistle [Ephesians] exhibits the One Ecclesia as made up of many Ecclesiæ. To each local Ecclesia St. Paul has ascribed a corresponding unity of its own; each is a body of Christ and a sanctuary of God: but there is no grouping of them into partial wholes or into one great whole. The members which make up the One Ecclesia are not communities but individual men" (p. 168). "Thus there is a multiplication of single Ecclesiæ. We need not trace the process further. We find St. Paul cultivating the friendliest relations between these different bodies, and sometimes in language grouping together those of a single region; but we do not find him establishing or noticing any formal connexion between those of one region, or between all generally" (p. 227). Whether this was anything like modern Congregationalism or not, it certainly was very unlike to modern diocesan episcopacy, or a National Church system.

carried on correspondence in their own name with sister Churches. It has been well said: "An ecclesiastical office endowed with independent authority could not exist along with this self-government. It could only take the form of a ministry whose warrant rested from day to day on the voluntary approval of the members."[1]

VI.

By way of conclusion to this part of the subject we have now only to add that *the practical consequences of the theory of Apostolical Succession—the estrangement, exclusiveness, and intolerance engendered by it—are presumptive evidence against it.* It is true that for the purpose of mitigating its seeming intolerance the theory is sometimes advanced with an air of pious humility. For example, in 1836 Dr. Pusey wrote to a friend as follows: "Apostolic Succession, what is this but to say that we have a privilege which scarcely any other body of Christians has in the West, which is freed from the corruptions of Rome. Or again, if we speak of it with reference to Dissenters, with what real sorrow we ought to feel their loss, and with what humility our own privileges!"[2] Mr. Haddan again sought to lessen the appearance of assumption by making pious concession: "The Churchman," he says, "often may well feel that he must watch and labour and pray if he would rival many a Dissenter in spirituality and holiness. But the truth is unaltered none the less; nor is the vantage ground both of faith and of grace diminished upon which the Churchman stands and by which he will be

[1] Weizsäcker's *Apostolic Age*, bk. v. c. ii. 2, § 1.
[2] *Life of Pusey*, vol. i. 403 (E. B. P. to J. F. Russell, Dec., 1836).

judged."[1] Men who have lived in a clerical atmosphere for the greater part of a lifetime can, no doubt, write in this way with the most perfect sincerity, believing that they, and they only, are commissioned and privileged from heaven. But pious concession is not the best substitute for sound argument, and we cannot forget that the artifice of inculcating absurdities by the use of "an awful and reverential manner" has been said to be the approved receipt for sanctifying, in the eyes of the timid and credulous, the most enormous deviations from truth and common sense. Imitators are seldom equal to those they imitate. It is difficult for Anglican writers to rival the Jesuits in the subtle art of propounding doctrines subversive of Scripture and insulting to human reason with an air sanctimonious and a show of pious gravity. It might well be supposed that so able a writer as the one just quoted would have some misgivings as to his theory, if, as he says, a Churchman with his supernatural privilege would have to strive so resolutely in order to rival in spirituality and holiness many a Dissenter who on his hypothesis was destitute of this privilege. There must be serious lesion somewhere.

While there is an air of piety in this way of putting the case, there is also the appearance of resolute fidelity to truth in the manner in which responsibility for the consequences of the theory is disavowed. In Tract No. 4 of the *Tracts for the Times*, Hurrell Froude first raised the question as to whether by accepting Apostolic Succession they did not unchurch all Christians who have no bishop, and then answered his own question by saying, "We are not judging others, but deciding on

---

[1] *Apostolic Succession in the Church of England*, by Arthur W. Haddan, p. 73.

our own conduct. We do not pass sentence on other persons, but we are not to shrink from our deliberate views of truth and duty because difficulties may be raised by such persons. To us such questions are abstract, not practical, and whether we can answer them or no, it is our business to keep fast hold of the Church Apostolical whereof we are actual members." In like manner Mr. Haddan also defends the exclusiveness of his party by saying that "truth is none the less to be held fast because there are good men who, unhappily for themselves, do not hold it; least of all, truth that forms part of the elementary creed of Christendom." Archbishop Bramhall, less courteous, puts the matter more brusquely: If continental Protestants, or Dissenters at home, go wrong, that is their affair, not his. "What have I to do with the regulations of foreign Churches, to burn mine own fingers with snuffing other men's candles? Let them stand or fall by their own master."[1] In company with these writers Canon Gore, also, has no misgiving on the score of uncharitableness. He declines to discuss the question as to whether Churches calling themselves Episcopal, but not Anglican, have really the historical succession, but he has not a vestige of doubt about others: "It will appear at once as a consequence of all this argument that the various Presbyterian and Congregational organisations, however venerable on many and different grounds, have, in dispensing with the episcopal succession, violated a fundamental law of the Church's life. . . . It follows, then, not that God's grace has not worked and worked largely, through many an irregular ministry, when it was exercised or used in good faith, but that a ministry

[1] *Warning against Scottish Discipline.*

not episcopally received is invalid, that is to say, falls outside the conditions of covenanted security, and cannot justify its existence in terms of the covenant."[1]

On reading this one is disposed to ask where is this covenant to be seen, the "terms" of which seem to be known in episcopal circles, but nowhere else? What are "uncovenanted mercies," and if, as it seems, they reach even to the salvation of a man's soul and to the building of him up in nobleness of Christian life and character, wherein do they differ from mercies that are covenanted? The only covenant we who read our Bibles know of is that new covenant, the "terms" of which were first set forth by the prophet Jeremiah (xxxi. 31–34), and afterwards more clearly and fully stated by the writer of the Epistle to the Hebrews (viii. 6–13), and of which Christ Himself is the Mediator. This only covenant of which we know anything in these New Testament days has for its "terms": that God's great law of life and truth is now to be no mere external law written on tables of stone, but a law inscribed by the living Spirit on the inward heart; that to men thus illumined the promise is made, "I will be to them a God, and they shall be to Me a people"; that there shall be a universal reign of light, so that "they shall not teach every man his neighbour and every man his brother, saying, Know the Lord, for all shall know Him from the least to the greatest"; and finally this new, this better covenant, carries this gracious promise, "I will be merciful to their unrighteousness, and their sins and their iniquities will I remember no more." There is nothing here, not a word, which authorises any man to narrow the flowings forth of Divine grace to an official

[1] *The Ministry of the Christian Church*, pp. 344–45.

line of priests. The only priest with whom this covenant is concerned is the one great Mediator, the Lord Jesus Christ Himself, who entered in once into the Holy Place, having obtained eternal redemption for us. If there is any other covenant in existence by which the Eternal has promised to tie Himself down to the communion of the Anglican Church, it is high time it was produced, that its credentials may be examined. We know nothing of it, and it appears that the Pope of Rome, the great authority on all matters of ecclesiastical etiquette, knows nothing of it either. In terms, the meaning of which cannot possibly be mistaken, he has decided, as we have seen, that Anglican Orders for the last three hundred years have been and are absolutely null and void, altogether invalid. Canon Gore cannot place the non-episcopal Churches lower down in the scale than the Pope places the Church to which Canon Gore himself belongs. Canon Gore will probably reply to the Pope that his assumptions do not alter facts; we say precisely the same thing to Canon Gore and those who are with him. The mere fact that ordinations have been performed by bishops for a given number of centuries is nothing to the purpose in face of the further fact that diocesan bishops were unknown for two centuries after the time of the apostles, that what bishops there were were simply individual pastors of separate Churches, with no more authority than a simple pastor has to-day. An exclusive theory of the ministry on which such momentous results are made to depend should surely have a broader and deeper foundation to stand on than a metaphor or a hint, a guess or a criticism. It cannot be shown when the commission for which so much is claimed was first given, or to whom, how it was passed on, or along what line it came, and yet on such frivolous grounds Christian men are insolently consigned to uncovenanted mercies, and bidden to withdraw from the Holy Place to the Court of the Gentiles. A vigorous writer of half a century ago said then what needs to be repeated now, that the strongest and most irrefragable argument against so-called Church principles is not so much their absurdity, though that is flagrant enough, but their essential uncharitableness. One stands absolutely confounded at the fatuity of men who, with the New Testament in their hands, are ready to fraternise with Rome while they treat Lutheran and Presbyterian with scorn and contumely; who for the sake of mere figments remorselessly exclude a large portion of the communities of Christendom from the very name, rights, and privileges of Christian Churches; who can imagine the great doctrines in which both they and their opponents coincide, and which form the theme and triumph of inspired eloquence, of less moment than doctrines and rites on which Scripture is ominously silent, or which seem to stand in shocking contrast to the moral grandeur and magnanimous spirit of the Christian institute.

The facts of life and of the spiritual world cannot be explained on the theories of these men, and may well give them pause. There have been and are saintly men and women by thousands who show all the graces of the Christian life, and whose Christian character is unimpeachable, who yet have remained outside the episcopal communion all their lives. There are thousands of godly ministers, whose work God has graciously owned in the saving and upbuilding of men, who can point to the fruits of their ministry and say, "Need we, as do some, epistles of commendation ? Ye are our epistles, written in our hearts, known and read of all men ; being made manifest that ye are an epistle of Christ, ministered by us, written not with ink, but with the Spirit of the living God ; not in tables of stone, but in tables that are hearts of flesh." On the other hand there have been numbers of clerics, it is no breach of charity to say, who have gone through all the forms of initiation into the episcopal ministry, and yet, so far as men could judge, were mere blind leaders of the blind. The facts of life make havoc of the fictions of priests. God refuses to be bound by the narrow notions of half-enlightened men. What they please to call His "uncovenanted mercies" are only His own Divine way of showing to these men, as He showed to Israel of old, that He will not be restrained within the pitiful metes and bounds which men in their pride and prejudice are for ever rearing. The love of God is broader than the measures of man's mind ; and, throwing down the middle walls of partition built up by men in their littleness, He says sublimely, " I will have mercy on whom I will have mercy, and I will have compassion on whom I will have compassion. The same Lord is Lord of all, and is rich unto all that call upon Him : for whosoever shall call upon the name of the Lord shall be saved."

LECTURE IV

EARLIEST FORMS OF CHURCH LIFE

LECTURE IV

EARLIEST FORMS OF CHURCH LIFE

THUS far in our inquiry we have found not a few weighty reasons for hesitating to accept that mechanical conception of the Church and the ministry involved in the idea of Apostolical Succession. Let us now turn to the more positive aspects of the question, in the hope of discovering, if we may, what the primitive constitution of the Church really was. We ought to set forth on our search by laying aside, as far as we can, our own preconceived ideas ; for though these may harmonise with our own preferences, they may not necessarily correspond with facts. With all their serious defects the Tubingen School rendered us one important service—they stated the problem of Primitive Church History in clearer and more tangible form than it had been stated before. Their main contentions have now been discredited and left behind, but Baur has the credit of being the first writer who asked himself, not what does Early Christianity prove, but what was it like? Let us ask the same question. It is direct and to the purpose, and has the advantage of clearing away much useless discussion and leading us to a straight issue.

But when we have resolved to keep to the simple question, What was Early Church organisation like? we ought to define what we mean by the word "early." Clement of Rome and Cyprian of Carthage are sometimes quoted in a general way as if they were contemporaries, whereas there was a century and a half between them—a century and a half of most eventful years during which momentous changes were made. It is not enough therefore to go back merely to Cyprian's time and to his treatise "de Unitate" in our search for what was primitive. More than forty years ago Bunsen drew attention to the fact that the Tractarian Party, while exalting "tradition" and "antiquity," reserved for themselves the task of determining, by a process of picking and choosing, what should be accepted as valid tradition and decisive antiquity. This he called introducing "Popery without authority." To avoid laying ourselves open to the same objection let us take the earliest time of all, the century and a half after the founding of the Church at Pentecost. There is nothing arbitrary in this selection, for this was the period immediately under the formative influence of the apostles or of men who knew them, and it is sufficiently long to give definite character to Church life. It may fairly be claimed that whatever was unknown to the Church in the first century and a half of its existence cannot be regarded as indispensable to its integrity through subsequent ages. Divine authority can no more be claimed for later innovations than it can be claimed for any ecclesiastical invention of our own times.

The period being thus restricted, the materials for judgement, so far as they have been preserved to us, are brought within definite and reasonable compass. The works thus included as being original sources are, of course, the Gospels, the Acts of the Apostles, and the Epistles of the New Testament; following these in sub-apostolic times we have the two documents improperly called the Epistles of Clement; the recently discovered "Teaching of the Twelve Apostles"; the Epistle of Barnabas; the Shepherd of Hermas; the Epistle to Diognetus; the Apologies of Aristides and Justin Martyr; the fragments of Papias and Hegesippus, and the Letters from the Churches of Lyons and Vienne, preserved by Eusebius; the writings of Irenæus; the Apostolic Canons and portions also of the Apostolical Constitutions, though these were not collected in their present form till a much later date. The Epistles of Ignatius and Polycarp, for well-known reasons, stand by themselves and require separate consideration.

In dealing with a period like that we have marked out for ourselves, where materials are scanty and uncertainties are many, we are under the necessity of feeling our way from the known to the unknown. It so happens that, as far as Church organisation is concerned, the time of which we know least is the critical and important period between the death of the Apostle Paul (c. 64 A.D.) on the one hand, and the time of Justin Martyr (c. 150 A.D.) on the other hand—a period, speaking roughly, of between eighty and ninety years. If the actual arrangements of those years could be made clear, many of our difficulties would vanish. But failing this, if we could gain something like certain knowledge on Church organisation as it existed midway between these two points, we should have gained a great step in advance. From this vantage ground we could look back to the state of things as described in Paul's Epistles to the Corinthians and the Ephesians, and forward to the conditions of Church life as described by Justin Martyr in his Apology, and if we found anything like continuity and agreement from point to point we should have reasonable presumption of something like certainty. Now it so happens that the discoveries of recent years have placed us in this fortunate position of being able to look both backward and forward from a midway point. The coming to light of the little manual known as the Didachê or "The Teaching of the Apostles," or "The Teaching of the Twelve Apostles," as it is variously described, constitutes a new era in our knowledge of the Early Church. It may therefore be worth while to give some brief description of the work before proceeding to use it.

In the quarter of Constantinople know as Phanar, inhabited almost exclusively by Greeks, is the patriarchal church and the residence of the Greek Patriarch. Here too is the confused and irregular mass of buildings belonging to the Patriarch of Jerusalem and forming what is called the Jerusalem monastery of the Holy Sepulchre. The building, a stone's throw to the east, has been for years the residence of Philotheos Bryennios, Metropolitan of Diocletian's ancient capital, Nicomedia. He is second only in ecclesiastical rank to the Patriarch, and eminent among his countrymen for his learning. In 1873, while looking over the MSS. in the Jerusalem monastery at Constantinople, he came upon a small bulky volume he had not noticed before. To his great surprise and satisfaction he found therein, in complete form, the two so-called Epistles of Clement. So occupied was he with these that he failed to notice the Didaché, which was in the middle of the book; and it was not till 1880 that, looking again at the little treatise, he began to realise the value of the find he had made. In 1883 he published the work, together with an introduction and copious notes, and since then the original MS. has been removed to Jerusalem, to the headquarters of the fraternity. The volume in which it was found comprises 120 leaves of vellum, or 240 pages, contains seven different works, including the Didaché, and ends with a colophon stating that it was "finished in the month of June, the 11th day, Tuesday, the ninth year of the Indiction in the year 6564" (*i.e.*, A.D. 1056) "by the hand of Leo, notary and sinner." This Didaché with which we are now specially concerned is admitted to be a very early Christian book, its probable date being c. 95 A.D. Zahn and Lightfoot both place it between 80 and 100 A.D.; Funk, Langen, De Romestin and others content themselves with placing it in the last quarter of the first century. It has been long known that there had been such a book. As early as 200 A.D. Clement of Alexandria quoted it as Scripture, regarding it as semi-apostolic and semi-inspired; Eusebius also speaks of it in the same way. Dr. Taylor has shown from the writings of Justin Martyr that he was probably familiar with it; and Professor Rendel Harris notes that it was current in the second century in Rome, Ephesus, Corinth, and Alexandria, and indeed was more widespread than almost any other early document that can be compared with it. It was incorporated into patristic writings and Early Church manuals; it is the basis of the seventh chapter of the Apostolic Canons; and a sermon by Boniface, the apostle of Germany, shows that he was familiar with it from beginning to end, using it almost as a text-book, so that it seems to have been known along the banks of the Rhine as late as the beginning of the eighth century.

This little manual had, therefore, a remarkable record to begin with; and it was no sooner published on its re-discovery in 1883 than scholars at once recognised its great importance. Dr. Lightfoot stated that the interest and value of the work were proved to exceed the highest expectations. It was accepted as a genuine fragment of the earliest traditions of the Church. Dr. Schaff, after a careful analysis of language and substance, pointed out that it bore close affinity in style and vocabulary to the writings of the New Testament, as distinct both from classical and patristic Greek; that while its vocabulary comprises 552 different words, of these 504 are New Testament words. Then, as to its substance, he showed that there is nothing in the Didachê which could not have been written between 70 and 100 A.D. On the one side there are no allusions to facts, movements, customs, and institutions known throughout Christendom from the middle or beginning of the second century; there is no mention made of a New Testament canon or of any New Testament book, except the Gospels. It is silent on the Easter controversy, which in the second century became a burning question in the Church, and it is silent also on certain ascetic practices which began to prevail. Then, on the positive side, it is seen to present Christian teaching and Christian institutions in primitive, childlike simplicity. The love-feast and the Eucharist, which from the beginning of the second century were gradually separated, in the Didachê were still one; there was no class distinction between clergy and laity, no mention made of ordination or of the three orders of which so much was made later, and there was still room left for extemporaneous prayer in the worship of the Church which had not yet stiffened into fixed liturgical form. From the general consensus of opinion as to the genuineness of the Didachê there was only one dissentient voice, that of Dr. Krawutzcky, of Breslau, who, as a Roman Catholic writer, felt that its theology did not come up to the orthodox churchmanship of Peter, and assigned it to an Ebionitizing source, c. 200 A.D. On the other hand, another Roman Catholic writer (*Dublin Review*, October, 1884) speaks enthusiastically of the work as a compendium of the apostolic teaching, as accepted in 140 A.D., but which presented a state of things which had already died out in a great part of the Church, thus resembling, as he said, that cathedral of St. Magnus, in the capital of the Orkneys, which witnesses at this day to a survival of Norman architecture in a remote district after it had ceased in England.

Enough has been said to show that Harnack does not use too strong language when he describes this book as of "epoch-making importance for the understanding of the earliest history of the Church constitution." We may now proceed, therefore, to the fuller consideration of that passage in the Didachê, of which he said that "in the whole of Early Christian literature there is no other passage so important for the initial history of the Catholic episcopate." This occurs in the fifteenth chapter, where, after speaking of the reception accorded to apostles, prophets, and teachers, the manual charges the brethren thus: "Appoint for yourselves, therefore, bishops and deacons worthy of the Lord, men who are meek and not lovers of money, and true and approved ; for unto you they also perform the service of the prophets and teachers. Therefore despise them not ; for they are your honourable men [or men to be honoured], along with the prophets and · teachers." Taking this passage with what had gone before, we arrive at this result, that at the end of the first century there was a twofold organisation in the early Churches, one based on the ministry of the Word, and regarded as directly from God—God-endowed and God-commissioned, belonging to all the Churches, and consisting of apostles, prophets, and teachers ; the other part an organisation fixed and local, chosen by the individual congregation, having for its function the management of the affairs of the community, and consisting of bishops and deacons. It is clear from the Didachê that the latter were regarded as inferior to the former. It was necessary to urge that they were not to be despised, but to be regarded with honour along with the prophets and teachers ; for indeed, probably in the absence of these, they also performed the service of the prophets and teachers.

The vital question now to be asked is, Does this twofold division of Church officers correspond with what we find in the Scriptures in the matter of Church organisation? In seeking an answer to this question we note first that both in the Didachê and the Scriptures the place of honour is assigned to the teachers rather than to the administrators of the Church. The Didachê says : " My child, thou shalt remember him that *speaketh unto thee the Word of God* night and day, and shalt honour him as the Lord ; for whencesoever the Lordship speaketh there is the Lord " (c. 4). In like manner in the Epistle to the Hebrews we read: "Remember your rulers who *spake unto you the Word of God*" (xiii. 7). The same Greek phrase is in both places, and also in the Epistle of Barnabas, as if it were a technical expression: "Thou shalt love as the apple of thine eye every one that *speaketh unto thee the Word of the Lord*" (xix. 19, 10). Then, when we come to differentiate these teachers, we again find the Didachê and the Scriptures agreeing. The Didachê speaks of apostles, prophets, and teachers: "Concerning the apostles and prophets, so do ye according to the ordinance of the Gospel. Let every apostle when he cometh unto you be received as the Lord" (c. 11). "Every true prophet desiring to settle among you is worthy of his food. In like manner a true teacher is also worthy, like the workman, of his food" (c. 13). Turning now from the Didachê to the Acts of the Apostles, we find that in the Church at Antioch, besides the Apostle Paul, there were prophets and teachers, Barnabas and Symeon, Lucius and Manaen (xiii. 1). In the First Epistle to the Corinthians also we read that "God hath set some in the Church, first apostles, secondly prophets, thirdly teachers," after which mention is made of helps, governments, and other special and temporary charismata (xii. 28). To the same purport it is said in the Epistle to the Ephesians that Christ at His ascension gave gifts to men: "He gave some to be apostles; and some, prophets; and some, evangelists; and some, pastors and teachers; for the perfecting of the saints, unto the work of ministry, unto the building up of the body of Christ" (iv. 11, 12). Further, in this same Epistle, it is said that Christian men are "of the household of God, being built upon the foundation of the apostles and prophets" (ii.

20). The prophets here spoken of are usually taken to be those of the Old Testament, but they are named after the apostles, and later on in the same Epistle it is said that the mystery of Christ, long hidden, "hath now been revealed unto His holy apostles and prophets in the Spirit," which can only mean prophets in Christian times. Tertullian says that Marcion, quoting the passage "built upon the foundations of the apostles and prophets," erased the words "and prophets," "forgetting that the Lord had set in His Church not only apostles, but prophets also," and "fearing, no doubt, that our building was to stand in Christ upon the foundation of the ancient prophets" (*Adv. Marcion*, v. 17). Thus both the New Testament and the Didaché agree in recognising three classes of propagandists or teachers God-commissioned for all the Churches, and not officially connected with any one Church—apostles, prophets, and teachers. Alike in the Epistle to the Hebrews (xiii. 7, 17, 24), the Epistle of Clement (xxi. 6), and in the Shepherd of Hermas (Vis. iii. 9, 7) they are spoken of as "rulers," "leaders" (ἡγούμενοι), as distinguished from the permanent officers or "elders" (πρεσβύτεροι). Clement urges the Corinthians to reverence their rulers (προηγουμένους) and to honour their elders (πρεσβυτέρους). This, he said, they had done in their better days; they walked after the ordinances of God, "submitting yourselves to your rulers [ἡγουμένοις] and rendering to the presbyters the honour which is their due" (c. 1); while Hermas distinguishes between "rulers" and those "elders" who, as in the synagogue, occupy the chief seats (πρωτοκαθεδρίταις). In Acts xv. 22 Judas and Silas are called chief men among the brethren (ἡγούμενοι), and ver. 32 explains in what way, "Judas and Silas, being themselves also prophets."

Harnack maintains that there is no passage in the whole of Early Christian literature from which we can safely identify "rulers" (ἡγούμενοι) with "elders" (πρεσβύτεροι); that in all places where the word occurs before Hermas, namely, in the Acts of the Apostles, the Epistle to the Hebrews, and the Epistle of Clement, it refers only to the teachers and preachers, the spiritual guides of the community.

Of the three classes—apostles, prophets, and teachers —thus designated as "rulers" or "leaders" the *apostles* take precedence. Of course, when apostles are mentioned we naturally think of the Twelve appointed by our Lord Himself. But even before the discovery of the Didachê Dr. Lightfoot pointed out that the term "apostle" was not restricted to the Twelve, and that the case of Paul himself shows that the original number was broken in upon.[1] Speaking of the appearances of Christ after His resurrection, it is said (1 Cor. xv. 6, 7) that He showed Himself to the Twelve, and after that "to all the apostles," as if there were others besides the Twelve. Andronicus and Junias are spoken of as "of note among the apostles," the most natural interpretation of which indicates a considerable extension of the term, and was so understood by Origen and Chrysostom. Barnabas also is described as an apostle, and even mentioned as such before Paul, and Paul himself designates his missionary assistants, Timothy and Silvanus, not merely as apostles of the Churches, but as apostles of Christ (1 Thess. ii. 6), and it is evident from the way he speaks of Barnabas and Apollos that he so regarded them also. It would appear, indeed, that apostles in the later sense of the word, that is, as missionaries

[1] *Ep. to the Galat.*, pp. 92 sq.

opening new fields of service, were so numerous that unworthy men could pass themselves off as such. Paul speaks of "false apostles, deceitful workers, fashioning themselves into apostles of Christ" (2 Cor. xi. 12, 15); and in the Apocalypse (ii. 2) it is said of the Church at Ephesus "thou didst try them which call themselves apostles, and they are not, and didst find them false." From all this it would appear that the New Testament recognises the existence of such apostles as we find spoken of in the Didachê—men outside the circle of the Twelve, and continuing after they were gone. They could not, of course, stand as witnesses of the life, death, and resurrection of our Lord, as did the Twelve whom Paul calls chiefest apostles ($\dot{v}\pi\epsilon\rho\lambda\iota\alpha\nu$ $\dot{\alpha}\pi\dot{o}\sigma\tau o\lambda o\iota$, 2 Cor. xi. 5, xii. 11), but they were as the Twelve in being travelling missionaries, propagandists of the new faith, preachers of Christ's Gospel in the new fields of service to which they were the first to go. Of course we are not to regard Paul as founding his claim to be an apostle on this practice of appointing additional apostles; his title to stand on the same footing as the Twelve resting on higher grounds and springing from a special Divine call. But this practice does account for the condition of things existing at the end of the first century, and regarded by the Didachê as recognised by the Churches. The looser and more general meaning of the word held its place side by side with its special and distinctive application.

Next, after the apostles, the Didachê speaks of the *prophets* as the spiritually endowed teachers of the Church. While the apostles go to uninstructed heathen peoples, the prophets have their mission to the Christian communities already gathered, for the purpose of building up the Church in knowledge, and faith, and holiness. The first prevailing idea concerning the prophet was that his function was that of prediction; then came the conception which was mainly true that his work was rather that of forthtelling than of foretelling, and that prophesying meant preaching. There needs still another modification of the idea before we arrive at the exact truth. The prophet in the Early Church differed from the preacher, inasmuch as his utterance was the spontaneous prompting of the Spirit. The afflatus comes upon him and he speaks because he cannot refrain. He was not a Church officer in the ordinary sense, inasmuch as the Divine gift bestowed upon him was not official but personal. "No prophecy ever came by the will of man: but men spake from God, being moved by the Holy Ghost." Such were the prophets meant by the Didachê, which represents them as playing a more important part than either the apostles or teachers with whom it associates them. Prophets are mentioned fifteen times in its few pages, apostles and teachers only thrice each. They are the chief priests of the Christian community. While a form for celebrating the Supper of the Lord is given, the Church is to "permit the prophets to offer thanksgiving as much as they desire." An apostle may not stop more than one day in a community, or two at most, whereas the prophet may settle for a length of time if he so desire. If he decides to settle he is to be duly cared for: "Every firstfruit of the produce of the winevat and of the threshing-floor, of thy oxen and of thy sheep, thou shalt take and give as the firstfruit to the prophets; for they are your chief priests. If thou makest bread take the firstfruit and give according to the commandment. In like manner, when thou openest a jar of wine or of oil, take the firstfruit and give to the prophets; yea, and of money, and raiment, and every possession take the firstfruit as shall seem good to thee, and give according to the commandment" (c. 13). Since he speaks under a Divine influence he is not to be judged by ordinary standards: "Any prophet speaking in the Spirit ye shall not try nor discern; for every sin shall be forgiven, but this sin shall not be forgiven" (c. 11). Still, while his utterances may not be judged he himself may. If he teaches truth and yet lives not the truth he teaches, he is a false prophet. This testing of the man by his life is spoken of in other writings of the time besides the Didaché. In the "Shepherd" Hermas says: "As I shall tell thee so shalt thou test the prophet and the false prophet. By his life test the man that hath the Divine Spirit. He that hath the Spirit which is from above is gentle and tranquil and humble-minded, and abstaineth from all wickedness and vain desire of this present world, and holdeth himself inferior to all men"; the false prophet, on the contrary, "exalteth himself, and desireth to have a chief place, and straightway he is impudent, and shameless, and talkative, and conversant in many luxuries and many other deceits." "Being empty himself he giveth empty answers to empty inquirers," taking care to keep clear of righteous, discerning men: "He never approacheth an assembly of righteous men; but avoideth them and cleaveth to the doubtful-minded and empty, and prophesieth to them in corners, and deceiveth them, speaking all things in emptiness to gratify their desires." Among men who have the Spirit of God the mere pretender is emptied, struck dumb and altogether broken in pieces, being unable to utter a word. "Trust thou the Spirit that cometh from God and hath power; but in the earthly and empty spirit put no trust at all; for in it there is no power" (*Mand.* xi.).

That there were spiritually endowed prophets having great influence in sub-apostolic times in the Christian Church is not only to be gathered from the Didachê and the Shepherd of Hermas, but also even from a heathen writer like Lucian (c. 165–170 A.D.). In his *De Morte Peregrini* he brings his hero Proteus among the Christians, describes how he became a prophet among them, and as such was plentifully supplied with all he needed ; he tells how at one time he wandered about attended by a crowd of satellites, and at another, when cast into prison, the Christians visited him and ministered to him in many ways. Lucian meant to be sarcastic on what he thought to be the simplicity of the Christians ; incidentally he has, as an outsider, recorded a phase of their Church life.

If we now compare these statements from outside writings with those found in the books of the New Testament we shall find them to correspond. From the time of Pentecost this gift of prophesying, that is, the gift of free, spontaneous utterance of spiritual truth under Divine influence, was certainly possessed by many in the Church. The ancient promise was fulfilled—your sons and your daughters shall prophesy ; and the Church was charged not to resist this manifestation, not to undervalue it : Quench not the Spirit : despise not prophesyings, is the injunction given. But beyond the general gift thus bestowed upon the Church as a sign and token of the descent of the Spirit, there were some who were specially endowed, and were recognised as speaking the mind of the Spirit with exceptional power. The names have been preserved of several in the Church at Jerusalem specially designated as prophets. We read of Agabus, who, along with other prophets, went down from Jerusalem to Antioch (Acts xi. 27, 28; xxi. 10); of Judas and Silas, who, being themselves also prophets, exhorted the brethren at Antioch with many words and confirmed them (Acts xv. 32). Also in the Church of Antioch itself we read there were prophets and teachers, Barnabas, and Symeon that was called Niger, and Lucius of Cyrene, and Manaen the foster brother of Herod the tetrarch (Acts xiii. 1). These prophets are evidently not regarded as officials of the Church in which we find them. Their work is spiritual, incidental, voluntary, and for the universal brotherhood. God set some in the Church, first apostles, secondly prophets, thirdly teachers; or, as it is otherwise stated, on His ascension Christ gave some to be apostles and some prophets . . . for the perfecting of the saints unto the work of ministry, unto the building up of the body of Christ; and so the Church was built upon the foundation of the apostles and prophets, Christ Jesus Himself being the chief corner-stone. These prophets, moving from place to place, the servants of all the Churches, coming into community after community for instruction and enlightenment, formed an important element in, and a striking proof of, the corporate unity of the Church. They did much to bind the scattered, independent, self-governing communities into one great visible whole. Their selection was not determined by human choice. The gift was heaven-bestowed, and was at once recognised wherever it appeared, raising its possessor to influence and eminence in the Church.

Taking all the evidence, apostolic and sub-apostolic, which has come down to us, it is clear that after the Twelve had gone the prophet and not the bishop was the influential factor in Early Church life. In the New Testament Church, as in Judah of old, the prophet and not the priest was the formative force.

Then, finally, among the non-local spiritual leaders of the Church, along with apostles and prophets there were "thirdly *teachers*." There was both place and need for these as well as those. For Christianity, passing beyond Jewish life, was in many directions, entering that great Greek world which was intellectually educated and endowed with the literary instinct, a world where stress was laid upon a knowledge of the literature of the past, and upon the habit of cultivated speech in the present. For intellectual purposes teaching had come to be a lucrative profession, the teachers being recognised by the State and by the separate municipalities, and in consequence enjoying immunities from public burdens. The schools where these travelling professors or teachers exercised their calling were not confined to Rome or Athens. As early as the middle of the first century Marseilles was even more frequented than Athens, and there were great intellectual institutions at Antioch and Alexandria, at Rhodes and Smyrna, at Ephesus and Byzantium, and even as far West as Naples and Bordeaux.[1] Into a world thus quick with mental life Christianity went forth on its mission of winning all classes of men for Christ. Out of the ranks of these teachers it is probable there arose those apologists, those defenders of the Christian faith against the heathenism of the time, who made their appeal to

---

[1] *Hibbert Lecture*, by Dr. Hatch, p. 35.

Roman emperors and to the cultivated classes of the Empire. There was also the work of further instruction to be carried on amongst the new converts who had simply received the first principles of Christian truth. The difference between the prophet and the teacher was that the latter was more quietly didactic and systematic than the former. Chrysostom, in a homily on 1 Cor. xii. 27, explains the difference thus: " He that *prophesieth* speaketh all things from the Spirit, but he that *teacheth* sometimes discourses also out of his own mind." The Catechetical Schools were a prominent and important feature of the time; that of Alexandria has been described as the first Divinity Hall of the Christian Church, and we have in the Apostolical Constitutions (vii. 39) a sort of synopsis of the course of instruction pursued in these schools. The catechumen was to be taught "in the knowledge of the unbegotten God, in the understanding of His only begotten Son and in the assured acknowledgment of the Holy Ghost." He was to "learn the order of the several parts of creation, the series of providence, and the different dispensations of the Divine laws." He was to be taught " to know his own nature, of what sort it is ; also how God has punished the wicked and glorified the saints in every generation" ; and finally he was to be shown that even when the world had gone astray " how God still took care of and did not reject mankind, but called them from their error and vanity to the acknowledgement of the truth at various seasons, reducing them from bondage and impiety unto liberty and piety, from injustice to righteousness, from death eternal to everlasting life." After his initiation the young disciple was to be further "instructed in the doctrines concerning our Lord's incarnation, and in those concerning His passion and resurrection from the dead and ascension into heaven." The work of the teacher was thus not less living or less needful than that of the apostle or the prophet.

Having thus dealt with the spiritually endowed, the God-commissioned teachers of the community, we pass now to the *local officers of administration* elected by the Church and variously described as *presbyters, bishops, deacons, presidents* (προεστῶτες) and *rulers* (προϊστάμενοι). These had a different origin from the former. While it is said that "God hath set some in the Church first apostles, secondly prophets, thirdly teachers" and further "helps and governments," it is nowhere said that He gave presbyters, bishops, or deacons. These arose from the necessity which every society feels for some form of government, and they took shape according to local feeling and past association. The kingdom of God as a Divine society was set up in the earth, being planted in the hearts of believing men and the spiritual forces by which it was to be perpetuated and extended were provided in the shape of apostles, prophets, and teachers, while the machinery of organisation by which these believing men should become a self-governing society was left to be evolved according to local circumstances and the necessities of the case. In the constitution of the society by which the kingdom of God is to find human expression much has been left to the judgement and free action of spiritually enlightened men. While God bestowed the charismatic gifts, the Church elected its own administrative officers. The community chose the Seven to serve tables as described in the Acts of the Apostles, and the Didaché of a later date enjoins the

Churches as follows: "Appoint for yourselves therefore bishops and deacons worthy of the Lord, men who are meek and not lovers of money, and true and approved; for unto you they also perform the service of the prophets and teachers"; that is, as we may suppose, in the absence of itinerant prophets and teachers: "therefore despise them not; for they are your honourable men along with the prophets and teachers" (c. 15).

As we now enter a region which has long been one of thorny controversy we shall probably best disentangle the whole question if we first of all carefully draw a distinction which the Apostle Paul himself has drawn, and which has been too often overlooked—a distinction between Churches existing among different nationalities and in various countries. For national preference and local custom naturally exercised their influence on the ecclesiastical as well as on the civil life of the time. We have first the *Churches of Judea*, in which only Jewish ideas prevailed and where the administration was in the hands of presbyters or elders (Gal. i. 22; 1 Thess. ii. 14). Then besides these "Churches of God which are in Judea in Christ Jesus," we have *the Churches of the Gentiles* (ἐκκλησίαι τῶν ἐθνῶν), in which there was also often a considerable Jewish element, and in which the local administrators were "bishops and deacons"; these two classes of officers being described in one general term by the Gentile Christians as "rulers" (προϊστάμενοι) or "presidents" (προεστῶτες), and by the Jewish Christians, in one general term as "elders" (πρεσβύτεροι).

Let us now see how this distinction works itself out in fact, taking for our starting-point the "Churches of Judea." Remembering the central place in the national life of Palestine which was held by the synagogue, we might naturally suppose that the organisation of the Christian Ecclesia would be largely shaped by it. For in the centuries immediately preceding the Christian era the synagogue was more closely associated with the religious life of the people than even the temple itself. There was but one temple, to which the people repaired only at distant intervals, while there must have been thousands who, from infirmity or other causes, scarcely ever joined the pilgrimage to Jerusalem. On the other hand the synagogue was in every town and village, was, so to speak, at every man's door, and the elders who sat in the chief seats were the familiar objects of a lifetime. Week by week all the year round the people, young and old, repaired to the synagogue, not only on Sabbath and feast days, but also on Mondays and Thursdays, "the days of congregation," when the peasantry brought their produce to the market and their causes of dispute to the judgement of the elders.

What was true of the Jewish people generally was, of course, true also of our Lord and His apostles. In the synagogues they worshipped through the days of their youth; in the synagogues our Lord wrought some of His greatest works and spoke some of His most memorable words. After His ascension the apostles and early believers still kept up for a while their connexion with the Jewish services in synagogue and temple. It was the most natural thing therefore for them to repeat in the Christian Church the only organisation of which they had any practical knowledge. When, then, the necessity for further development arose, as it did in the matter of the daily ministration, the Twelve called the multitude of the disciples together and desired them to look out, from among themselves, *seven men* of good report, full of the Spirit and of wisdom, whom they, the apostles, might appoint over the business. The course suggested was the one they were accustomed to. The election of the elders of the synagogue depended on the choice of the congregation,[1] and the number elected for smaller towns and villages was usually seven. When Josephus organised Galilee he said, " Let there be seven men to judge in every city ; and these such as have been before most zealous in the exercise of virtue and righteousness."[2]

Following wonted use and custom, therefore, the apostles asked that seven men might be chosen for the *diakonia of tables*, while they gave themselves to the *diakonia of the Word*. (Acts vi. 1–6). Now what were these seven men ?—were they deacons or elders ? Those of us who have long been accustomed to regard the account in the sixth chapter of the Acts as precedent and warrant for the election of seven deacons in a Church may regard the question as superfluous. Yet the question is asked and there are substantial reasons for asking it. Vitringa[3] in the seventeenth century, and the learned canonist, Just Henning Boehmer,[4] and the historian Mosheim in the eighteenth, maintained that the seven were simply the elders of the Jerusalem Church. In our own time Lechler and others agree with this view, while Ritschl and Lange maintained that the office of the seven included both the eldership and the later diaconate. Apart, however, from the authority of names, let us see what are the facts.

The first thing to be noticed is that the seven officers

[1] Edersheim's *Life and Times of Jesus the Messiah*, i. 438.
[2] *Antiquities of the Jews*, IV. viii. 14.
[3] *De Synag. Vet.* iii. 926.
[4] *Dissert. Juris Eccles. Antiqui.*, Dissert. vii. 373.

elected are nowhere in Scripture described as deacons. They are simply called the Seven (Acts xxi. 8). So far as we know the first writer who spoke of them as deacons was Irenæus,[1] but this was a hundred and fifty years after the time of their election, and it was the description of a man who was familiar only with the Gentile Churches of Asia Minor and Gaul, and in Gentile Churches the local administrators were bishops and deacons. Dr. Lightfoot points out that though the word "deacon" does not occur the corresponding verb and substantive ($\delta\iota\alpha\kappa o\nu\epsilon\tilde{\iota}\nu$ and $\delta\iota\alpha\kappa o\nu\acute{\iota}\alpha$) are repeated more than once. On the other hand it must be noted that when these words do occur it is simply in the general sense of service, and the noun ($\delta\iota\alpha\kappa o\nu\acute{\iota}\alpha$) is applied to the apostles as well as to the seven, a contrast being instituted between the *diakonia* of tables and the *diakonia* of the Word. As a matter of fact the word "deacon" ($\delta\iota\acute{\alpha}\kappa o\nu o\varsigma$) never occurs in the Acts of the Apostles, and even in the Epistles it is in the original applied to those who certainly were not deacons in the ecclesiastical sense of the word. The magistrate is the "deacon" of God (Rom. xiii. 4); "what then is Apollos? and what is Paul? 'Deacons' through whom ye believed" (1 Cor. iii. 5). Elsewhere, still speaking of himself, Paul says: "in every thing commending ourselves as 'deacons' of God" (2 Cor. vi. 4); "are they 'deacons' of Christ? I more" (xi. 23); "the Gospel whereof I was made a 'deacon'" (Eph. iii. 7; Col. i. 23); he also calls Timothy "our brother and God's 'deacon' in the Gospel" (1 Thess. iii. 2). As describing the officer of a Church the word "deacon" is found in only three verses of the New Testament (Philip. i. 1; 1 Tim. iii. 8, 12); in

[1] *Adv. Hæres.*, i. 26. 3; iii. 12. 10; iv. 15. 1.

all three it refers to Gentile Churches, and in all three bishops and deacons are associated together, and there is no mention made of elders. The first reference occurs in a salutation to the Macedonian Church at Philippi, the other two in directions given to Timothy, whom he had exhorted to tarry at Ephesus (1 Tim. i. 3), that is, among the Greek Churches of Asia Minor. The diaconate, therefore, is a Gentile institution rather than Jewish.

Further, not only are the Seven never called deacons anywhere in the New Testament, but when for the first time officials are mentioned as existing in the Church at Jerusalem (Acts xi. 30), they are called "the elders" (τοὺς πρεσβυτέρους), the definite article being used as indicating an office already well known, and this though not a single word had been previously said as to the appointment of elders. Nor is this all: these officers are called elders in a case where the function of the deacon was specially concerned, for it involved the receiving and distributing of money to the poor in the Church. In a time of famine the disciples at Antioch, "every man, according to his ability, determined to send relief unto the brethren that dwelt in Judea, which they also did, sending it to *the elders* by the hand of Barnabas and Saul." If there were deacons in the Jerusalem Church why was not this money for the poor handed to them? Ritschl suggests that possibly by this time the office had fallen into abeyance,[1] but certainly long after this it had not fallen into abeyance in the Church either at Philippi or Ephesus, therefore this cannot be the explanation. Davidson thinks they were left out for the sake of brevity. Then further, if it is suggested that there

[1] *Entstehung der christliche Kirche.* 2te aufl., p. 355.

might be deacons as well as elders, the presbyters taking rank above the deacons, we are inclined to ask how is it, then, that if such an order had been created in the interim, the names of these elders were not given while those of the Seven are all carefully recorded? No mention is made of any appointment after that of the Seven, and no names are given of elders as being appointed. There is also another point. If there were deacons in the Church at Jerusalem as well as elders, it is remarkable that they are never mentioned on occasions when we should have expected they would have been. In the important conference recorded in Acts xv. mention is made of "the apostles and the elders with the whole Church" (xv. 22); of the "chief men among the brethren," afterwards described as "prophets," and no fewer than five times in the course of the chapter (xv. 2, 4, 6, 22, 23) "apostles and elders" are spoken of together. All this about elders in one chapter while deacons are not mentioned so much as once throughout the whole book. On a later occasion, when Paul and his fellow-travellers returned to Jerusalem, Luke says: "The brethren received us gladly. And the day following Paul went in with us unto James, and *all the elders were present* (Acts xxi. 18). Still not one word about deacons among the officers of the Church. The only conclusion we can come to, in the face of these facts, is that in the Jerusalem Church in apostolic times there were neither bishops nor deacons, that while apostles came and went on missionary work the Churches of Judea were each presided over by a body of presbyters or elders, as the synagogues had been in the times before them.

But it may be said that in coming to this conclusion

we are overlooking the fact that James, the brother of our Lord, and after him Symeon, the son of Clopas, are spoken of as bishops of Jerusalem. In reply it must be noted first that in the New Testament, which is our highest authority, neither James nor any other man is ever described as bishop of Jerusalem. Indeed, if we may make a short digression on an important point, nothing is more striking than the contrast between the portentous claims made by and for bishops in ecclesiastical history, and the extremely scanty references made to them in Scripture. First we have the verb "to oversee" (ἐπισκοπεῖν), which occurs only twice, once to urge men to *look diligently* lest any man fail of the grace of God (Heb. xii. 15); and once where Peter enjoins the elders to exercise the *oversight* of the flock, not of constraint but willingly (1 Pet. v. 2). Then we have the substantive "episcopate" (ἐπισκοπή), which occurs only four times, and twice out of the four it has no ecclesiastical bearing, but simply refers to a time of Divine *visitation* (Luke xix. 44 ; 1 Pet. ii. 12) ; of the remaining two instances one is a quotation from the Septuagint version of the Psalms (cix. 8), where it is said of a wicked man "let another take his *office*" (τὴν ἐπισκοπὴν), these words being quoted and applied to Judas (Acts i. 20). The remaining passage is the only one of the four having any reference to the function of a bishop, and says: "If a man seeketh the office of a bishop he desireth a good work"[1] (1 Tim. iii. 1). Finally, we come to the original word for bishop itself (ἐπίσκοπος),

---

[1] Dr. Hort translates this passage thus: "If any man seeketh after ἐπισκοπῆς (a function of oversight) he desireth a good work. He therefore that hath oversight must needs be free from reproach." He adds: "So I think we should naturally interpret the words in any case on account of the article" (*Christian Ecclesia*, p. 193).

and this occurs only five times in the whole of the New Testament. The first time it appears it is used by Paul in speaking of the work of men whom, a few verses earlier, Luke had described as the *elders* of the Church at Ephesus (Acts xx. 17, 28); it is used by him also in saluting the saints at Philippi "with bishops and deacons" (Phil. i. 1); in two other places it is used in describing the qualifications of bishops (1 Tim. iii. 2; Titus i. 7); and finally it is used when our Lord is described as "the Shepherd and Bishop of souls" (1 Pet. ii. 25). These being absolutely the only passages in the New Testament where the word for bishop is used in any of its forms and in any connexion it will be seen how slender is the foundation for the vast hierarchical pretensions of a later time.[1]

It will be seen also, to return to our point, that James, the brother of our Lord, is nowhere described in Scripture as bishop of Jerusalem. It is true he was

[1] Referring to Paul's address to the elders of Ephesus at Miletus Dr. Hort asks: In the sentence, "Take heed to yourselves and to all the flock in which the Holy Spirit set you as ἐπισκόπους," how are we to understand this last word? He replies: "No one, I suppose, doubts now that the persons meant are those first mentioned as 'elders of the Ecclesia.' Have we then here a second title? The only tangible reasons for thinking so are that in the second century the word was certainly used as a title, though for a different office; and that it was already in various use as a title in the Greek world. But against this we must set the fact that both in the Bible and in other literature it retains its common etymological or descriptive meaning 'overseer,' and this meaning alone gives a clear sense here. The best rendering would, I think, be, 'in which the Holy Spirit set you to have oversight,' the force being distinctly predicative."

Dr. Hort's further notes on Paul's address: "The elders are said to have been set in the flock of Ephesus to have oversight of it *by the Holy Spirit*. Neither here nor anywhere else in the address is there any indication that St. Paul himself had had anything to do with their appointment.... But the manner in which the Holy Spirit is elsewhere associated with joint acts, acts involving fellowship, suggests that here the appointment came from the Ecclesia itself" (*The Christian Ecclesia*, pp. 98-100).

a prominent person in the Church, though neither an apostle nor a bishop. He took an active part in the Conference at Jerusalem (Acts xv.), and Paul tells us that James and Cephas and John, "they who were reputed pillars," gave to himself and Barnabas the right hand of fellowship as they set forth to go to the Gentiles. But there is no reference to any official position as being held by James. He had great personal influence from his weight of character—he is spoken of in later times as James the Just—and from the fact that he was known as the brother of our Lord, and he may have been, in all probability was, the foremost man among the elders of the Church, but beyond this the New Testament itself tells us nothing. All else is mere tradition, the value of which may soon be estimated. Passing by the simple mention of James which Josephus gives of his being delivered to be stoned under Ananus the high priest, some time before the destruction of Jerusalem, the first reference to his position in the Church is that by Hegesippus which Eusebius has preserved ($H. E.$, ii. 23). He tells us that James, the brother of the Lord, "received the government of the Church with the apostles," that is, at the same time ($\mu\epsilon\tau\grave{a}$ with the genitive). Rothe has pointed out how carefully Hegesippus speaks in this case; and it is surely laying more stress upon the words than they will well bear when Dr. Lightfoot says "that the Church of Jerusalem presents the earliest instance of a bishop." This statement rests upon traditions preserved by Eusebius, and while there is a whole century between James's death and the time when Hegesippus wrote, there are two centuries and a half between James and Eusebius. The latter, therefore, compiled his history long after the episcopal idea had received wide development, and when the form of government in the Church at Jerusalem would be likely to be forgotten. Further, his source of information seems to have been the Ebionite writings known as the Clementines (*Clem. Recog.*, i. 68), of which Dr. Lightfoot himself has said, "the fictions of this theological romance have no direct historical value." Eusebius is evidently in a mist of uncertainty on the subject. He says (iv. 5) that he could not ascertain in any way that the times of the bishops in Jerusalem had been regularly preserved on record, but that he had learned from writers that down to the invasion of the Jews under Hadrian there were fifteen successions of bishops—that is, reckoning from Symeon, who died in the reign of Trajan, there were thirteen bishops in succession in less than thirty years, a fact which, as Lightfoot admits, throws suspicion on the accuracy of the list. Then as to James himself Eusebius is not consistent in his statements. He says that the episcopal seat was committed to him by the apostles (ii. 23), then that he received it from our Saviour Himself (vii. 19), and then that he received it after the ascension of the Saviour (iii. 5), while he preserves at the same time the statement of Hegesippus that James was in office in the Church along with the apostles; he also quotes Hegesippus further to the effect that in the reign of Domitian the grandchildren of Judas, called the brother of our Lord, "ruled the Churches (ἡγήσασθαι) both as witnesses and relatives of the Lord" (*H. E.*, iii. 20).

The evidence of Eusebius, therefore, is somewhat conflicting, and all that we know of James from other sources makes it improbable that he would be the man to introduce a Gentile office and title like that of bishop. For while he became a Christian disciple his sympathies remained strongly Jewish. Hegesippus relates that he was a consecrated Nazarene from his birth; that he drank neither wine nor strong drink, that a razor never came upon his head, that he wore only linen garments, that he alone was allowed to enter the holy places, and that he was often found upon bended knees in the temple alone. This traditional account of him is in agreement with what we find in the New Testament. For though in the Conference at Jerusalem (Acts xv.) he spoke on the side of granting tolerance to Gentile Christians in the matter of Jewish observances, he could be rigid enough when Jewish Christians were concerned. Paul tells us (Gal. ii. 12) that at first when Peter was at Antioch he did not hesitate to eat with Gentiles, but that when "certain came from James, he drew back and separated himself, fearing them that were of the circumcision." A further trace of the Jewish proclivities of James is found in the fact that his Epistle is addressed "to the twelve tribes which are scattered abroad greeting," that in it he speaks of the Christian place of meeting as "your synagogue" (ii. 2), and of its officers as "the elders of the Ecclesia" (v. 14). Looking at all these facts there is every probability that in the Churches of Judea, till the destruction of Jerusalem at all events, there were neither bishops nor deacons, but simply such elders as there were in the synagogues of the time.

But now, passing from the "Churches of Judea" to those communities described by Paul as the "Churches of the Gentiles," we find, as we might expect, that in Greek-speaking cities the Christian societies shaped

themselves very largely in accordance with Greek ideas.
For to begin with there was a certain analogy between
these societies and the free Greek cities of the time.
The Christian Churches formed such a federation of free
democracies as the Greeks had striven to realise; each
Church being self-disciplining and possessing authority
over its officers, yet maintaining brotherly fellowship
with the other Churches. It was only natural, therefore,
that where Greek ideas prevailed Greek titles and offices
should obtain in the Churches. This really seems to
have been the case. Dr. Hatch has, no doubt, connected
the title of bishop too closely with the part which that
officer took in the finances of the Church, but he has
made quite clear that "episkopos" was a well-recognised
title of office in the contemporary non-Christian associations of Asia Minor and Syria, that is, among the nearest
neighbours of the Christian organisations. The term
was in use not only in private associations, but also in
public municipalities as descriptive of well-known
officials. "Episkopos," bishop, overseer, was a title
which designated commissioners appointed to regulate
a new colony; inspectors whose business it was to report
to the Indian kings; magistrates who regulated the sale
of provisions under the Romans; and certain officers in
Rhodes whose functions are unknown. Further, as
Professor Ramsay has shown, episkopoi were known as
the officers of the Greek religious fraternities (θίασοι) of
the time; and what is even more to the purpose still, in
the inscriptions of south-west Phrygia of the pre-
Constantinean period, that is, till the beginning of the
fourth century, when we meet with diakonoi or episkopoi
they are usually the officials of a pagan temple, not of a
Christian Church. A diakonos inscription was found at

Cyzicos, and two others at the metropolis of Ionia, which are to be seen in the museum and library at Smyrna. Episkopoi occur not rarely in Syrian pagan inscriptions of the third century. In his third volume Waddington has given us copies of several of these found at Bostra, Salkhad, Mdjemir, and elsewhere. And apart from all other considerations of familiarity and fitness, there was in times of persecution an element of safety in using titles that were in common use. Professor Ramsay has shown that it was part of the policy of the Christians during the years when persecution had come, or might come any time, not to make themselves or their institutions too prominent. They put nothing in public documents, such as their epitaphs, which could be quoted as evidence of Christianity, and if an official was mentioned, a title common to the pagans, like that of episkopos, was used.[1]

It will be seen from all this that before ever there was a Christian Church in existence the titles episkopoi and diakonoi were in common and familiar use both in secular and religious life, and that they did not come into Christian use till the Church had passed beyond Judean boundaries into the great Grecian world outside. We do not find them in the New Testament at all till Paul salutes the Macedonian saints at Philippi "with bishops and deacons," or sends to the elders at Ephesus to come to him at Miletus, or gives direction to Timothy and Titus concerning Church officers in Ephesus and Crete, telling them what kind of men episkopoi and

---

[1] *Voyage Archéologique en Grèce et in Asie Mineure*, par Philippe Le Bas, Paris, 1870. Inscriptions, tome iii.—Syrie. Nos. 1911, 1989, 1990, 2298. Hatch, *B. L.*, p. 37; Lightfoot, *Ep. to Philippians*, p. 93. Ramsay's *Cities and Bishoprics of Phrygia*, vol. i. pt. ii., 1897, p. 494.

diakonoi ought to be (Phil. i. 1; Acts xx. 17, 28; 1 Tim. iii. 1–13; Titus i. 7).

But while Greek ideas and titles naturally prevailed in the Churches founded in Greek cities, we need not be surprised to find at the same time Jewish terms and titles taking their place alongside with them. For Christian Churches, as we know from the Acts of the Apostles, often took their rise in those Jewish synagogues scattered through the empire, and in very many places Jews and Jewish proselytes formed the nucleus of Christian communities. It would be quite natural for a Jew to describe in a general way as elders those officers of the Church whom a Greek would describe more specifically as episkopoi and diakonoi. And while the Jew had his general term elders, that is, presbyters, the Greek would have his when he wished to speak of the episkopoi and diakonoi as the officers in a body. He would describe them as "those who are over us in the Lord," or as "the rulers" (προϊστάμενοι, 1 Thess. v. 12; Rom. xii. 8; 1 Tim. iii. 4, 12); or he might describe them as "presidents" (προεστῶτες), as Justin Martyr did (*Apol.*, i. 65, 67); or as "presiding elders" (προεστῶτες πρεσβύτεροι), as Paul did (1 Tim. v. 17), or as Hermas did (*Shep.* v. 2. 4). So that just as there was one term, "leaders" (ἡγούμενοι), to describe the spiritually-endowed apostles, prophets, and teachers when spoken of together, so there were general terms for describing the administrative officers, bishops, and deacons when they were spoken of together. Among the three general terms just referred to the Jewish word "presbyter" held the field and took permanent place in the Church, first as presbyter, then as priest.

The classification thus given is not mere guess-work.

Chrysostom, writing in the fourth century, says that "originally (τὸ παλαιόν) the presbyters were called bishops and deacons of Christ and the bishops presbyters;" Epiphanius also, in the same century, tells us that in the apostolic age there were some Churches with presbyters and no bishops, and others with bishops and no presbyters (*Hær.* 75). The former would be Jewish Christian Churches and the latter Gentile. Evidence that the term "presbyter" in Gentile Churches was a general term for bishops and deacons taken together may be briefly stated as follows:—

First, where presbyters are spoken of there is no mention of bishops or deacons. This will be found to be the case with the Acts of the Apostles, the Epistle of James, the First of Peter, the Second and Third of John, and with the Apocalypse. And when Paul tells Timothy (1 Tim. v. 17, 19) that elders ruling well are worthy of double honour, and that he is not to receive a charge against an elder except at the mouth of two or three witnesses, he mentions no other Church officers besides. Then, *secondly*, where bishops and deacons are mentioned elders are not. In 1 Tim. iii. 1–13 Paul describes the necessary qualifications for bishops and deacons, and if there were elders besides them in the Church there would be no reason for not describing their qualifications also; the title was not unknown to him, as the fifth chapter shows, but he says nothing about them here. Then again, when he salutes the officers of the Church at Philippi (Philip. i. 1) he mentions only bishops and deacons, he does so without using the article before these words, the absence of the article showing that the summary of the persons constituting the Christian Church at Philippi was complete. So again in a later time with the Didachè. In this manual the Churches are enjoined to appoint for themselves bishops and deacons worthy of the Lord, and to despise them not, for they are men to be honoured along with the prophets and teachers, but from first to last no mention is made of presbyters. In Hermas, too, presbyters are not mentioned together with apostles, prophets, and teachers, but bishops and deacons, so that presbyters are not designated except as they come under the term bishops and deacons. This important fact, as Harnack points out, cannot be explained by those who adhere to the strict identity of presbyters and bishops.

Thirdly, the general terms for Church officers are not confused with those by which they are particularised. We have apostles and elders together and bishops and deacons together, but never bishops and elders, or deacons and elders. This confusion came later, and came in the wake of further ecclesiastical development. Polycarp, if his Epistle to the Philippians may be taken to be genuine, was the first to speak of presbyters and deacons together (c. 5.), and after him Clement of Alexandria (*Strom.*, vii. 1, 190–210 A.D.).

Fourthly, elders are mentioned in one place and bishops and deacons in another in such a way as to show they mean the same thing. For example, Luke tells us in the Acts of the Apostles (xiv. 23) that, as Paul and Barnabas returned on their route through Lystra, Iconium, and Antioch, they appointed for them *elders* in every Church, the word used ($\chi\epsilon\iota\rho\sigma\tau\sigma\nu\eta\sigma\alpha\nu\tau\epsilon\varsigma$) indicating election by vote.[1] When we turn to that early Christian document, the Epistle of Clement

[1] Ramsay's *St. Paul, Traveller and Roman Citizen*, pp. 121-2.

(95 A.D.), we find it said that the apostles "preaching" everywhere in country and town, they appointed their firstfruits (τὰς ἀπαρχὰς), when they had proved them by the Spirit, to be "*bishops and deacons* unto them that should believe" (c. 42). These men thus appointed by them, or afterwards in continuance, and who have ministered unblameably to the flock of Christ, he considers to have been unjustly thrust out from this ministration of theirs in which they offered the gifts of the *bishop's* office unblameably and holily. They were happy, he thinks, who lived before the restless times came on. " Blessed are those *presbyters* who have gone before, . . . for they have now no fear lest any one should remove them from their appointed place" (c. 44). It is plainly implied that the presbyters in the one passage are the bishops and deacons of the other. This account given by Clement agrees also with what Paul says when he speaks of his "well-beloved Epaenetus, who is the *firstfruits* (ἀπαρχὴ) of Asia unto Christ" (Rom. xvi. 5), and also when he says to the people of Corinth: " Ye know the house of Stephanas, that it is the *firstfruits* of Achaia, and that they have set themselves to minister unto the saints" (1 Cor. xvi. 15). It would appear from this there were several who were regarded as superintendents or overseers in the Church, and whose influence rested on the fact of their being the first believers in the place, and upon their maintaining the Church by their ministry. This position of theirs, therefore, was not so much a question of an instituted office as of a relationship that had grown out of fact, was founded on voluntary work, and was constantly dependent on the goodwill of the community.

Thus, then, if in our one inquiry as to what the

Churches of the first century were really like, we have at all made the position clear, it seems to be this : common to all the Churches, both those of Judea and those of the Gentiles, and moving to and fro among them, were certain God-commissioned, spiritually-endowed propagandists and instructors who received their call with their gift direct from God, whom the Churches could recognise or reject but not appoint, and who were known as apostles, prophets, and teachers. Then next there were local officers in each of the Churches, who had charge of the administration of affairs, including worship and discipline, who were elected by the voice of the people, and who were known among the Churches of Judea as the elders, and among Greek - speaking Gentile Churches as bishops and deacons, these bishops and deacons being sometimes described together in general terms as presbyters or elders, and sometimes as presidents or rulers.

The differentiation of the administrative officers in Gentile Churches as bishops and deacons implies distinctive functions and a division of labour. What the distinction was may not have been very clearly defined at first. The qualifications for bishops laid down by Paul to Timothy (1 Tim. iii. 1–13) are not very different from those he gives for deacons. Probably the difference between the two offices was, at the beginning, rather personal than official. The bishops may have been those among the elders of greater age and standing than the deacons. Tertullian says : " The tried men of our elders preside over us, obtaining this honour not by purchase, but by character, for there is no purchase in the things of God " (*Apol.*, 39). Speaking for a somewhat later time, the Apostolical Constitutions say that a pastor who is to be ordained a bishop must be unblameable and unreprovable, and not under fifty years of age, for such an one is in good part past youthful disorders. But if in a small place one advanced in years is not to be found, then let some younger man who has a good report among his neighbours, and is esteemed by them worthy of the office of a bishop, be ordained in peace (ii. 1). Clement of Alexandria, at the end of the second century or the beginning of the third, says that in the Church "presbyters attend to the department which has improvement for its object and the deacons to the ministerial," by which is no doubt meant in the one case spiritual teaching and leadership when that of apostles, prophets, and teachers became less frequent, and in the other the management of the more secular affairs of the community. It would fall to the bishop or to the bishops in turn, if there were several, to preside over the services at the meetings of the brethren. Justin Martyr has indicated a difference of function at the Lord's Table. He says "there is brought to that one of the brethren who presides bread and wine, and he taking them gives praise and glory to the Father of the universe through the name of the Son and of the Holy Ghost, and offers thanks at some length for our being counted worthy to receive these things at His hands, the people expressing their assent to the prayers and thanksgivings by saying Amen. This being done, those who are called by us deacons give to each of those present to partake of the bread and wine, and to those who are absent they carry away a portion" (*Apol.*, i. 65). In a following chapter Justin adds that after the communion "they who are well to do and willing give what each thinks fit, and what is collected is deposited with the president (προεστώς), who succours the orphans and widows, and those who, through sickness or any other cause, are in want, and those who are in bonds, and the strangers sojourning among us, and in a word takes care of all who are in need" (c. 67). Tertullian, with a little more detail, says: "These gifts are, as it were, piety's deposit fund. They are taken to support and bury poor people, to provide for boys and girls destitute of means and parents, for old persons confined to their homes, and for such, too, as have suffered shipwreck ; and if there happen to be any in the mines, or banished to the islands, or shut up in the prisons, for nothing but their fidelity to the cause of God's Church, they become the nurslings of their confession" (*Apol.*, 39). Besides the oversight of this kindly Christian service, the presiding elders had to discharge the important duties of hospitality to brethren of other Churches coming and going. Those Christians driven from city to city by persecution, wandering as outcasts or refugees, found with fellow-Christians welcome and hospitality. Hermas (*Shep.* ix. 28) speaks of "bishops, hospitable persons, who gladly received into their houses at all times the servants of God without hypocrisy." Besides these duties of benevolence, the elders had to see to the discipline of the community, to administer rebukes and sacred censures. "For," says Tertullian, "with a great gravity is the work of judging carried on among us, as befits those who feel assured that they are in the sight of God ; and you have the most notable example of judgement to come when any one has sinned so grievously as to require his severance from us in prayer, and the assembly and all sacred intercourse" (*Apol.*, 39).

Passing from the bishops to the deacons, we find that, besides receiving the elements and distributing them to those who were present at the Lord's Table, and conveying them to those who were absent, they were the assistants of bishops in the benevolent work referred to, and were, so to speak, their executive, seeking out the cases of those who were in distress, and inquiring, as a court of first instance, into charges involving the discipline of the Church. Judging from the Apostolical Constitutions at a later period, they stood in relation to the services of the Church, too, very much as the tithing-man of a New England town or the churchwarden of an English parish in days when discipline was stricter than it has since become. It is enjoined that when an assembly of the Church is called the bishop, " as one that is the commander of a great ship, is to charge the deacons as mariners, to prepare places for the brethren as for passengers with all due care and decency." " If any one be found sitting out of his place let him be rebuked by the deacon, and be removed into the place proper for him ; . . . let the deacon be the disposer of the places, that every one of those that come in may go to his proper place, and may not sit at the entrance. In like manner, let the deacon oversee the people, that nobody may whisper, nor slumber, nor laugh, nor nod ; for all ought in the Church to stand wisely and soberly and attentively, having their attention fixed upon the Lord " (bk. ii. 57). So, again, as to those who come from other places, and are receiving hospitality : " If any brother or sister come in from another Church bringing recommendatory letters, let the deacon be the judge of the affair, inquiring whether they be of the faithful and of the Church. When he is satisfied that they are really of the faithful and of the same sentiments in the things of the Lord, let him conduct every one to the place proper for him" (ii. 58). These directions belong, however, as we have said, to a more organised and later time than that with which we are specially dealing. Here, to conclude with, is the description of ideal deacons of the earlier time as given in one of the two documents which form the basis of the Apostolic Canons: "They are to have good testimony from the congregation, to be honourable, gentle, quiet, not quickly angry; they are to be intelligent, encouraging well to secret works while they compel those among the brethren who have much to open their hands; also themselves generous, communicative, honoured with all honour and esteem and fear by the congregation, carefully giving heed to those who walk disorderly, warning the one, exhorting the other, threatening the third." If the deacons of the early time answered to this description, or came at all near it, they did indeed, as Paul says, serve well as deacons, gaining to themselves a good standing and great boldness in the faith.

LECTURE V

THE IGNATIAN EPISTLES

LECTURE V

THE IGNATIAN EPISTLES

SAILING past the Western Islands of Scotland the voyager, after leaving Ardnamurchan Point, comes within sight of that Scuir of Eigg which is to the geologist both an object of interest and a source of perplexity. A mountain wall, or hill-fort, rising a thousand feet high, resting not on granite foundations, but on the remains of a prostrate forest, it seems to form no natural combination of outline with the island on which it stands. And while thus isolated in the general landscape it is at the same time composed of porphyritic material the like of which is not to be found in the whole of Scotland besides. This hill-fort, or natural tower, standing thus solitary in the landscape and inexplicable, may furnish an illustration of the position held in the Christian literature of the second century by the much-debated Epistles of Ignatius.

The New Testament, the Epistle of Clement, and the Shepherd of Hermas, when read in the light thrown upon them by the Didachê, reveal, as we have seen, a twofold division in the ministry of the Early Church: the first embracing apostles, prophets, and teachers, divinely called, spiritually endowed, and moving to and fro among the Churches at large; the second consisting of a body of presbyters or elders, who, for the better way of meeting the needs of local church life, were differentiated as bishops and deacons. We have no sooner, however, taken this into our thought than we are confronted by the Epistles of Ignatius, supposed to have been written within twenty years of the Didachê, but on reading which we find ourselves face to face with an altogether different conception of Church organisation. In these Epistles everything is made to turn upon the office of one bishop as the centre of unity in each Church. He is spoken of as supreme in authority, as the representative of God and Christ, and as the guardian of truth. In writing to Polycarp Ignatius charges him as bishop of Smyrna to vindicate his office with all diligence (c. 1). "Let nothing," he says, "be done without thy consent, and do thou nothing without the consent of God" (c. 4). To the people he says: "Give heed to your bishop that God also may give heed to you. I give my life for those who are obedient to the bishop, to presbyters, to deacons. With them may I have my portion in the presence of God" (c. 6). Then also not only in this letter to Polycarp, which may be regarded as having more of a personal character, but in most of those he sends to the Churches, we find the same strenuous claims insisted on. "Every one," he says, "whom the Master of the House sendeth to govern His own household we ought to receive as Him that sent him; clearly, therefore, we ought to regard the bishop as the Lord Himself" (*Eph.* 6). Those "live a life after Christ" who "obey the bishop as Jesus Christ" (*Trall.* 2). "It is good to know God and the bishop, he that honoureth the bishop is honoured of God; he that doeth anything without the knowledge of the bishop serveth the devil" (*Smyr.* 9). He who obeys his bishop obeys "not him, but the Father of Jesus Christ, the Bishop of all"; while, on the other hand, he that practises hypocrisy towards his bishop "not only deceiveth the visible one, but cheateth the Invisible" (*Magn.* 3). "Do ye all follow the bishop as Jesus Christ followed the Father" (*Smyr.* 8). "As many as are of God and of Jesus Christ are with the bishop" (*Philad.* 3). The Ephesians are commended because they are so united with their bishop "as the Church with Jesus Christ, and as Jesus Christ with the Father." "If," he adds, "the prayer of one or two has so much power, how much more the prayer of the bishop and of all the Church" (*Eph.* 5). "Wheresoever the bishop shall appear there let the people be; even as where Jesus may be, there is the universal Church" (*Smyr.* 8). "Let no man do anything pertaining to the Church without the bishop" (*Magn.* 4, *Philad.* 7). "It is not lawful either to baptize or to hold a love-feast without the bishop, but whatsoever he may approve this also is well-pleasing to God, that everything which is done may be safe and valid" (*Smyr.* 8). Those who decide on a life of virginity must to the bishop only disclose their intention; and those who purpose marrying must obtain his consent to their union, that their "marriage may be according to the Lord, and not according to concupiscence" (*Poly.* 5). It was not of mere motion from himself, "it was the preaching of the Spirit who spake on this wise, Do nothing without the bishop" (*Philad.* 7).

Well might Milton exclaim on reading all this: "Surely no Pope can desire more than Ignatius attributes to every bishop; but what then will become of the archbishops and primates if every bishop, in Ignatius' judgement, be as supreme as the Pope?" Even Dr. Lightfoot, while, with the scholarly labour of years maintaining the genuineness of these Epistles, felt himself compelled to describe the language of Ignatius as "strained to the utmost," and to say how "subversive of the true spirit of Christianity in the negation of individual freedom, and the consequent suppression of direct responsibility to God in Christ, is the crushing despotism with which this writer's language, if taken literally, would invest the episcopal office."[1]

This Ignatian enigma, around which the battle of controversy has been so long and so hotly waged, is not a question of merely academic or literary interest. The keenness of the conflict reveals the practical character of the issues involved. Bishops like Ussher and Pearson and Lightfoot contended for the authoritative character of the Ignatian Epistles as being the corner-stone of the Episcopalian polity. It is of consequence, therefore, for us to ask, Are these Epistles a genuine product of the earliest age of the Church? Who was their author, and is he a reliable witness as to a state of things which actually existed in sub-apostolic times? And, finally, if genuine and reliable, do they honestly and fairly bear the construction Episcopalians put upon them?

I.

In seeking answers to these questions let us first examine the form in which the Ignatian Epistles have come down to us, and see what is known of the writer. These letters have reached us, as is well known, in three

[1] *Essay on the Christian Ministry*, pp. 234-5.

different forms: there is a longer recension containing fifteen letters, eight of which are admittedly spurious; then there is the middle or Medicean recension, sometimes known as the Vossian, which contains the remaining seven of the fifteen; and, finally, there is a shorter form in Syriac, known as the Curetonian, which contains only three letters. This last recension Canon Cureton contended was the original version, holding the Vossian to be merely an interpolated expansion. On the other hand, Dr. Lightfoot maintained that the Vossian is the true original, and the Syriac simply an epitome. More recently Professor Völter, of Amsterdam, has drawn a distinction between the six Asia Minor letters out of the seven and the remaining Epistle sent by Ignatius to the Romans. He regards the latter to be a forgery, but the other six to be genuine. His reason for making this further division is that he finds distinct differences between the Roman Epistle and the other six. For example, while in the Roman letter the writer twice announces himself emphatically as bishop of Syria, the other six contain no such title, but rather seem to imply that the writer was not a bishop. In four of the Asia Minor letters he mentions "the Church which is in Syria," but the words which designate him as bishop are wanting. On the contrary, he unites himself with the congregation in contrast to the episcopal office. In his Epistle to the Ephesians he says: "Let us therefore be careful not to resist the bishop, that by our submission we may give ourselves to God" (c. 5); and, again, "plainly therefore we ought to regard the bishop as the Lord Himself" (c. 6). "Remember in your prayers the Church which is in Syria, whereof I am not worthy to be called a member, being the very last of them" (*Trall.* c. 13). Then there are two or three other passages which Völter has not noticed, but which seem to sustain his contention that Ignatius was not a monarchical bishop. The form of the sentence appears to associate him with the deacons of the Church: "There is one bishop, together with the presbytery, and *the deacons my fellow-servants*" (*Philad.* c. 4). " I salute your godly bishop and your venerable presbytery and *my fellow-servants the deacons*" (*Smyr.* c. 12). He speaks also of " my fellow-servant Burrhus, who by the will of God is your deacon" (*Eph.* c. 2). Then, too, Völter contends there is a quite different tone in the one letter from that in the six. In the Epistle to the Romans there is an almost fanatical desire for martyrdom, which he is afraid the Romans, in mistaken kindness, may seek to frustrate; while in the others the writer speaks on the subject in a manner much more measured. In the Asia Minor letters his imprisonment is so little burdensome that he has no cause to complain. He rejoices in complete freedom of epistolary and personal intercourse. Quite other is the letter to the Romans. While, like the six, supposed to be written from Smyrna, it is full of complaint of the inhuman cruelty of his guards, of whom he speaks thus: " From Syria even unto Rome I fight with wild beasts by land and sea, by night and by day, being bound amidst ten leopards, even a company of soldiers, who only wax worse when they are kindly treated" (*Rom.* c. 5). On such grounds as these Völter comes to the conclusion that the cardinal mistake of previous investigators has been made in presupposing the unity of the Seven Epistles; that it is better to regard the six as the true recension, and the

Epistle to the Romans as spurious.[1] At the opposite pole to Völter is Renan, who held that the Epistle to the Romans is the only one of the seven that is genuine, the remaining six being spurious.

Then, while there is this initial embarrassment arising from competing recensions of the documents themselves, there is also a certain air of mystery about the writer. Of the origin, birth, and education of Ignatius we know absolutely nothing. The earliest tradition makes him to be the second bishop of Antioch, or if, as some, Peter be reckoned the first, then that he was the third. This tradition is derived through Origen, who wrote a century and a half later than the time at which Ignatius is supposed to have been martyred. On the other hand, Chrysostom, who lived at Antioch a century and a half later still, makes Ignatius to be the immediate successor of Peter at Antioch; while the Apostolical Constitutions (vii. 46) represent him as being ordained by the Apostle Paul. The tradition as to the date at which he became bishop of Antioch is equally uncertain. His accession is placed about 67 A.D. Yet Ignatius being either second or third bishop it would be difficult to reconcile such accession with what we find in Acts xiii. 1., where the Church at Antioch is described about 44 A.D. as being under the spiritual direction of prophets and teachers such as those we find in the Didachè, and where, so far as appears, there was no bishop at all. Dr. Lightfoot, after careful investigation, comes to the conclusion that of the accession of Ignatius we simply know nothing whatever, and that of his administration at Antioch all that has come down to us is the improbable tradition

[1] *Die ignat. Briefe, auf ihren Ursprung untersucht.*, von Daniel Völter, Professor der Theologie in Amsterdam. Tübingen, 1892.

preserved by Socrates (*H. E.*, vi. 8) to the effect that Ignatius saw a vision of angels praising the Holy Trinity in antiphonal hymns, and that he introduced the practice into the Church at Antioch, from whence it spread to all the Churches.

If, then, Ignatius be a real personality, all that can be known about him now must be gathered from the Epistles which bear his name. From these we learn that he was being sent to Rome as a condemned prisoner for the execution of his sentence. Under what circumstances he was arrested and condemned we are not told. One legend makes the Emperor Trajan himself to have taken action against him while on a visit to Antioch, another that he did so in Rome. There is nothing to be learnt from the Epistles about this journey of Ignatius till we find him at Philadelphia, in the heart of Asia Minor. Shortly after he was hospitably entertained at Smyrna by Polycarp and the Church in that city; and here representatives from the Churches of Ephesus, Magnesia, and Tralles came to greet him on his way. At Smyrna he wrote four of the seven Epistles to the Churches which had sent representatives to be taken back by them; and one to the Church in Rome, to be sent on in advance. This Epistle to the Romans says nothing about Church affairs, mentions no bishop as being at Rome, asserts no episcopal authority, and is the only one that bears a date, that date being August 24th, the year not being mentioned. From Smyrna the soldiers in charge took him to Troas on the Ægean, where he was overtaken by two deacons from the Church at Antioch, and where he wrote three more letters, two of these to the Churches of Philadelphia and Smyrna he had just left behind him, the third to Polycarp, the bishop of Smyrna. Starting somewhat suddenly from Troas, he crosses the sea to Neapolis and thence to Philippi, where he was welcomed and afterwards escorted on his journey by the brethren there. From the moment he left Philippi we lose all farther trace of him. We know nothing more either as to the rest of his journey or his fate at the end; his death by martyrdom is spoken of by anticipation, but nowhere recorded. The whole of the supposition of the Epistles is that he is going to be martyred in Rome, yet in the later decades of the fourth century his grave was shown outside the Daphnitic gate at Antioch; and Chrysostom, when presbyter at Antioch, accepting the story of the translation of his bodily remains, in one of his sermons draws an imaginary picture of Ignatius being borne aloft on men's shoulders from city to city like a victor returning in triumph amidst the applause of the bystanders: "ye sent him forth a bishop, ye receiveth him a martyr; ye sent him forth with prayers, and ye received him with crowns." As these words were spoken rhetorically more than two centuries and a half after the event to which they are supposed to refer, perhaps no great historical importance can be attached to them.

The earliest mention we have of the Epistles themselves is in the Epistle of Polycarp to the Philippians. Next after this there are allusions in three writers—Irenæus, Origen, and Eusebius. Irenæus, who lived nearest to the time when Ignatius is supposed to have been martyred, does not mention him by name, but merely says: "As a certain man of ours said when he was condemned to the wild beasts because of his testimony with respect to God: 'I am the wheat of Christ [God] and am ground by the teeth of the wild beasts that I may be found pure bread [of God].'" These words occur in the Ignatian Epistle to the Romans (c. 4), but as Irenæus represents the martyr as *saying* this it has been held by some that it may merely refer to some utterance preserved among the Christians, and does not necessarily make it certain that Irenæus had seen the Epistle itself. Then later (253 A.D.) Origen twice mentions Ignatius by name, referring to a passage in the Epistle of Ignatius to the Romans (c. 7) and to one in the Epistle to the Ephesians (c. 19). It is to Eusebius, however, writing some seventy years later than Origen, we are indebted for more distinct information. He knew of seven Epistles, the same in number and name as those included in the Vossian recension, and he gives considerable quotations from them, supplying a catalogue of the letters which, in his opinion, are correctly ascribed to Ignatius. All later references down to the ninth century, when these Epistles passed into oblivion, were almost certainly mere quotations from the history of Eusebius, and therefore destitute of independent value. After slumbering in forgetfulness for centuries these Epistles came unexpectedly to life again in a remarkable way. In the fifteenth century William de Wideford produced a passage from them for the purpose of confuting the position taken by John Wickliff. Two hundred years later Archbishop Ussher happened to meet with this quotation, which suggested to him the possibility of these Epistles being still in existence somewhere. Inquiries which he set on foot resulted in the discovery of a Latin version in the library of Caius College, Cambridge, which was published in 1644. This was followed two years later by the publication of the original Greek text by Isaac Voss at Amsterdam. Then again in 1842 after two centuries more, the short Syriac recension of three Epistles was found in a monastery in the Nitrian desert by Dr. Tattam, Archdeacon of Bedford, who had been sent out in search of MSS. by the trustees of the British Museum. By the publication of this shorter recension by Canon Cureton in 1845 the Ignatian Controversy was once more set aflame, and can scarcely be said to have slumbered since.

Having thus referred to the documents themselves, let us notice briefly the difficulties many have felt in accepting the Ignatian Epistles as genuine.

Dr. Lightfoot, with prodigious learning united to the patient labour of thirty years of life, has strenuously maintained that these Epistles, so far as the middle recension is concerned, are entirely genuine and trustworthy. Harnack, too, whose knowledge of Early Christian literature is perhaps unrivalled in our time, says that after repeated investigation, he feels the hypothesis of their spuriousness to be altogether untenable. On the other hand writers like Canon Cureton can only accept these Epistles in part. For them the historical situation is beset with difficulty. For example, while Ignatius is supposed to be hurried along by soldiers, whom he describes as leopards, and who treat him with severity, they note that he is at the same time represented as receiving visitors from Churches far and near, to whom he writes elaborate Epistles in return. Also while thus hurried along, no time being lost, intelligence yet overtakes him at Troas that the persecution at Antioch has ceased. So that immediately after the soldiers and their prisoner had started for Rome Trajan must have suspended hostilities against the Christians in that city, without reversing or mitigating the cruel sentence against Ignatius himself. It is curious too and improbable that the Church at Philadelphia should have received an account of the condemnation of Ignatius at Antioch, a city situated some four hundred miles to the south-east of their city, and have so timed their embassy as to meet him at Troas about two hundred miles to the north-west, as he was passing through on his journey to Rome. Thus considerable deputations are supposed to meet him both at Smyrna and at Troas at a time when open profession of Christianity might cost a man his life. There is also another point of difficulty. In his Epistle to the Ephesians (c. xx.) Ignatius expresses his intention to write a second little book specially for them, in which he will set forth the dispensation, of which he had begun to speak to them relating to the new man in Christ Jesus, especially if the Lord should reveal aught to him. That a man condemned to death and in the close custody of ten soldiers by whom, as he says, he is "harassed by day and night, by sea and land," should be able to write even one such Epistle as that which he had sent to the Ephesians seems sufficiently remarkable; but that while the day of his martyrdom is drawing nearer, and he is being hurried to Rome to undergo a sentence of death, he should still further think of writing a second little book to send to people with whom he seems to have had little to do except to receive a deputation from them in the person of Onesimus, is so much more remarkable as to seem almost incredible.

The question is naturally asked, too, why the zeal of this writer is so exclusively directed to other Churches than his own? After weeks of separation under painful circumstances, and after the remarkable change which is supposed to have come over their fortunes, has he no word of counsel or congratulation or of farewell for his own Church of Antioch? So strongly was it felt there was something halting here that the forger who made the addition of eight admittedly spurious Epistles to the seven held to be genuine, undertook to supply what was felt to be a want, and in the name of Ignatius fabricated a letter to the Antiocheans. There is also another point to be noted in passing. In the Epistle to Polycarp, "who is bishop of the Church of the Smyrneans," the writer forgets himself for a moment, and urges this Polycarp, who is a bishop himself, to give heed to the bishop, that God also may give heed to him (c. 6).

Such are some of the difficulties involved in this Ignatian question, and there are others on which it is not needful to enlarge. So many are they that while Lechler admits the genuineness of these letters, he at the same time confesses, so grave have been his doubts for years, that if, between 118 A.D., when they are supposed to have been written, and 170–175 A.D., when the monarchical idea of the episcopate had come to be asserted, a point of time, an occasion, and a person could be found for the authorship of the letters in case they were forged, he should cease to accept them.[1] On the other hand, Dr. Killen thinks he is able to fix the forgery both as to time and person. In the early part of the third century, he says, there was a mania for this kind of thing, as the spurious writings attributed to Clement of Rome clearly show. Certain features in the case, he suggests, point to Callistus, whom Hippo-

[1] *Apostolic and Post-Apostolic Times*, by G. V. Lechler, p. 326. Edin., 1886.

lytus describes as a man of great versatility of talent allied to deep cunning and much force of character; and of whom he says further that he was given to intrigue, and so wily in his movements that it was not easy to entangle him in a dilemma. It is suggested that it might occur to such a man to endeavour to strengthen the growing pretensions of the hierarchy by a series of letters in the name of an apostolic father, exalting the bishop and vigorously asserting his claims.[1] Practices of the kind certainly did exist as early indeed as the second century. Dionysius, who was bishop, that is, pastor of the Church of Corinth about 170 A.D., wrote a series of Epistles, as Eusebius tells us, to the Lacedæmonians, the Athenians, to the Nicomedians, to the Churches of Crete, to the Romans, and to several other communities; and even in his own lifetime these were tampered with for a purpose: " As the brethren desired me," he says, " to write Epistles, I wrote them ; and these the apostles of the devil have filled with tares, taking out some things and adding others. To whom a woe is reserved. Not wonderful, then, is it, if some have also endeavoured to corrupt the writings of the Lord, since this has been done with others not to be compared with these " (Euseb., *H. E.*, iv., 23). It might also be said that an age which extended the seven Epistles of Ignatius to fifteen by forgery, was perhaps not unequal to forging the seven to start with. The Decretals of Isidore of a later time, by which the Papacy fraudulently supported its claim for centuries, did their work effectively, though now for years past even Roman Catholics have renounced them as forgeries.

[1] *The Ignatian Epistles Entirely Spurious*: a Reply to Dr. Lightfoot, by W. D. Killen, D.D., 1886.

The question of the *Date* of these Epistles has also been matter of keen controversy as well as that of the authorship. Dr. Lightfoot placed them in the early years of the second century, taking up a middle position between Wieseler, who fixed the martyrdom of Ignatius in 107 A.D., and Harnack, who some years ago was in favour of 138 A.D. He thought that we should be doing no injustice to the evidence by setting the probable limits between 100 and 118 A.D., without attempting to fix the year more precisely, but evidently inclining to the later of these years. He held that these Epistles accord with everything else we know of the beginning of the second century; that all the evidence, without one dissentient voice, points to episcopacy as the established form of Church government among the Churches of Asia Minor from the close of the first century.

The evidence in support of this strong statement is the testimony of Irenæus to Polycarp, the Epistle of Polycrates of Ephesus to Victor of Rome, and a passage in the writings of Clement of Alexandria. On the other hand, Harnack, who thoroughly accepts the Ignatian Epistles as genuine, maintains that these witnesses are not valid for the purpose for which Lightfoot uses them, for the simple reason that they all belong to the end of the second century or to the beginning of the third, when it is admitted that the episcopal idea had received considerable development. He very decisively sums up his judgement thus: "*Apart from the Epistles of Ignatius we do not possess a single witness to the existence of the monarchical episcopate in the Churches of Asia Minor as early as the times of Trajan and Hadrian.*"[1] The italics are his, and he goes on to say

[1] *Expositor*, Third Series, iii. 16-22.

that these Epistles, as a source of information, stand alone, not only in assuring us that the monarchical episcopate was thoroughly naturalised in the Churches of Asia Minor of his day, but also in testifying to the existence of that episcopate at all. Such a conception of the bishop as that held by Ignatius, so far as Early Christian literature is concerned, Harnack contends has its earliest parallel in the Apostolic Constitutions of the next century, and that from what we know from other sources of Early Church history, no single investigator would assign the statements about the bishop to the second, but at the earliest to the third century.

In his latest work Harnack informs us that he has seen reason to change his mind as to the matter of the date of the Ignatian Epistles. He holds now that both these Epistles and that of Polycarp were almost certainly composed in the last years of Trajan's reign, that is, between 110 and 117 A.D., possibly between 117 and 125 A.D.; not impossibly, but certainly not probably, later still. But while thus coming round to agree with Lightfoot in accepting the early date, he still maintains, as against him, it is only from the Ignatian Epistles that we know at all of the existence of the monarchical episcopate in Asia Minor as early as the time of Trajan and Hadrian.[1]

The evidence on which those who contend for the genuineness of the Ignatian Epistles is regarded by Dr. Lightfoot as so complete, that no Christian writings of the second century, and indeed few other writings of antiquity, are so well authenticated. First, we have Polycarp, a contemporary, saying in his Epistle to the

---

[1] *Die Chronologie der altchristlichen Litteratur bis Eusebius*, 1er Band, s. 396. Leipzig, 1897.

Philippians that he received letters from Ignatius, which he is sending to them along with his own, at their request, and asking them if they have any further news of Ignatius and his companions since they left Philippi, to be sure and certify him of the same. It may well be said, with Lightfoot, that if this letter of Polycarp's can be accepted as genuine, the authentication of the Ignatian Epistles is perfect. And there is good reason for so accepting it, since it is vouched for by Irenæus, a most reliable witness, who knew Polycarp personally, and was a pupil of his. Irenæus tells us (*Hær.*, iii. 3, 4) that Polycarp wrote an eminently satisfactory letter to the Philippians, from which those who wish may learn the character of his faith. To the existence of this letter Eusebius in his history also bears testimony, though of course he is merely repeating the statement of Irenæus. There can be no question that Polycarp was referring to Ignatius the martyr, for in this letter to the Philippians he rejoices that they hospitably received the followers of the true Love and escorted them on their way—those men who are encircled with saintly bonds which are the diadems of them that be truly chosen of God and our Lord. He exhorts them to the obedience and endurance which they saw with their own eyes in the blessed Ignatius and Zosimus and Rufus, yea, and in others also who came from among themselves, who are now in their due place in the presence of the Lord, with whom also they suffered.

It must be admitted that while Polycarp's Epistle is, so far as external evidence goes, the bulwark of the Ignatian Epistles, that Epistle itself is exceptionally well attested, so that only the very strongest internal evidence, such as serious anachronisms, should shake our confidence in it, whereas such anachronisms as were supposed to exist have vanished before a more critical examination. Several years ago Harnack said that after repeated investigations the genuineness of these Epistles seemed to him beyond doubt, and the hypothesis of their spuriousness to be untenable. The inner grounds for accepting them as genuine are only capable, he thought, of being fully realised by the careful investigator, but to him they are overpowering. Zahn's arguments, as confirmed by Lightfoot's investigations, and consisting as they do of careful deductions regarding the historical situation, the individuality of each separate Epistle, especially that to the Romans, and also the route travelled, and the relation of these Epistles to the New Testament, he held to be so many incontestable proofs of their genuineness.[1]

This writer has not changed his mind in this respect. In his great work on the Chronology of Early Christian Literature, recently given to the world, he maintains that there are no productions in that early literature more splendidly attested from without than are the Ignatian Epistles by the Epistle of Polycarp, nor more satisfactorily confirmed from within by the consistency of the writer's ideas, his conceptions, his theological position, and even his very peculiarities. He holds that the unity of style, both as to form and content, and the freedom with which the writer bears himself, makes it more than ordinarily improbable that we have here before us a mere skilful fabrication. The difficulties connected with the routes traversed he holds not to be of serious sort or incapable of explanation, and they are

[1] *Expositor*, Third Series, iii. 10, 15.

decreased tenfold by the way in which details scattered here and there through the various Epistles are yet found to harmonise with each other. The very differences existing between the Epistle to the Romans and the six Asia Minor letters, instead of exciting suspicion, really tend to prove that the letters as a whole are not the product of the brain of some clever schemer; for, while nearly all the drift and tendencies of the six are wanting in the one, nearly every line of the one shows that it came from the same author as the six.[1]

II.

And now comes the important practical question, Supposing these Epistles are genuine, what do they prove? Do they furnish a solid foundation for exclusive episcopal claims? It is this ecclesiastical bearing which has turned the literary inquiry into a burning controversy. But for the way in which the claims of the diocesan bishop are asserted by the Established Church on the one side, and challenged by the Free Churches on the other, these Epistles might have slumbered for ever beneath the dust under which they had lain for centuries before Ussher and Voss brought them forth once more to light. So far as the historical basis is concerned, do they settle the controversy?

By way of obtaining an answer to this question let us look at the alternatives. Either these Epistles are (1) altogether genuine, as Lightfoot and Harnack contend; or (2) only the three Epistles of the short Syriac recension are genuine, as Cureton, Bunsen, and Ritschl maintain; or (3) the seven are genuine, but have been interpolated by the insertion of the episcopal passages, as Canon

[1] *Die Chronologie*, pp. 389, 399, 400.

Jenkins and others believe; or (4) they are altogether spurious, the work of a fabricator like Callistus, as Dr. Killen maintains. Practically it comes to this—if these Epistles are spurious, or if they can be proved to be interpolated or extended for a purpose, they cease to be of any value. The controversy in that case is at an end, and we simply fall back upon that portion of the Christian literature of the second century which is admittedly genuine, and from thence gather our knowledge of the Christian Church of the time. But there remains the other alternative, that they are neither spurious nor interpolated, but absolutely genuine. Suppose this is freely conceded what will follow? What will be the effect of this concession on the episcopal claim to Apostolical Succession?

1. The Ignatian Epistles furnish evidence of *the existence elsewhere of other forms of Church government* besides the monarchical episcopate obtaining at Antioch and among the Churches of Asia Minor. It has been shown that the one external support on which the advocates of genuineness mainly rely is the Epistle of Polycarp to the Philippians. Now the tone of this letter, so far as the monarchical episcopate is concerned, is widely different from that of the Ignatian Epistles, there being no mention of a bishop in it from first to last. Indeed, Dr. Lightfoot himself has said that it "has proved a stronghold of Presbyterianism;" and he points out the awkward dilemma in which the French writer Jean Daillé found himself while contending against the genuineness of the Ignatian Epistles because of the countenance they were supposed to give to episcopacy. If he admitted the genuineness of Polycarp's Epistle he could not do this without ad-

mitting at the same time the genuineness of the Ignatian Epistles. If, on the contrary, he denied the genuineness of that Epistle, while a member of the Reformed Church of France, he would be giving up what was, or what seemed to be, one of the principal evidences that the presbyterial form of government existed in the earliest time. But it may be replied that if Polycarp's Epistle had a double edge for Daillé as a Presbyterian, it had a double edge also for Lightfoot as an Episcopalian. For if he sets this Epistle aside he sets aside the strongest evidence he has in favour of the Ignatian Epistles, and if he admits it, he admits a document which he has himself described as a stronghold of Presbyterianism, and as containing no mention of a bishop from first to last. On reading it we find that its ecclesiastical conceptions are those of the Didachè and the Epistle of Clement. It begins thus: "Polycarp and the presbyters that are with him unto the Church of God which sojourneth at Philippi;" he describes the qualifications of elders and deacons as they are described in the Pastoral Epistles; he urges the Philippians to submit themselves to the presbyters and deacons as to God and to Christ; while he has not one word as to the respect due to a bishop, or as to his qualifications, or even as to his existence; he expresses his grief over the lapse of Valens, who aforetime was a presbyter among them, and he urges the Church not to hold this man and his wife as enemies, but to restore them as frail and erring members. Judging from Polycarp's letter, the monarchical episcopate had no existence as yet, either at Smyrna or Philippi. So, again, with Ignatius' own Epistle to the Romans. Like the Epistle of Clement to the Corinthians, it is addressed not to any official, but to the Church itself. He sends greeting "to the Church that is beloved and enlightened through the will of Him who willed all things that are; even unto her that hath precedence in the country of the region of the Romans, being worthy of God, worthy of honour, worthy of felicitation, worthy of praise, worthy of success, worthy in purity, and having precedence in love, walking in the law of Christ, and bearing the Father's name; which Church also I salute in the name of Jesus Christ the Son of the Father." In this Epistle, as in that of Polycarp, there is not the slightest mention of a bishop from first to last, yet courtesy would have demanded this had there been a bishop in Rome at the time this letter was written, which evidently there was not.

There is another point not altogether irrelevant. Dr. Lightfoot imagined that he had found reference to the case of Ignatius in Lucian's satire, "De Morte Peregrini," which describes the career of a charlatan who was first a Christian and afterwards a cynic. He describes how in his Christian days he was thrust into prison on account of his faith; how the Christians regarded this as a calamity for the whole brotherhood, doing all they could to rescue and serve him; and how from certain cities in Asia there came deputies sent by Christian communities to assist and console him. From the fact that these details correspond in some respects with the experience of Ignatius, to whom representatives of Churches were sent while he was at Smyrna and Troas, Dr. Lightfoot infers that Lucian may have been acquainted with the story of Ignatius, if not with the Ignatian letters. But probably most will agree with Professor Ramsay [1] that Lucian's satire may not refer

[1] *The Church in the Roman Empire*, p. 366.

to any particular case, inasmuch as the facts referred to were the regular and characteristic practice of the Christians ; and that the only safe inference from Lucian's words is that the picture of life given in the letters of Ignatius is true. But if Lucian had any knowledge of the Church life of the Christians about the middle of the second century, as he evidently had, though he may be no witness to the historical character of the Ignatian story, he may furnish evidence as to the Church constitution of the time. The Church as Lucian describes it is just such a simple, loving brotherhood as Justin Martyr sets before us, and as the Didachê exhorts, the members of which stand loyally by each other in time of trouble. His hero Peregrinus becomes such a prophet among them as we find described and honoured in the Didachê. He associates himself with their priests and scribes, by which terms, familiar to a heathen writer, he might very well mean the presbyters, that is, the bishops and deacons of the community. Be that as it may, the Christian communities which Lucian knew seem not to have been under the presidency of a monarchical bishop.

2. Notwithstanding the extravagant terms in which Ignatius speaks of the bishop, it is clear that *he did not mean a diocesan bishop, but simply the pastor or overseer of one individual Church community*. Of a diocese in the modern sense of the word there is not, as Lightfoot himself admits, so much as a trace in the Ignatian Epistles. Three letters out of the seven are inscribed as being sent to three neighbouring Churches— those at Ephesus, Magnesia, and Tralles. Each of these Churches is spoken of as having a bishop, yet Tralles was only about fifteen miles from Magnesia, and Magnesia

about the same distance from Ephesus, so that within a range of about thirty miles there were no fewer than three bishops. It would seem that the bishop of Ignatius was after all simply a Congregational pastor whose office he had unduly and unscripturally magnified. Even Canon Gore makes a similar admission. "The bishop," he says, "according to the early ideal, was by no means the great prelate ; he was the pastor of a flock, like the vicar of a modern town, in intimate relations with all his people (p. 104). To the same effect Dr. Hatch informs us that "there was a bishop wherever in later times there would have been a parish church. From the small province of Proconsular Asia, which was about the size of Lincolnshire, forty bishops were present at an early Council ; in the only half-converted province of North Africa 470 episcopal towns are known by name" (*B. L.*, 79). This view is sustained by the early document known as the Apostolic Church Order, which assumes that the smallest Church will have a bishop of its own. It provides, as we have seen, that if in any given Church there are fewer than twelve persons who are competent to vote at the election of a bishop, they shall write to some neighbouring Church, which shall send three selected men to examine carefully whether the man they are about to choose is worthy, that is, if he has a good report among the heathen. The Apostolical Constitutions too, describe "a pastor who is to be ordained a bishop for the Churches in every parish ;" and provides that if a parish is so small that a person sufficiently advanced in years to be a bishop cannot be found in it, a younger man, after due inquiry, is to be ordained in peace (ii. 1). Even with Ignatius, notwithstanding his extravagant utterances, the bishop is

only the pastor of a single Church and by no means
entirely autocratic. Office, says he, is not everything;
'Let not office puff up any man, for faith and love are
all in all, and nothing is to be preferred before them"
(*Smyr.* 6.) He assumes that there will be other officers
associated with the bishop in the government of the
Church having joint authority. He speaks of the bishop
and them that preside over you" (*Magn.* 6). The
brethren are to be obedient to the bishop, and to one
another, obedience in the latter case qualifying and
defining that in the former (*ib.*, c. 13). The Trallians
are to be "obedient also to the presbyters as to the
apostles" (c. 2). The Philadelphians are to give heed
to the bishop and presbyters and deacons" (c. 7):
"there is one bishop together with the presbytery and
the deacons, my fellow-servants" (c. 4); and he is
devoted, he says, to those who are subject to the
bishop, the presbyters, the deacons" (*Polyc.* 6).

3. Then again, while there is no recognition of
diocesan episcopacy in the Ignatian Epistles, *neither is
there any trace of the later idea of Apostolical Succession*,
or of the bishop as being instituted by the apostles.
According to Ignatius it is the presbyters, not the bishop,
who take the place of the apostles. There is godly
concord in a Church, "the bishop presiding after the
likeness of God, and the presbyters after the likeness of
the council of the apostles, with the deacons who are
most dear to me" (*Magn.* 6). In the Epistle to the
Trallians the idea takes a somewhat varied form: he
would have the brethren "respect the deacons as Jesus
Christ, even as they should respect the bishop as being
the type of the Father, and the presbyters as the council
of God, and as the college of apostles" (c. 3). The

Smyrnaeans, again, are to follow the bishop as Jesus Christ followed the Father and the presbytery as the apostles (c. 8). All through these Epistles the same idea prevails. While exalting the bishop or pastor as the New Testament never does, the writer does not make him the successor of the apostles or trace back to them the institution of his office. The bishop has his place "not of himself or through men, nor yet for vainglory, but in the love of God the Father and the Lord Jesus Christ" (*Philad.* 1).

This is what we might expect. For if the Epistles are genuine they are of Eastern origin, the work of the pastor of the Church at Antioch. But the theory that the bishop succeeded to the office and authority of the apostles took its rise in the West. In the East it came much later and spread but slowly. Harnack has reminded us that even in the original of the first six books of the Apostolic Constitutions, composed about the end of the third century, and representing the bishop as mediator, king, and teacher of the community, his office is still not yet regarded as apostolic. Here, as in the Ignatian Epistles, it is the presbyters who are regarded as continuing the work of the apostles.

4. Again, while in the Ignatian Epistles the bishop is simply a pastor, the president of a Congregational Church, and the elders are looked upon as the representatives of the apostles, to quote Dr. Lightfoot, "*there is not throughout these letters the slightest tinge of sacerdotal language in reference to the Christian ministry.*" The only passage in which there is any mention of a priest or high priest is in the Epistle to the Philadelphians (c. 9), and it reads as follows: "The priests likewise were good, but better is the High Priest,

to whom is entrusted the holy of holies ; for to Him alone are committed the hidden things of God ; he Himself being the door of the Father." No exegesis is worth a moment's consideration which refers these priests to the Christian ministry. The writer is simply contrasting the Old Dispensation with the New, and while he allows the worth of the former he claims superiority for the latter. By "priests," as the connexion shows, he could only mean the Levitical priesthood, the mediators of the old covenant ; while the High Priest referred to is none other than Christ the mediator of the new. It is simple literal truth to say that Ignatius never applies the term "priest" to the ministers of the Christian Church. Nor does he represent them as performing priestly functions, as transmuting the simple elements used at the Lord's table. Only the most strained interpretation, such as would pervert the meaning of any writings, can bring the modern priestly ideas out of his words. If he speaks of an altar, it is a symbolic reference to our Saviour Himself: "Come as to one altar, even to one Jesus Christ" (*Magn.* 7). When he says (*Ephes.* 5), "If any one be not within the precinct of the altar he lacketh the bread," the context plainly shows that what he meant was that if a man keeps back from Church fellowship he loses the blessing which Church fellowship is fitted to give. When he speaks of the blood of God he clearly means His unspeakable love ; for as the blood is the life, life is love and love is life. "I have no delight," he says (*Rom.* 7), "in the food of corruption or in the delights of this life. I desire the bread of God, which is the flesh of Christ who was of the seed of David ; and for a draught I desire His blood, which is love incorruptible." To the same spiritual purport he says (*Trall.* 8), " Arm yourselves with gentleness and recover yourselves in *faith which is the flesh of the Lord,* and in *love which is the blood of Jesus Christ.*" His great concern is to prevent the one local community in any one given place from being split up into parties, and observing the communion in sections, of which there appears to have been some danger in his time. " Let that be held a valid eucharist which is under the bishop" (*Smyrn.* 8); " come as to one altar, even to one Jesus Christ" (*Magn.* 7); " be ye careful to observe one eucharist (for there is one flesh of our Lord Jesus Christ and one cup unto union in His blood ; there is one altar as there is one bishop, together with the presbytery and the deacons my fellow-servants)" (*Philad.* 4).

The simple truth is that while men have used these Epistles as the bulwark of diocesan episcopacy, they have been unwarrantably reading into them the ecclesiastical ideas of a much later time—ideas of which, it is safe to say, Ignatius knew nothing whatever. What he was concerned about was, not to show that there are three Orders in the Church of Divine authority, but to secure peace and unity in each individual Church. He is simply saying in effect, what it is a good thing to say to any Church—rally round the officers you have chosen and keep together. In the concentrated individuality of each single community he sees the safety of the Universal Church. To quote all the passages in proof of this would be to quote a large part of the Epistles. A few taken here and there may suffice for our purpose. " Some persons," he says, " have the bishop's name on their lips but in everything act apart from him. Such men appear to me not to keep a good conscience, forasmuch as they do not assemble themselves according to commandment" (*Magn.* 4). "Let there be nothing among you which shall have power to divide you, but be ye united with the bishop and with them that preside over you, as an ensample, and lesson of incorruptibility" (c. 6). "Attempt not to think anything right for yourselves apart from others; but let there be one prayer in common, one supplication, one mind, one hope, in love and joy unblameable, which is Jesus Christ, than whom there is nothing better. Hasten to come together all of you, as to one temple, even God; as to one altar, even to one Jesus Christ who came forth from one Father, and is with One, and is departed unto One" (*Magn.* 7). He salutes the Church of the Philadelphians, "more especially if they be at one with the bishop and the presbyters who are with him, and with the deacons that have been appointed according to the mind of Jesus Christ." "As children of light shun divisions and wrong doctrines. ... For many specious wolves with baneful delights lead captive the runners in God's race: but where ye are at one they will find no place" (c. 2). "Assemble yourselves together in common, every one of you severally, man by man, in grace, in one faith and one Jesus Christ, who after the flesh was of David's race, who is Son of Man and Son of God, to the end that ye may obey the bishop and the presbytery without distraction of mind" (*Eph.* 20).

Making allowance for a tone of oriental exaggeration here and there, we feel that Ignatius in these and such like utterances gives sound advice to the Churches of his time. His principle is that the right men should be chosen by the society as its officers, and then that they should have its confidence and support when chosen. It may be there was special need for this reiterated exhortation to unity and concert of brotherly action. Indeed, such exhortations are seldom out of place at any time, human nature being what it is. Still, judging these Epistles by their general tenour, it is obvious that Ignatius had no more thought of setting up an autocratic diocesan bishop than he had of setting up a world-controlling, infallible Pope. The one would have been an anachronism as well as the other. Professor Ramsay quite expresses one's own feeling when he says: "I can find in Ignatius no proof that the bishops were regarded as *ex officio* supreme even in Asia, where he was evidently much impressed by the good organisation of the Churches. His words are quite consistent with the view that the respect actually paid in each community to the bishop depended on his individual character" (*C. R. E.*, p. 371).

It is a further point of great importance that the only idea Ignatius has of the relation of the separate Churches to each other is that which manifested itself simply in brotherly intercourse, and in the possession of a common ideal and a common hope. He knows nothing of a union of the different communities into one Church, organised under a diocesan bishop and guaranteed by law and office. With him the bishop is of importance only for the individual community, and has no official control beyond the Church of which he is pastor. Dr. Loening, who in addition to his great ability and learning has had the advantage of being trained in *Kirchenrecht*, or canon law, and therefore has a keen appreciation of everything of the nature of constituted authority, distinctly says that of organised union of separate communities Ignatius knows nothing. While united in the bonds of a common faith and love, in constitution they are independent.[1] Each separate community is an image of the Universal Church, and is complete in itself. The elders are attuned to the bishop even as its strings to a lyre, therefore, in their concord and harmonious love Jesus Christ is sung. The people and officers of each separate Church are to form themselves into a chorus that, being harmonious in concord and taking the keynote of God, they may in unison sing with one voice through Jesus Christ unto the Father (*Eph.* 4). Beyond the law and authority of Christ there is for Ignatius no control of the Christian communities from without. At the same time there is most real union maintained among the Churches. The Ignatian Epistles show in what way brotherly intercourse was kept up. As the martyr was on his way to Rome from city after city the Churches sent deputations of honoured brethren to greet him on his way and to assure him of their love and sympathy. Intercourse was also kept up by means of letters, hospitality and brotherly conferences on matters relating to the common welfare. There was real living congregational union while the Churches were separate and self-governing.

To sum up the whole question then, if we remember that with Ignatius the bishop meant the pastor of a Church, that his exhortations to honour bishops and presbyters were exhortations to Christian men to rally round the Church and the Church officers, with

[1] *Die Gemeindeverfassung*, s. 120 : "Alle Schreiben des Ignatius sind erfüllt von dem Gedanken, dass die christlichen Gemeinden ihr Haupt und ihren Mittelpunkt in dem Bischof zu finden haben. Eine Verfassungsmässige, organisatorische Vereinigung der einzelnen Gemeinden unter einander kennt er nicht. Die einzelnen Gemeinden sind mit einander vereint durch das Band des gemeinsamen Glaubens und der Liebe, aber der Verfassung nach stehen die einzelnen Gemeinden selbstständig und unabhängig von einander."

which they had voluntarily connected themselves; that there is nothing in his letters favouring Apostolical Succession or sacerdotalism, or the organisation of many Churches under one government—when these things are remembered, it will be seen that Congregationalists, least of all people, have anything to fear from the establishment of the genuineness of the Ignatian Epistles. With utmost complacency and calmness of mind we can afford to stand by while great scholars of the English Church like Ussher and Pearson and Lightfoot learnedly labour to prove that Ignatius actually lived and wrote the Epistles which bear his name. The toil of battle has been theirs, the spoils are ours.

LECTURE VI

THE TRANSITION FROM PROPHET TO PASTOR

LECTURE VI

THE TRANSITION FROM PROPHET TO PASTOR

PAUSING for a moment at the point of transition between the first century and the second, let us note how the various Christian Churches had by this time come to be organised in the leading cities of the empire. Till the flight of the Christians to Pella, previous to the destruction of the city, the Mother Church in Jerusalem seems to have retained the form of organisation brought over from the synagogue; that is, as a self-governing community they were presided over by a number of presbyters or elders chosen by themselves. The connexion of the apostles with the Church was only temporary. Within a few years of Pentecost they had left Jerusalem for other lands as propagandists of the faith. On the outbreak of Herod's persecution of the Church (Acts xii.), so far as we can see, of the Twelve only Peter and James were left in the city. James was slain, and Peter, on his release from prison, "departed and went to another place." The next time we hear of him he is at Antioch. It would seem, therefore, there were only elders left, of whom James, the brother of the Lord, may have been one. At Alexandria, also, next to Jerusalem the most Jewish city of the empire, the same arrangement prevailed. We have already learnt from Eutychius that till 188 A.D. "there were no bishops in the whole of provincial Egypt," and that the custom in the Church at Alexandria was for the twelve presbyters there to choose from their own number a patriarch as president, whom they themselves set apart by laying on of hands. Then, crossing from Alexandria to Rome, even there we as yet find no trace of episcopal organisation. The letter sent from this Church to that at Corinth in the year 95, was, as tradition affirms, written by Clement, but whether he was anything more than a leading presbyter does not appear, inasmuch as he is not described by any official title. Even twenty years later, Ignatius, in his Epistle to the Romans, makes no mention of any bishop as existing among them, a fact difficult to account for, if there were one. What is thus true of Jerusalem, Alexandria, and Rome, we find to be true also of Corinth. We gather from Clement's Epistle that the management of the affairs of this Church was in the hands of a body of elders. At Thessalonica, again, we have Paul's Epistles to the Church there, but in them no mention of any bishop. He states that he had sent Timothy to them as God's minister in the Gospel of Christ to establish and comfort them, but, as the context shows, it was only on a temporary visit. There are local officers who labour among them and are over them in the Lord, as there were at Corinth, rulers ($\pi\rho o \ddot{\iota} \sigma \tau a \mu \acute{\epsilon} \nu o \iota$) whom they are to know and esteem highly in love for their work's sake; prophesyings are heard in their Church gatherings, which they are not to despise; but there is no salutation to any bishop or presiding officer either in Paul's first Epistle or his second, his salutation being to the Church only. Still keeping in Roman Macedonia and passing from Thessalonica to Philippi, the apostle salutes the saints there with the bishops and deacons. But sixty years later (117 A.D.) Polycarp, writing to this same Church, urges them to submit themselves to the presbyters and deacons as to God and Christ, and charges the presbyters to be compassionate and merciful towards all men, visiting the infirm and showing themselves not unmindful of the widows, the fatherless, and the poor. We can only conclude that the bishops and deacons at Philippi in Paul's time were the presbyters of Polycarp's time, and *vice versâ*.

The cities we have thus gone over were the great leading centres of the civilised world — Jerusalem, Alexandria, Rome, Corinth, Thessalonica, Philippi, yet in none of them have we found so much as a trace of that episcopate which the modern Episcopalian believes to be absolutely essential, not only to the *bene esse*, but the *esse* of a Church. It is only when we come to Syria and the Churches of Asia Minor that we find a bishop spoken of separately from the presbyters and deacons; but as we have seen from the Ignatian Epistles—absolutely the only literature of that time in which this form of organisation is spoken of—this bishop is simply the presiding pastor of a single Church, the presbyters and deacons sharing the administration of affairs with him.

The process of transition from a government by elders, like that in Jerusalem, to that by bishop, elders, and deacons, as found at Antioch and in Asia Minor, is necessarily somewhat obscure. The period between 70 A.D., the date of the destruction of Jerusalem, and 95 A.D., the date of the Epistle of Clement and the

Didaché, is the darkest time of all. We have scarcely a gleam of light, and can only feel our way. Perhaps our safest course will be to follow the fortunes of the Church in Jerusalem, about which Hegesippus tells us all that can now be known. From the fragments of his writings which Eusebius has preserved for us, he supplements the account we find in the New Testament. For long after Pentecost the Christians, as we know, while having their own meetings apart, still repaired for worship to the temple. They are described as day by day continuing steadfastly with one accord in the temple and breaking bread at home (Acts ii. 46, *R.V.*). The apostles Peter and John were going up into the temple at the hour of prayer, when they found the lame man at the temple gate. In the outer court of the temple, as a convenient place of concourse, they preached to the people. "Go," said the angel to the apostles he had released from prison—"go ye and stand and speak in the temple to the people all the words of this life"; and they entered into the temple about daybreak and taught. At a later time we find Paul, with the four men who had a vow upon them, going into the temple, purifying himself with them, declaring the fulfilment of the days of purification, until the offering was offered for every one of them (Acts xxi. 26). He tells us also that he was praying in the temple when he fell into the trance in which he received his Divine commission to the Gentiles (xxii. 17).

This connexion, more or less intimate, was probably kept up till the martyrdom of James, the brother of the Lord, as described by Josephus and Hegesippus. After his death and before the outbreak of the war (66 A.D.) "respected men" (δοκίμοι) among them led the Christians to the land east of Jordan, where they settled at Pella, from whence they spread over the Hauran and to the lands still further east. The great tract of country south of Damascus, still called the Hauran, was at that time thickly inhabited and well garrisoned by Roman soldiers. Strabo tells us that the garrisons thus maintained by Rome had produced a feeling of security which tended greatly to prosperity, and the point to be noted especially is that in this same district to which the Jerusalem Church was transplanted during the stormy years when their own city was desolated by war, the term bishop was the usual title for municipal officials, and in no other part of the Greco-Roman world is this title so often found in inscriptions.[1] The whole district abounds in ruins, and not only in Bozra, its ancient capital, but in numerous towns and villages, frequent Greek inscriptions have been found by recent explorers. It is, perhaps, not without significance that in this same region, where the title of bishop is more frequently found than elsewhere as that of a municipal functionary, the Jerusalem Church found its settlement. Hegesippus tells us (*H. E.*, iv. 22) that all those who had gone forth into Pella and the neighbourhood chose Symeon, the son of Cleopas, as their head, he being the cousin of our Lord. James's position also had previously rested on his relationship to Jesus, and on personal regard. Hegesippus gives him no title, as holding no formal office; it is only when the Church has gone into the country east of the Jordan, where episkopos was the common title of a public officer, that Hegesippus gives the title episkopos to Symeon, the

---

[1] Le Bas et Waddington, *Inscriptions Grecques et Latines*, vol. iii. Nos. 1911, 1989, 1990, 2070, 2298, 2308, 2309, 2310, 2412.

successor of James, though whether he received the title at the time or not is not certain. What the organisation of this Church continued to be like cannot be inferred from the list of bishops of Jerusalem given by Eusebius; for since he gives a list of thirteen bishops in twenty-eight years, as Loening says, it is impossible to say whether this is an arbitrary list or a combination of lists, or whether it contains the names of presbyters. But it is not improbable that from this Church at Pella, where one presbyter became president with the title of bishop, this arrangement passed to the Church of Antioch, and thence to the Churches of Asia Minor. Very little importance can be attached to the statement that episcopacy was introduced into Asia Minor by the Apostle John, resting as it does on a single passage in Clement of Alexandria (*Quis Divus* c. 42), and on the common desire of all the Churches of a later time to trace their origin to some apostle or other. It is true that Tertullian maintained that John made Polycarp bishop of Smyrna, but Irenæus, who knew Polycarp personally and who refers to the succession of pastors in the Churches, says nothing of this.

While the Church in Jerusalem gives us only problematical hints as to the transition from government by a body of elders to that by a body of elders presided over by a pastor or bishop, there is one Church —that of Corinth—where we are on surer ground. There we can distinctly trace the existence of three successive forms of Church organisation within the space of about a century. Let us, therefore, follow the course of events in this Church as far as we can with the materials at our disposal.

1. Taking the year 53 as the probable date of Paul's

First Epistle to the Corinthians, we can, from the 11th, 12th, and 14th chapters, with tolerable certainty, infer the kind of arrangement prevailing at that time. On reading these chapters we are struck by the absence of any mention of the official element as such, and by the active part taken in the worship by the various members of the Church. There are diversities of gifts, diversities of ministration, and diversities of workings. To each one is given the manifestation of the Spirit to profit withal. The human body, of which each part has some function to serve, is the analogy employed to describe the organic life of the Church. Ye are the body of Christ and severally members thereof. There is special mention made of the fact that God hath set some in the Church, first apostles, secondly prophets, thirdly teachers, the same spiritually endowed leaders, in short, whom we find forty years later described in the Didachê as itinerant teachers among all the Churches. But unless described under the general terms "helps and governments," presbyters, bishops, and deacons are not so much as mentioned; indeed, neither presbyters nor bishops are named even once in either of the two Epistles to the Church at Corinth.

While at the time Paul wrote these Epistles the service of the Christians was not unlike that of the synagogue, inasmuch as many took part in it, the Christian service was yet fuller, richer in devotional feeling, and more varied than that of the synagogue. It was still the time of that great efflorescence of spiritual power bestowed at Pentecost, meant rather for temporary sign than for permanent continuance. "When ye come together each one hath a psalm, hath a teaching, hath a revelation, hath a tongue, hath an interpretation." "To one is given through the Spirit the word of wisdom; and to another the word of knowledge according to the same Spirit: to another faith in the same Spirit, and to another gifts of healings in the one Spirit; and to another workings of miracles; and to another prophecy; and to another discernings of spirits; to another divers kinds of tongues; and to another the interpretation of tongues."

It needs scarcely be said that prayer and praise entered largely into the worship of that early time. Paul places praying and prophesying side by side, and elsewhere he urges the Christians to speak to one another in psalms and hymns and spiritual songs. Probably the spiritual song was generic, the psalm and hymn specific; the psalm designating a composition which took its character from the Old Testament Psalms, though not confined to them, the hymn being a song of praise. Pliny says that the Christians in Bithynia sang hymns responsively (*secum invicem*) to Christ as God; and referring to a much later time, Tertullian, speaking of the Agapé, says that as it commenced with prayer, so with prayer it was closed, and that each one was asked to stand forth and sing, as he can, a hymn to God, either one from the Holy Scripture or one of his own composing (*Apol.*, 39). Hippolytus, too, speaks of the enemies of the Christians as watching for a fit time, and entering the House of God while all are there praying and praising God, seizing some of them and carrying them off.

To these ordinary forms of worship there seem to have been added in the Corinthian Church certain ecstatic and extraordinary manifestations of the Spirit. The speaking with tongues was a form of endowment in which the man appeared to pass out of himself into an ecstatic condition. It does not seem that we are to regard this gift, as exercised at Corinth, to be the same as that manifested by the disciples on the day of Pentecost. The narrative in the latter case seems to imply utterance in an intelligible language other than the speaker's own. The miracle at Pentecost was special for a special occasion, as was that in the house of Cornelius, and also that in the case of those disciples at Ephesus who had previously known only the baptism of John. At Corinth, on the contrary, speaking with tongues appears to have been a form of speech not understood without interpretation by those standing near. The man was speaking to God in an ecstatic manner to be distinguished as different from ordinary speech. It was prayer offered in those exuberant moods of soul when the new faith found common modes of expression insufficient for its exalted condition. To the bystander it appeared like soliloquy. "He that speaketh in a tongue speaketh not unto men, but unto God: for no man understandeth; but in the Spirit he speaketh mysteries. He that speaketh in a tongue edifieth himself, but he that prophesieth edifieth the Church." Therefore it was unintelligible to others; could be compared only to the use of an instrument, a pipe or harp giving no distinction in sounds, to a trumpet giving an uncertain voice. It was a sign, being marvellous, but only to unbelievers; believers gained no edification from it. Paul had the gift himself in even eminent degree, but he did not greatly value it. "I thank God," he says, "I speak with tongues more than you all: howbeit in the Church I had rather speak five words with my understanding that I might instruct others also, than ten thousand words in a tongue." Still, this mysterious gift in one man must have produced impressions sufficiently definite in another for that other to be able to interpret it. To one was given divers kinds of tongues, on another was bestowed the interpretation of tongues. "If any man speaketh in a tongue let it be by two, or at most by three, and that in turn; and let one interpret: but if there be no interpreter let him keep silence in the Church, and let him speak to himself and to God." Paul had drawn from this source in his own inner life; but he felt that it was not unattended with danger. It came perilously near that mysterious borderland of the spiritual nature where excitement oft repeated breaks down the will-power and generates disease, and where prayer is apt to degenerate into mere phrenzy. It was destined to pass away after doing certain needed work as a sign. The attempt Edward Irving made to revive it in our own century proved, as might be expected, a conspicuous failure. "Whether there be tongues, they shall cease." The fulness of the Spirit showed itself also in simpler and more didactic forms. "What shall I profit you unless I speak to you either by way of revelation, or of knowledge, or of prophesying, or of teaching?" "To one is given through the Spirit the word of wisdom"— the power to understand and expound the Divine conception of the world, its progress, God's purpose concerning it, and the regulation of human life in accordance with that purpose: "to another the word of knowledge according to the same Spirit"—that higher enlightenment we receive through Christ—the knowledge of the glory of God in the face of Jesus Christ.

2. Such were the conditions of Church life and worship at Corinth in the year 53 A.D. as we gather them from Paul's Epistle. They were characterised by many-sidedness, by great fulness and variety of spiritual life; but also by phenomena which from their very nature could only be temporary. It was inevitable that they should sooner or later give place to those more important and permanent forms of the Spirit's action on the souls of men which belong to all time and all lands. Let us now, while still keeping to the Church at Corinth, pass from the year 53 A.D. to the year 95 A.D., from Paul's Epistle to the Epistle of Clement. During these two and forty years a whole generation has passed away, and the inevitable change in Church life has become an accomplished fact. Tongues and the interpretation of tongues are now a thing of the past, and Church life has settled down into more ordinary grooves. The Church, for how long we know not, has been presided over by presbyters who have "ministered unblameably to the flock of Christ in lowliness of mind, peacefully and with all modesty, and for long time have borne a good report with all." But at the time of the writing of this Epistle, and indeed as the occasion of its writing, an unworthy revolt had sprung up against these presbyters on the part of some in the Church. "We see that ye have displaced certain persons, though they were living honourably, from the ministration which had been respected by them blamelessly." "It is shameful, dearly beloved, yes utterly shameful and unworthy of your conduct in Christ, that it should be reported that the very stedfast and ancient Church of the Corinthians, for the sake of one or two persons, maketh sedition against its presbyters." "It will be no light sin for us,

if we thrust out those who have offered the gifts [τὰ δῶρα] of the episcopate unblameably and holily." Their good name has been tarnished "through the unholy sedition, so alien and strange to the Elect of God, which a few headstrong and self-willed persons have kindled." "Men were stirred up, the mean against the honourable, the ill-reputed against the highly-reputed, the foolish against the wise, the young against the elder. For this cause righteousness and peace stand aloof." Their brethren in Rome plead with them to return to a better mind: "For Christ is with them that are of a lowly mind, not with them that exalt themselves over the flock. He Himself came not in the pomp of arrogance or of pride, though He might have done so, but in lowliness of mind." Let us walk worthily of Him. "Let us reverence our rulers [προηγουμένοι], let us honour our presbyters." "We ought to do all things in order, as many as the Master hath commanded us to perform at their appointed seasons. And where and by whom He would have them performed, He Himself fixed by His supreme will: that all things being done with piety according to His good pleasure might be acceptable to His will. They, therefore, that make their offerings at the appointed seasons are acceptable and blessed; for while they follow the institutions of the Master they cannot go wrong." "Who, therefore, is noble among you? Let him say: 'If by reason of me there be faction and strife and divisions, I retire, I depart, whither ye will, and I do that which is ordered by the people: only let the flock of Christ be at peace with its duly appointed presbyters.'"

The drift of all this is clear enough, and also the

form of Church organisation which it assumes. We have here in the year 95 A.D. a self-governing Church, over which there are rulers described by the same term (προηγούμενοι) as that applied in the New Testament and the Didachê to those itinerant spiritual leaders, the apostles, prophets, and teachers. But besides these rulers who are to be reverenced there are also presbyters who are to be honoured, these being local church officers chosen by the people and apparently also set aside by the people, presbyters "who have offered the gifts," that is, discharged the functions, "of the episcopate unblameably." There is nothing in this Epistle of Clement to indicate that up to this point at least, any one presbyter had taken precedence of the rest as presiding bishop or pastor. Here, then, we have what we may describe as the second stage of Church organisation in Corinth, the form prevailing at the end of the first century and the beginning of the second.

3. Once more we take a step forward of half a century or more in the history of this Church, and again we find a change has taken place in the interval. About the year 150 A.D., Hegesippus, quoted by Eusebius (*H. E.*, iv. 22), tells us he went to Corinth, where he found Primus taking the oversight of the Church (ἐπισκοπεύοντος), with whom he had familiar conversation, passing many days with him as he was on the point of sailing for Rome. He found the Church at Corinth had continued in the true faith, and while he was with Primus, "we were mutually refreshed," he says, "in the true doctrine." Some time later Primus was followed in the pastorate of this Church by Dionysius (*H. E.*, iv. 23), who imparted freely, Eusebius tells us, not only to his own people, but to others abroad also, the

blessings of his disinterested labours. He seems to have been a public-spirited man, a leader among the Churches, being most useful of all in the general Epistles he addressed to various Churches—to the Lacedæmonians, instructing them in the true religion and inculcating peace and unity; to the Athenians, urging them to the faith and life prescribed by the Gospel; to the Nicomedians, in which he refutes the heresy of Marcion and sets forth the standard of truth; and also to the Church at Cortyna, congratulating Philip, their bishop, on the many instances of fortitude evinced by the Church under his care. He wrote also to the Churches at Amastris and Pontus, mentioning that Bacchylides and Elpistus had urged him to write. These letters do not assume any authoritative control on his part over these Churches, inasmuch as we find him writing also to the Church in Rome, in which he mentions that in his own Church at Corinth they still continue to read Clement's letter of seventy years ago, on the Lord's Day, and also that which Soter, the Roman pastor, had sent them; and he commends them for their kindness in sending contributions to many Churches in every city. By thus refreshing the needy in their want and sending to the brethren condemned to the mines what was necessary, they were, as Romans, keeping up the time-honoured custom of their Roman ancestors. Nothing is left of these Epistles of Dionysius beyond the fragments preserved by Eusebius, who places him in his Chronicon under the year 171 A.D., as a sacred man celebrated at that time. But they were regarded as of sufficient authority to make it worth while to interpolate them and they are interesting as throwing considerable light on the state of the Church at the time they were written. They show, for example, that it was the custom of the Churches to read letters from other Churches in public assembly and to maintain brotherly relations with each other. But the point to be specially noted is that the Churches far and wide have pastors or bishops presiding over them. This is not only the case in Asia Minor as the Ignatian Epistles have shown us at an earlier time, but also in Rome, Corinth, Athens, Sparta, Nicomedia, Cortyna, and the Churches in Crete. Still, even at this time (171 A.D.) the importance of the pastor or bishop continues to be subordinate to that of the Church over which he presides. All the Epistles of Dionysius, including that to Rome, are addressed in each case to the Church, not to the pastor; and the one to Rome shows that Soter's letter to the Church at Corinth, like the earlier one of Clement, was written not in his own name, but in that of the Church at Rome of which he was pastor. The Epistles of Dionysius may seem to be an exception, being written in his own name, he using the first person singular, but this is explained by his telling us that he wrote these Epistles at the request of certain brethren, some of whom he names; they were, therefore, not communications from a Church, but from an individual.

Thus, then, following the development of the Church at Corinth, and trying as far as we can to keep to known and assured facts, we find that by about the beginning of the last quarter of the second century there was at the head of this Church a presiding pastor or bishop, and we gather from his letters that the other Churches to which these letters were written had also each of them a presiding pastor or bishop. The important question now arises for consideration—how did it come about that one presbyter began to take precedence of the rest and to occupy the position of presiding pastor or bishop, and what, mainly, were the forces which contributed to this result?

1. Dr. Hatch's theory, as to how the change probably came about, is well known. He makes it to turn very largely upon financial considerations. The offerings of the Christians in the time of Justin Martyr were made, as he tells us, not privately but publicly, not directly to those who had need, but to the presiding officer in the general assembly of the brethren. The officer thus presiding received the offerings and then and there solemnly dedicated them to God, uttering over them words of thanksgiving and benediction. The president thus became the responsible treasurer of the Church, and his functions, as such, were of great importance. He had to care for the poor, for those who were outcasts because of their confession of faith, for those who were sent to prison or sold into captivity, above all for the widows and orphans of the Church. Then, too, there were brethren from other Churches passing from city to city, who were to be received with Christian hospitality. All this involved a large amount of ecclesiastical administration, of which the episkopos or presiding presbyter was the pivot and centre ; and while, no doubt, there were other duties to be discharged, these were primary and fundamental. In support of this view, Dr. Hatch mentions an inscription in which it is recorded that by a resolution of the municipal authority the episkopoi of the city are directed to accept of a certain offer and to invest the money. In other inscriptions found in the Haurân this title seems to be used of the financial officers of the temple of the gods.

Possibly not a few will agree with Loening that, in this argument of his, Dr. Hatch is dazzling rather than convincing. This writer contends that the Haurân inscription is too vague for the stress laid upon it, and he quotes Waddington (iii. 147) to the effect that while that inscription seems to show that the episkopoi exercised some sort of surveillance over the revenues of the temple, the expression used (τὰ τοῦ θεοῦ) might apply to certain taxes imposed by the episkopoi for the reparation of the temple.[1] Kühl[2] also maintains with great force, that Hatch's basis is not broad enough for his conclusions, resting as they do upon one, or at most two passages where the episkopos acted in a financial capacity; that there is no reason to hold that the episkopoi mentioned in the inscription quoted were *permanent* officers of finance; and that so general a name does not suit so narrow an office. This objection urged by Kuhl is sustained by the researches of Foucart,[3] who found the episkopoi to be those officers who had to examine candidates for admission to the Greek Associations. In another case on which Hatch relies, where episkopos was the title of a municipal officer sent by the Athenians to subject states, it would rather seem that the man was a special commissioner sent to reduce conquered cities to order; this, therefore, was an exceptional case on which no general conclusion can be founded. Dr. Lightfoot's examination of the word as found in the LXX. also shows that it had more than a financial significance. In some instances it signifies "inspectors, superintendents, taskmasters" (2 Kings

---

[1] *Die Gemeindeverfassung des Urchristenthums*, s. 22.
[2] *Die Gemeindeordnung in den Pastoralbriefen.* Berlin, 1885.
[3] *Les Associations Religieuses Chez les Grecs*, 1873.

xi. 19; 2 Chron. xxxiv. 12, 17; Isa. lx. 7). In others it is a higher title, "captains" or "presidents" (Nehem. xi. 9, 14, 22). Of Antiochus Epiphanes it is recorded that, in order to carry out the overthrow of the worship of Jehovah, he appointed episkopoi over all the people to see that his orders were obeyed. The word, therefore, has a wider signification than Dr. Hatch's argument would seem to imply.

2. Professor Ramsay,[1] while not ignoring the duty of the presiding elder or bishop in the Christian Church to care for the material wants of the flock, regards the main part of his function, as lying in a different direction to that indicated by Dr. Hatch. With him the central idea in the development of the episcopal office lay in the duty of each community to maintain communication with other communities. The destruction of Jerusalem having annihilated all possibility of one localised centre for Christianity, it was made clear that the unity of the Churches must henceforward be maintained by a process of intercommunication and brotherhood. He thinks it scarcely possible to exaggerate the share which frequent intercourse between the congregations, from a very early stage, had in moulding the development of the Church. Most of the documents in the New Testament are the products and monuments of this intercourse. He holds the Ignatian Epistles to be genuine, but whether genuine or not, they bear witness to a state of things known to exist, and bring out into strong relief the close relations existing between different congregations. Without any power of legislation or external authority, there was real congregational union and true brotherly intercourse. The Epistles represent the most cordial welcome as

[1] *Church in the Roman Empire*, pp., 361, seq.

being extended to Ignatius all along the route he travelled. He, too, sends loving messages to the Churches, and receives the deputations sent from them to meet and convoy him. These and similar details presuppose intimate knowledge of each other's affairs, a regular system of intercommunication, and brotherly union of the closest kind along the great routes across the Empire.

All this being so, Professor Ramsay thinks that this close connexion could not be maintained by mere unregulated voluntary efforts, that organised action alone would be able to keep it up. It was work to be left not in many hands, but in one. Episkopos merely means overseer, and any presbyter to whom a definite duty was assigned by his brethren would be an episkopos for the occasion; therefore, any presbyter might become an episkopos for the occasion, and he, by proved aptness and power in some one thing, might come to have executive duties often assigned to him, and in this way the tried episkopos would tend to become permanent. Still, for a long time his authority was delegated, and his influence depended not so much on his official position as on his personal qualities. It became his duty to maintain hospitality towards the brethren coming from other Churches, and to compose the letters sent in the Church's name to sister communities. Still, in the earliest time his position was co-ordinate, not supreme. He was simply a presbyter on whom certain duties had been imposed; he was far removed from the monarchical bishop of A.D. 170; and there is no trace of anything to suggest that he exercised any authority *ex officio* within the community. He was the representative of the Church, and the letters he wrote were written, like Clement's Epistle, in their name, not his, and their contents referred solely to the brethren, not to himself. Even in the Ignatian Epistles Professor Ramsay sees no proof that the bishops were regarded as supreme even in Asia. What Ignatius says is quite consistent with the view that the respect paid to the bishop in each community depended on his individual character rather than on his official position.

3. There is much to be said for the view thus presented. The presiding elders of the scattered communities chosen, as they were, as being men of character and position, and acting, as they did, as leaders in facing the storms of persecution which ever and again broke over the hapless suffering brethren, they would naturally be the medium of communication between the various Churches. Still, while Professor Ramsay's theory probably thus comes nearer to the facts of the case than that of Dr. Hatch, we have a sort of feeling that it is defective in an important sense. For it lays too much stress on the external relations of the Churches, and too little on the internal life and worship of each separate Church. Yet the latter is vital and primary, while the former, though important, is secondary and subordinate. The permanent instruction and edification of the Church, the maintenance and extension of Divine truth, and the efficient observance of public worship were of paramount importance. Yet there were causes at work which were beyond all human control, and which tended to place this department of service in the hands of the local leaders of the various Churches.

(*a*) The gradual cessation of the extraordinary gifts of the Spirit, possessed, as we have seen, by nearly all the members of such a Church as that at Corinth, for example, would necessarily issue in the brethren at large taking a less prominent and active part in the worship and instruction of the Church. The special manifestations of the Spirit were intended to be but temporary, and were to disappear before those ordinary influences which, if less striking, were more important and more permanently influential. Even when the extraordinary charismata were at their highest point of affluence the apostle sought to prepare men's minds for a time when these would cease to be. He taught that to speak the truth in love is better than to speak it in many tongues ; that charity is greater than intellectual gifts ; and that faith would live on when prophecy had ceased. When this change had come the power of service would inevitably pass, as to its more public forms, from the many to the few.

(*b*) While the charismata declined among the brethren at large, the same cause would be at work affecting the spiritually endowed apostles, prophets, and teachers who moved about among all the Churches. These prophets were probably not very numerous at any time, and they would probably be growing fewer at the very time that the Churches were increasing in number. More and more those functions of the prophet which were essential to the welfare of the Church would come to be discharged by the local officers, the bishops and deacons, " for they also minister to you the ministry of the prophets and teachers." The future was on the side of the regular and permanent authority rather than with the extemporaneous and enthusiastic. But the permanent office rose in dignity and importance as the temporary institution of prophecy declined. Next in importance to the apostles in the Primitive Church stood the Christian prophets, and what was of permanent value and importance in the work of the prophet was passed on to the bishop or pastor. Thus, in its most spiritual element the gift of prophecy has never ceased in the Christian Church. "Age after age has seen the rise of great teachers, alike within and without the ranks of the regular ministry—men who were dominated by a sense of immediate mission from God, and filled with a conviction which imparted itself by contagion to their hearers. Prophecy as an institution was destined to pass away, leaving those of its functions which were vital to the Church's well-being to be discharged as a rule by the settled Ministry, which rose to its full height only on its rival's fall."[1]

(c) The formation of the New Testament Canon, again, had a decided, though indirect, influence in the elevation of a settled ministry in the Church. On the one hand, when these writings became a recognised and authoritative standard of Divine truth they gradually "put an end to a situation where it was possible for any Christian under the inspiration of the Spirit to give authoritative disclosures and instruction;" and, on the other hand, possessing these, the permanent leaders of the Church were enabled to unfold and enforce the mind of the Spirit with assured confidence. It is not a mere coincidence that the gradual formation of the New Testament Canon synchronised to a large extent with the gradual elevation of one presbyter from among the rest to be the presiding bishop or pastor of the Church. At the beginning of the last quarter of the

[1] Prof. J. Armitage Robinson, paper on *The Christian Prophets*, 1895.

second century both processes were at work; at the end of that century both processes were complete.

While in the way thus indicated the prophet was merged into the pastor, and the pastor succeeded to the function of the prophet, it must not be overlooked that the germ of the prophet's function was to be found in the office of the presbyter or bishop from the beginning. A presbyter took higher rank if he could both teach and exhort as well as take the practical management of the affairs of the Church: " Let the elders that rule well be counted worthy of double honour, especially those who labour in the Word and teaching." He is to be "apt to teach," but this qualification is merely given in a list of thirteen or fourteen others (1 Tim. iii. 3–7; v. 17). In the same way, in the ancient document worked into the Apostolic Canons it is said of the bishop that "it is good if he is educated, in a position to expound the Scriptures, but if he is unlearned, then he must be gentle and filled with love to all, so that a bishop should never be as one accused of anything by the multitude." When we come to the Apostolic Constitutions, that is to such portions of them as experts regard as being genuinely ante-Nicene, we find that a great step forward has been taken in the way of assimilating the function of the ruling elders to that of the presiding bishop or pastor. " The bishop to be ordained should be patient and gentle in his admonitions, well instructed himself, meditating in and diligently studying the Lord's books, and reading them frequently, so that he may be able carefully to interpret the Scriptures, expounding the gospel in correspondence with the prophets and with the law, and to let the expositions from the law and the prophets correspond to the gospel.

For the Lord Jesus says, 'Search the Scriptures, for they are those which testify of me.' . . . Be careful, therefore, O bishop, to study the Word, that thou mayest be able to explain everything exactly, and that thou mayest copiously nourish thy people with much doctrine and enlighten them with the light of the law" (ii. 5).

Thus rose as a permanent office in the Christian Church the important function of the Christian pastor, "not out of the apostolic order by localisation, but out of the presbyteral by elevation; and the title, which originally was common to all, came at length to be appropriated to the chief among them."[1]

It is here, then, in the transition from the temporary to the permanent forms of the Spirit's action, that we come upon the great epoch-making change in Church organisation, the importance of which has not always been realised. The cessation of supernatural charismata, the withdrawal of those special gifts which from Pentecost onwards had played so important a part in Church life and worship, would necessarily create a new era in ecclesiastical history. Other changes in after-centuries were brought about by officials, synods, and councils of human institution, but this, as it were, by an ordinance of Heaven itself. Not that spiritual gifts were now to cease. They were as needful as ever " for the perfecting of the saints unto the work of ministering, unto the building up of the body of Christ." They will be needful until the end, " till we all attain unto the unity of the faith and of the knowledge of the Son of God, unto a full-grown man, unto the measure of the stature of the fulness of Christ." But while the gifts are con-

[1] Dr. Lightfoot, *Essay on Christian Ministry*, p. 194.

tinued, their form is changed. Out of that community of spiritual men known as the Church there were to be raised up from time to time men endowed for service by the Spirit of God, those whose gifts of guidance, edification, instruction, persuasion, and conviction, coming to be recognised by the brotherhood, caused them to be placed in the forefront as the men of light and leading. These, rather than the diocesan bishops of a later time, who are brought but little into contact with the great body of the people, are the true bishops of the Church, doing their work under the inspiration and guidance of the one Chief Shepherd and Bishop of souls.

The Christian pastor or bishop, then, while succeeding to the work of the ruling presbyter of the first century, succeeds also to the function of the prophet of the New Testament times, even as the New Testament prophet succeeded under new and enlarged conditions to the work of the prophet of God in ancient Israel. The Jewish priest passed altogether away, his work being consummated and superseded by that of the great High Priest, who has passed into the heavens. But the prophet having permanent relation to the spiritual needs of human life, has, of necessity, permanent place in the Church of Christ. The work done by the prophets of God in Israel is one that needs doing in every age and among all nations. They rebuked evil and inspired to good; they reminded the people of God's purpose concerning them, and were the corrective of that proneness to superstition so often seen in the nation's life. It has been well said that Israel's ritual always remained Israel's peril, the peril of relapsing into Paganism. In the path of a people drifting again and again into idolatry, with its attendant uncleanness, the prophet confronted them and said, " I am full of power by the Spirit of the Lord, and of judgement, and of might, to declare unto Jacob his transgression, and to Israel his sin." Over against the priest multiplying ceremonies and sacrifices appeared the prophet, saying, " He hath showed thee, O man, what is good ; and what doth the Lord require of thee but to do justly, and to love mercy, and to walk humbly with thy God." It was Israel's salvation, so far as salvation was then possible, that she had men among her who did not permit themselves to be carried away by the general infatuation, but who looked facts in the face, penetrated to the centre of the national life, and became the spiritual and intellectual leaders of the time. The prophets did this. They represented the genius of the Israelitish spirit in its purest and grandest forms, and long even after its political annihilation, Israel stood, and indeed still stands, under their influence.[1]

But the spiritual work of the prophet, so far as teaching is concerned, did not cease when he himself had ceased. It passed over into the synagogue. Jewish tradition speaks of the institution of preaching in terms that may even be described as extravagant. To say that it glorified God and brought men back to Him, or that it quenched the soul's thirst, was as nothing. A city weak and besieged, but delivered by the wise man in it, was a picture from the life of the benefit the preacher brought to his hearers. Upon him rested the Divine Spirit, and his office conferred upon himself as much merit as if he had laid the choicest sacrifices on the altar of burnt-offering. In both the Jerusalem and

[1] Kittel's *History of the Hebrews*, iii. 4, 65.

Babylon Talmud the "Sabbath-observance" and the Sabbath-sermon are identified.[1]

So again when that silence of the prophet, which had lasted for centuries, was broken at length, and John the Baptist appeared, it was not as a priest, but as a preacher of repentance he came. He was a voice crying to men's consciences with direct and solemn power. And when the One greater even than he appeared, our Lord Himself, it was as a prophet and a preacher of righteousness, as well as a redeeming Saviour. The Sermon on the Mount was the manifesto of His kingdom; His parables were revelations, the utterance of things hidden from the foundation of the world; His chosen disciples were charged to go forth and teach all nations; His Church was to be edified by the truth; the earliest converts continued steadfastly in the apostles' teaching. When these apostles went forth on their world-mission they erected no altars, assumed no priestly power, enjoined no elaborate ceremonies—they simply went everywhere preaching the Word. The greatest of them all, the man of Tarsus, deliberately set Christian preaching above Christian baptism. Christ, said he, sent me not to baptize, but to preach the Gospel. By that which some men thought the foolishness of preaching, it was God's good pleasure to save them that believe. As long as he had liberty he preached, and when liberty was denied him he went on teaching men by those Epistles which are a possession for ever to the Church of God.

The weapon thus prized by apostolic men has ever been a weapon of power in the Church's warfare. When preaching gave place to mere ceremonialism,

[1] Edersheim's *Life and Times of Jesus the Messiah*, i. 446.

religion degenerated into mere superstition ; when
teaching went down, the life of the Church went down
with it. On the other hand, when living men proclaimed a living message, an era of revival began to
dawn. This is true all along the line. Even a Roman
Catholic writer has expressed his conviction that "when
the history of preaching in Italy at the time of the
Renaissance is written, it will be seen that the free and
fervent exercise of this office is one of the most cheering
signs in an age clouded with many shadows." In
a time which, he says, was a melancholy period of
almost universal corruption and torpor in the life of
the Church, which from the beginning of the fourteenth
century had been manifesting itself in the worldliness of
the clergy and the debasement of the people, it was the
preaching of the Friars which stirred the stagnant pool
of the nation's life as with the breath of God. Men like
Bernardine of Siena, Alberto da Sarteano, Antonio di
Rimini, Giovanni di Prato, Antonio di Vercelli among
the Franciscans ; and Giovanni di Napoli, Gabriele Bar-
letta, and especially Girolamo Savonarola among the
Dominicans, were to that age what the prophets of
old were to Israel, voices, even when disregarded, still
pleading for God and the right.[1]

With true instinct the Reformers of a later time
also made powerful use of the living voice. By this
Wickliff prepared the way for that Reformation which
changed the face of England. It was complained
against him that his preachers went through the
realm from county to county and from town to town,
preaching from day to day, not only in churches and
churchyards, but also in market-places and public

---

[1] *History of the Popes*, by Dr. Ludwig Pastor, Professor of History, University of Innsbruck, 1885.

thoroughfares. Luther, Calvin, Knox, and the other Reformers again in their time, Wesley and Whitfield in theirs, brought in a new era by giving forth the revealed truth of God with the persuasive power of the living voice. This stirs the world as no mere pageant, no magic, no miracle, ever can.

But special missions and movements, from their nature, can only be limited in their action, and temporary. It is necessary that the revelation of God should be brought to bear upon human life universally and continuously. The Church of God is to be the pillar and ground of the truth, sustaining it as a pillar sustains the roof, or a foundation the building. To this end there must be an abiding ministry of truth, delivering its testimony all the year round to all the continually changing generations of men. Christianity has no priestly caste, but as one of its most distinctive features it has a ministry of reconciliation, whose work shall be continuous till our Lord shall come again. "The idea of a distinct use of human life, devoted, as to its governing and engrossing object, to a perpetual agression against human ignorance and human sin,—of an occupation as definite and as binding as a soldier's, in which teaching, comforting, warning, elevating human souls, should have the place of the ordinary pursuits of life,—of a call and mission which set before a man as his appointed work in the world the communication, to all whom he could reach, of the grace and truth and peace of Christ "[1]—this idea first took abiding shape and form when the functions of the presbyter and of the prophet of the earliest time came together into the hands of one man, that man thus becoming the bishop or pastor of the local, self-governing Church.

[1] R.W. Church, *The Purpose of the Christian Ministry*, p. 127.

LECTURE VII

HIERARCHICAL DEVELOPMENTS IN THE CHURCH

LECTURE VII

HIERARCHICAL DEVELOPMENTS IN THE CHURCH

IN the course of our inquiry as to the form taken by primitive Church organisation we have now reached the end of the second century. We have found the Churches still separate and self-governing, each with its own presiding pastor or bishop, to whom is committed that work of teaching and edifying the Church once discharged by charismatic apostles, prophets, and teachers. It is still true, to use Dr. Hort's words of the earlier time, that "each local Ecclesia has a unity of its own; each is a body of Christ and a sanctuary of God: but there is no grouping of them into partial wholes or into one great whole." The arrangement was simple enough, yet it seems to have been as effective as it was simple. The Churches had no codified laws beyond that summary which runs all law into love of God and man. They had no visible God and no prescribed ritual, for their God was within them, and they were themselves sanctuary, priests, and sacrifice. Yet they went forth to reorganise the world by the principle and example of self-government, based upon self-control within and the extinction of the selfish will. The conditions were so simple as, to some minds, to seem hopeless, yet they were the very pledge of vitality and ultimate success.[1] For to a marvellous extent succeed they did. In that defence of the Christians which Tertullian addressed to the persecuting rulers of the Empire, he urges them to look facts in the face and consider whether they are not vainly striving to drive back the oncoming waves of the sea. "The outcry is," he says, "that the State is filled with Christians—that they are in the fields, in the citadels, in the islands; that both sexes, every age and condition, even high rank, are passing over to the profession of the Christian faith" (*Apol.*, i.). He reminds the magistrates of Carthage that when Arrius Antoninus was driving things hard in the province of Proconsular Asia, the whole body of the Christians in one united band presented themselves before his judgement seat. "If," said he, "we should take it into our heads to do the same thing here in Carthage, what would you make of so many thousands, of such a multitude of men and women, persons of every sex, and every age and every rank? How many fires, how many swords would be required? You would decimate the city and would have to recognise among the confessors and martyrs your own relatives and companions, men of your own order, noble ladies, leading persons, kinsmen or friends of those of your own circle. We are but of yesterday, yet we have filled every place among you—cities, islands, fortresses, towns, market-places, the very camp, tribes, companies, palace, senate, forum—we have left you nothing but the temples of your gods." These are contemporary statements, made by a man who had means of knowing, they were made to public authorities who had means of testing their accuracy, and they lead

[1] Bunsen's *Hippolytus*, i. 151.

to one somewhat obvious reflection. We are sometimes told that nothing but an organised hierarchical system could have preserved Christianity in those dark and stormy times through which it has come to us. But the days when the Church advanced to spiritual victory and spread among the nations in the manner Tertullian here describes were days when the great persecutions of the Roman Empire were running their course; they were also days when the Churches were separate and self-governing and when diocesan bishops had not as yet appeared above the horizon.

What we have now to do is to discover, if we can, how the hierarchical system came to prevail, and how these separate Churches lost their self-government and became the great organisation known as the Catholic Church. We shall find a variety of causes at work producing this result, some of them worthy and honourable, others the reverse. We shall have to consider also whether all the changes that were made carry, of necessity, Divine authority with them, such as that all subsequent generations must needs accept them as part of the will of Heaven. Dr. Hort was of opinion that we find the *jus divinum* of the Church in the lessons of history and experience. But it is possible to read these lessons differently. Even Divinely guided men are not always obedient to guidance, and have sometimes to get wholesome discipline out of their own mistakes. We should have to accept some very wild conclusions did we believe all ecclesiastical developments to be Divine. To be authoritative they must be in accordance with the essential principles of the Church, not a reversal of its essence. It has been well said that there is far clearer evidence that the great Church systems teach what is essentially different from the teaching of Christ, than there is that Christ ever promised to protect any external institution from falling into error. We have better means of access to Christ's own teaching than we have evidence of the Divine character of any organisation that professes to speak in His name.

In further pursuing our inquiry, we shall come upon three important changes in Church life and organisation: *First*, the change of emphasis from spiritual life to orthodox doctrine ; *Secondly*, the consequent development of clerical claims ; and *Thirdly*, the transition from independence in the several Churches to centralised government.

I.

We find first *a gradual change of emphasis from spiritual life to orthodox doctrine as the condition of Church fellowship.* Nothing could be simpler or more spiritual than the bond of union at first. "We are," says Tertullian, "a body knit together as such by a common religious feeling, by the Divine quality of discipline and by a common hope. (*Corpus sumus de conscientia religionis et disciplinæ divinitate et spei foedere.*) We meet together as an assembly and congregation that, offering up prayer to God as with united force, we may wrestle with Him in supplications. This violence God delights in." "How fittingly," says he again, "are they called and counted brothers who have been led to the knowledge of God as their common Father, who have drunk in one spirit of holiness, who from the same abyss of a common ignorance have agonised into the same light of truth" (*Apol.*, 39). The bond of brotherhood, therefore, was not external, mere might of law, but internal—the Holy Spirit, who, dwelling in the heart by faith, placed all in immediate communion with Christ the Head. In process of time this basis of fellowship was changed for another.

Historians are agreed that the first assault upon the early simplicity came from the side of the Gnostics. It is not easy to classify the various thinkers of this school. The best of them, looked at on their best side, may be described as men earnestly in search of a philosophy of religion. Ever since thoughtful men began to face themselves and that system of the universe in the midst of which they found themselves, they have felt "the burthen of the mystery . . . the heavy and the weary weight of all this unintelligible world." Confronting the mystery it was inevitable they should persist in trying to solve it. This is the rationale of the *Gnosis*. The earliest seeds of it are said to have been originally of Indian growth and to have been carried westward by the influence of that vast Buddhist movement which, in the fifth century B.C. had overspread the East from Thibet to Ceylon. The general name, however, is used to designate various sects that sprang up in the eastern parts of the Roman Empire about the time that Christianity set forth on its mission. It is a misleading view of Gnosticism to regard it as a mere offshoot and corruption of Christianity, the mere outcome of disappointed ambition on the part of unworthy apostates from the religion of Christ. According to his contemporary, Clement of Alexandria, Basilides seems never to have been a Christian. Dying in Alexandria (133 A.D.), he was succeeded by Valentinus, a man of Jewish parentage, brought up in that city, and whom Irenæus describes as the chief of the Gnostics. In Syria other sects were

founded about the same time, taking their names from
Marcion and Bardesanes, both Persians by origin, and
therefore Magians in religion. The leading Gnostics
came to Christianity with opinions already formed,
which they sought to graft upon it; they were not
apostates from it. Origen, who was a keen observer,
and had the best opportunities of knowing, tells us that
not only people of the labouring class, but also many
from the cultured classes of Greece, came to see something honourable in Christianity, and sects arose not
from a mere love of controversy, but with a desire to
penetrate deeper into the truth of Christianity, and
these sects took the name of men who admired the
religion of Christ in its essence, but from various
causes had arrived at different conceptions concerning
it (*c. Cels.*, iii. 12). Speaking of these men, Jerome said
that it requires a gifted man, a man of ardent mind, to
construct a heresy, and such, he adds, was Valentinus,
such was Marcion, such was Bardesanes, philosophers to
be admired for their intellectual force. Whatever, therefore, may be said of some of the Gnostics, and however
true it may be that in their writings the most sublimated
spiritualism enters into the strangest union with a crass
superstition based on Oriental cults, it cannot be said that
the foremost of these men were mere ignorant declaimers.
They have been described as the theologians of the first
century, the first to transform Christianity into a system
of doctrine, to work up tradition systematically, and to
present Christianity as an absolute religion in definite
opposition to Judaism and other religions. Yet, with
all their ability and earnestness, they wrought havoc
among the Christian Churches by presenting their
own speculations concerning the universe and man's

life as on the same level of authority with Divine Revelation. Their aim was to found Christianity, not on historical facts, but on ontological ideas. They further claimed to have received special revelations of their own. Hippolytus (*Refut.*, vii. 8) says that Basilides and his disciple Isodorus professed to have received from Matthias secret discourses which he, being specially instructed, had heard from the Saviour—these secret discourses as a matter of fact being nothing more than a mere amalgam of the ethics of Aristotle and the teachings of Christ. Ideas and principles utterly foreign to Christianity were imported into it, so that it required more than common discernment to say what was true Christianity and what was not. It was hard to draw the line between the ordinary Christian and the Gnostic who called himself a Christian. Moreover, the better sort of these men were accompanied by a left wing who crowned the image of Jesus along with the images of Pythagoras, Plato, and Aristotle, and who again shaded off into a motley crowd of magicians, soothsayers, sharpers, and jugglers who, under the honoured name of Christianity, deceived the people with their unintelligible formulæ and scandalous ceremonies. It was an epoch-making crisis in the history of the Christian Church. We cannot read the treatise "Against Heresies" of Irenæus, or the "Refutation of all Heresies" by Hippolytus, without realising how acute was felt to be the danger threatening Christianity, and how important it was to make the line between the Gospel of Christ and the perversions and adulterations of these men sharp and clear. At a time when copies of New Testament books could only have been the possession of the few, ordinary people were anxiously asking how they were to discern between what was really apostolic teaching and what was not. The answer made to this inquiry was simple and direct. The apostolic teaching, they were told, is that which has been handed down in the Churches planted by apostolic men. Irenæus, in the preface to his third book, urges his friend faithfully and strenuously to resist the false teachers " in defence of the only true and life-giving faith which the Church has received from the apostles and imparted to her sons. For the Lord of all gave to his apostles, the power of the Gospel, through whom also we have known the truth, that is, the doctrine of the Son of God." " How stands the case ? " asks he. " Suppose there arise a dispute on some important question among us, should we not have recourse to the most ancient Churches with which the apostles held constant intercourse, and learn from them what is certain and clear?" Among these Churches there is definite consensus of belief. " The Church, though dispersed throughout the whole world, even to the ends of the earth, has from the apostles and their disciples received this faith. . . . Though the languages of the world are different the tradition is one and the same. The Churches which have been planted in Germany do not believe or hand down anything different ; nor do those in Spain, nor those in Gaul, nor those in the East, nor those in Egypt, nor those in Libya, nor those which have been established in the central regions of the world. As the sun, that creature of God, is one and the same throughout the whole world, so also the preaching of the truth shineth everywhere and enlightens all men that are willing to come to a knowledge of the truth " (i. 10, 1, 2). Also about the year 150, or some five-and-thirty years before Irenæus wrote his great work, Hegesippus tells us he himself made a journey of inquiry from the East, by way of Corinth, to Rome, and everywhere he found the same doctrine prevailing among the Churches. This unanimity he regarded as proof that these Churches possessed the apostolic tradition. For, as Tertullian afterwards puts it—" Is it probable that so many Churches, and they so great, would all have gone astray into one and the same faith? Error runs many ways, truth but one. When, therefore, that which is deposited among many is found to be one and the same, this unanimity is not the result of error, but of tradition."

It was inevitable that the Church should contend earnestly for the faith once for all delivered to the saints, should lay great stress upon a correct belief as a condition of Christian fellowship. But it was attended by one serious danger from which the Church did not long escape. For by the end of the second century the early Christian enthusiasm had begun to die down, giving place to a more reflective piety, and too often the centre of gravity in the Church was shifted from holiness of life to correctness of creed. At a time when Christian men had to contend for the apostolic tradition as for dear life, it was perhaps natural that orthodoxy rather than spiritual life should come to be regarded as the determining test of Christian fellowship. If a man assented to the creed the more important matter of a new life was in danger of being taken for granted. And as it is easier to give intellectual assent to a proposition than to enter into living union with Christ, diminished reality naturally brought spiritual decline. As we learn from Tertullian, by the beginning of the third century there were Churches where mutual recognition and brotherly intercourse were made to depend on assent to doctrinal formulæ. The change came about gradually, of course, and varied according to men and place, but it did come about that, without inquiring very closely into the reality of a great spiritual change, if a man gave intellectual assent to the traditional formula, he became entitled to the salutation of peace, the title of brother, and the participation of hospitality. In this way there was reached what has been described as "the most fatal turning-point in the history of Christianity."

II.

Consequent on the change of emphasis from life to doctrine came *the development of clerical claims.*

The apostolic tradition, the orthodox faith, having, as we have seen, come to be looked upon as the breakwater against the on-coming waves of Gnosticism, it was felt important to have it made secure beyond all possibility of doubt or uncertainty. It was thought this could best be done by showing that there was not only a consensus of belief among the Churches referred to, but that these Churches also had had a succession of pastors going back to the beginning and following close upon each other (*ordo episcoporum per successionem ab initio decurrens*). As early as between 181 and 189 A.D. Irenæus speaks of "that tradition which originated from the apostles, which was preserved by means of the succession of the presbyters in the Churches" (iii. 2, 2); and Tertullian maintained that the Christian Churches could do what the Gnostic communities could not—they could produce their original records; they could unfold the roll of their pastors running down in due succession from the beginning, in such manner that the first of these shall be able to show for his predecessor some apostle or some apostolic man who continued steadfast with the apostles (*De Præscr.*, 32). At first sight this might seem as clear a passage as the strongest believer in the modern doctrine of Apostolical Succession could desire. But an examination of the context shows at once that Tertullian's point is not that some supernatural commission of grace or authority has been handed on from man to man, but that the apostolic tradition goes right back to the beginning, and because older is therefore truer than the Gnostic heresy. Immediately before the passage just referred to he says: "Let me discuss the priority of truth and the comparative lateness of falsehood... From the actual order it becomes clear that that which was first delivered is of the Lord, and is true, whilst that is strange and false which was afterwards introduced. This opinion will keep its ground in opposition to all later heresies" (c. 31). If these Gnostics venture to claim that they go back to the apostolic age, let them, he says, prove it—let them produce their original records; let them unfold the roll of their bishops going back to the beginning. Earlier still he had spoken of the actual things accomplished: he points to the Gospel preached, to the sinners who had become saints, to the thousands who were baptized, to the works of faith which had been wrought, to the spiritual gifts in active exercise, to the ministries of mercy instituted, and, to sum up the whole, to the martyrs crowned: and he asks, "Where was Marcion *then*, that shipmaster of Pontus? Where was Valentinus *then*, the disciple of Platonism? These men lived not so long ago, as late indeed as the reign of Antoninus. People are still living who remember them, their own actual disciples and successors, who cannot therefore deny that these men were but of yesterday." Further, in the last of his five books against Marcion, Tertullian mentions that in his " Prescription against all Heresies," that is, in the passage just referred to, he had fixed his criterion of truth in the testimony of time, claiming *priority* as the test of truth, and alleging *lateness* to be the characteristic of heresy (v. 19). His point therefore was that the truth now taught was the truth first taught, and this fact was guaranteed by the succession of pastors from the time of the apostles (*ab initio*).

But while the *priority* of the apostolic truth, and therefore its *genuineness*, was supposed to be established by the succession of pastors, by way of making the rule of faith (*regula fidei*) more absolutely certain a further supposition was introduced. It came to be assumed that the episkopoi or pastors of these Churches had, in succeeding to their office, received some special supernatural endowment guaranteeing the truth. So far as we know the idea first appears in Irenæus's great book against heresies (iv. 26, 2, 5). "Since God," he says, " hath placed in the Church, first apostles, secondly prophets, thirdly teachers, there where the gifts of the Lord have been placed it behoves us to learn the truth, that is, from those who possess that succession of the Church which is from the apostles, men of blameless lives as well as of incorrupt teaching. It is incumbent upon us to obey the presbyters who are in the Church, those who possess the succession from the apostles, those who together with the succession of their office have received the certain gift of truth (*certum veritatis charisma*) according to the good pleasure of the Father."

Probably all that Irenæus meant by this was that the pastors of these Churches had been called to their office as being men endowed by the Spirit with special discernment in spiritual things. But one step prepares the way for another, and some five-and-thirty years later we find Callistus, bishop of Rome in 220 A.D., contending that the bishops had not only come into possession of apostolic truth by virtue of due succession, but also into the place of government and full authority (*potestas*) of the apostles, which they could transmit to their successors. There were, no doubt, contributing influences, but so far as the formulating of the claim to Apostolical Succession can be traced to one man, that one man was Callistus, who was bishop of the Church in Rome from 218 to 222 A.D., in succession to Zephyrinus. The discovery and publication in 1850 of eight out of the ten lost books of the treatise of Hippolytus, entitled "The Refutation of all Heresies," has thrown new light on the generation between 190 and 220 A.D., a period which has been described as that in which the secularising of the Church made the greatest strides. Bunsen goes so far as to say that the ninth book of this treatise has doubled our knowledge of this period. The account which Hippolytus here gives of Callistus, damaging as it is, has been accepted as trustworthy by Bunsen and Bishop Wordsworth, but demurred to as *ex parte* and prejudiced by Dr. Döllinger. What Hippolytus says about Callistus is that he was a man cunning in wickedness, subtle where deceit was concerned, and impelled by a restless ambition. At the end of the

second century, as bank manager for Carpophorus, a
Christian man of influence among the brethren, he was
charged with embezzling the money entrusted to him
by the Christians, and though the charge was not
pressed against him, he was subsequently, under the
prefecture of Fuscianus, scourged and sent as a convict
to the mines of Sardinia. On his release, finding his
way to Antium (Porto d'Anzo) he there made the
acquaintance of Zephyrinus, and, being the stronger
man of the two, acquired complete ascendency over
him. On the death of Victor in 202 A.D. Zephyrinus
succeeded as bishop of the Church in Rome, whither
Callistus went with him, and here for the next sixteen
years the two were in closest relationship, Callistus
acting as coadjutor to Zephyrinus. What may have
been the condition of the Church in Rome at this time
we do not know, but Hippolytus gives us a poor account
of their bishop. He describes Zephyrinus as a stupid
and illiterate person who, being fond of money and
accessible to bribes, was played upon by Callistus, who
did with him what he liked, shaped his policy, and
eventually contrived to succeed him. Having, in 218
A.D., climbed into the place of Zephyrinus, the pretensions of Callistus grew with his position. Among
other things he claimed the right to forgive sins by
virtue of his office. Up to his time the Church upheld her title to be considered a fellowship of saints.
Sinners of the grosser sort came under public discipline. Penitents were restored to fellowship only after
public confession of sin. Tertullian describes these
penitents as casting themselves before the brethren and
beseeching them to pray for them. The darker forms
of sin were severely dealt with. Whoremongers,

adulterers, murderers, idolaters, were refused re-admission to the Church, and by stern judgement upon evil the boundary-line between the Church and the world was faithfully maintained. Callistus, by way of strengthening his own party, set about changing all that. As a right appertaining to the bishops as successors of the apostles, that is, as possessed of the spirit and the power of the keys, he claimed to be able to forgive sins and to re-admit men of gross and evil lives to the fellowship of the Church. Hippolytus says of him (ix. 7) : " He first invented the device of conniving with men in regard to sensual indulgence by saying that all had their sins forgiven by himself." He further daringly declared that "if a bishop were guilty of any sin, even that unto death, he ought not to be deposed." Like some others since his time, Callistus sought to justify lax procedure by perversions of Scripture. Did not the apostle say, "Who art thou that judgest another man's servant?" Did not Christ say, " Let the tares grow along with the wheat," and does not this mean let sinners remain in the Church? Was not Noah's ark a symbol of the Church, and did it not contain dogs and wolves and ravens—all things clean and unclean? In regard to this man Callistus, and his time Harnack says significantly : " The complete adoption of the episcopal constitution coincided with the introduction of the unlimited right to forgive sins." The claim thus made was, however, not permitted to go undisputed. Tertullian maintained that with the Church as a whole, not the bishops, was the power to bind and loose : " For the entire Church is properly and principally the Spirit Himself. He combines that Church which the Lord has made to consist in three. From that time forward every company who have combined together in the faith is accounted a Church from its Author and Consecrator. Thus the Church, it is true, will forgive sins, but it is the Church of the Spirit by means of a spiritual man; not the Church which consists of a number of bishops. For the right and arbitrament is the Lord's not the servant's, God's Himself, not the priest's" (*De pudic.*, xxi). In the same treatise he explains what he understood to be meant by the power of the keys, the power of loosing and binding spoken of by Christ to Peter. He held that what followed showed what was meant. When Peter preached the Gospel on the day of Pentecost he was the first to unbar the entrance to the heavenly kingdom in which was " loosed " those sins which aforetime were " bound " in accordance with true salvation. He " bound " Ananias with the bond of death, and the lame man at the temple gate he " loosed " from the infirmity of a lifetime. So again he " loosed " Gentile believers from the narrowing observances of the Jewish law by protesting against the imposition upon them of a yoke which neither the Jews themselves nor their fathers were able to bear. " This sentence," adds Tertullian, " both ' loosed ' those parts of the law which were abandoned, and ' bound ' those which were reserved. Hence the power of loosing and binding committed to Peter had nothing to do with the serious sins of believers."

Still, in spite of protests from men like Tertullian and the Montanists generally, and in spite of the fact which we infer from the writings of Clement of Alexandria that the novel claim made by Callistus was for long scarcely heard of in some Churches, this claim once made fell in with the growing ecclesiastical temper of the time, and began to be taken up and asserted by others. In a Council of eighty-seven bishops held at Carthage in 256 A.D., to consider the question of the re-baptism of those who came over from heretical communities, we find the claim put forward as a matter of course by Clarus of Mascula, a city of Numidia. "The judgement of our Lord Jesus Christ is sufficiently plain," he said, "when He sent His apostles and accorded to them alone the power given to Him by His Father; and to them we have succeeded, governing the Lord's Church with the same power." These eighty-seven bishops were all unanimous in asserting that baptism administered by bishops in the Church carried with it the effectual remission of sins, but administered by others outside was entirely destitute of any such result. Some of these brethren had a very direct way of coming to the point. Quintus of Aggya said: He can give something who has something, but what can heretics give who it is plain have nothing? Secundinus of Carpi asked: "Are heretics Christians or not? If they are Christians why are they not in the Church? If they are not Christians how come they to make Christians?"[1] Those who thus spoke were African bishops, but these opinions were not confined to them. Far away to the north, at Cæsarea in Cappadocia, was Firmilian, who in his celebrated letter to Cyprian about the action of Stephen of Rome plainly asserts that "the power of remitting sins was given to the apostles and to the Churches which they, sent by Christ, established, and to the bishops who succeeded to them by vicarious ordination" (*ordinatione vicaria*), that is, as

[1] Seventh Council of Carthage, Routh's *Reliquiæ Sacræ*, iii. 130 *sq.*

one person succeeds another in his office (*Epp. Cyp.*, 75).

From this it is clear that not only the power to forgive sins was claimed, but also a much more important power. The idea had now gained a footing in the Church, and was well on its way to universal acceptance, that the bishops had also succeeded to the power of the apostles to confer spiritual gifts, to bestow supernatural grace by ordination or confirmation, so that from them the Holy Spirit entered into the souls of others. This acceptance, however, was only gradually accorded. The power to forgive sins was not formally recognised till about the fifth century, while the completest form of the more advanced claim, to be able to pass on the Holy Spirit and to confer supernatural grace, is not found till we are on the threshold of the Middle Ages: "It was received as a doctrine by the Council of Paris in A.D. 829; it forms the basis of several arguments in the pseudo-Isidorian decretals; it passed at length into the ordinals; and it still survives."[1]

III.

The gradual assent to the supernatural claims of the clergy prepared the way for a *gradual transition from self-government to centralisation in the Churches*.

Milman described the time of the Decian persecution (A.D. 249–251) as the birth epoch of Latin Christianity, and Cyprian as its true parent. Certainly, if the more advanced conception of Apostolical Succession may be traced to Callistus of Rome, the developed idea of the Episcopate as the centre of Unity in the Church may

[1] Dr. Hatch's *Bampton Lecture*, p. 109.

be regarded as mainly the work of Cyprian of Carthage; and though they were widely different men the one prepared the way for the other. Cyprian, perhaps the most influential Church leader of his time, remained a heathen till he had reached the mature age of forty-six; and he had been but a short time a Christian when by the suffrages of the people he was chosen bishop of Carthage. The circumstances attending his election had much to do with making the maintenance of unity an all-important question in Church life. For five of the presbyters of his Church resisted his appointment, were never reconciled to it, and before long set up a rival bishop in the person of Fortunatus, in which act they were joined by several African bishops who were at variance with their colleagues. Desiring to bring over to their side Cornelius, the bishop of the important Church in that city, they sent deputies to Rome bringing certain charges against Cyprian. This called forth a vehement letter from Cyprian to Cornelius (*Ep.* 54) urging him to defend the unity of the Church as founded on the union of the bishops. He reminds him that the origin of heresies and schisms is the spirit of disobedience to God's priest, and that men like these opponents of his do not consider that there is one priest, for the time priest in the Church, and for the time judge in place of Christ (*judex vice Christi*), whom the whole fraternity ought to obey. He writes, he says, as a man provoked, grieved, constrained. For he had been chosen in time of peace by the suffrage of the entire people, had been faithfully linked with his colleagues, approved by his flock during a four years' pastorate, and in time of trouble had been demanded in the circus "for the lions" by the clamours of the heathen. Was it right that he should be superseded by Fortunatus, a mere standard-bearer of sedition, who had been set apart by five bishops brought to Carthage for the purpose, and this through the action of men who had set up for themselves a conventicle outside the Church and opposed to the Church? Were the dignity of the Church, the faithful and uncorrupted majesty of the people within, and the priestly authority and power to be set aside that those without might judge concerning a ruler within—heretics judging a Christian, lapsed men one who is faithful, a criminal his judge, the sacrilegious a priest? We can only infer what the charges were which these men brought against Cyprian from a letter written by him to Pupianus, one of his opponents, who seems to have been a reasonable man, and to have enjoyed high consideration among the Christians as having witnessed a good confession even under torture. It appears Pupianus had told Cyprian that he felt scruples which must be removed before he could hold communion with him as a bishop; he plainly says that the Church had been scattered by his action, and reminds him that the ministers of Christ should be lowly-minded, for both our Lord and His apostles were. Cyprian retorts that as to lowliness of mind Pupianus himself displays considerable arrogance of soul in thus calling rulers and priests to his judgement-seat. As to the Church being scattered by him, *they* are the Church who are a people united to the priest, the flock which adheres to its pastor, and he ought to know that the bishop is in the Church and the Church in the bishop, and that if any one be not with the bishop he is not in the Church. In this autocratic spirit Cyprian met the opposition to himself.

This secession at Carthage was not long after followed by that at Rome which was led by Novatian, and which was intended as a protest against the lax reception again into the Church of those who had fallen back into idolatry during the time of persecution. Novatian may be described as a puritan contending for the purity of the Church against the decay of discipline. Of strong convictions and ardent in their assertion, those who took the same views placed him at their head, and compelled him against his will to assume the position of rival bishop to Cornelius. Both parties naturally sought the countenance and support of the leading Churches of Alexandria, Antioch, and Carthage. So far as Carthage was concerned Cyprian as bishop threw the weight of his influence on the side of Cornelius and denounced Novatian as a disturber of the unity of the Church, as one who set himself against a bishop regularly chosen and appointed by God Himself. On the other hand Novatian maintained, that since purity and holiness are essential marks of a true Church, every community which neglects the right use of discipline and tolerates gross sins in its members, in that very fact ceases to be a true Church, and forfeits its rights and privileges. It is not schism but a simple duty to separate from such a community, for the Church is a holy Church only when the members of the brotherhood are living pure and righteous lives. In reply to this Cyprian and Cornelius maintained that the Church is pure and holy apart from its members, in that it is carried on and sustained by a succession of bishops, deriving its predicates of purity and holiness from that notion.

The Unity of the Church thus became the burning

question of the time, and it was then and under these circumstances that Cyprian wrote his celebrated treatise " De Unitate Ecclesiae." Up to this point all separations had been on the ground of doctrine, this of Novatian was a question of discipline and organisation. Hitherto if a man held the apostolic faith he belonged to the Church, now it was established that a man must not only be a Christian and accept the apostolic tradition, he must first and foremost be obedient to the bishop. Without the latter the former counted for nothing. In the treatise referred to Cyprian places the centre of Unity for the Church, not in the possession of a common life of the Spirit, or in the holding of the apostolic tradition of truth, but in the cohesion of the bishops. He held that what the bishop was in the individual Church of which he was pastor, that the whole body of bishops was to the universal Church. The episcopate, he says, is one, each part of which is held by each one for the whole. The Church also is one which is spread abroad far and wide into a multitude by an increase of fruitfulness. As there are many rays from the sun yet but one light, many branches on a tree yet but one tenacious root, many streams from one spring, yet is unity preserved in the source ; so if you separate a ray from the sun its light is gone, or a branch from the tree its fruit is gone, or a stream from its fountain its waters are dried up. In like manner whoever is separated from the Church is separated from the promises of the Church ; who forsakes the Church of Christ attains not to the rewards of Christ ; he is a stranger, he is profane, he is an enemy. He can no longer have God for his father who has not the Church for his mother. The Lord says, "I and the

Father are one," and it is written of the Father and of the Son and of the Holy Spirit—" And these Three are One." Does any one believe that this unity which thus comes from the Divine strength and coheres in celestial sacraments can be divided in the Church and separated by the parting asunder of opposing wills? He who does not hold this unity does not hold God's law, does not hold the faith of the Father and the Son, does not hold life and salvation.

Nothing, he says, can be a sufficient substitute for a proper obedience to the duly constituted ecclesiastical authority. A man may be of pure life, of sound faith, may even surrender his life rather than his faith, yet it profits him nothing: the stain is not even washed away by blood, the inexpiable and grave fault of discord is not even purged away by suffering. He cannot be a martyr who is not in the Church; he cannot attain to the kingdom who forsakes that which shall reign there. They cannot dwell with God who are not of one mind with God's Church. They may be given to the flames or thrown to the wild beasts, that act of devotion will yet not be the crown of faith, but the punishment of perfidy; not the glorious ending of religious valour, but the destruction of despair. Does he think he has Christ who acts in opposition to Christ's priests, who separates himself from the company of His *clerus* and people? He bears arms against the Church, he fights against the Divine Order; an enemy of the altar, a rebel against Christ's sacrifice, for the faith faithless, for religion profane, a disobedient servant, an impious son, a hostile brother! Despising the bishops and forsaking God's priests, he dares to set up another altar, to make another prayer with unauthorised words, to profane the truth of the Lord's offering by false sacrifices—does he not know that he who strives against God's appointment will be punished for his daring by Divine visitation?

Thus, by the middle of the third century (251 A.D.), Cyprian had advanced the claims of ecclesiastical authority about as far as they can well be carried. As we read all this we feel that we have travelled far from the days of Clement of Rome and the Didachè; far also from the days of Justin Martyr and Irenæus; far, indeed, even from the days of Tertullian, whom yet Cyprian professed to call master. And now the question arises, What precisely did Cyprian mean by making the Unity of the Church consist in the Unity of the Episcopate? It was only five years before that, as a convert to Christianity, he had come over from paganism with all its associations and its organisation of priests. Moreover, he wrote his " De Unitate " in the heat of the Novatian controversy, when personal issues were being keenly contested. Did he mean all that he seems to mean? The late Archbishop Benson, in a Life of Cyprian, on which, as he tells us, he had been engaged, more or less, for thirty years, gives us what he regards as Cyprian's meaning and Cyprian's position on the question before us.[1] Dr. Benson first calls attention to the place the pastor or bishop of each individual Church had come to occupy in Cyprian's time in the view both of his own people and of the outside world. As a congregational pastor he was chief of the Christian society; the confiscation of his property was the first, for a time the only, edict of persecuting magis-

---

[1] *Cyprian: his Life, his Times, and his Work*, by E. W. Benson. Macmillan, 1897.

trates; in the assembly of the elders his presidential chair was already the symbol of his authority; he was specially the preacher in his Church, the chief instructor; he was principal arbitrator in disputes; as to morals and discipline, whether clerical or lay, he was judge in Christ's stead of disqualifications for communion, propriety of restoration, suitableness for office. Having given us this description of what a bishop was in Cyprian's time to his own congregation, which he calls his diocese, Dr. Benson proceeds to ask: " Was there anything which for the whole Church Catholic corresponded to the bishop's position in respect of his own diocese? The Cyprianic answer is absolutely clear: What the bishop was to his own diocese that the whole united body of bishops was to the whole Church." He explains that when our Lord gave His commission to Peter alone, in that fact He indicated the oneness or unity of the commission itself: "So ever since, this tangible bond of the Church's Unity is her one United Episcopate, an apostleship universal, yet only one—the authority of every bishop perfect in itself and independent, yet not forming, with all the others, a mere agglomeration of powers, but being a tenure upon a totality like that of a shareholder in some joint property." Having thus given us what he holds to be Cyprian's meaning, Dr. Benson asks: Was Cyprian an Expounder or an Inventor of the Oneness of the Church? and he describes Cyprian's relation to the evolution of the episcopal idea thus: "Cyprian formulated the 'Theory' as Brahe, Copernicus, or Newton gave the 'Theory' of the Solar System. He 'constructed the Hypothesis,' he 'superinduced the conception upon the facts.' The conception was that the one undivided episcopate constituted not the authority only, but the Unity of the Church. Then that followed which follows always in Science. The conception is a secret which, once uttered, cannot be recalled, even though it be despised by those to whom it is imparted. As soon as the leading term of a new theory has been pronounced and understood, all the phenomena change their aspect. There is a standard to which we cannot help referring them." He further says of this theory of an undivided episcopate: "still *that* is the 'Theory' which underlies Christendom to-day."

According to this hypothesis, just as there were certain ascertained facts in the starry heavens out of which Newton deduced his theory of the Solar System, so there were certain Scriptural revelations from which Cyprian deduced his episcopal theory of Church organisation. The point to be inquired into is, Do Scripture teachings sustain Cyprian's theory as effectually as astronomical facts sustain Newton's? Dr. Benson found in Cyprian's writings from the first the idea of the Church Universal—an Ideal more complex or more abstract than that of parishes or individual congregations. The use of the term "Ecclesia" in the narrower sense of a "congregation" or "diocese" is, he says, not earlier than its broader, aggregate sense as meaning the "Whole Body of the Faithful." To show that this is the case, he gives the following references to Cyprian's works: *Testimonies* i. 19, 20, ii. 19; *De Habitu Virginum* 3, 10; *Epistles*, x. 5, i. 1, 2, iii. 3, ii. 2. When we turn to these we find they speak of the Israel of the Old Testament as the Ecclesia of God; of the Seven Churches of the Apocalypse meaning by seven a perfect whole; and of the comparison of the Church as the

Bride, the Lamb's Wife. This is the conception in all the references given—the Church as one united whole, the one universal Ecclesia of which Paul speaks in the Epistles of the first Roman Captivity. No doubt Cyprian held this view from the time he became a Christian, for the unity of all believers is one of the great regnant thoughts of Scripture; but it is surely a long step to take in advance to suppose that the Unity of the Whole Body of the Faithful consists in the Unity of the Whole Body of Bishops. This is precisely the point to be proved if Cyprian's "Theory" is to be worth anything at all.

Against this theory that the Unity of the Church consists in the unity and authority of the bishops is the simple fact that, even according to Cyprian's own writings, the bishop derives his authority from the people, and is very far from being an absolute autocratic official. Writing to the elders and deacons of his own Church at Carthage while away from them, he says (*Ep.* v.): "I have not been able to reply by myself, since from the outset of my pastorate I made up my mind to do nothing on my own private opinion without your advice and without the consent of the people." Again, he places the ultimate power over the bishop in the hands of the people. He says (*Ep.* lxvii.): "A people obedient to the Lord's precepts and fearing God ought to separate themselves from a sinful prelate (*praepositus*), and not to associate themselves with the offerings of a sacrilegious priest, especially since they themselves have the power of choosing worthy priests (*sacerdotes*), or of rejecting unworthy ones."

Then, again, as to the Unity of the Bishops themselves, we find that no one of them has a right to assume authority over another; every bishop governs his Church in his own way, and there need be nothing like uniformity among them. Cyprian himself presided at the Seventh Council of Carthage held in A.D. 256. In opening that Council he said: "None of us sets himself up to be a bishop of bishops (*episcopus episcoporum*), nor by tyrannical terror does any compel his colleague to the necessity of obedience; since every bishop, according to the allowance of his liberty and power, has his own proper right of judgement, and can no more be judged by another than he himself can judge another." There were therefore to be no archbishops and no Lincoln Judgements as in later days. There was also to be no Act of Uniformity. Speaking in one of his Epistles (*Ep.* 71) of some bishops who still retained certain things in their Churches peculiar to themselves, he says: "In this case we neither do violence to, nor impose a law upon any one, since each ruler has in the administration of the Church the exercise of freedom, as he will give account of his conduct to the Lord."

It is, moreover, to be observed that, so far from the Unity of the Church being dependent on the confederated unity of the Episcopate, there was never a time when all Christian Churches of acknowledged orthodoxy, and even of episcopal organisation, were within that confederation. Cyprian's theory never actually corresponded to the facts. Dionysius, bishop of Alexandria, tells of meeting with whole Churches in Arsinoë (A.D. 260-268) who stood apart from the main body, whose presbyters and teachers of the brethren in the villages he called together, and of whose constancy, sincerity, docility, and intelligence he speaks in the highest terms.¹ We may also recall the case of the Novatians, who had separated from the older Church in Rome on the ground of purity of communion. There is a treatise by Novatian himself on the Trinity, and there are other proofs manifold that they held, even more faithfully than the Church they separated from, to the apostolic faith. Acesius, a Novatian bishop in Constantinople, held in great esteem by the Emperor Constantine, was invited by him to the Nicene Council, and accepted the Nicene Creed unconditionally, saying that it embodied the universal belief since the time of the apostles.² If any of these people returned to the general body of the Church they were received without re-baptism, and the Council of Nicæa directed that if in any city or village there existed only Novatian clergy, they were to retain their offices, so that a Novatian bishop of an entirely Novatian district remained a regular bishop when he re-entered the older Church. As late as A.D. 383 also, the Emperor, while forbidding other sectaries, allowed the Novatians to retain possession of their churches, to hold their services, and to ordain their ministers. They were indeed a great Church confederation, and claimed the title "Ecclesia Catholica." They possessed many churches in Rome itself, which were attended by large congregations. In Constantinople, too, they had numerous following; for under Chrysanthus, their bishop, who had formerly held military appointment at the palace, was subsequently Governor of Italy and Lieutenant-Governor of the British Isles, their Churches were established and greatly augmented. Socrates tells us also of Paul,

---

[1] Euseb., *H. E.*, vii. 24.
[2] Socrates, *H. E.*, i. 10, Sozomen, i. 22.

another of their bishops, who died in 438 A.D., and who was held in such universal esteem that all sections of the Church seemed united at his funeral, attending his body to the tomb chanting psalms together. As a community of Churches they were so numerous and widespread as to form a considerable rival body to those who called themselves the Catholic Church. In the East they had Churches in the principal cities of the Empire, with a regular succession of bishops renowned for their piety. They had Churches even in Scythia; and in Asia Minor they are said to have been as numerous as the community which called itself the Catholic Church. Epiphanius says that in Thyatira for more than a century the Christians in that city were all Novatians. Augustine also is our authority for saying that they were widely spread in Northern Africa, and in the south of Gaul and the north of Italy and Spain they had taken root as firmly as in Phrygia and central Asia Minor. And they were not only widespread, but also long-lived, as is shown by the fact that as late as A.D. 692 they are mentioned in the 95th canon of the Trullan (Quinsext) Council. Neander was of opinion that along the line of Priscillianism, Adoptianism, and Claudius of Turin there may be a point of contact between these Novatians of primitive times and the Waldenses and Albigenses of the Middle Ages.

If we knew all we should probably find many other bishops or pastors besides those of the Novatians, and thousands of sincere Christians who, either from remoteness or other causes, remained aloof from any such confederation as is implied in the Unity of the Episcopate, who yet were quite as Christian and apostolic in their faith as were those who found place within it. And if we come still farther down, the separation between the Church of the East and that of the West, which after centuries of time is as wide as it ever was, shows how little reality of spiritual sort there has ever been in the Unity of Bishops as the basis of the Unity of Christendom. It never has, with anything like sufficiency, represented the greater, Diviner unity of the whole Church of Christ. It is a mere expression the spiritual significance of which evaporates the more closely we look into it.

Thus much may be conceded that towards the close of the third century the bishops of certain Churches came to form themselves into a close ecclesiastical corporation, refusing recognition to all outsiders. Claiming the Church they represented to be the foundation of the Christian religion, they claimed also that all the arrangements made by them from time to time, their functions, institutions and liturgies were, from the source from which they were derived, holy and apostolic. When this confederation, rather than that of the Novatians, was the one chosen by the Emperor Constantine as the Church to be united with and supported by the State, their Councils ceased to be merely deliberative, but became legislative, and were enforced by the authority of the State. In this process the self-governing power of the Churches was lost in the centralised power of those bishops who met in Council and determined under what conditions and with what discipline of penance the people should be governed. The canons of these Councils have been described as the milestones marking the line of advance along the road over which ecclesiastical power increased and the liberties of the people were lost. Formerly, as in the days of Clement of Rome, all communications were between Church and Church; eventually they were between bishop and bishop; and when the bishops met in Council, no longer as mere representatives, but as absolute rulers, and their decisions were registered and enforced by the State, the transition from self-government to centralised power may be said to be complete.

That this change has been for the benefit of spiritual religion may well be doubted. Though some have professed to regard Church Councils as the organs by which the Holy Spirit guided the progressive movement of the Church, their mode of procedure has not always presented the most edifying spectacle. Some of those who have had most experience of them when possessed of legislative power, have had least faith in them. Said Gregory Nazianzen: "I am so constituted that, to speak the truth, I dread every assembly of bishops. I salute them afar off, since I know how troublesome they are. For I have never yet seen a good end of any of them, never been at a synod which did more for the suppression than it did for the increase of evils; for an indescribable thirst for contention and for rule prevails in them."[1] To this it may be sufficient to add the testimony of a prominent churchman of our own time, who was also an eminent ecclesiastical historian: "A General Council," says Dean Milman, "is a field of battle in which a long train of animosities and hostilities is to come to an issue. Men, therefore, meet with all the excitement, the estrangement, the jealousy, the antipathy engendered by a fierce and

[1] *Ep. ad Procop.*, 55.

obstinate controversy. They meet to triumph over their adversaries, rather than dispassionately to investigate truth. Each is committed to his opinions, each exasperated by opposition, each supported by a host of intractable followers, each probably with exaggerated notions of the importance of the question, and that importance seems to increase, since it has demanded the decision of a general assembly of Christendom." [1]

[1] *Latin Christianity*, i. 156.

LECTURE VIII

THE IMPERIAL CHURCH

LECTURE VIII

THE IMPERIAL CHURCH

THE Archbishop of York recently controverted the dogma of the Immaculate Conception of the Virgin Mary on the reasonable ground that it was a human addition to the body of divinely revealed truth. He held that "nothing but a special revelation from God could have made known to mankind a fact which could only be one of the deepest secrets of His Divine operation." This dogma, he declared, "is no part of the truth into which the Holy Spirit was to lead the Church. It is a new gospel, a new order of humanity; it is something added to the words of the Book."[1] May we not say that this vigorous utterance is as true of the episcopal doctrine of Apostolical Succession as of the papal dogma of the Immaculate Conception? For the mysterious transmission of supernatural grace along an official line of priests, if it be a fact, must also be one of the secrets of God which could only be made known by special revelation from God. It is contrary to the analogy of faith; if it be a gospel, "it is a new gospel, a new order of humanity, something added to the words of the Book." While on the one hand this doctrine is pro-

[1] *Sermon in Westminster Abbey*, July 1, 1897. Opening of the fourth Lambeth Conference.

mulgated without special authority from heaven, on
the other we can see how the merest human influences
account for its appearance, how it grew up as other
errors have grown up, one misconception preparing the
way for another, and one departure from the right
bringing others in its train. When acceptance of an
intellectual creed, or a mere Church system, became
a substitute for spiritual life as a qualification for Church
fellowship; when the power of the clergy had steadily
increased at the expense of the loss of self-government
on the part of the laity; and when the Unity of the
Church was made to consist in the Unity of the Episcopate rather than in common participation of a Divine
life, the Church was well on its way towards that
mediæval ecclesiastical system from which the Reformation at length brought deliverance.

When we pass, as we do now, from the third century
to the fourth, we enter upon that important epoch in the
history of the Church when she not only ceased to be
persecuted by the rulers of the Empire, but even entered
into close alliance of friendship with them. Naturally
a change so momentous profoundly affected the fortunes
of the Church. Some will contend that it affected them
for good, bringing Christianity into wider fields of influence. On the other hand it may be clearly shown
that the Church was seriously secularised, and the
priestly spirit greatly intensified by this alliance. In
showing this it is not necessary to maintain that the
resulting changes were altogether the outcome of evil
design and priestly ambition, or their consequences evil
and only evil. Though as time went on the ideals of
the New Testament were left far behind, this should not
prevent us from recognising the good that mingled with

the evil, or from seeing that here, as elsewhere in the great drama of human history, conflicting forces were made to work out certain beneficial results. In spite of its serious corruption and its growing superstition the Imperial Church rendered important services to humanity. What it might have done if it had remained pure and true to its own spiritual principles can only be surmised now, but with all its drawbacks it did much to educate and discipline the wild strength of nations that now sway the destinies of the world, and so laid the foundations of our modern civilisation. It guided the youth of these nations; by canonical law and church regulation it habituated them to legal order and prepared them for settled habits and peaceful industry. In spite of many serious evils also it may be admitted that the Western Church advanced beyond the Eastern in that it did not conceive of Christianity as mere matter of knowledge or of speculation, but as that which concerned the will. It was thus raised above mere theory into a Divine rule of life for all nations, and its ethics received a higher significance. Its mistake consisted in identifying that canon law which was its own creation with the Divine law, and in its confounding the supremacy of the Church and its rulers with the supremacy of God over the hearts and inmost souls of men. It must be an evil thing when the spiritual blessings which the Church has to make known to the people are simply transformed into instruments of ecclesiastical power and hierarchical rule.

The evils of ecclesiasticism, it must be further remembered, were kept in check and to some extent neutralised, by the power of personal Christian life. So Divine a thing is the Church of God that as in the first three centuries despotism could not crush it, so neither in after time could corruption wholly destroy it. The heavenly fire was kept burning on the altar of lowly hearts even when evil and unscrupulous men were working havoc in the high places of the Church. The true victories of the Gospel are not to be sought for in the *haut politique* of worldly and ambitious ecclesiastics. Again and again when the times have been evil that breath of God which blows where it lists has brought freshness to stagnant places and created lives beautiful with the beauty of Christ. The religion of the people has often saved the Church from the irreligion of its rulers. Upon the rock of Christian lives, not upon Church organisation, our Lord has founded that Church of His against which the gates of hell shall not prevail.

We now pass to consider what further influences were at work, from the time of the Imperial Church onwards, strengthening and intensifying the priestly idea of the ministry of the Church.

I.

The first influence of this kind we have to notice is *that which resulted from the Union of the Church with the Empire*. Probably at the time this union seemed both natural and desirable. To men whose lives had been desolated by the awful cruelties of the Diocletian persecution, and who were only too familiar with the sad story of the long list of other persecutions by which that was preceded, it must have seemed too good to be true that the Emperor Constantine had taken the much-suffering Church to his favour and protection. "When the Lord turned again the captivity of Zion, we were like unto them that dream." Even we, who have only read the story which the Churches of Lyons and Vienne sent to their brethren in Asia Minor, of fearful suffering endured with heroic fortitude ; or that other record also preserved by Eusebius of the martyrs of Palestine—even we may realise to some extent the sense of relief and overmastering joy ushered in by the new era of religious freedom. But we must ourselves have lived through those awful days fully to sympathise with Eusebius as he exultingly exclaims : " Now a bright and splendid day, with no overshadowing cloud, irradiated the Churches in the whole world with its celestial light ! "

Then, too, there was nothing specially novel or startling to citizens of the Roman Empire in the thought of ministers of religion being taken into favour and invested with special functions by the State. For in the religious system of Ancient Rome the hierarchy was the State itself in its religious capacity. There was no conflict between an order of priests and the officers of the Republic, for the simple reason that those officers themselves, as they reached certain stages, became ministers of the gods, and were clothed *ex officio* with a certain sacred character. But though the association of religion with State policy was not unfamiliar, it was no less fraught with evil results to the Church of Christ. She was no longer left free to develop herself outwardly from her own inward principle, and she came under the temptation of employing worldly force for the accomplishment of spiritual ends. The worst forms of the evil resulting from the alliance did not show themselves till those later centuries when the princes of the Frankish Empire acquired a dominating influence over the Church. They did so by claiming to nominate the bishops who by that time had, according to the existing polity, the entire governance of the Church in their hands; and thus by the manner in which they obtained their places the bishops became subservient to the princes. Still, even in the earliest days of State connexion, its consequences began to be felt in every part of the Church constitution, and its influence in various ways reached to the whole course and shaping of the Church development. To begin with, the further organisation of the Church was carried out simply on the lines of the Empire—that is to say, it was conformed to the existing secular system. As Gregorovius has described it, the new Church was in her outward form a Latin creation, having the Empire for her type.[1] The second canon of the Council of Constantinople developed the fourth and sixth canons of the Council of Nicæa as to the territorial arrangements of the Christian hierarchy, conforming the ecclesiastical to the civil arrangements. From the time of Constantine onwards the Imperial State was divided into Præfectures and Diœceses, and the Imperial Church into Patriarchates and Diœceses. The Patriarchs of Rome, Alexandria, Antioch, and Constantinople corresponded to the Prætorian Præfects of the East, of Illyricum, of Italy, and of Gaul; while the bishops corresponded to the Vicarii or Vice-Præfects of the Diœceses into which the Præfectures were sub-divided. Thus it came about that "diocese," which was at first a political term, began to have an ecclesiastical signification.

It followed naturally from this that Churches secured

---

[1] *History of the City of Rome in the Middle Ages*, by Ferdinand Gregorovius, vol. i. p. 11.

precedence and importance not from spiritual pre-eminence, but according to their civic greatness. The 28th canon of the Council of Chalcedon recognised the maxim that "the city which was honoured with the sovereignty and the Senate should also be magnified in ecclesiastical matters." When Damasus, as bishop of Rome, in 378 A.D. petitioned the Emperor Gratian to give to him a wider jurisdiction than he had hitherto possessed, Gratian readily consented, on the principle that it was due to him as Emperor that his bishop should hold a higher dignity and position than the rest of bishops, and he enacted that all metropolitans of the Western Empire and all bishops who chose were to be tried before the bishop of the Imperial city; and that all civil officers of the Empire were to bring the metropolitans to Rome by force if they resisted his decree. Constantinople, the rival Imperial city, made similar request. In 445 Leo had obtained from Valentinian a confirmation and enlargement of the right derived from Gratian's law, by which the bishop of Rome further extended his authority over five dioceses not his before; and in 451, or six years later, the Church of Constantinople, by the 28th canon of the Council of Chalcedon, obtained permission to exercise authority over Pontus, Asia, and Thrace. It need scarcely be said that there was nothing specially sacred or authoritatively Divine in all this. It was simply a political arrangement. The Church followed the lines of the Empire in its organisation; of that Church the universal Emperor was the recognised head, and the Œcumenical Councils which gave it unity were summoned under Imperial authority. The clergy acknowledged the Emperor to be their highest judge, and none ventured to call in question his supreme authority. The Imperial laws, even when affecting the interests of the Church, were received by the bishops with implicit obedience, and publicly read by them in the churches. Because they had been anointed, the later Emperors seriously laid claim to priestly dignity. "Both king and priest am I," wrote Leo the Isaurian to Gregory II. Power on the one side too often secured subserviency on the other. The fact that the Emperor exercised great influence in filling up the most important bishoprics, in even deposing and appointing bishops without further ceremony, gave him largely the direction of ecclesiastical affairs and the submission of the clergy.[1]

While these close relations between Church and State acted in several ways to the deterioration of the spiritual idea, what we are specially concerned with now is their influence in fostering the priestly pretensions of the clergy. The tendency already at work to regard the ministers of religion as a separate class and caste became greatly strengthened; for no sooner had the State taken the Church under its protection than it granted to her ministers those important immunities which had been previously enjoyed by the priesthood of the heathen temples. The purpose of this, as stated by Constantine himself to Anulinus, one of his pro-consuls, seemed commendable enough on the surface. "It is my will," he says, "that these men within the province entrusted to thee in the Catholic Church over which Cæcilianus presides, who give their services to this holy religion, and whom they commonly call clergy, shall be held totally free and exempt from all public offices to

[1] Gieseler's *Ecclesiastical History*, i. 422-3.

the end that they may not by any error or sacrilegious deviation be drawn away from the service due to the Divinity, but rather may devote themselves to their proper law without any molestation" (Euseb., *H. E.*, x. 7). Though subsequent edicts did not exempt ecclesiastics from burdens which fell upon them as landowners when they possessed estates, they were freed from some of the public imposts and municipal burdens, besides having granted to them a stated allowance of corn from the public granaries. This had a twofold result—utterly worldly and unspiritual men came into the ranks of the clergy for the most worldly reasons, and the clergy themselves were more and more separated as a class from the rest of the community. Eusebius, who was always ready to eulogise Constantine and his policy, could not help saying that among the grievous evils of the time, of which he himself was eye-witness, was the indescribable hypocrisy of those who gave themselves out as Christians merely to obtain some worldly advantage. For the sake of escaping burdensome offices of State, which often entailed upon their holder ruinous personal expenditure, men utterly unsuitable for the position sought ordination in the Church. The endowments of the State made some of the higher offices of the Church prizes not to be despised. Prætextus, a pagan magistrate, sarcastically told Bishop Damasus that he would turn Christian himself if he might have the bishopric of Rome. This had become a prize so much to be coveted, that men considered respectable put themselves at the head of armed factions to gain and win it at the price of riot, bloodshed, and executions. On the occasion of the bloody contest between Damasus and Ursicinus concerning the episcopal chair in Rome, the historian Ammianus Marcellinus remarked —" When I consider the splendour of civic life, I can understand these men in the desire to attain their object, striving with all the strength of their party; since, could they attain their end, they might be sure of becoming rich through the presents of matrons, of driving in lofty carriages, of dressing in splendid garments, of having such sumptuous meals that their tables surpass those of princes" (xxvii. c. 3). Jerome, too, in a celebrated letter of his (*Ep.* 22), has described the clerical manners of the time with a pen which Juvenal might envy.

The result of all this—the immunities granted to the clergy, freeing them from burdensome and costly service; the increase of their wealth; the placing them under ecclesiastical judges and beyond the jurisdiction of the ordinary courts; and the gradual enforcement of celibacy—made of them a separate caste in the community, and the caste feeling naturally intensified priestly pretension and created a widening gulf between the clergy and the laity. The influence of this could not but be harmful to the spiritual interests of the Church. Guizot has remarked that the separation of the governing and the governed, the non-influence of the governed in their government, is more disastrous in its effect upon the religious than it is upon the political life of a people. For there are greater interests at stake —the reason, the conscience, future destiny—all that is most near, most individual, and most free. Evils great enough may result when a man abandons to an external authority the direction of his material interests and his temporal destiny; but when it extends to the conscience, the thought, the internal existence, to the abdication of self-government, the delivering oneself to a foreign power, this amounts to moral suicide, a servitude a hundred times worse than that of the body or the soul.[1] Strangely enough, Harnack contends[2] that when the rights of the people had been usurped by the clergy a Church had been created within which the pious layman could find a holy place of peace and edification. With priestly strife he had then nothing to do, and the religion of the laity attained freedom in proportion as it became impossible for them to take part in the establishment and guardianship of the official Church system. It is only necessary to apply this principle to political life to see how fallacious it is. It would then follow that when a people are deprived of all political rights and are handed over to despotism, benevolent or otherwise, they are under more healthful civil conditions than when enjoying the educating and elevating influences of self-government. "From the root of a protectorship upsprings a tyrant," was a discovery made by the political experience of Ancient Greece, and is a discovery often re-discovered in later times. It is a serious evil to a nation when political questions vitally affecting the nation's life are denied free discussion, and are withdrawn from the action of public opinion. It is an evil more serious still when Christian men take part in Church life merely as spectators; when the idea practically prevails that the great questions of theology and the spiritual life are the privileged domain of the clergy, and that the function of the laity is simply to hear and to obey. This feeling, the result of priestcraft on the one hand and of idle indifference on the other,

---

[1] *Hist. of Civilisation in Europe*, Lect. vi.
[2] *Hist. of Dogma*, ii. 127.

has worked irreparable mischief in the Church of God, and has created a debased spiritual condition from which there is only slow and painful recovery.

Further, the State did much to strengthen the priestly pretensions of the clergy by *forcibly repressing all opinions and teachings contrary to those of the prevailing Church*. Of course the Church, of itself, as it became more centralised, brought pressure to bear upon all dissentients from its doctrine and discipline, but that pressure naturally became more urgent and intense when the State proceeded to enforce the decisions of synods and councils by means of the civil power. This enforcement was not much felt during the reign of Constantine and his sons; for Constantine, after his victory over Licinius, proclaimed full toleration for all religions, protected even heathen priests in their prerogatives, and still retained for himself, as Emperor, the heathen dignity of Pontifex Maximus. In this policy he was followed by Jovian, by Valentine I. in the West, and Valens in the East. Gratian was the first to decline the Pontificial title; he also, to the great grief of the Senate, removed the altar of Victory from the Senate House and all privileges from pagan worship; it was Theodosius I., however, who brought firm even pressure to bear both against heresy and heathenism, and by fifteen repressive edicts in the fifteen years of his reign determined to secure absolute uniformity of religious life and worship. In 392 A.D. he set about the extermination of the ancient religion of the Empire by force. He enacted that any one daring to kill or sacrifice a victim, or derive auguries by the accustomed rites, should be held to be guilty of treason.[1] His

[1] *Cod. Theod.*, xvi. 10, 12.

son Honorius went still further. In 408, addressing Olympius, Master of the Offices, he said : [1] "We forbid those who are enemies of the Catholic sect to serve as soldiers in our palace. We will have no connexion of any kind with any man who differs from us in faith."

One does not need to sympathise with heathenism in order to sympathise with heathen men who, trained from childhood in the ancient religion of Rome, refused to be made Christians by coercion instead of conviction. Cases like that of Generidus present the persecuted heathen in a more dignified attitude than the persecuting Christian. A brave and honest soldier who still adhered to the religion of his forefathers, when the law was passed forbidding one not a Christian to remain in the service of the Emperor, Generidus handed back his belt, the emblem of military office, and retired into private life. But a desperate crisis came in the fortunes of the Emperor, under pressure of which he entreated Generidus to return and take the command of troops in Pannonia and Dalmatia. This officer replied by reminding Honorius of the law which forbade a heathen like himself to serve the State. Honorius said at once that while the law must remain in force special exemption should be made in his favour. "Not so," rejoined the soldier; "I will not be a party to the insult thus put upon my brave heathen comrades. Restore them to the rank which they have forfeited because they adhere to the religion of their forefathers, or else lay no commands on me." [2]

But it was not merely in the case of heathen men and heretics who denied the faith of Christ that the power of

---

[1] *Cod. Theod.*, xvi. 54, 5.
[2] Zosimus, *Hist. Roman Emperors*, v. 46.

the State gave support to the dominant Church. There is a case on record where a number of Christian Churches in Africa held that the rest of the Churches with which they had been in association were too lax in their terms of communion. Their contention was simply for greater purity in Church fellowship, and their soundness in the faith was beyond question. They tried first to convince their brethren in the associated Churches, but failing in this they finally resolved to secede and meet together as a separate confederation, the basis of which should be greater purity of life ; and, as Dr. Hatch has said, but for the interference of the State they might have lasted as a separate confederation to the present day (*B. L.*, 179). All similar divergences were dealt with in the same way. In 408 A.D. an edict went forth that no one who dissents from the priest of the Catholic Church shall have leave to hold his meetings within any city, or in any secret place in our dominions. If he attempts it, the place of meeting shall be confiscated and he himself driven into exile.[1] In 410 the order was given, " Let the houses of prayer be utterly removed within which the superstitious heretics have furtively crept to celebrate their rites, and let all enemies of the holy law know that they will be punished with proscription and death if they shall any longer attempt in the abominable rashness of their guilt to meet together in public."[2] Nor were these mere idle words. Under the name of heresy was included the least deviation from the doctrine or discipline of the larger confederation which the State had chosen to uphold. The churches of such persons were confiscated and often their private property also ; they were made in-

---

[1] *Cod. Theod.*, xvi. 5, 45.
[2] *Ibid.*, xvi. 5, 51.

capable of bequeathing or receiving money by will; they or their teachers were banished from cities by law, and even those who availed themselves of the permission which Jovian had given them to hold assemblies outside the walls of the city were punished by deportation; they were sometimes branded as "infames," were fined and excluded from the service of the State; their books were sought and burnt, one edict making concealment of these a capital offence; while provincial judges and governors were fined if they showed favour or lenity to the accused. As late as 729 A.D. the Emperor Leo I. endeavoured to force the Montanists to embrace the creed of the dominant Church, but so devoted were they to their faith that, rather than yield, they assembled in a building, and having set it on fire, perished in the flames.[1] Yet the Montanists, notwithstanding some enthusiastic opinions held by them, were much better Christians than many of their persecutors, and much nearer in their faith and practice to apostolic times. Even the bishop of Rome had once acknowledged the prophetic gifts of their leaders and had bestowed his peace on their Churches in Asia and Phrygia; and the saintly confessors of Lyons and Vienne openly advocated their cause and published the letters of their martyrs. Much has been made of the enthusiastic opinions of the Montanists, but it is not difficult to see that the real reason for seeking to stamp them out was their maintaining that the dominant Church was far from being composed of Christian men and that the true hierarchy of the Church was a hierarchy of the saved and spiritually

[1] *History of the Later Roman Empire*, by J. B. Bury, M.A., 1889, ii. 423.

enlightened. Men with such opinions naturally came into conflict with ecclesiastics who principally aimed at securing a firm footing in the world, and regarded the possession of the Divine force of Christianity as guaranteed by the transmission and succession of bishops. The Montanists taught that it is not the grace that is communicated by office that is the *essentia* of the Church, but the piety of the individual members who receive spiritual guidance. A man, they said, might be in office and yet be a merely psychical person, or only spiritual in the narrowest sense, whereas it is the spiritual man who is the only rightful possessor of the power of the keys.[1] Other reasons have been industriously given for the treatment they received, but these anti-hierarchical opinions of theirs really constituted the head and front of their offending. As Dr. Hatch has said, in the last stages of the struggles for purity of life the party which endeavoured to preserve the ancient ideal was treated as schismatical.[2]

As much has been made of the continuity and solidarity of that which calls itself the Catholic Church, it may be well to show somewhat further that long before the days of Arnold of Brescia, or of the Waldenses and Albigenses, and long before the establishment of the Inquisition, the Unity of the Church was sought to be maintained by ruthless repression of all attempts at Church reform and all endeavours after greater simplicity and purity in Church life. By way of illustration let us take the case of Priscillian, bishop of Avila, whom Gibbon des-

[1] *Die Geschichte des Montanismus*, von G. Nathanael Bonwetsch, Erlangen, 1887, pp. 13, 116.
[2] *Hibbert Lecture*, p. 164.

cribed as a man who adorned the advantages of birth and fortune by the accomplishments of eloquence and learning. Not finding the Church of his own day sufficiently pure from the world, he established meetings among his followers, not with the view, as it would appear, of separating them from the Catholic Church, but of raising them to a higher level of Christian life. As these conventicles drew some away from services elsewhere they gave great offence to those in authority, and Hyginus, bishop of Cordova, laid an information before the metropolitan, Idacius of Merida. Thereupon a Council, at which twelve bishops attended, was held at Saragossa (380 A.D.) to consider the matter of these irregular proceedings. At this Council eight canons were passed, not imputing false doctrine on the part of the Priscillianists, but censuring the meetings, and eventually a rescript was obtained from the Emperor Gratian banishing the offenders from the Empire. Under the succeeding Emperor, Priscillian and two of his followers were put to death by the sword. These three martyrs of 385 A.D. stand out in history as the first Christians who suffered death for their opinions at the hands of their fellow-Christians. But neither the canons of the Church, nor the rescript of the Emperor, nor the sword of the executioner succeeded in immediately crushing out these opinions. Priscillianism ramified into Aquitaine, and though it never took deep root north of the Pyrenees, it spread through most of the provinces of Spain, especially in the cities, and in spite of persecution lingered on till the middle of the fifth century.

Besides Montanists and Priscillianists, those early times saw another body of men, the Paulicians, who also were charged with erroneous opinions, but whose real offence seems to have been their opposition to the priestly claims and the hierarchical organisation of the dominant Church. They also held their ground, with more or less of success, for three centuries at least (668–976 A.D.). They took their rise somewhat as follows. A teacher of the name of Constantine, belonging to some Gnostic sect, happened for the first time in his life to come into possession of a complete copy of the New Testament. The reading of this, especially of the Pauline Epistles, made a deep impression upon his mind and led him to stand forth as a reformer both of his own sect and of the larger Church. It was the special devotion of this man and his followers to the teachings of the apostle which led to their being called Paulicians; and it was by the Christianity drawn from these writings mainly, but apprehended under the form of Gnostic dualism, that they from that time onward were led to aim at the reformation of the Church and the restoration of apostolic doctrine. Constantine's successor was Sergius, a young villager of Galatia, who meeting with a woman who belonged to the Paulicians, was asked by her if he had ever read the Gospels. He replied he had not, for that the mysteries of the Holy Scriptures were too exalted for laymen, and belonged exclusively to the clergy. She on the contrary maintained that the Scriptures were intended for all men, and were open to all, for God wills that all should come to the knowledge of the truth, and that the clergy kept back the mysteries of the Divine Word from the laity lest they should find out how many corruptions had been introduced into the Church. This conversation led Sergius, as Constantine had been led before him, to a diligent study of the writings of the Apostle Paul, and to a consecration of the remaining years of his life to the mission of restoring the life and manner of the Church to apostolic simplicity. He and his followers contended that multiplied rites and ceremonies had stifled the true life of religion, and they protested against the superstition of relying on the magical effect of external forms and sacraments. Indeed, like George Fox and his followers in much later days, they rejected the outward celebration of the sacraments altogether, holding that the true baptism was that of the Spirit, and that the true eating of the flesh and the drinking of the blood of Christ consisted in coming into vital union with Him through His teachings and His Word, which were His true flesh and blood. They eschewed the name of temples for their places of assembly, simply calling them places of prayer. They especially regarded the Christian priesthood as they saw it in the Church, founded upon the pattern of the Old Testament, as one of the foremost corruptions of the Christian element; and they held that it was of the very essence of Christianity that it made no distinctions between clergy and laity, but sought to establish a higher fellowship of life among all men.

The numbers of these men eventually became formidable. With varying fortunes they spread through all the provinces of Asia Minor; by way of Thrace, Macedonia, and Epirus they passed into Europe; they crossed the Balkans into Bulgaria, and along the Danube through Hungary and Bavaria into Germany; by Lombardy into Switzerland and France; and by the Mediterranean to Venice, Italy, and Sicily. The ecclesiastical authorities took alarm and resolved that no quarter should be given to such men or to such obnoxious opinions. Royal commissioners were sent against them whose measures of severity have been described by the Byzantine chroniclers as memorable triumphs. They made converts to Catholicism after the manner in which the Turkish Sultan has made converts to Islam in these later days. Those who resisted the Imperial invitation to ecclesiastical union were plied with the usual arguments. We read of hanging, crucifying, beheading, drowning. It is calculated that more than one hundred thousand of these people perished at the hand of their persecutors. When we are told of the solid unity of the hierarchical Church, and of its continuity through centuries, we recall the methods by which that unity was forced upon the nations, and that continuity maintained. Recalling these methods, we can see nothing in them of the Spirit of Christ; nothing that gives the priest a moral and spiritual right to demand that all men shall acknowledge his authority and recognise the divinity of his claim.

II.

We now come to notice the stimulating effect on *the growth of priestly ideas in the Church through the contact of the Church with Paganism on the one side, and Gnosticism on the other.* As in the construction of the great Church of St. Sophia in Constantinople there were introduced marble columns from the heathen temple of Diana at Ephesus; as in the basement of the church of San Clemente in Rome there is still to be seen an altar to Mithras; and as on the chair claimed to be that of St. Peter there were found, when it was uncovered some thirty years ago, diminutive arabesques descriptive of centaurs, and ivory panels on which were engraved the labours of Hercules, so in the Church itself after its alliance with the Empire, along with the substance of the Christian faith there came to be large admixtures of pagan superstition. For, though the Empire nominally became Christian under Constantine, paganism lingered on for generations, and while transformed it never altogether died out. Even the emperors of the family of Constantine, though presiding over the Councils of the Church and settling disputed points of Christian doctrine, did not refuse to bow themselves in the House of Rimmon, and they so far honoured the fanatical heathenism of Old Rome as to accept some of the titles and even perform some of the sacrificial rites which had marked the semi-religious character of the heathen emperors who had preceded them. Around the person of the Emperor, among the highest officials of the Court, believers in the old religion as well as the new, pagans as well as Christians were to be found together. As we gather from the memorable treatise of Pope Gelasius, addressed to Andromachus, head of the Senate and defender of the heathen festival of the Lupercalia, so obstinately did the traditions of the ancient religion still linger among the aristocracy, and so deeply rooted was paganism among the members of the Senate, that a hundred and eighty years after the supposed conversion of the Empire consuls could still be found who observed the omens of the sacred hens, the auguries and other ancient ceremonies which the religion of their forefathers had associated with their office. A strong minority of the Roman aristocracy took no more kindly to the religion of Christ than did the Pharisees of Jerusalem. A God whom they would have to worship in common with the plebs was an offence to their pride ; and the democratic principles of Christianity, the ideas of equality, freedom and brotherhood which threw down the barriers between master and slaves at the table of the Lord, were at variance with their life-long prepossessions and prejudices. The intellectual circles of Rome, the authors and rhetoricians clung to their old associations with the ancient literature and philosophy in which they had been educated, and still adhered to the pagan faith. Even as late as the reign of Theodosius (379–395 A.D.), many of the small band of literary men who flourished in the latter days of the Empire remained faithful to the old superstitions. Ammianus Marcellinus, Zosimus, Priscus, and possibly also Procopius, the chief historians of the period, were all pagans.[1] Even when convinced of the truth of Christianity men of this class were either half ashamed or half afraid to avow their change of faith. Augustine in his " Confessions " (viii. 3, 4) describes the attitude of Victorinus, a man skilled in the liberal sciences, the instructor of many noble senators, and of so much reputation that his statue was erected in the forum of Trajan. Having searched into the Christian writings he "said to Simplicianus (not openly but privately as a friend), ' Understand I am a Christian.' Whereto he answered, ' I will not believe it, nor will I rank you among Christians unless I see you in the Church of Christ.' The other in banter replied, ' Do walls then make Christians ? ' " He often said he was already a Christian yet as often declined to avow himself; "for," says Augustine, "he feared to offend his friends, proud dæmon-worshippers, from the

---

[1] Hodgkin's *Italy and her Invaders*, ii. 568.

height of whose Babylonian dignity he supposed the weight of enmity would fall upon him."

Even Christian men could not altogether shake off the glamour of the old system, its culture, its charm, and its early associations; they were still conscious of a certain hankering after the classical art whose subject-matter was pagan myth and pagan history. Augustine felt the thrill, but felt also a secret misgiving that the thrill was sinful. Jerome could not resist the fascination of the old writers even when he felt that they might be harmful to his Christian faith; and one Germanus had to confess with many tears that often while he was engaged in prayer the old heroes and heroines would pass into his soul, and the remembrance of the ancient gods disarranged his thoughts of the God in whom he had come to believe.[1] As late as 467 A.D., amidst the festivities on the accession of the Emperor Anthemius, historians have told us how the pagan festival of the Lupercalia with all its indecencies was actually celebrated under the eyes of Emperor and Pope, and before the Christians of Rome, according to the ancient custom. Down to the days of Chrysostom (390 A.D.), Antioch, where the disciples were first called Christians, contained as many believers in Jupiter as in Christ. At Rome even the drastic laws of Theodosius had failed to suppress either the pagan cult or the pagan party in the city. The frequent edicts commanding the temples to be closed and the altars and images to be removed clearly show that throughout the provinces, pagan shrines and pagan observances still lived on. In contradiction to the Imperial edict which prohibited heathen sacrifices, sacrificial priests (*sacerdotes*) were appointed

[1] Bury's *History of the Later Roman Empire*, vol. i.

in the fifth century; the chapels of the compitalian Lares still stood at the corners of the streets; and the Christian poet Prudentius complained that Rome had not one but several thousand genii whose portraits and symbols were to be found over doors of houses and baths, and in every corner of the city. In 392 A.D. the Senate, taking advantage of the murder of Valentinian, temporarily restored the ancient religion. The statue of Jupiter, which had been thrown down, once more stood erect, the altar of Victory was once more placed in the Curia, the ancient ceremonies were again celebrated in Rome, and in 394 the Consul Flaminius publicly attended the festivals of Isis, the Magna Mater, and the Lustration of the city. The term pagan ("paganus," villager) indicates, of course, that the ancient cult lingered longest in rural places, in lonely glens and unfrequented pasture lands. But there does not seem to have been much to choose between rustic and citizen in the matter. The life of St. Barbatus describes the people of Benevento, the capital of the duchy of that name, though calling themselves baptized Christians, yet as given over to the most absurd superstitions, worshipping the image of the viper and devoutly paying homage to a "sacrilegious" tree not far from the walls of their city. The childish credulity of idle Naples (*otiosa credidit Neapolis*) of which Horace spoke centuries ago remains indeed unaltered to the present time. Down to the end of the sixth century and the beginning of the seventh, Gregory the Great, as we learn from his Epistles, was still engaged in rooting out paganism from parts of Italy and the islands of Corsica and Sardinia. He finds it necessary to rebuke landowners, some of them even bishops, who allowed their peasants to continue in heathenism, and official persons who were bribed into conniving at it. The feast of Bota in honour of Pan and of Brumalia in honour of Bacchus were still observed, and at the gathering in of the vintage the god Dionysius was still invoked. As late as the Council of 692 A.D. it was still necessary strictly to prohibit the heathen custom of kindling illuminating fires in front of houses and shops and leaping over the flames. Thus for nearly three hundred years after the Empire was supposed to be converted to Christianity the old religion still lived on, with its tenacious belief in priests and sacrifices, omens and auguries. It not only lived on among its own votaries, but it profoundly affected the life of the Church. The persecuting edicts of Theodosius and Honorius forced crowds of heathen men and women into the Church who brought their superstitions with them, and the population of the Roman Empire was then superstitious indeed. Ghosts and genii peopled their imagination ; tales of witchcraft and magic, marvellous transformations, prodigies and apparitions fill the literature of the period. It is in such soil that priestcraft attains its rankest growth. These believers in priests and sacrifices, flamens and augurs, forced into Christianity while still clinging to all their heathen associations, had much to do with the turning of Christian presbyters into something not very unlike to pagan priests.

Then, too, by way of conciliating the heathen, large concessions, well meant but disastrous in their result, were made by the Church itself. Every concession thus made to superstition was so much ground permanently lost, while the feeble protests and cautions by which these concessions were accompanied were soon forgotten ; if indeed they were always thus accompanied, which is doubtful. For the official guardians of the truth were themselves in sore need of guardianship. The ministry of the Church had undergone a process of deterioration. Professor Ramsay has reminded us of the great contrast between the Church of the fourth century and that of the earlier period. From being the champion of education it became more and more its opponent, looking on culture, literature, and art with growing disfavour. Its bishops were worse educated, or scarcely educated at all. At the Synod of Constantinople, held in 448 A.D., a Phrygian bishop, Elias of Hadrianopolis, was unable to sign his own name (*eo quod nesciam literas*).[1] Others, not quite so bad as this, betrayed their credulity by their proneness to rely on spurious authorities like the Sibylline books, and to believe any strange story that seemed to favour religion or make for the power of the Church. The majority lived in an atmosphere of prodigies, and even men of master minds, like Gregory the Great, as we gather from the four volumes of his dialogues, showed a credulity which to us in these days is simply astounding.

The worship of relics was fully developed already in Gregory's time, attracting pilgrims from far and near. Filings from the chains of St. Peter, or shavings of iron from the fabulous gridiron of St. Lawrence, were worn round the neck as amulets; the dogma of purgatory dates from the days of Gregory, and it was he who gave to the service of the Mass nearly the same form it still bears in the Roman ritual. In the next century after his a pope and a patriarch believed in the power

[1] *Cities and Bishoprics of Phrygia*, p. 509.

of painted Virgins to heal the sick and the maimed, and
to exude unearthly balsams, and men did not hesitate
to believe the legends that certain pictures, regarded
with peculiar veneration, had been manufactured in the
workshops of heaven.[1]

As captured Greece enslaved her conqueror, so did
heathenism the Church. In pagan temples the altars
were illuminated with candles; the more honoured
the shrine, the greater the multitude of tapers. The
Christians of the earlier time laughed at this folly.
"Their gods," said Lactantius (vi. 2), "stand in need
of lights that they may not be in darkness. If they
would contemplate that heavenly light which we call
the sun, they would see at once that God has no need
of their candles, who has Himself given so clear and
bright a light for the use of man. The light He requires
of us is of another kind—the light of the mind." Two
centuries after Lactantius wrote thus, Christians had
begun to copy pagans, and were burning candles on
their own altars in the daylight. In the Early Church
there was no Host, that is, no sacrificial victim, uplifted
for adoration. "Shall I offer victims and sacrifices to
the Lord," asks the Roman Christian in Minucius Felix,
"when the victim fit for sacrifice is a good disposition
and a pure mind and a sincere conscience? He who
cultivates justice makes offerings to God; he who
abstains from fraudulent dealing propitiates God; he
who saves his brother from danger slaughters the most
acceptable victim. These are our sacrifices, these our
rites in the worship of God." The uplifting and adoration of the *hostia*—the sacrificial victim—comes not
from Christian, but from pagan thought. One has only

[1] Bury's *Hist. of the Later Roman Empire*, ii. 387.

to read the account by Apuleius (*Metam.*, xi.) of priests and processions, and of the mysteries of Isis in the last age of paganism, to understand how the Host came to be lifted up in church, or carried in procession in golden pyx or monstrance, on Corpus Christi Day.

There is yet another aspect of the influence of non-Christian faiths upon the Christian Church which requires consideration—that, namely, *arising from the Greek Mysteries, and coming into the Church from the side of Gnosticism.*[1] In entering upon this it is necessary to realise, as far as we can, the spirit of the age when ceremonies began more and more to dominate the worship of the Church. It was the age of mysteries and mystic tendencies. While superstition of the grosser kind already alluded to prevailed mainly in the West, these subtler tendencies prevailed chiefly in the East, and were one side of that Hellenising process by which the Church was so profoundly affected. From a time prior to that of Herodotus down to the year 396 of the Christian era, when the temple at Eleusis was destroyed by Alaric and his Goths, the Greek Mysteries were celebrated with much solemnity and great splendour. One cannot even now stand on the plateau of Eleusis in the midst of those magnificent ruins of its great temple, which have been excavated since 1882, or look out from its noble portico of Doric columns across the waters of the bay of Salamis without feeling how much there was in the surroundings to lend impressive-

---

[1] *Das antike Mysterienwesen in seinem Einfluss auf das Christentum*, von Gustav Anrich. Göttingen, 1894. *The Eleusinian Mysteries*, a Study of Religious History, by François Lenormant, *Cont. Rev.*, vols. xxxvii. and xxxviii., 1880. *The Influence of the Mysteries upon Christian Usages*, by Dr. Hatch (Hibbert Lecture, 1888), pp. 283-309. *Mysteries*, by Prof. Ramsay, *Encycl. Brit.*

ness to a celebration which continued through so many centuries. Serious authorities speak respectfully of these mysteries. Cicero, who in his time was one of the initiated, held that they taught their votaries to live happily and to die with a fairer hope. They were believed in not only by the mass of the people, but by many of the most thoughtful and educated intellects in successive generations, and have been described as one great attempt made by the Hellenic genius to construct for itself a religion that should keep pace with the growth of thought and civilisation in Greece. Unlike the common religion of the people, they attempted to deal with the deeper questions which troubled the minds of more thoughtful men—the questions of sin, of a future life, and of the punishment of guilt. There were the greater and the lesser mysteries. At the greater mysteries there were purifications in the waters from which those who had been initiated into the lesser mysteries were supposed to come up new men as from a laver of regeneration, the purification being followed by a sacrifice called the "sacrifice of salvation." In the last stage of the mysteries the initiated were led in the darkness of night into the lighted interior of the sanctuary, where with great splendour was enacted the drama of Demeter and Korê, meant to signify the passing of the Earth through its yearly periods. It was the drama of Nature enacted year by year as every winter turns to spring, the drama of human life in its course, the soul rising from a lower self to a higher, death giving place to life. The significance of these ceremonies (never seen but by the initiated), the point they had in common both with the ceremonies of Gnosticism and those of the Catholic Church, was that they were supposed to confer purity of soul and secure salvation. Sopater taught that this initiation established kinship with the Divine nature, secured immortality and a joyful resurrection. The author of the Homeric Hymn (*In Cer.*, 480-2) exclaims at its close : " Happy is he among men who has seen the mysteries ; but he who is not initiated, who does not participate in the sacred rites, will not enjoy the same destiny after his death in the abodes of darkness." It is not to be supposed that these ancient mysteries were consciously and directly imitated by the Church ; at the same time their influence upon it was very real, though it only came through the medium of Gnosticism, which formed a sort of half-way house between the pagan temple and the Christian Church. In common with the Greek Mysteries, Gnosticism had its ceremonies, by means of which it promised to give to the initiated that purification which was deemed essential to immortality, and to secure to them a joyful resurrection in the after-life. We are at a disadvantage in trying to gain an accurate knowledge of the various systems classed together under the term Gnosticism, from the fact that our information comes mainly from the writings of opponents who undertook to refute its heresies. One original treatise—the " Pistis Sophia "—has, however, come down to us, and perhaps it will be best to derive our evidence mainly from that.[1]

[1] The only MS. of the " Pistis Sophia " known to exist was bought by the trustees of the British Museum from the heirs of Dr. Askew some time last century [*Add. MSS.*, 5114]. Where he found it or bought it, or when the Museum authorities acquired it, is not known. It is a Coptic MS. in the Thebaic dialect, written in double columns on vellum, and is in good preservation. Woide, whose knowledge on such matters was considerable, was the first to call attention to it, which he did in 1778 in Cramer's *Beiträge zur Beförderung theologischer Kenntnisse* (iii. 82 *sq.*).

From this document we find how much stress was laid upon ceremonies and mysteries by the Gnostics. The author asserts the necessity of the mysteries to salvation, and that the work of Christ consists solely in having brought these mysteries into the world. As with the Greek Mysteries, their general aim was to procure eternal life and blessedness for man, and the degree of blessedness in a future life was made to depend on the degree of the knowledge of the mysteries attained in this. Jesus is made to say to His disciples: "Cease not day and night to seek until ye have found the mysteries of the kingdom of light, which will purify you and transform you into pure light, that ye may be brought to the kingdom of light." "It is because of sin that I have brought these mysteries into the world, for the remission of all sins which have been committed from the beginning." No matter what a man may be, if he has not gone through the ceremonies there is no hope for him: "I say unto you, even though a righteous man have not committed any sin at all, it is impossible to take him into the kingdom of light, because the sign of the kingdom of the mysteries

No one seems to have noticed it again till 1847, when Ed. Dulaurier gave a detailed account of it, with two specimens of the text in a French translation, in the *Journal Asiatique* of that year (pp. 534-548). The first thorough investigation of the work was made by K. R. Köstlin in Baur and Zeller's *Theologische Jahrbücher* for 1854 (pp. 1-104; 137-196).

In 1851 a complete edition of the Coptic text, with a Latin translation, was prepared by M. G. Schwartze, and edited by Petermann (Berlin), the Latin translation being again issued separately in 1853. The Coptic is held to be a translation from a Greek original, many of the Greek terms being retained in it. Mr. G. R. S. Mead, B.A., M.R.A.S., who has recently published an English translation of Schwartze's Latin version, with an Introduction, for the Theosophical Society (Lond., 1896), is of opinion that the original was no other than the famous Apocalypse of Sophia, composed by Valentinus, and that the "Pistis Sophia" was compiled in the latter half of the second century, perhaps in Alexandria.

is not with him. In a word, it is not possible to bring a soul into the light without the mysteries of light." These mysteries help the soul to escape the cosmic powers between earth and the pleroma: "He who shall accomplish that first mystery of the ineffable in all its configurations and all its types, after this at any moment when he shall name that mystery he shall be saved from all that might have befallen him at the hands of the rulers of fate. In that moment he shall depart from the body of the matter of the rulers and his soul shall become a great light stream, it shall soar into the height." Mary is represented as asking Jesus, "Do the mysteries of the baptisms cause the sins which are in the hands of the workmen of wrath to disappear so that they forget them?" To which He replies: "These workmen are ever in the judgement, seizing and rebuking every soul that sinneth and that hath received no mystery; they keep them in chaos and chastise them; but these receivers of wrath cannot go beyond chaos, so as to enter into the orders which are higher than chaos." The baptized, therefore, are safe. "When a man receiveth the mysteries of the baptisms, those mysteries become a mighty fire, exceedingly fierce, which burneth up sins; they enter into the soul occultly and devour all the sins which the spiritual counterfeit hath implanted in it." Hearing this, Mary exclaims, "Now I can interpret Thy former words, 'I am come to send fire on the earth!'"

While the Gnostics thus regarded ceremonial purification as a necessary condition of immortality and a joyful resurrection, and believed that such purification was secured by baptism, they associated magical and mechanical ideas with the Eucharist also, and transformed this into a mystery. According both to Irenæus (vi. 34) and Hippolytus (i. 13, 2) the Marcosians believed in the transubstantiation of the elements at the word of invocation, holding that some kind of grace dropped down at that moment into the cup of wine, giving it special powers, and that to obtain this mercy those present must hasten to drink. Both these writers assert there was deliberate deception; that Marcus, the leader, taking the cup of white wine infused some drug into it, and prolonging the Eucharistic prayer to more than its usual length, to give time for its operation, changed the colour of the wine to purple or red, thus leading his followers to believe that some supernatural grace had descended, giving to the potion its blood-red potency. Incomprehensible sounds were heard, words spoken, and signs made, all derived from the *magica scientia* of the period. The practice also of fasting before the Eucharist, according to Porphyrius, was by the Gnostics associated with the idea of dæmon powers: "When we eat, evil dæmons come into the body: we must therefore abstain from food before the sacraments to drive them away." The Valentinians held that bread, oil for anointing, and baptismal water, while remaining outwardly the same, after being exorcised by invocation received the power of imparting holiness. Lipsius quotes such prayers as these: "Come, water from the living waters, power of salvation from yonder power . . . come and dwell in these waters that herewith the gift of the Holy Spirit may be imparted;" "in Thy name, O Jesus, may the power of grace and thanksgiving come and dwell in this bread, so that all souls that partake thereof may be renewed, and their sins forgiven."[1] Thus the communication of spiritual bless-

---

[1] *Apokr. Apostelgg.*, i. 333, 340.

ing was regarded as a physical process, and it is manifest that Gnosticism was, in an important sense, an anticipation of later Church developments, and that there were manifold correspondences between them. Time brought many changes. The beginning and middle of the second century were characterised by a moral conception of Christianity, but from the fourth century onwards—that is, from the time when under the influence of the persecuting edicts there was a great influx of the heathen into the Church—we find an increasingly elaborate system of mysterious ceremonies, and baptism and the Lord's Supper especially became important connecting-links in the Hellenising of Christianity.[1]

Apart from Gnosticism, there were tendencies in the Church itself, especially in Alexandria, which greatly helped the process. The literary tendency to allegorical treatment of Scripture, the finding of an occult meaning in the plainest statement, accompanied by the remark, "the initiated understand this," and the growing up of that *disciplini arcana* which turned Gospel facts into secret mysteries, necessitating jealous exclusion of the uninitiated and symbola or pass-words for others, prepared the way for all the innovations which Gnosticism brought in. In the introduction of the word "sacrament," which regarded the holy thing as a secret, unapproachable, inconceivable, a long step was taken in the treatment of Gospel truths as mysteries. It was inevitable that the Alexandrian conception of religion as we find it in Clement, and his successor Origen, should affect those acts of worship which were supposed to veil mysterious truths. The act must be performed,

[1] Anrich, *Das antike Mysterienwesen.*

even though the performer may not know what is
meant by it. All must comply, says Origen, bending
the knee and turning to the east, even though they do
not understand. The ritual of the Lord's Supper took
on an air of mystery it had not at first, and began
to excite such feelings as were characteristic of the
Greek Mysteries, but foreign to the early Christian
celebration. There came also to be some idea of a
connexion between taking the elements at the Lord's
Supper and the future resurrection of the body. This
which had been first hinted at by Ignatius, Irenæus,
and the Alexandrian Clement, by the fourth century
had become generally accepted, and by Gregory of
Nyssa developed in the crudest way. It was this idea
which gave birth to the practice of administering the
sacrament to those who were at the point of death as
a *viaticum mortis*, and even sometimes to those who
were actually dead.

Once this kind of thing had begun to prevail the
door was opened to many other practices associated
with heathen mysteries and superstitions. If the uninitiated among the heathen ventured to intrude upon
the Eleusinian mysteries, their crime was punished
with death; so, too, if the uninitiated among the
Christians partook of the Lord's Supper they incurred the penalty of everlasting guilt. Out of this
came the further thought of the sanctity of the
altar-space both in the temple of the mysteries and
the Christian Church. The heathen temple at Samothrace, as recent excavations have shown, had its semi-
circular apse, that at Hierapolis and that at Eleusis
their sacred daïs, which only the chosen priests might
tread, long before there was an apse or railed-off altar-

space sacred to the clergy in the Christian Church. The custom of carrying lighted candles or torches in Christian processions had begun by the fourth or fifth century, and these had been used time out of mind in almost all the heathen mysteries. The watchings through Easter night, followed by the illumination of the Churches, also find their parallel in these mysteries. The rogation or gang-week of the Christian Church, consisting of processions through the fields for a blessing on the fruits of the earth, was really, if traced far enough back, a continuation of the ambervalia of those *fratres arvales* who led a sacrificial victim three times round the cornfields before the sickle was put into the corn. In the month of January, year by year, the dwellers in Rome and the neighbourhood send their horses, asses, and other beasts of burden to the convent of St. Anthony, where, for a small gratuity, they are sprinkled with holy water and blessed by a surpliced priest. In this they are but following the custom of their heathen ancestors, who had their cattle and sheep lustrated at the festival of the Palilia, that is, sprinkled with water by means of a branch of laurel or olive, to preserve them from accident, contagion, and disease. Finally, the Italian peasant who puts his faith in this Madonna or that, in the San Cristoforo of one village, or the San Lorenzo of another, is only filling up with new saints that ancient Pantheon of the gods whom his fathers worshipped. The names are changed, the underlying ideas of polytheism remain much the same.

LECTURE IX

THE DEVELOPMENT OF THE PAPACY

LECTURE IX

THE DEVELOPMENT OF THE PAPACY

IN the history of the ecclesiastical theory of Apostolical Succession a prominent place, of necessity, must be assigned to the bishop of Rome. For the highest claim of all, to apostolic grace and power, is that made by the Pope. He claims not merely, as other bishops, to be a successor of the apostles, but to be the direct successor of Peter, the chief of the apostles, and as such Christ's special vicar and vicegerent upon earth. The present Pope, as we have seen from his recent Encyclical, has emphasised this claim in a very decisive way. He declares that if other bishops deliberately secede from Peter and his successors, they are by that very fact deprived of the right and power of ruling; that the Episcopal Order separated from the Papacy becomes nothing better than a mere lawless and disorderly crowd. It is important, therefore, to inquire how far this claim is historically valid, and on what foundation it rests. For all other claims to Apostolical Succession hang by this. If this is not valid neither are they. The Anglican Church, of necessity, derives through the Roman, therefore for all its bishops and priests the Pope becomes the *fons et origo* of whatever priestly power and sacramental grace they are supposed to possess.

The first fact which meets us in our inquiry is that at the outset the Bishop of Rome derived his importance from the Church, not the Church from the bishop. The Church was in all probability founded by those 'sojourners from Rome" who were converted at Pentecost, and it came to have an honourable primacy of spiritual life and Christian character before any mention is made of a bishop as presiding over it. It had, therefore, been in existence some twenty years when the apostle in his Epistle to the Romans says of it: "I thank my God that your faith is proclaimed throughout the whole world" (i. 8); "your obedience is come abroad unto all men" (xvi. 19); "I am persuaded of you, my brethren, that ye yourselves are full of goodness, filled with all knowledge, able also to admonish one another" (xv. 14). The Christian reputation thus early won seems to have been long maintained. Sixty years later Ignatius in his Epistle to the Romans also addresses this community as a "Church that is beloved and enlightened, . . . even her that hath the presidency in the country of the region of the Romans, being worthy of God, worthy of honour, worthy of felicitation, worthy of praise, worthy of success, worthy in purity, and having the presidency of love, walking in the law of Christ, and bearing the Father's name." Again, about half a century later still, Dionysius, the pastor of the Church at Corinth, bears the same honourable testimony to their Christian zeal and consistency of life. Writing to the Church in Rome he says: "For this practice has prevailed with you from the very beginning, to do good to all the brethren in every way, and to send contributions to many Churches in every city. Thus refreshing the needy in their want, and furnishing to the brethren condemned to the mines what was necessary, by these contributions which ye have been accustomed to send from the beginning, you preserve as Romans the practices of your ancestors the Romans, which was not only observed by your bishop Soter, but also increased, as he not only furnished great supplies to the saints, but also encouraged the brethren that came from abroad, as a loving father his children, with consolatory words." Eusebius (iv. 23), quoting this letter of Dionysius, adds that the practice of the Romans, therein commended, had been retained down to the persecution in his own time, that is down to the year 300.

Thus this Roman Church early became the foremost Church in Christendom, and acquired influence in the most legitimate way, by Christian character and brotherly service. In the mere matter of numbers it was strong and vigorous. Tacitus describes the Christians of Rome in the days of Nero as a "vast multitude" (*Ann.* xv. 44). Not only were they numerous, but faithful also, standing firm to their principles in that awful time of the Neronian persecution. Some of their brethren, sewn in the skins of wild beasts, had been torn to pieces by dogs, others crucified, and yet others wrapped in tar-cloth and set on fire as living torches to illuminate the Emperor's gardens, yet the main body still remained steadfast. The fiery storm through which they had to pass only made their fortitude and fidelity the more conspicuous. And while they thus stood loyally by their Master, in after days, as Dionysius tells us, they stood loyally also by their brethren in tribulation in other cities, sending financial help to those imprisoned or condemned to the mines, and also to smaller Churches struggling with difficulties. Again, in the middle of the third century. Dionysius of Alexandria writing to Stephen, Bishop of Rome, refers to " all the provinces of Syria and Arabia which at different times you supplied with necessaries, Mesopotamia, Pontus, and Bithynia" (*Euseb.* vii. 5); and as late as the fourth century Basil speaks gratefully of Roman help sent to Cappadocia " to redeem captives " (*Ep.* 70). The Roman Church, too, from her position and wealth, naturally became a bureau of intelligence and a centre of communication for the universal brotherhood. There were members in her fellowship who had come from various Churches in many lands; brethren also who were temporarily in Rome were received to hospitality ; news from all the Churches came to Rome as to a universal centre ; and, as we learn from the Epistle of Clement, when there was dissension or trouble of any kind, the Roman Christians sent brotherly letters by honoured brethren, seeking to reconcile differences and restore peace. When great questions of Church doctrine or Church discipline arose, the weaker Churches naturally turned to their stronger sister for counsel and guidance. Thus gradually influence came to this Church as influence always comes when men sincerely, and in a spirit of unselfishness, are trying to bear one another's burdens, and so fulfil the law of Christ. Beyond doubt the Roman Church possessed an acknowledged primacy, but, as Harnack has said, " it was the primacy of active participation and fulfilled duty."

Two things are, however, to be specially noted about this primacy : first, it was the primacy of the Church, not merely of its bishop, the creation of the faith and love, the earnestness and zeal of the whole brotherhood; and next, it was a primacy yielded freely out of respect and esteem, not demanded as a *legal* right. So far as we know, Victor (189–199 A.D.) was the first bishop to claim authority for himself apart from the Church. He appears to have been the first Latin bishop of Rome, and the first who is known to have had relations with the Imperial Court. His claim to something like universal dominion was made in connexion with the Easter question. Contrary to the custom elsewhere, the Churches of Asia Minor celebrated Easter on the 14th of the month Nisan, whether it fell on a Sunday or not. Victor wrote to them, apparently in terms which they resented, rebuking them for this. Polycrates, bishop of Ephesus, replied that, in acting as they did, they were but following the ancient Scriptural usage, and were not to be intimidated by threats. "Upon this, Victor the bishop of the Church of Rome forthwith endeavoured to cut off the Churches of all Asia, together with neighbouring Churches as heterodox, from the common unity. And he published abroad by letters and proclaimed that all the brethren there are wholly excommunicate" (*Euseb.* v. 24). This was a new departure, a transition from the pre-eminence of a Church to the personal ascendancy of the bishop of the Church. As such it was resented not merely by Polycrates, whom it affected, but also by Irenæus. This eminent Church father wrote to Victor in the name of the Churches of Gaul, and extracts from his letter have been preserved by Eusebius He himself, he says, agreed with Victor as to the time of keeping Easter, but he plainly tells him that he had exceeded his right in thus cutting off whole Churches of God who observed what they regarded as the tradition of an ancient custom. He reminds him, too, how differently his predecessors had acted : "those presbyters who presided over the Church before Soter, and over which you now preside." Speaking thus of all the bishops of Rome down to the year 189, as simple presbyters, not as popes, Irenæus says that though they did not observe Easter after the Asian manner, they were not the less in peace with those from Churches where it was so kept, neither did they at any time cast off any merely on this point of ritual. This narrative of Eusebius may be regarded as more than usually significant. It would seem that the first time a bishop of Rome separated himself from the Church in his action, and played the pope on his own account, he was openly rebuked by men so conspicuously eminent in the Church as Polycrates, the bishop of Ephesus in the East, and Irenæus the bishop of Lyons in the West.

Victor was succeeded by the weak and foolish Zephyrinus in 199, and he again by Callistus in 218 A.D. It was this last-mentioned bishop, as has been previously mentioned, who first formulated the theory of Apostolical Succession, and laid claim to the power of forgiving sins. The power thus claimed by Victor in 190, and strengthened by Callistus in 220, received further advancement by Cyprian's theory of the Unity of the Episcopate enunciated in 251. In accordance with this, it will be remembered, each bishop is regarded as not merely the bishop of this or that single community, but as a bishop of the Church at large, a joint shareholder in a universal episcopate. But then the question arose, how can unity be secured in the Church with such a plurality of rulers ? If Cyprian's theory is to be made to work, it must be carried a step further. Thus it came to be maintained that in several senses every bishop is a successor of Peter, and therefore to every bishop belongs the episcopate of Peter. But Peter's episcopal throne, the throne upon which the whole Church rests, has its foundation at Rome, Rome is therefore the *ecclesia principalis*, the Mother Church and root of the entire Christendom. And since every bishop shares Peter's Episcopate, upon that episcopal throne sits not merely the Roman bishop, but every bishop. The throne of Peter is the one episcopal throne of Christendom. It has become necessary to multiply that throne because the Churches have multiplied; still through that very process of multiplication each several bishop has come to possess the Roman episcopate. Through this identity of the Episcopate universal Christendom becomes an undivided community, and of the world episcopate of Peter every bishop possesses an undivided portion.[1] This idea of unity is ingenious, but it is not the Scriptural idea, and no man can honestly claim for it that it came into the world by Divine revelation. A mere afterthought to give plausibility to a system, it carries with it no more authority than that of the ecclesiastics who invented it.

The process by which the lesser Churches became subject to the greater, and the greater to the authority of Rome, was a gradual work of time, and the result of a combination of influences. Till the middle of the third century the number of predominant communities and bishops was still comparatively small. In the whole of the Eastern part of Africa there was only one leading congregation, that of Alexandria, and in West Africa

[1] *Kirchenrecht*, von Rudolph Sohm, ss. 345-6. Leipzig, 1892.

that of Carthage. In Italy there was only Rome, while in Spain no single congregation occupied a position of pre-eminence, and in Gaul only that of Lyons. In the Greek-speaking East influential congregations were more thickly scattered. We find them at Corinth, Philippi, Thessalonica, Ephesus, Tarsus, Cæsarea in Cappadocia, Cæsarea in Palestine, Jerusalem, and at Antioch. Each of these leading Churches acquired influence over the smaller communities around them, but as yet there was nothing like a complete network of provincial organisation, no legally established privileges, or formal control of one Church by another. The period of this further development is to be looked for in that long breathing-time of more than forty years between the end of the Valerian persecution and the beginning of that under Diocletian, (260-303 A.D.)[1] Eusebius (viii. 1) gives us a vivid description of this time with its lights and shadows. During these forty years, he says, the heathen emperors even entrusted Christian men with the government of provinces and laid no commands upon them as to sacrificing to the gods. Officials in the Imperial palaces, and even the emperors themselves, allowed their servants liberty to declare their religion freely. Privileges were granted to the officers of the Churches everywhere, these officers being also treated with great deference by the rulers and governors of the State. The natural result of this change after the death of Valerian was seen in large accessions to the Christian congregations in the Empire. "Who," exclaims Eusebius, "can describe those vast numbers of men that flocked to the religion of Christ, the multitudes that came crowding in from every city, the magnificent

[1] Sohm, ss. 368-9.

congregations in the houses of prayer?" The places of worship were not large enough to contain the numbers that came, and new and spacious edifices had to be erected in all directions. But human nature cannot long bear up under continued prosperity. The brighter the light the darker the shadow which it casts. Conflict within the Church succeeded to persecution from without and was more spiritually disastrous. Says Eusebius sadly, "by reason of excessive liberty we sank into negligence and sloth." Like the first disciples, there came strifes among them as to who should be greatest; men were struggling for pre-eminence in the Church, for official place and power, "assailing each other with words as with darts and spears, prelate inveighing against prelate and people rising up against people." Eusebius mourns over it all and seems to anticipate the lament of Gregory Nazianzen at Constantinople, a century later: "Would to Heaven," cries he, "there were no primacy, no eminence of place, no tyrannical precedence of rank; that we might be known by eminence of virtue alone!" "Some that appeared to be our pastors, deserting the law of piety, were inflamed against each other with mutual strifes, accumulating quarrels and rivalries, anxious only to assert the government as a kind of sovereignty for themselves." In this way the original equality of all congregations and all bishops, which had been hitherto maintained as a fundamental principle, came to give place to something very different. An elaborate organisation arose, a systematically ranged and legally united ecclesiastical body.

The process of absorption of the lesser Churches by the greater was of course only gradual. First a finger was seized, then the hand, then the arm, and then the whole body. There was a sort of friendly arrangement at first that leading congregations and their bishops should have some part in choosing and recognising bishops for the smaller communities. This was not a formal or legally defined recognition, and till the middle of the third century the separate communities, in principle, still retained their freedom. When they had elected a bishop the result was simply communicated to the bishop of the neighbouring leading community without any express confirmation being asked for or granted. But in the period of inner conflict in the second half of the third century, to which reference has just been made, two things happened. First the bishop of the leading community claimed the right of conducting the election of a pastor in the smaller Church and also of confirming it, a choice made without this concurrence coming to be regarded as invalid. Next, when a smaller Church became vacant, a larger community with its bishop would claim the right of filling up the vacancy themselves, and following upon the right to elect, the right also to dismiss. Under the plea of rendering assistance they went so far as to elect a bishop or pastor in their own congregation and sent him to the vacant Church without its being allowed to have any voice in the matter. Of course there were instances when this interference was resented and when the Church refused to accept the bishop appointed for them. In this way arose conflict between one community and another and between one bishop and another.[1] Still the practice obtained, and so one bishop came to have judicial supremacy over other bishops. Evidence of

[1] Sohm, 370-1.

this may be gathered from the 18th canon of the Synod of Ancyra held in the year 314, and Eusebius, in the appendix to his eighth book, refers sorrowfully to the unlawful ambitions of those heads of the Churches who from being shepherds of the intelligent flocks of Christ became lords over God's heritage. He prefers, he says, to draw the veil of silence over the ambitious aspirings to office, and the injudicious, unlawful ordinations which took place.

It was the great Council of Nicæa—the first Council summoned by the Emperor after the union of the Church with the Empire—which gave formal sanction to this mode of proceeding and turned custom into law. This Imperial synod, or, as it came to be called, this Œcumenical Council of A.D. 325, had for its main object the settlement of the great dogmatic controversy concerning the Person of Christ; but it also entered upon the question of the organisation of the Church, and the action it took on this matter marks the transitional stage in the attainment of supremacy by one bishop over another. For the principle of the ecclesiastical constitution it laid down, and made authoritative by canons 4 and 5, was that in each of the provinces of the Empire the bishop of the chief city should have authority, as metropolitan, over all the rest of the bishops and Churches in the province. Previously the custom had been, in the case of the election of a bishop for any of the Churches, that it was deemed sufficient if three bishops were present at the synod called for election. The change now introduced by the Council was to the effect that *all* the bishops, if not present at the synod, should afterwards express their concurrence in the election before the ordination could be proceeded with. If two or three of these bishops should refuse their consent this would not invalidate the election, provided that a majority consented. But if the metropolitan objected, his objection alone was fatal to the election. With him rested the right of confirmation or veto, and without his consent no one could be ordained as a bishop in the province. This right of confirmation or veto was the only right granted by the Council to the metropolitan as such, and nothing was said about giving him power of ordination. This right, however, as a new departure, had far-reaching results. For not long before, Diocletian by a process of sub-division had greatly increased the number of provinces in the Empire, and in the Church the metropolitans of all the smaller provinces thus created became possessed of metropolitan rights.

It is to be noted also that in the larger capital towns of entire great divisions of the Roman Empire, there were already Churches which had attained a special pre-eminence and dignity, either from their civic importance, or because Christianity had extended itself from them in wider circles. The sixth canon of Nicæa simply confirmed this already existing pre-eminence. The Churches mentioned are those of Rome, Alexandria, and Antioch, the Churches of the three great capitals of the Roman Empire. The canon runs thus: "Let the ancient customs prevail—namely, those in Egypt, Lybia, and Pentapolis—that the bishop of Alexandria have authority (ἐξουσίαν) over these, since the same is customary for the bishop of Rome. Likewise in the case of Antioch and other provinces, let the privileges (τὰ πρεσβεῖα) be secured to the Churches." Some higher rank was clearly intended, and as the political officers of these larger provinces were styled *Exarchs*, the bishops or metropolitans who presided over the ecclesiastical administrations were styled *Exarchs* also, choice, however, being subsequently made of the more ecclesiastical title of *Patriarch*. Some years later, when the city of Byzantium had, under the name of Constantinople, become the seat of government of the Roman Empire in the East, and the second capital of the entire Roman world, it was thought necessary that this Church, as the Church of the second Imperial residence, should receive the rank of a Patriarchate also. Accordingly, at the second (Ecumenical) Council of Constantinople, held A.D. 381, it was decided that the bishop of Constantinople should take rank next after the bishop of Rome, not for any ecclesiastical reason, but simply because Constantinople, as the Eastern seat of government, was New Rome. The Council of Chalcedon in the following century (451 A.D.), by its twenty-eighth canon, confirmed this decision in a manner which showed that pre-eminence was accorded purely on political grounds. The canon runs thus: "The fathers rightly conceded that rank to the episcopate of Old Rome *because it was the Imperial city*, and the hundred and fifty bishops [at Constantinople] being moved with the same intention, gave equal privileges to the holy seat of New Rome [Constantinople], judging with reason that the city which was honoured with the sovereignty and senate and enjoyed equal privileges with the elder Imperial Rome, should also be magnified like her in ecclesiastical matters, being the second after her."

Returning now to the sixth canon of the Council of Nicæa, we can see that from it certain important inferences clearly follow: (1) That the authority of the bishop of Rome, which had extended to districts beyond his own province, needed no confirmation on the part of the Council ; it was evidently already accepted in the Church. In this respect he was in advance of the bishops of Alexandria and Antioch. (2) That these two last-mentioned Churches had confirmed to them by the Council the authority which custom had already assigned to them, and for the reason that the bishop of Rome already enjoyed similar authority, his position being taken as the model for theirs. (3) Since that position was .thus taken as the model for theirs, and since the authority of Alexandria and Antioch was restricted to a certain definite area, it follows further that the anthority of the bishop of Rome was also restricted to a certain definite area, an area the extent of which was determined by custom. Rufinus, writing some seventy-five years later than the Nicæan Council, explains its sixth canon as meaning that "at Alexandria and in the city of Rome the ancient custom must be observed, that the former (bishop) should take care of Egypt, and the latter of the *Suburbicarian* Churches" (*H. E.*, x. 6). That is, that Alexandria should have authority over Egypt, Libya, and Pentapolis, while the bishop of Rome should exercise supervision either over the four provinces nearest to Rome, or over the region under the jurisdiction of the civil officer known as the *vicarius urbis*, that is, over the seven continental provinces of Middle and Southern Italy, together with the islands of Sicily, Sardinia, and Corsica. We thus arrive at this very obvious conclusion : If the authority of the bishop of Rome was thus limited to a certain definite area, and that area was merely determined by custom, it follows of course that the bishop of Rome in the year 325 was not in any sense a universal governor, that his authority did not come of Divine right, or because he was the successor of Peter, but simply because Rome was the great metropolis of Empire and the seat of government. As Canon Bright puts it in his *Notes on the Canons*: " If the bishops of Nicæa had believed Sylvester, then bishop of Rome, to be the divinely appointed ruler of the whole Church, the one universal overseer, and the fountain of all episcopal jurisdiction, they could not have been content to say that the bishop of Alexandria ought, according to custom, to have power in one region *because* the bishop of Rome had similar power in another. It would have been impossible to use his patriarchal status as a precedent without a saving clause acknowledging his unique and sovereign position as the one Vicar of the Church's Divine Head, and pointing to it as the true source of all patriarchal and metropolitical jurisdiction."

The next landmark of importance in the history of Papal development, after the sixth canon of Nicæa, is a letter of Julius, bishop of Rome, of the year 340. When the dominant party of the Eastern Church had deposed Athanasius of Alexandria from his office, Julius invited both parties to present the matter, by their delegates, before an assembly of the Western Church. To this the Eastern bishops convened at Antioch replied, bluntly telling him that it did not belong to him, a foreign bishop, to set himself up as a judge in the affairs of the Eastern Church; that he, as bishop of a larger city, was no more than other bishops; that his predecessors had never thought of interfering in the interior affairs of the Eastern Church any more than the older bishops of the East had constituted themselves judges in the controversies of the West. Notwithstanding this reply, Julius convoked a synod of Italian bishops, who found the charges against Athanasius to be baseless, and he then wrote a carefully worded letter to the Eastern bishops, a complete copy of which Athanasius has preserved for us in his "Apologia contra Arianos."[1] This letter is dealing with men who claim that all bishops have the same and equal authority, and are not to be ranked according to the magnitude of their cities. The question of right is openly thrown into the arena. And it is to be specially noted that in reply to these men Julius does not claim supreme power for himself as bishop of Rome. He claims that according to the canon the result of the Eastern synod should have been made known "*to us all*, that so a just sentence might *proceed from all*." The proceedings, to be valid, ought to be universally accepted, and without him the recognition was not universal. He claims that in demanding to be consulted in any case affecting the Church of Alexandria he has the warrant of *custom*, and he claims to have *traditions* received from St. Peter. These are the claims he makes, but he does *not* claim to have any jurisdiction derived from Peter or to have any right to judge the case on his own authority. This letter, put forward under hostile challenge, has been well described as showing the high-water mark of the Papal tendency down to 340, and as being in marked contrast to the tone of his successors later on in the same century.

As marking another stage in the history, three years after the letter of Julius we come upon the canons of the Council of Sardica, now Sofia in Bulgaria, which

[1] Nicene and Post Nicene Library, vol. iv.—*Athanasius*, p. 113.

was held in 343. The re-instalment of Athanasius by the Roman bishop was not recognised by the Eastern Churches. In this time of conflict the Council of Sardica undertook to grant to the Roman bishop jurisdiction over the whole Church. According to canons 3, 4, and 5, this Council decreed: (1) That when a bishop is condemned in a matter, and he believes that injustice has been done him, the synod which judged him shall write to the Roman bishop Julius; so that, if necessary, a new inquiry may be made by the bishops of the neighbouring province, he himself to name the judges; (2) in such a case, no other person shall be nominated to fill the place of the deposed bishop until the Roman bishop shall have received notice of it and decided on the point; (3) if in such a case the deposed bishop appeal to the bishop of Rome, and he considers a new investigation to be desirable, he shall commit such investigation to the bishops of the neighbouring province, and may also send some of his own presbyters to assist. It will be seen that these canons, in the case of deposed bishops, assign to the Roman bishop a certain supreme power of jurisdiction and right of revision, a right to receive appeals and to deal with them at Rome. The underlying thought of the decrees of Sardica is that if the Pope has accepted the decision of a synod the Church has completed its acceptance; is so far embodied judicially in the person of the Pope; and has so far received a Head invested with judicial power. The Council of Sardica, for the first time, although within narrow limits, admits a judicial power of the Roman bishop over all Christendom; and he appears for the first time as Pope, as Primate of the whole Ecclesia.[1]

[1] Sohm, 416-17.

The value of the decrees of Sardica is, however, heavily discounted when we remember that though this Council was intended to be œcumenical, it really was not. For the bishops were divided on the question of faith, and this division rent the Council asunder, so that the Arian bishops of the East withdrew to Philippopolis to hold a separate synod there. In addition to the Western bishops, only those from the East remained who had been condemned and deposed there by the party hostile to them. It was to their interest to increase the powers of the Pope, since he, as the champion of the Nicene party, stood their friend. Under these circumstances the decrees were not accepted in the East, and even in the West they carried but little weight in succeeding times.

But though these decrees did not carry weight, they furnish an illustration of the way in which Rome has so often been willing to support her power by resort to doubtful and disreputable means. Cases frequently occurred where clergy in the North African Church, who had been deposed for their offences, appealed to the Roman Church and were received to protection. Hearing of this, the two Councils of Carthage of 407 and 418 decreed that whoever thereafter, instead of appealing to the jurisdiction of their own Church, should appeal to one beyond the sea, should be severed from the fellowship. In spite of this decree, however, in 418 a deposed presbyter did make his appeal to Zosimus, the bishop of Rome, who was willing to deal with the matter before his own tribunal. The Carthaginians at once protested against their own authority being thus set aside. By way of establishing his right to receive appeals, Zosimus fell back upon the recited canons of Sardica, but instructed his delegates to present them at the Council of Carthage, in 419, as canons of the great Council of Nicæa. The African bishops were amazed, having never heard of such canons before. They therefore communicated at once with the bishops of Constantinople, Alexandria, and Antioch, asking for reliable copies of the genuine canons of Nicæa. When these were examined they were found to contain no such decrees as those upon which Zosimus relied for his authority, and they turned out to be only the Sardican decrees under an assumed name. Still, in spite of this exposure, in 425 Leo I. again appealed to them, in the case of Flavian of Constantinople, and again appealed to them as Nicene. He did this again and again, and there is an ancient collection of canons published in the appendix to his works where these Sardican canons are formally ascribed to the Council of Nicæa. Further, the canon authorising an appeal to be made to "*Julius*, bishop of Rome," was deliberately altered to "*Sylvester*, bishop of Rome," to suit the alteration of time from 343 to 325.

Still, while there were side issues, the main issue of the time was between Arian and Athanasian, and Rome won the victory at length, as the great power that bore aloft the banner of orthodoxy in the Church. The theological battle of the time ended in the defeat of Arianism, and the victory of the Nicene faith was the victory of the Roman power. As Sohm puts it (s. 417): " It was not the decrees of Sardica nor any other outward authority which spoke the decisive word. It was the doctrinal power of the Roman bishop which at this critical moment soared by the force of an inward

might to the power of judicial rule." The position thus
gained by theological considerations was further confirmed by Imperial enactment. The Emperor Theodosius,
who, as a Spaniard, belonged to the Nicene party, issued
in 380 his celebrated edict, in accordance with which all
the world was commanded to accept that religion which
the Romans had received from the Apostle Peter. This
edict was at first only to apply to Constantinople, but
in the following year it was extended to the whole
Empire, and the principle was laid down that those
only should be acknowledged as Catholic Christians
who held to the faith of the co-essential Trinity as it
had been taught by Peter to the Romans, and as it
was then held by Damasus, bishop of Rome, and
Peter, bishop of Alexandria.

Thus from the all-important victory of the Athanasian
party over the Arian, followed by the decisive edict of
Theodosius, we may safely date the authoritative ruling
power of the Pope, not merely over Italy, but over the
West generally. Consequent upon this fact is the rise
from this time of those Roman decretals which formally
asserted the Roman power, which were issued in the full
consciousness of authority, and were so accepted by
those to whom they were addressed The first genuine
decretal was issued by Siricius, bishop of Rome, in 385.
It was addressed to Himerius, bishop of Tarragona, in
answer to a series of questions sent by some Spanish
bishops to Damasus, but as they only reached Rome
after that bishop's death, they were answered by his
successor Siricius. This decretal of his stands first in
the later canonical collections. There had been other
authoritative decrees issued long before in the third
century, but these are passed by to begin with that of

Siricius, as being the first issued and accepted as emanating from legislative power. In this he answers questions as to certain doubtful points of usage, the validity of heretical baptism, the treatment of apostates, and the steps by which the clergy were to pass from the lower to the higher ranks. Answering these questions, he speaks in a tone of full authority. He styles it arrogant presumption in the Spanish priests that they should baptize multitudes of people at Christmas, at the feast of Epiphany, and at the festivals of the apostles and martyrs, as well as at the other regular times, and decrees that henceforth, except in cases of necessity, baptism shall only be administered at the festivals of Easter and Pentecost.

The most important part of this decretal, however, related to the great question of the celibacy of the clergy. On this point Siricius was very peremptory. He ordered that presbyters and deacons should separate from their wives; that such as had before violated this rule through ignorance might be allowed to retain their places, but only on condition of observing continence and without hope of promotion; that any one attempting to defend the contrary practice should be deposed; that no man who had married a widow, or who had been more than once married, should be eligible to the ministry; and that clergy contracting such marriages should be deposed. Thus by this decretal a growing practice was established as an authoritative law, and this law remains unrepealed. It is a law which again and again has been defied, infringed, eluded, but it remains, and more than anything else has resulted in separating the priestly order from the rest of society into a caste by themselves, and apart from common human sympathies, interests and affections. It has, as Milman says, justified them to themselves in assuming a dignity superior to the rest of mankind, and seemed their title to enforce acknowledgment and reverence for that superior dignity. It was a perpetual appeal to their pride, and the clergy were taught to assert this departure from a Divine institution as at once a privilege, a distinction, and as the consummation and the testimony to the sacredness of their order.

In this decretal of his Siricius began the practice of dating decretals by the consul of the year, after the manner in which the Imperial rescripts or laws were dated. It thus assumed an authoritative legal form, and it was written in the tone of one who expects the usages of the Church of Rome to be received as those of Christendom. It was to be communicated beyond the province of Tarragona to the rest of Spain—to Carthagena, Baetica, Lusitania, Galicia, and even to Southern Gaul. From this time the title of Pope must be accorded to the bishop of Rome, and with the decretals of Siricius the formal papal jurisdiction over the West may be said to be established. The Imperial recognition of the position thus gradually attained came later. It was in the next century, in 445, that Leo I. obtained from the feeble and contemptible Emperor Valentinian III. that important Imperial rescript which ran as follows : " We decree by a perpetual edict that nothing shall be attempted contrary to ancient custom, either by the Gallican bishops, or by the bishops of other provinces, without the authority of the venerable man, the Pope of the Eternal City ; but whatever the authority of the Apostolic See has sanctioned or shall sanction, let that be held by them and by all for a law, so that if any of the bishops shall neglect, when summoned to come to the tribunal of the Roman prelate, let him be *forced* to come by the civil government of the province." This rescript of Valentinian, on behalf of Leo, must be set side by side with Leo's own letter to the Illyrian bishops in which he claims for himself "that on him, as the successor of the Apostle Peter, on whom, as the reward of his faith, the Lord had conferred the primacy of apostolic rank, and on whom he had firmly grounded the universal Church, was devolved the care of all the Churches, to participate in which he invited his colleagues, the other bishops" (*Ep.* xi.). During the period of sixty years which commenced with the first decretal of Siricius in 385 and closed with the rescript of Valentinian in 445, followed as it was by the autocratic letter of Leo I. to the Illyrian bishops, we may say the papacy was erected and the Roman bishop was transformed into the spiritual ruler of Christendom.

It is sometimes said that the papacy was an inevitable product of the condition of things in the early Middle Ages; that it was not created by designing priests any more than by the Founder of Christianity; and that its growth was due to the fact that the bishop of Rome was the one rallying-point in a world of confusion, the one centre of order amid chaos, the one central light in a night of darkness. It is contended that no order or authority remained save that which rested in the person of the bishop of Rome, who thus became the exalted head of the Holy Roman Church; in other words, that it was the downfall of the Western Roman Empire, when barbarians swarmed over Italy, that created the supremacy of the Roman bishop. There is enough truth in this to make the general statement misleading.

We must, if we would be accurate, distinguish between the temporal dominion and the spiritual authority of the Pope. He had attained priestly supremacy before the barbarians had really brought chaos and desolation to Italy. During the first six hundred years of the Christian era there were only two really great bishops of Rome, Leo I. (440–461) and Gregory I. (590–604). In the time of Leo, the spiritual supremacy was attained, and in the time of Gregory the temporal dominion of the Pope was established. From the traditional episcopate of Peter until the entrance of the Goths into Rome forty-five bishops are said to have succeeded each other in the Eternal City. Of many of these we are told but little indeed, and what little we are told is not always reliable. Their biographies were in some cases compiled by monkish chroniclers for the Liber Pontificalis very much as Agnellus, with surprising candour, tells us he prepared the lives of some of the bishops of Ravenna. When he could find nothing authentic about them either from tradition, or history, or the monuments, " in such a case," he says, " that there might not be a break in the series, I have composed the life *myself*, with the help of God and the prayers of the brethren."[1] Possibly of some of the bishops of Rome there may be biographies equally pious with those of the bishops of Ravenna, and equally worthless, but we are upon surer ground in laying stress upon Siricius and Leo before the fall of Rome, and upon Gregory after that great catastrophe had reached its consummation.

Five great invasions by Visigoths, Huns, Vandals, Ostrogoths, and Lombards, extending over a hundred and sixty years, and therefore over five generations of

[1] Muratori's *Scriptores Rerum Italicarum*, ii. 62.

men, mark the memorable period which has been called the *Death of Rome*. It was during this century and a half, and after *spiritual* supremacy had been attained, that the bishop of Rome achieved *political* supremacy and laid the foundations of the Temporal Power. Other causes besides invasions were at work contributing to this result. In 423 the Emperor Honorius died in his fortieth year, the male line of the great Theodosius thus becoming extinct and the Western Empire left without any appointed successor. Under these circumstances the activity of the Roman bishop became the sole animating power in the history of the city. In 440 Leo I. was unanimously elected to the episcopate, and in him the hour and the man came together. While the Imperial power tottered to its fall, and province after province became the prey of the German tribes, Leo, a born leader of men, bent his full strength to make the Roman dogma felt to its full extent, and to win supremacy for the Roman Chair. In a still later time the process commenced by him was continued by others. In 475 Romulus Augustulus, the last Roman Emperor, was proclaimed, but he had scarcely put on the purple before he was overthrown by the same rebellious mercenaries to whom he owed the dignity. The following year Odovakar was proclaimed King of Italy by his motley army, but he had no idea of setting himself up as Emperor of the West, or of making Italy an independent Teutonic kingdom apart from the Empire. He merely set up a barbarian military monarchy without foundation and without stability. The extinction of the Imperial power caused Rome to sink to the position of a provincial town, and her last political and civil life died out. Then, no longer dominated by the Emperor of the West, the Papacy assumed the place of the Empire, and filling for a time the void caused by the disappearance of the Imperial power, it formed a bridge between the ancient and modern world.[1] Hodgkin[2] goes so far as to say that the proclamation of Odovakar in 476 was in its indirect consequences a revolution which affected most powerfully the life of every inhabitant of Mediæval and even of Modern Europe. For by it the political centre of gravity was changed from the Palatine to the Lateran, and the bishop of Rome, now beyond comparison the most important personage of Roman descent left in Italy, was irresistibly invited to ascend the throne and to wrap himself in the purple of the vanished Augustus. The fact that the Gothic rulers continued to reside at Ravenna, and that, as Arians, they remained outside the Roman Church, was really advantageous to the Pope, who as head of Catholic Christendom felt himself raised above the heretical kings of Italy, and came to have a more and more influential voice in the internal affairs of the city. By a rescript of Athalaric the Roman bishop was appointed arbitrator in all disputes between the clergy and the laity, and any one refusing to submit to the decision of the Pope was sentenced to be fined ten pounds in gold. This decree practically amounted to an exemption of the clergy from all secular jurisdiction and laid the foundation of the political power of the papacy. With the advent of the Lombards and the overthrow of the Goths the political life of Rome came to its close, and she entered upon the period of her papal Middle Ages.

[1] Gregorovius, vol. i.
[2] *Italy and her Invaders*, ii. 544.

The papacy rose to still greater power and entered upon that struggle with Byzantium which became a revolution, and out of which the Church issued a rich temporal power and mistress of the Eternal City.[1]

While the beginnings of the Temporal Power of the papacy had been made by previous Popes, it was Gregory the Great (590–604), however, who may be said to be its real founder. Under his rule, coming as he did at a time of civil desolation, religious interests thrust civic affairs into the background. There were no longer any public festivals but those of the Church, and the only events which occupied the minds of men were of ecclesiastical sort. Gregory took full advantage of the opportunities thus afforded, and made the Temporal Power the permanent object of aspiration. Pope Pelagius (555–560) had in his time called in the assistance of military officers against bishops who resisted his authority, but Gregory went beyond this. He himself appointed the officers both civil and military. He nominated Constantius Tribune of Naples when that city was hard pressed by the Lombards; he entrusted the administration of Nepi in Southern Tuscany to Leontius, and made peace on his own account with the Lombards.[2] He extended the boundaries of the Patriarchate of the West far beyond the limits of Constantine and founded that supremacy of the Roman bishop over the Western Church which was to last a thousand years.[3] Leo I. and Gregory I. established the supremacy of the apostolic chair; the continuous energy of sagacious Popes then succeeded in giving political

---

[1] Gregorovius, vol. ii.
[2] Bury's *History of the Later Roman Empire*, ii. 157.
[3] Hodgkin's *Italy and her Invaders*, v. 279.

existence to the Church and in creating a permanent ecclesiastical State. Uniting royalty to the priesthood, they brought the greatest and most honourable period of the history of the Roman Church to an end. As Gregorovius has said: the essentially contradictory nature of their twofold character drew the bishops of Rome ever deeper and deeper into the vortex of political ambition. In the demoralising struggle for the maintenance of their temporal title, they became involved of necessity in intestine strife with the citizens of Rome, and in lasting quarrels with the political rivals of the time. From the foundation of the ecclesiastical state, for centuries three forces were in perpetual conflict—the ancient municipal right of the people, the ancient right of the Imperial monarchy, and the acquired right of the papacy.[1]

The claim to supremacy of spiritual sort—and it is with this rather than with that to Temporal Power we are especially concerned—was from the first contested by the Patriarch of Constantinople, on behalf of the Eastern Church. The year 595, in which Gregory began seriously to prepare his scheme for the conversion of Britain, was also the year in which he formally entered the lists with John the Faster, who as bishop of Constantinople had revived the claim to the title of Universal Bishop, conceded by courtesy to some of his predecessors. John wrote to Gregory a letter in which in almost every line he called himself Ecumenical Patriarch. Gregory wrote back protesting against this "wicked word" (*sceleste vocabulum*, Ep. v. 19 [45]), and telling him that he had forbidden his *responsalis* Sabinianus to communicate with him till he had amended

[1] Gregorovius, vol. ii.

his error. When the Emperor entreated Gregory not to cause the scandal of a quarrel for the mere adoption of a foolish title (*frivoli nominis*), Gregory replied: "I beg the Imperial Piety to consider that some frivolous things are quite harmless, and others grievously hurtful. . . . But I say with confidence that whosoever calls himself Universal Bishop (*sacerdos*), or desires to be so called by others, in his elation is a forerunner of Antichrist, because in his pride he exalteth himself over all others" (*Ep.* vii. 33 [30]). When, however, the Patriarchs of Constantinople continued to use the objectionable title, the Roman Pontiffs, finding they could not prevent its use by their rivals, proceeded to adopt it for themselves. About the year 682 the Popes began to style themselves Ecumenical Bishops or Ecumenical Popes. For centuries two rulers of the Church alike claimed universal jurisdiction ; and in the Church of Rome Pope after Pope assumed a title which in the judgement of their greatest predecessor was a distinct mark of the precursor of Antichrist.

The further development of the Temporal Power of the Popes belongs rather to the general domain of mediæval history than to the inquiry with which we are here specially concerned. To say the least it was never a popular government. Revolution succeeded revolution with bewildering frequency, and when at length, in our own day, the rule of the Pope, along with that of the Bourbons, fell before the discontent of its own subjects and the national aspirations of a united Italy, it fell never to rise again. The *spiritual* authority of the Roman See, on the other hand, was attained before the *temporal*, and has outlived it. It is still a force to be reckoned with in modern diplomacy, and it is still the highest embodiment of the claim to apostolic power and grace.

The history of the growth of power on the part of the bishops of Rome has not thus far been eminently suggestive of what is specially supernatural and Divine. There are certain other considerations to which we must now also briefly advert which may serve still further to shatter the tottering edifice of Apostolical Succession in the Roman Church, and by consequence in the Anglican also, which derives through the Roman.

1. It must be admitted that there is nothing specially Divine or apostolic in the way in which the Roman Church has allowed her claim to be supported by means of frauds and forgeries. The series begins with the Clementine forgeries, which, though not a production of the Church at Rome, but of some Ebionitish heretic of the second century, yet did much by its acceptance in the third and following centuries to favour the Roman claim. In some respects it is opposed to that claim inasmuch as it speaks of James as "the lord and bishop of bishops who rules Jerusalem, the holy Church of the Hebrews and the Churches everywhere;" but at the same time it represents Peter as laying hands on Clement in the presence of the Church at Rome, as their bishop, and saying: "To him I entrust my chair of discourse, I communicate to him the power of binding and loosing, so that with respect to everything which he shall ordain on earth it shall be decreed in heaven" (*Ep. of Clem. to James*, c. ii.). But for the acceptance of this fiction as genuine history the world would probably not have heard of the Chair of St. Peter.

It is otherwise with that Donation of Constantine of which no trace is to be found till the middle of the eighth century, and by virtue of which Constantine, immediately after his baptism, and to show his gratitude for the cure wrought by Silvester, gave to that Pope and his successors many comprehensive and civil rights and to the Roman clergy many eminent privileges, but most of all made over Rome and Italy to the Pope. Dr. Döllinger was of opinion that the document was fabricated in Rome by some Roman ecclesiastic between 750 and 775 and that it had for its aim the setting up of a great kingdom embracing the whole of Italy under the rule of the Pope instead of an Italy divided between the Lombards and the Greeks.[1] It ordained not merely the sovereignty of the Pope over Rome and the provinces, cities, and towns of the whole of Italy, but decreed that the Chair of Peter shall have supreme authority over the patriarchal Chairs of Alexandria, Antioch, Jerusalem, and Constantinople, and over all Churches in the world; and that it shall be judge in all that concerns the service of God and the Christian Faith. No pains were taken at first to make it well known, but after its incorporation into the forged Decretals of Isidore, that is, from 840 onwards, it began to be treated as authentic by Aneas, bishop of Paris, and Hincmar, bishop of Rheims; and in 1054 Leo IX. recited nearly the whole text of the Donation openly and confidently to the patriarch Michael Cerularius; on the other hand Gregory VII. was ominously silent concerning it, though he must have been under great temptation to use it. However, from the twelfth century to the fourteenth its authority was in the ascendant and made the basis of higher and constantly increasing claims. Historians were more cautious than ecclesiastics in

---

[1] *Fables respecting the Popes of the Middle Ages*, 1871, pp. 117-18.

using it, some of them leaving the question open, others making a compromise. The boldest position of all was taken when in 1245 Innocent IV. declared it was an error to suppose that Constantine was the first to confer Temporal Power on the Roman See; for before this Christ Himself entrusted *both* powers to Peter and his successors, the sacerdotal and the royal, and the reins of both kingdoms, the earthly and the heavenly. All, therefore, that Constantine did was merely to resign an unlawfully possessed power into the hands of its lawful possessor, the Church, and had received it back from the Church. In like manner Tolomeo of Lucca explained the Donation as a formal abdication of Constantine in favour of Silvester, and thence draws the conclusion that the power of all temporal princes derives its strength and efficacy solely from the spiritual power of the Popes.

This falsehood, which had attained such vast proportions, was first assailed by the lawyers, not for ecclesiastical reasons, but on the obvious legal ground that from the first the Donation was legally null and void, inasmuch as an Emperor could only enlarge not diminish the Empire. A mutilation of the Empire, of which he was only the administrator, could be set aside by any one of his successors as null and void. Still while saying this even the lawyers conceded that long prescription had conferred legal validity. It was not till the fifteenth century that this imposture came to be dealt with on historical grounds by Reginald Pecock, bishop of Chichester, Cardinal Cusa, and Lorenzo Valla. At their hands it received its *coup de grâce*. Canonists and jurists still tried to hold on to its genuineness, but when Cardinal Baronius once for all confessed its unauthenticity all voices in its favour were finally silenced.

Besides the Donation of Constantine the false Decretals of Isidore, which embodied that Donation, played an important part in supporting the papal theocratic system. Following in the wake of previous collections, these later forgeries fell in with the prevailing spirit of the age and acquired great authority by assuming the names of former bishops of Rome. Towards the end of the fifth century Dionysius, a Scythian monk settling at Rome, undertook to edit a systematic compilation of the canons of previous Councils, more accurate and complete than any previously existing. This collection met with so much favour that he proceeded to make a second in which were interwoven with the one already issued the decretal letters of the Popes from Siricius down to Anastasius II. By thus systematising these decretals he assimilated them to the rescripts of the Emperors, and, which was a point of great importance, he thus placed the letters of Popes, written in answer to questions addressed to them, on a level with the canons of Councils. Dionysius died in 556, and in the following century Isidore of Seville, a name venerated in the Church, issued a Spanish recension of this collection with the addition of later ecclesiastical ordinances. This prepared the way for a spurious collection which in the ninth century was palmed upon the world under the name of Isidore. It consisted of sixty letters professedly from bishops of Rome, all of them fictitious, certain conciliar decrees, and a third part which contained decretals of Popes down to Gregory II. The first of these was the genuine decretal of Siricius, others were partly genuine, while the rest were shameless forgeries which an uncritical age received with simple credulity.

Simple indeed was the credulity and benighted the

age which accepted these decretals as authoritative documents. For early bishops of Rome were made to quote Scripture from a Latin translation made long after they were in their graves; Victor, bishop of Rome, is made to write a letter on the celebration of Easter to Theophilus, bishop of Alexandria, who lived two hundred years after him; Scripture is mutilated and altered in the most shameless manner to suit the forger's purpose; things utterly incongruous with the age in which they were supposed to be written are retained in the most careless manner; and passages are patched together without any intelligible connexion. But these forged decretals supported the papal theocratic system, and that was enough to make them welcome to a Church never very scrupulous as to the weapons she uses, or the auxiliaries she employs. They pushed the papal system and the priestly idea to an extent never embodied in ecclesiastical laws before. The conception of an inviolable caste of priests was held up and defended from the Old Testament in a manner utterly foreign to the spirit of the Gospel. The supremacy of the Popes, the dignity and privileges of the bishop of Rome, the whole hierarchy from the highest to the lowest degree, their sanctity and immunities were upheld and glorified. The priests were represented as the very apple of God's eye, they were the *spiritales* as opposed to the laity, who were only *carnales*, and if ever a man sinned against them he sinned against God Himself. Even bad priests, if they do not fall from the faith, must be tolerated as sent by God. And if priests were to be thus regarded much more were bishops to whom power to bind and loose had been given by Christ. Even if they were to make an unjust decision men were bound to respect it; their persons were to be inviolable and maintained independent of the secular power, the only judge over them in the last resort being the Pope, from whom there could be no appeal. The drift of the Pseudo-Isidorian decretals is that there is by Divine right a coherent organism of ecclesiastical powers in regular gradation; bishops over priests, metropolitans over bishops, primates and patriarchs over metropolitans, but finally over *all* the bishop of Rome, on whom had been conferred in particular the power to bind and loose, and who was directly constituted head over all by Christ Himself. The importance of this forgery lay in this—that the ideal of the future was represented as a fact of the past, and the papal primacy was set forth as an original institution of the Church of Christ. The end of the century in which these decretals appeared was a time of wild confusion, and when the Empire and the papacy at last revived, two centuries of disorder threw a halo of immemorial antiquity around these pious frauds. They appeared about 850 A.D., and it was not till the fifteenth century that Nicholas of Cusa began to express historic doubts concerning them. During the next hundred years after him Erasmus, the Magdeburg Centuriators, and, above all, the Calvinistic pastor, David Blondel, proved conclusively that they were mere forgeries. Even Rome herself has long since given them up, though, characteristically, she has never ceased to profit by them.

2. There is a further consideration of importance. If we accept the claim of the Pope to apostolic succession and apostolic authority, we must at the same time accept, as authoritative, teachings distinctly contrary to those set forth by the apostles themselves. Even Romanists

do not pretend that all the doctrines of their Church are to be found in the Scriptures. Cardinal Wiseman, for example, explains in one of his "Lectures on the Doctrines and Practices of the Roman Catholic Church," the process by which Catholics become Protestants. The process, he says, in every case, is simply this: Somehow the man comes to be possessed of a Bible, and on reading it he is surprised to find no mention of transubstantiation or auricular confession; not one word about purgatory or the worship of images. "He goes to his priest and tells him that he cannot find these doctrines; his priest argues with him and endeavours to convince him that he should shut up the book that is leading him astray: he perseveres; he abandons the communion of the Church of Rome — that is, as it is commonly expressed, the errors of that Church — and becomes a Protestant. Now in all that the man was a Protestant before he began his inquiry: he started with the principle that whatever is not in that book is not correct—that is the principle of Protestantism." (p. 12.) Of course, in the Cardinal's judgment, this is a wrong principle, and we are to infer that the so-called successors of the apostles do not pretend to narrow themselves down to apostolic teaching. It seems to some of us that they do not expand it so much as directly contradict it. It certainly must be a strange process of mind which can succeed in reconciling the doctrine of Justification by Faith as taught in the Epistle to the Romans with that taught by the Church of Rome; or Peter's teaching as to the Forgiveness of Sins through repentance and faith with the Roman Catholic doctrine of Penance for sin. Indeed, one may apply this remark to most of the doctrines regarded as distinctive of the Papal Church—

the infallibility of papal decisions, auricular confession to, and absolution by, a priest, the invocation of saints, the sacrifice of the Mass, and the pains of purgatory. The doctrine of Indulgences as coarsely and even scandalously expressed by Tetzel roused Luther to indignation and action, but even as defined by Leo X. in a decretal addressed to Cardinal Cajetan in 1518 it amounts to a gross contradiction both of the letter and spirit of Scripture. That decretal declared that by the power of the Keys committed to Peter and his successors the guilt of sin could be remitted by the sacrament of penance; and its temporal punishment by Indulgences, which proceeded from the superabundant merits of Christ and the Saints; that the authority of the Pope could confer an Indulgence by means of absolution, and could transfer it to those in Purgatory by means of intercession.

Then, again, take the worship of the Virgin. Striking indeed is the contrast between the simple, beautiful womanliness of Mary, as we see her in the Gospel story, and the fulsome and even blasphemous adulation of her which has culminated in the dogma of the Immaculate Conception. This cult of the Virgin has grown to something inconceivable and incredible. She has been made to invade and possess the very throne of God Himself. She is called our "Co-Redemptress"; she is even said to be "Co-present" in the sacrament of the Eucharist. Dr. Faber declared that "to St. Ignatius was shown at Mass the very part of the Host which had once belonged to Mary." "Here in England," Faber goes on to say, "Mary is not half enough preached. Thousands of souls perish because she is withheld from them." So that she who was once set forth as Mediatrix with the Redeemer is now declared to have been even our Co-Redemptress. The evidence for this is to be found not in the mere loose talk of ignorant priests, but in the formal answers from archbishops and bishops to the Pope as to what they desired in regard to the declaration of the Immaculate Conception as an Article of Faith. The Archbishop of Syracuse, the bishop of Asti, of Cariati, of Almeria, and others justified the attributes "Companion of the Redeemer," "Co-Redemptress," "Authoress of Everlasting Salvation."[1] Such wild and unwarranted talk on the part of archbishops and bishops was outstripped by Pope Pius IX. himself. It is with a shock of painful surprise that, in the Salon Podesti of the Galleria Pia in the Vatican, one comes upon the vast fresco painted by order of this Pope to celebrate the promulgation of the Dogma of the Immaculate Conception in 1870. In the upper half of this fresco there are three thrones; on the right is the representation of God the Father, on the left that of God the Son, and *in the central place* between them is Mary. Her figure is the same height as theirs, and together with them she forms a new Trinity, the Spirit in the form of a dove hovering over her head. Trede has well said that Michel Angelo would never have painted a fresco like that to any man's order.[2]

3. Among the Notes said to be characteristic of a true Church there are two to which the papacy lays special claim—*Unity* and *Sanctity*. Let us examine this claim. First as to *Unity*. The first thing that suggests

---

[1] *An Eirenicon*, by E. B. Pusey, D.D., 1865, p. 151.

[2] *Das Heidentum in der römischer Kirche*, von Th. Trede, 1890, ii. 341. I first saw this fresco during a visit to Rome in 1889. A photograph of it, obtained from Spithoever, the bookseller in the Piazza di Spagna, is before me as I write.

itself as we examine the facts is, that such Unity as there is was only attained after several centuries, and was attained by the destruction of the liberties of other Churches and the forcible absorption of rights all along the line. The Churches were gradually brought under the control of bishops, bishops were subjected to metropolitans, metropolitans to primates and patriarchs, and finally these were in their turn subjected to the Pope. The individuality of the various National Churches was merged into Unity by gradual encroachments on the part of Rome. And this not without resistance and ever-recurring conflict. Even the Unity which is supposed to be created by having one Head, in the person of the Pope, will not bear very close examination. If we take the period of four centuries and a half before the Reformation, during which the papacy attained to its greatest height of power and splendour, the Unity is seen to be but of chequered and uncertain sort. Even before we reach the Great Schism of 1378, when for six-and-thirty years there were two separate and opposing lines of Popes, one at Rome and one at Avignon, again and again we come upon rival Popes, both claiming to be the successor of Peter and possessor of Peter's authority. From 963 A.D., when Benedict V. was set up as anti-pope to Leo VIII., down to 1328 A.D., when Nicholas V. became the rival of John XXII., there were no fewer than nineteen anti-popes, each of them the leader of a hostile party and each in succession claiming to be the only lawful Head of the Church, in opposition to nineteen others. A Council of the Church sat from November, 1380, till March, 1381, for the purpose of determining which was the real Pope — Urban VI. or Clement VII. In 1411 there were three claimants to the papacy all at once. Earlier still, in 1044, Benedict IX. and his family having filled Rome with robbery and murder, the populace rose in furious revolt, drove him out of the city, and elected Sylvester in his place. After forty-nine days the friends of Benedict reinstated him, but again he was compelled to abdicate; before doing so, however, he unblushingly sold the papacy to Gregory VI., like a piece of merchandise, for money. All three Popes were living in Rome at the same time; one in the Lateran, another in St. Peter's, and the third in the church of St. Maria Maggiore.[1] In 1061 Anselm of Lucca was placed upon the papal chair by means of the arms of Richard of Capua as Alexander II.; on the other hand the German and Lombard bishops, assembled at Basle, raised the Veronese Cadalus to the papacy as Honorius II. These two Popes, the one in Rome, the other on the farther side of the Alps, were each busily engaged making warlike preparations to drive his rival from the Lateran by force of arms. It was no mere personal question. Behind the two Popes were the two world-powers themselves—the Roman Church and the Roman Empire—and their struggles for the tiara deluged the city with blood. For more than a year Rome was the scene of a terrible civil war, while the two Popes, on whose behalf it was waged, sat one in the Lateran, the other in Hadrian's fortress, singing masses, issuing decrees and bulls, and heaping anathemas on one another's heads.[2]

Turning from the note of *Unity* to that of *Sanctity*, so far as the Popes themselves are concerned, we are still less impressed with their claim to apostolic power and

---

[1] Otto of Friesing, *Chron.*, vi. 32.
[2] Gregorovius iv. 144.

grace. In every Church, no doubt, there have been unworthy men, and Churches must not be altogether judged by individuals; still, when, as in the case of Rome, there is one definite line of men who, above all others, claim to have possession of Divine powers and to be the exclusive channels of supernatural grace, and on that account refuse to recognise as Churches of Christ all communities not subject to themselves, it becomes both a right and a duty to test their pretensions by the standard which Christ Himself has given us. The unvarying natural law is that men do not gather grapes of thorns, or figs of thistles; our Lord therefore said of the ecclesiastics of His own time—" by their fruits ye shall know them." This test commends itself to every man's common sense, and we may fairly apply it to the Popes in view of the supernatural claims they make for themselves. Exalted claims need to be supported by exalted signs. Let us see how far this has been the case.

There have been between four and five hundred bishops of Rome within historic times. Some of them were scarcely seated on the pontifical throne before they were called away by death or were overthrown by sedition. Among the rest there were men of conspicuous power, like Leo I. or Gregory I. or Gregory VII., born leaders of men, who left their mark on their time, but who may be described as statesmen rather than as theologians, and whose triumphs were in the secular rather than in the spiritual sphere. Others were men of simple piety, but not remarkable for special force in any way; while others again were men of the world, fighting for worldly ends with the most carnal of weapons. There have been Popes of

Rome endowed with more of the military instinct than the apostolic. Benedict VIII. (1012–1024), inheriting the warlike tendencies of his kinsmen, the Counts of Tusculum, led his troops in person against the Crescentii in the Sabina; and Innocent II. (1130–1143) spent much of his life as a general in military expeditions. In 1139 we find him collecting an army and marching to S. Germano against King Roger of Sicily. When in 1378 Count Robert of Geneva was elected Pope as Clement VII., he was chosen by the cardinals as a man of vigour. The fact which recommended him to their favour was, that the previous year, as Legate in North Italy, he had put down a rising of Cesena against his soldiers by a pitiless massacre of the whole city. For three days and three nights the carnage raged inside, while the gates were kept shut so that none could escape. Five thousand perished in the slaughter of that awful time. Again, we find Julius II. marching against Perugia in 1509, mounted on horseback and wearing a rochet: before him was carried a cross, and a bishop bore the Host, the symbols of the broken body and shed blood of Him who said, "My kingdom is not of this world: if My kingdom were of this world, then would My servants fight." Julius made no secret of his preferences. When Michael Angelo, modelling his statue, suggested that the left hand might hold a book, "Nay," said this Vicar of Christ, "give me a sword, for I am no scholar." At the siege of Mirandola in 1511 he was in person in camp, roundly abusing his generals for their incapacity, "with copious garniture of military oaths and coarse jests." We find him presiding at councils of war, arranging the position of cannon, directing military operations and inspecting his troops.

While some of the Popes were more military than ecclesiastical, others, like Nicholas I. and John VIII., were mere politicians, totally absorbed in aims of temporal dominion, and drawing the papacy deep into the current of Italian politics. Hildebrand, as Gregory VII., aimed as resolutely at the sovereignty of the world and trampled on the neck of princes as absolutely as ever did Napoleon himself. Out of his vast ambitions there came a struggle between the Imperial crown and the papal tiara longer and more terrible than the Thirty Years' War of centuries later. Besieged in S. Angelo by Robert Guiscard, who took Rome by storm for his rescue, it has been well said that Gregory in the burning city—burning on his account—was as terrible a man of destiny as Napoleon, calmly riding over bloody fields of battle, the horrors committed by both ending in exile and death for both.

So again, if we turn to the elementary principles of simple morality, we find that many of the Popes fall below the most ordinary standard. Take the description which a modern historian has given of Æneas Sylvius, who, as Pius II., was Pope from 1458 to 1464. He had lived, says Creighton, amongst dissolute companions, and had been as dissolute as the worst among them. He cannot be said to have had any principle in life except that of making himself comfortable wherever he was. In those days chastity was a mark of a saintly character, and Æneas never professed to be a saint. He took no other view of life than that of a selfish voluptuary, for whom the nobler side of things did not exist.[1] Gieseler (v. 12) has quoted part of a letter of his written to his father, announcing the birth of a natural son, in

[1] *History of the Papacy*, ii. 245, 279, 477.

which he openly treats the most ordinary rules of chastity as counsels of perfection, meant only for exceptional men.

Yet loose as were the principles of Pius II. before his elevation to the pontificate, he may almost be called a saint when placed in comparison with some who sat in Peter's Chair before and after him. In 955 John XII. was elected Pope at the early age of eighteen. From the beginning he plunged into the most unbridled sensuality, made the gilded youth of the city his daily companions, and turned the Lateran palace into an abode of riot and debauchery. In 963 the licentious life of the Pope was reported to the Emperor by the Imperial agents. They told how he had squandered towns and estates upon his mistresses, and how that no respectable woman dared any longer to make a pilgrimage to Rome for fear of falling into his power. A synod was called, and a citation issued, in which it is said to John : " Charges so disgraceful are laid to your account, that were they reported of even a comedian, they would make us blush for shame . . . Learn, therefore, that you have been accused, not by a few persons only, but by the world at large, by laity as well as clergy, of murder and perjury, of sacrilege and of incest." This successor of Peter thus accused, returned this brief answer : "John, Bishop, servant of the servants of God, to all the bishops —We have heard that you wish to appoint another Pope. If you do so, I will excommunicate you by the Almighty God, and you shall neither confer Orders nor celebrate Mass" (*Liutprand*, c. 13).

In the following century the overthrow of the Crescentii in Rome left the field vacant for the Counts of Tusculum, who transformed the Chair of

Peter into an hereditary possession from 1012 to 1048. The third Pope of this Tusculan house was Benedict IX. (1033-1048). He was only twelve years old when he was made head of the Church and Vicar of Christ upon earth, and at the hands of this child bishops were not ashamed to receive consecration and the symbols of their dignities. With the development of his physical powers the young Pope entered upon a career of shameless profligacy. One of his successors in the pontificate, Victor III. (1086), relates how Benedict robbed and murdered in Rome. He shuddered, he says, to confess how profligate and vicious this man's life had been; and Rudolf Glaber, a monk of Cluny, and a contemporary, has painted the hideous form of this monster against the background of his time when pestilence and famine were devastating Europe.

It is not necessary to go on to speak of Alexander VI. The world has heard enough, and more than enough, of Rodrigo Borgia and his son Cæsar, the cardinal. Their names have become a very synonyme for lust and rapine and murder. They and others of their kind, who with them have sat in the loftiest hierarchical places, seem as if they were meant to serve as bitter satire on the sheer emptiness of all priestly claims. Nor need we show how utterly foreign to the spirit of Christ have been those who have organised persecution and massacre against the saints of God. The great body of thoughtful men will never accept as the only representatives of Him who came to seek and save, the Popes who blest Philip of Spain as he set up his Council of Blood, and sent fire and sword through the Netherlands; who gave benediction to that King of France who organised and relentlessly carried out the massacre of St. Bartholomew; who smiled upon the Inquisition; and beneath whose favour the valleys of Piedmont were desolated with cruel slaughter. It is useless to say these men were only acting in the spirit of their time. They themselves created that spirit, and created it even while they were claiming to be the sole keepers of that Church whose aim and mission is to set up God's kingdom of the heavens upon this earth of ours.

LECTURE X

THE ANGLICAN CHURCH IN TUDOR TIMES

LECTURE X

THE ANGLICAN CHURCH IN TUDOR TIMES

IN the fall, first of Pagan and then of Papal Rome, history in one respect repeated itself. For it was Germany, in the person of the Goths, that, after centuries of powerful rule, brought the first Rome to its end; and again, a thousand years later, it was Germany, in the person of Luther, that shook the second Rome to its foundations, after generations of masterful sway. The first Rome fell not merely because the Goths were at the gates, but because its work was done. It had done much. It had taught the nations the art of government and given to them a great and enduring system of law. But it had also robbed these nations of liberty; and as century was added to century, the virtues of free men were being more and more effaced by the habit of blind submission to authority. The hour had come for the sturdy nations of the north to emerge from obscurity and rejuvenate the world. In like manner when Luther appeared the time had come for the nations to rise from the long sleep of ages and create a new era of freedom and spiritual life.

Incomplete as was the Protestant Reformation, it marks the transition from the mediæval to the modern world. In England it arose under different conditions and took a different course from that which it took on the continent of Europe. On the Continent the reformation of doctrine came first and the separation from Rome followed as a consequence. In England, on the contrary, the separation from Rome preceded the reformation of doctrine. We may safely say that, even if Henry VIII. had not broken with Rome on the matter of the divorce, the Reformation would have come sooner or later. The feeling was in the air, and the process of preparation had been going on for centuries. The seed sown by the Lollard preachers, the propaganda of the Christian Brothers, and the placing of the New Testament in the hands of the people by William Tyndale, had not been in vain. It would have come, therefore, even if there had been no divorce of Katharine; but coming as it did accounts for the fact that the separation from Rome was made absolute and complete in the reign of Henry VIII., and the reformation of doctrine and worship, so far as it went, was not carried out till the reign of Edward VI.

The policy of Thomas Cromwell in bringing about a severance from Rome effected a complete revolution both in the civil and ecclesiastical government of the country, but the ecclesiastical revolution was very much the more thorough and complete of the two; and we have now reached the point when it may be well to inquire how far that revolution affected the question of Apostolical Succession in the Anglican Church.

The continuity of the Church of England before and after the Reformation will be regarded differently by different men according to their Church relations and personal prepossessions. The Anglican Churchman maintains that the changes made were not such as to destroy the identity of the Church; and that the English Reformers themselves had no intention of setting up a new institution in place of the old. On the other hand, Dr. Makower, an eminent German jurist, being unaffected by Anglican influences, and having, after the German manner, made an exhaustive study of the constitutional question,[1] arrives at a different conclusion. When it is said that the transition from the old to the new was made in valid form, and that there is no material difference in character between the English Church before and after the Reformation, this writer contends that in neither of these two senses is it true that the development of the Reformation period was in uninterrupted connexion with the past. For so far as the form is concerned in which the change was made, two important facts have to be noted: (1) As to the independence of the ecclesiastical authorities in England, the power of the Pope to govern and make rules had been recognised for centuries by decisive acts of State; therefore, when England, by resolution of her national representatives, renounced for the future all acknowledgment of the papal authority, the step thus taken at the Reformation must be accounted revolutionary and indicative of a distinct breach with the past. Then (2) as to the relations of the State to the English authorities of the Church. According to constitutional law as it prevailed before the Reformation the State was not entitled to issue ordinances upon purely ecclesiastical matters; the exclusive right of the Church to make

[1] *Die Verfassung der Kirche von England*, von Felix Makower, Dr. Jur. Berlin 1894.

such ordinances was not contested by the civil power, but was regarded as a right inherent in the Church, and not dependent on the consent of the State. Whereas in the days of Henry VIII., Edward VI., and Elizabeth important laws were passed, the Royal Supremacy was imposed, and the reformed Prayer Book introduced by the sole act of the civil power, Convocation being either not consulted or expressedly hostile to the measure adopted. So that the " prerogatives of the Crown " and the "laws and customs of the land" bore a totally different meaning after the Reformation from that which they had before it, and this change in meaning was brought about by a legal rupture, and the statutes by which that rupture was effected remain permanently operative. Such being the fact, the changes made consisting in the complete abolition of all papal authority in England and in the transference of almost all rights of government previously exercised by the Pope to the English sovereign, these changes involved an alteration of the constitution of the Church in the very point which must be regarded as decisive. For the peculiar *essentia* of the Roman Church consisted not so much in the distinctive character of its offices as in the existence of a central power outside the various nations, and which claimed to stand above them. The Reformation in England struck directly at this power, and must be regarded as having produced a *fundamental change* in the constitution of the Church; therefore, from the standpoint of legal history, the doctrine of continuous development must be rejected.

The truth is, the only way in which the identity of the English Church before and after the Reformation can be maintained is by regarding the people, the

Christian Commonalty, and not the succession of bishops as constituting the Church. However smoothed over, the breach between the Old Church and the New was as complete as it could well be made. On one side, that of king and Parliament: the Act of Appeals, the Act for the Submission of the Clergy, the Act for restraining the payment of Annates, and that restraining the payment of Peter's-pence, and other exactions of the Pope had made an end of all existing relations between the Church of England and the Papal See; while the great Act of Supremacy had, so far as legislation could do it, transferred the papal authority to the king. Then on the other side, as far as the Pope was concerned, by his bull of excommunication and deposition against the king and all his abettors, Paul III. made the separation final and complete.

To this the Anglican Churchman will probably reply that the changes thus brought about did not affect the spiritual authority of the Church, which was passed on from generation to generation by means of the succession of bishops; and that the commission from Heaven remains unaffected by mundane revolutions and the decrees of kings and popes. This would be a valid and sufficient answer if only the reality of Apostolical Succession, and of the transmission thereby of supernatural power and grace, had first been shown to be established on something like solid historical foundation. This, however, is precisely the thing we have hitherto sought for and have not found. So far as we have seen, the continuous life of Christ in the world has not been perpetuated through the succession of diocesan bishops, but along the unbroken line of believing Christian men; the spiritual influence there is in the world comes direct from the Spirit of God; and the Divine commission and personal qualifications of every true minister of Christ take their rise from the personal contact of the living soul with the living God. In the light of these facts we are entitled to ask: Is there anything in the history of the Anglican Church since she separated from Rome at the Reformation which can supply the evidence hitherto so conspicuously wanting? Is there anything in her formularies or in the course taken by her leaders which may satisfy any fair-minded inquirer that by virtue of her organisation she possesses a certain mysterious, supernatural grace which other Churches, not so constituted, do not possess?

As soon as we set forth in search of an answer to these questions the first thing which forcibly strikes us is the fact that the Anglican claim to Apostolical Succession, with all it is supposed to involve, is a thing comparatively recent and modern. By this, of course, we do not mean that episcopacy, government by bishops, was a new thing in the Church, for this went on after the Reformation as before. But episcopacy as a convenient system for administering Church life and worship is one thing, and episcopacy as laying claim to exclusive supernatural powers quite another. It is this latter claim we maintain to be recent and modern. It is safe to say that, for more than half a century after England broke with the See of Rome, no such claim to power and grace, conferred *jure divino* by means of the hierarchy, was ever made. Further, when towards the end of the sixteenth century it began to be made it was made only by a particular school or party, polemically, as the best way of counteracting the claim to Divine right made for their own system by the Presbyterians. For long after it was put forward it was not regarded seriously or widely accepted. The Anglican School can scarcely be said to have taken its rise till the first three decades of the seventeenth century. Towards the end of that time—the time of the Laudian reaction—Apostolical Succession began to be the watchword, ecclesiastically, of the comparatively small party in the State which, politically, held to a belief in the Divine right of kings, and taught in their extremest form those doctrines of passive obedience and non-resistance which Mr. Gladstone has described as "the plague-spot of the Church of England." After the convulsion produced by the Civil Wars, and the changes introduced by the Commonwealth and the Revolution of 1688, the doctrine was revived by the Nonjurors, and feebly maintained on into the eighteenth century by that mistaken and moribund party. Practically it is only within the last sixty or seventy years, that is, since the rise of the Oxford Movement, that it has been advanced with anything like boldness and persistence by any considerable party in the Church.

To establish this position is, in view of present-day controversies, of more than ordinary importance. To make it quite clear, therefore, let us (1) examine the formularies of the Church after the separation from Rome; (2) mark the Erastian character of the newly-established Church; (3) recall the known opinions of the Elizabethan divines; and (4) trace the policy pursued by the authorities of the Church in relation to foreign Protestant Churches and Presbyterian Orders.

I.

First, then, let us examine the authoritative documents and formularies of the newly-organised Church. To begin with, we will take the important period between 1534, when England was formally separated from the See of Rome, and 1553, when the death of Edward VI. put a stop for a time to the work of Reformation. Naturally, from the way the change was brought about by Henry VIII., these documents were much less Protestant in tone in the earlier part of this period than they became in the later. The Ten Articles of 1536, for example, are very different from the Forty-two of 1552, which became the Thirty-nine of 1563. This difference in the Articles is simply a reflection of the difference in the feeling of the nation. It was not till 1546 that even Cranmer and Latimer gave up their belief in the actual corporal presence of Christ in the Eucharist; and Hooper, writing to his friend Bullinger in that same year, can only say: "Our king has destroyed the Pope but not popery. . . . The impious Mass, the most shameful celibacy of the clergy, the invocation of saints, auricular confession, superstitious abstinence from meats, and purgatory, were never before held by the people in greater esteem than at the present moment."[1] Bonner and Gardiner, who burnt Cranmer and Latimer in Mary's time, sat on the same Commissions with them in Henry's time. It is important, therefore, carefully to note dates and observe the progress of events and opinions at a time when men's minds were undergoing rapid changes, as they do in a period of convulsion and transition. The

[1] *Zurich Letters*, 1537-1558, p. 36.

Ten Articles of 1536, the first document we come to after the eventful year 1534, had very little that was Protestant about them. They were drawn up in the king's own handwriting, introduced in Convocation July 11th, and agreed to the same day, so that the clergy did little more than register the opinions of a king who, so far as doctrine was concerned, was never a Protestant at heart. These Articles of Faith and Ceremonies teach—that children dying without baptism could not be saved; that confession to a priest is necessary; and that the words of the priest pronouncing absolution "are the very words of God Himself, as if He should speak unto us out of heaven;" transubstantiation was left unchanged; and it was affirmed that we may pray for the dead, and offer Masses for the repose of their souls; finally, superstitious ceremonies, such as sprinkling holy water, bearing candles on Candlemas Day, giving ashes on Ash Wednesday, bearing palms on Palm Sunday, and creeping to the cross and kissing it on Good Friday, were enjoined to be kept as being good and laudable.

These Ten Articles gave satisfaction to neither side. They went too far for some and not far enough for others, so that while they were issued under the title, "Articles to stablish Christian quietness," they only produced deeper discord. It was found they would not do; the following year, therefore, a special Commission was summoned to meet at Lambeth to prepare a fuller Manual of Faith, as an official exposition of the doctrine of the English Church. This Manual, issued in 1537 under the title *The godly and pious Institution of a Christian man*, and popularly known as "The Bishops' Book," was again a compromise between two contending parties ever growing wider apart. Cranmer, Latimer, and Barlow were on one side, Gardiner and Stokesly on the other; and, as Strype says, "In the course of the work Gardiner, the Pope's chief champion, with three or four other bishops, went about with all subtle sophistry to maintain all idolatry, heresy, and superstition."[1] When the bishops had finished with it the king took the book in hand and altered it to his liking, with the result that the archbishop "disliked some of the things the king wrote."

Three years later it was found that this Manual also needed revision. In 1540, therefore, a second Commission was instituted, which showed a great and memorable change of opinion on the part of Cranmer and some other bishops. Certain subjects in the form of Queries were proposed beforehand to the members of this Commission, on which, at a time specified, they were to give in their opinions in writing. In the seventeenth century Bishop Stillingfleet found these Answers to the Queries at Lambeth, and Bishop Burnet printed them in the Collection of Records at the end of the first volume of his *History of the Reformation*, as the Stillingfleet MSS. The ninth Query propounded was as to whether the apostles made bishops themselves because there happened to be no Christian king to make them, or by authority from God. On this point the two archbishops were at issue. The Archbishop of York was of opinion that the apostles had power to make bishops, priests and deacons, which power they derived from Christ and Christ alone. On the other hand, Archbishop Cranmer held that "all Christian princes have committed unto them immediately of God

[1] *Life of Cranmer*, fol. 1694.

the whole cure of all their subjects, as well concerning the administration of God's Word for the cure of souls as concerning the ministration of things political and civil governance." Also that while in the admission of the clergy to their functions "divers comely ceremonies and solemnities be used, this is not of necessity, but only for good order and seemly fashion; for if such offices and ministrations were committed without such solemnity, they were nevertheless truly committed; and *there is no more promise of God that grace is given in the committing of the ecclesiastical office, than it is in the committing of the civil office.*" Barlow, the bishop of St. David's, agreed that the apostles ordained other bishops because in their time there lacked a Christian prince to do it. Dr. Cox, afterwards bishop of Ely, held that "the apostles had authority of God to exhort and induce men to set forth God's honour and so to make them priests." On the other hand, the Archbishop of York, with several others, held that the apostles made bishops by authority given them from God. The Archbishop of Canterbury, in reply to further questions, held that "bishops and priests were at one time and were no two things, but both one office in the beginning of Christ's religion;" and that "he that is appointed to be a bishop or a priest, needeth not consecration by the Scripture, for election or appointment thereto is sufficient." So also thought Barlow and Cox, while others held consecration to be requisite. The bishop of London was of opinion that bishops came first, yet he thought it "not of importance whether the priest then made the bishop or else the bishop the priest."

The book for which these queries and answers prepared the way occupied these divines some three years in the making, being published in 1543 under the title of *A Necessary Doctrine and Erudition for any Christian Man.* The preface was written in the name of the king, and, according to the title-page, the book was "set forth by the King's Majesty of England," in distinction from the "Bishops' Book" of 1537; therefore it was popularly known as the "King's Book," and was regarded as an authorised statement of the Teaching of the Church. It consisted of various parts, one of which was the Apostle's Creed and in the ninth article of that Creed, on the Holy Catholic Church, according to Bishop Burnet, it defines that Church "as comprehending all assemblies of men over the whole world that receive the faith of Christ; who ought to hold an Unity of love and brotherly agreement together, by which they become members of the Catholic Church." [1]

In its final form portions of the "King's Book" expressed the reactionary opinions of the king rather than those of the archbishop. Strype says (p. 100): "For indeed there were some parts therein which the archbishop himself did not approve of; foisted into it by Winchester's means and interest at that time with the king [*i.e.*, by Bishop Gardiner]. He knew well enough that Winchester's hand was in it; and so he told him plainly in King Edward's time, telling him in relation thereto that he had seduced the king."

---

[1] Dr. Hort, in his *Ecclesia*, p. 2, says: "*Congregation* was the only rendering of ἐκκλησια in the English New Testament as it stood throughout Henry VIII.'s reign, the substitution of *Church* being due to the Genevan revisers; and it held its ground in the Bishops' Bible in no less primary a passage than Matt. xvi. 18, till the Jacobean revision of 1611, which we call the Authorised Version."

When we arrive at the reign of Edward VI., we find that while there was no addition to legislation so far as the Church was concerned, there were great and important changes in the doctrine of the Church, and that in a Protestant direction. The documents of special significance belonging to this time were the two Prayer Books of 1549 and 1552, the Articles of the Church, and the Ordinal, or "Form and manner of making, ordaining and consecrating of Bishops, Priests, and Deacons."

The publication of the Prayer Book of 1549 has been described as probably the most important event which had taken place in the English Church since the Synod of Whitby in 664, A.D.[1] "In 1549," says Strype, "the Common Prayer Book, by the great care and study of the archbishop, was now furnished and settled by Act of Parliament." Important as the book was, it is extremely doubtful whether it ever received the sanction of Convocation. There is no mention of any debate upon it in any contemporary records. It was mainly Cranmer's work, and while it was a compilation from the various Service Books already existing in the Church, it was mainly a revision and translation from the Latin of the breviary and missal and pontifical according to the Use of Sarum, with additions, some of which were from the reformed Roman breviary published by Cardinal Quignon in 1535, some from contemporary Lutheran sources, the rest being the composition of Cranmer himself. The Communion Service was almost wholly adopted from the Sarum Missal with some very important alterations and omissions. The preparation of

[1] *History of the Church of England*, by H. O. Wakeman, 4th ed., 1897, p. 274.

the priest both before he began Mass, and before the oblation of the elements called the lesser oblation, was almost entirely omitted, also the ceremonies of the fraction and the elevation of the host and the kissing of the pax; moreover, the whole of the service was to be said or sung plainly and directly instead of being said secretly as before; and further there was a careful exclusion of such words of the Mass as had become associated with the doctrine of transubstantiation. Other changes also were made in other parts of the book. Only the names of such saints as were mentioned in the Scripture were admitted, and there was left out all direct invocation of saints and all mention of purgatory.[1] The Prayer Book of 1549 was a distinct harking back to Scripture, primitive teaching and usage.

If this is true of the Prayer Book as published in 1549, still more is it true of it as it was revised and issued in 1552, when, though brought nearly to its present form, it was made more thoroughly unsacramentarian than it has ever been since. Cranmer was the active agent in the revision, as he had been in the compilation, and all the time he was in close intercourse with the foreign Protestants; with Peter Martyr, who was Professor of Divinity at Oxford, and with Martin Bucer, who held the same position at Cambridge; while John à Lasco, Paul Fagius, Peter Alexander, Bernardinus Ochinus, and others were his honoured guests at Lambeth. The influence of these men, about whose thorough Protestantism there can be no mistake, is very manifest in the revision of the Prayer Book of 1552. Strype[2] tells us that when Cranmer had completed his own part

[1] *Wakeman*, 275-8. [2] *Life of Cranmer*, fol. ed., p. 210.

in that work he desired Bucer to examine the book and make suggestions, which he did: "and such deference was given to his judgement that most of the things that he excepted against were corrected accordingly." On Peter Martyr also being asked for his opinion: "he agreed clearly with Bucer, disapproving of the things of which Bucer had disapproved." The changes thus made are most significant, for they were all in an anti-sacerdotalist direction. The expression, "the *priest* shall first receive the communion in both kinds," was altered to "the *minister* shall first receive, &c."; the sentence, "when he delivereth *the sacrament of the body of Christ*," was made to read, "when he delivereth *the bread*"; the expression in the Communion Service, "the body of our Lord Jesus Christ preserve thy body and soul to eternal life," took this form, "Take and eat this *in remembrance* that Christ died for thee and feed on Him in thy heart by faith with thanksgiving"; and similarly also on taking the cup—" Drink this *in remembrance* that Christ's blood was shed for thee and be thankful." An Anglican of to-day admits that the Prayer Book of 1552 "marks the extreme point to which the Church of England ever went in the direction of compromise with those who held Zwinglian or Calvinist views."[1]

When we turn from the Prayer Book to the Articles the same strong Protestant tendency is clearly manifest. In the Parliament of 1549 an Act was passed "that the King's Majesty may nominate and appoint thirty-two persons to peruse and make ecclesiastical laws." No steps were, however, taken under this Act till 1551 when a Commission was appointed consisting of the

[1] *Wakeman*, p. 295.

archbishop and the following bishops: Goodrich, Ridley, Poynet, Coverdale, Barlow, Hooper, Latimer, and Scory—all of them, except perhaps Barlow, men of deepening Protestant convictions. Among others on the Commission along with the bishops were John à Lasco and Peter Martyr, as foreign Protestants both of them Presbyterians. At the head of the Commission was, of course, the archbishop himself and among the works to which he applied himself was the drawing up of a code of "Articles of Faith for the Reformed Church of England." In the course of the following year, within the period allowed by the Act, he produced the Forty-two Articles, which in 1563 were shortened to the Thirty-nine. They were finally approved of and published in May, 1553, and put forth by the king's authority. The influence of the foreign Protestants is even more marked upon the Articles than upon the Prayer Book. They were based in great measure upon the Confession of Augsburg. Article XIX., defining the Church, is taken from Article VII. of that Confession, which says: "The Church is a Congregation of Saints in which the Gospel is rightly taught and the sacraments rightly administered"; Article XXIII., "Of Ministering in the Congretion," defines a minister in precisely the same way as Article XIV. of the Augsburg Confession, and merely says that no one should take upon himself the ministerial office till he is lawfully called by men who have public authority given unto them in the congregation, which is no more than every Presbyterian or Congregationalist would say, though they might differ as to what the public authority ought to be. Again, Article XXXVI., "Of Consecration of Bishops and Ministers," simply says that the Ordinal recently set forth, which indeed was Cranmer's own work, is sufficient and yet not superstitious ; it does not, any more than the Preface to the Ordinal, declare that ministers not episcopally ordained are not true ministers of the Gospel.

The new Ordinal, or Ordination Service, was published in March, 1550, after the first Prayer Book and before the second. The ordinale and pontificale according to the Use of Sarum formed its groundwork, and a recent Anglican writer claims that "all the essential parts of the old rites were most carefully retained."[1] On this point we may fairly refer him to the Pope, who in his "Letter Apostolic concerning Anglican Orders," issued in September, 1896, plainly and authoritatively declares that the essential parts were *not* retained. This is what the Pope says : " For the full and accurate understanding of the Anglican Ordinal there is nothing more pertinent than to consider carefully the circumstances under which it was composed and publicly authorised. The history of that time is sufficiently eloquent as to the animus of the authors of the Ordinal against the Catholic Church, as to the abettors whom they associated with themselves from the heterodox sects, and as to the end they had in view. Under a pretext of returning to the primitive form, they corrupted the liturgical order in many ways to suit the errors of the Reformers. For this reason in the whole Ordinal not only is there no clear mention of the sacrifice, of consecration, of the sacerdotium, and of the power of consecrating and offering sacrifice, but every trace of these things which had been in such prayers of the Catholic rite as they had not entirely rejected, was deliberately removed and struck out."

[1] *Wakeman*, p. 287.

II.

Passing now from historic documents to historic facts, we find that in the Tudor time the supreme place in the Church was accorded not to the bishops, but to the Crown. The sixteenth century has been described as the golden age of personal government, not in England alone but all over Europe; as a time when kings governed as well as reigned, and when "the king's will" was the *ultima ratio* with ministers, bishops, and judges alike. On an occasion when the question was argued before Henry VIII. as to whether the clergy were really amenable to the jurisdiction of the ordinary criminal law, he closed the arguments with the plain declaration: "By the permission and ordinance of God we are King of England, and the kings of England in times past had never any superior but God only." The act of 1531 made the king absolute as Supreme Head of the Church. How it appeared to outsiders may be gathered from the despatches of Chapuys to the Emperor Charles V. Under date February 14, 1531, he writes that "the clergy have been compelled, under pain of the law of Præmunire, to accept the king as head of the Church, which implies in effect as much as if they had declared him Pope of England."[1] A reference to the later Act of Supremacy of 1534 will show that this language is no exaggeration. It begins by saying that though "the King's Majesty justly and rightly is, and ought to be, the supreme head of the Church of England, and so is recognised by the clergy of this realm in their Convocations, yet nevertheless, for corroboration and confirmation thereof, and for increase

[1] *State Papers*, 1530-1.

of virtue in Christ's religion within this realm of England; be it enacted that the King, our Sovereign Lord, shall be taken, accepted and reputed the only supreme head in earth of the Church of England called *Anglicana Ecclesia*, and shall have and enjoy all honours, dignities, pre-eminences, jurisdictions, privileges, authorities, immunities, profits and commodities to the said dignity of supreme head of the same Church belonging and appertaining; and that our said Sovereign Lord shall have full power and authority from time to time to visit, repress, redress, reform, order, correct, restrain, and amend all such errors, heresies, abuses, and offences, whatsoever they be, which by any manner, spiritual authority or jurisdiction ought or may lawfully be reformed, repressed or amended most to the pleasure of Almighty God and the increase of virtue in Christ's religion." The clergy in Convocation had tried to soften the royal supremacy by the saving clause—" as far as the law of Christ may permit," but these words were omitted in the Act which became the law of the land, and the absorption of the powers of all " manner of spiritual authority " with the prerogatives of the Crown was absolute and complete.

The authority thus comprehensively claimed was no mere formal thing. In the Convocation of 1536, for the first time, the king's lay vicar-general, Thomas Cromwell, appeared and took his seat next the archbishop, and signed documents, so far as appears, even before him. The previous year also Cromwell, in his capacity as the king's vicegerent and vicar-general, was directed to make a visitation of the whole clergy, and at the same time an inhibition was issued to the bishops forbidding them to exercise any jurisdiction while the visitation was pending. When the rights of jurisdiction were again transferred to them, they were given as rights emanating from the Crown and subject to recall. The commission of the King to the bishop of Hereford is dated October 14, 1535, and gives him authority to ordain, institute, collate, invest, and remove in the diocese of Hereford. A similar commission for the exercise of episcopal functions was taken out by Bonner, as bishop of London, in 1539, which Burnet has printed in his *Collection of Records* (iii. 14); and it is said that even the archbishop himself took out such commission also. Thus the most comprehensive powers were placed in the hands of a lay sovereign and his lay vicar-general, who thus "as a matter of law invaded the region of hitherto exclusively clerical rights in a manner never before seen in the history of the Christian Church."

Take, again, the case of the Six Articles. These were in all probability Henry's own composition, represented exactly his own opinions, and were rightly regarded by the Protestants as reactionary. In the case of these Articles the supreme headship was shown to be a reality indeed. An emphatic and authoritative statement of doctrine was introduced into Parliament as "the king's will," a penal clause added because it is "the king's will," and it becomes the law of England binding upon clergy no less than laity. Yet all that Convocation had to do with it was that they were simply asked whether they approved of the doctrines. Even the ordinary forms of legislation in use in Convocation were omitted. The vicegerent comes and asks what the members think of the doctrine, and that is all, and if there was any deliberation it took place under the immediate superintendence of the lay vicar-general.[1]

[1] Child's *Church and State under the Tudors*, p. 84.

During the minority of Edward VI. the authority of the king was exercised by the Council of State. This was not less Erastian than Henry himself had been. At its very first sitting (February 2, 1547) an order was made that the bishops should renew their commissions. In this way they were shown that they held their authority simply from the Crown, and their episcopate, in virtue of the Act of Supremacy, was treated as only a creation of the royal pleasure. Their appointments were held to be ended by the death of the reigning prince, and were now renewed by letters patent, and to be continued during good behaviour.

Passing to the reign of Elizabeth, when the Church of England was practically made what she has since remained, it is needless to say that the new Queen retained the same absolute power in the Church which had been claimed in previous reigns. By the Acts of 1559 the Acts of the Royal Supremacy and of the Submission of the Clergy, which had been repealed in Mary's time, were restored in full, except that the Queen, while retaining the reality, declined the title of Supreme Head of the Church. The branches, sentences and words of the said several Acts were to extend as fully and largely to the new Queen as they ever did to her Highness's father; and ecclesiastical jurisdiction, all pre-eminences, spiritual and ecclesiastical, were united and annexed to the Imperial Crown of this realm as before.

Elizabeth was not slow to use the power she claimed. Even before the Acts of Henry VIII. had been restored she proceeded by proclamation to " tune the pulpits." She charged and commanded (December 27, 1558) " as well those that be called to ministry in the Church as all others, that they do forbear to preach or teach, or to give audience to any manner of doctrine or preaching, other than to the Gospel and Epistle of the day and to the Ten Commandments, without exposition or addition of any manner, sense or meaning to be applied and added." In a series of Injunctions issued by the Queen the following year, to be observed under penalty by her subjects, she commanded that "all ecclesiastical persons having the cure of souls should to the uttermost of their wit, knowledge, and learning," preach four times a year, at least, against all usurped and foreign power; that they should once a month, at least, purely and sincerely declare the Word of God, and exhort their hearers to works of faith, mercy and charity, and against pilgrimages, setting up of candles, praying with beads and such like superstitions. She further enjoins that in order "that the vice of damnable despair may be clearly taken away, and that firm belief and steadfast hope may be surely conceived of all their parishioners, being in any danger, the clergy shall learn and have always in readiness such comfortable places and sentences of Scripture as do set forth the mercy, benefits and goodness of Almighty God towards all penitent and believing persons."

When the Articles were revised for publication in 1563 she modified them herself both by insertion and exclusion. Dr. Lamb[1] has shown that it is almost a certainty that she alone was the author of the words in Article XX: "The Church hath power to decree rites or ceremonies, and authority in controversies of faith." For the clause was inserted there in the first printed copy of the Articles which was issued under the Queen's

[1] *Historical Account of the Thirty-nine Articles from* 1553-1571, by John Lamb, D.D., Master of Corpus Christi College, Cambridge, 1829.

authority in 1563, and was inserted after the Articles had passed the Convocation and before they could be published with authority. According to the requirements of the Act of Submission, in order to their having authority, it was necessary that the Great Seal should be attached to them, and to get this they came into the hands of the Queen. It is known that she kept the book for a twelvemonth, and before sending it forth she appended to it a statement that she had assented to it "after diligent reading and scrutiny by herself."

In 1566 an Act was passed declaring the making and consecrating of the archbishops and bishops of this realm to be good, lawful, and perfect; this Act alleging that the Queen, "by her supreme power and authority *hath* DISPENSED with all causes or doubts of any imperfection or disability that can or may in any way be objected against the same." Clerical orders of doubtful sort guaranteed and made valid by royal dispensation must be somewhat startling to believers in Apostolical Succession, yet the Act of 8 Eliz. c. i. remains to show that such things were not unknown in the days when the Anglican Church was in the process of being made what she has now become.

The truth is, it was Queen Elizabeth who was the formative force in shaping the Church of England, and all that her bishops could do was to stand by and let her have her way. Bishop Jewel, writing from Salisbury to his friend Bullinger in 1566, has to say: "I wish that all, even the slightest vestiges of popery might be removed from our churches, and above all from our minds. But the Queen at this time is unable to endure the least alteration in matters of religion."[1] All through

[1] *Zurich Letters*, 1558-1579, p. 149.

her reign her impetuous will was paramount. Convocation she made light of, and the bishops knew what it was to be browbeaten if they dared to cross her path. In 1576, for example, she commanded Archbishop Grindal to put a stop to the religious exercises known as " prophesyings," which were conferences of the clergy on portions of Scripture. The ministers of a certain division each gave in turn his explanation of a portion of Scripture agreed on beforehand, and then the moderator summed up the observations made and gave what he held to be the true sense. Grindal was unwilling to suppress these exercises. He thought they did the ministers good and the people too, who came in great numbers to hear and learn. He therefore declined to obey the Queen's command, respectfully giving his reasons, but it cost him his place as archbishop. For he was sequestered for six months in June, 1577, on account of non-compliance, and confined to his house. He afterwards submitted. Still he remained a nominal primate, without influence or power, until 1583, when he died; and this though in 1580 sixteen bishops of the province of Canterbury petitioned for his restoration, but in vain. There was arbitrary power on the one side and absolute submission on the other. Similarly in the case of Dr. Cox, the bishop of Ely. The Queen wished him to give up his palace in Holborn to a favourite of hers, Sir Christopher Hatton, and on his refusal, she, with a round oath, gave him to understand that as she had frocked him she would unfrock him unless he gave way, and eventually give way he did.

The age of the Tudors was the age of imperiousness on the part of the Crown, and acquiescence on the part of the subject. Even strong men were carried along with the stream. In 1536, for example, Miles Coverdale dedicated his translation of the Bible to Henry VIII., and in that dedication he plainly said that the Scripture declared most abundantly that the office and authority given unto kings is above all powers, "let them be Popes or Cardinals or whatsoever they will." In courtier-like fashion he goes on to say: "When your Grace's subjects read your letters, or begin to talk or commune of your Highness they move their bonnets for a sign or token of reverence unto your Grace, as to the most sovereign lord and head under God, which no man useth to do unto any bishop." By way of parallel to this, let us pass from 1536 to 1588, from Henry to Elizabeth, from Miles Coverdale to Dr. Hammond. Hammond was Chancellor of the diocese of London and an active member of the Court of High Commission. Men were beginning to talk in tentative fashion of the Divine right of bishops, and Lord Burleigh referred the matter to him for judgement. As a Church authority, and in judicial fashion, he gives it as his opinion that the name of bishops as importing superiority committed to a minister of the Word and Sacraments over many Churches and pastors is not to be found in the Scriptures; that the names of *episcopus* and *presbyter* imported one function, so that he that was a pastor or elder was also bishop, and the bishop in like sort called elder, and therefore the name of *episcopus* being no name of distinction in office from the elder, could not import superiority over elders. "For my part," he says, "I could yet never find one jot that signified a special authority of bishops and another of elders." As to the appoint under-officers in the execution of that government which he hath in ecclesiastical causes as well as he may do in civil matters, for the reason is all one in them both. . . . The bishops of our realm do not (so far as I ever yet heard), nor may not, claim to themselves any other authority than is given them by the statute of 25 Hen. VIII., recited in the first year of her Majesty's reign, or by other statutes of this land, neither is it reasonable they should make any other claim, for if it had pleased her Majesty to have used no bishops at all, we could not have complained justly of any defect in our Church ; or if it had liked them to limit the authority of bishops to shorter terms, they might not have said they had any wrong."[1]

III.

Thus Erastian principles prevailed in high places, and the bishops were subject to great pressure on the part of the Crown. Still, of course, it may be said that in spite of such pressure they themselves were believers in the doctrine of Apostolical Succession as now understood, and held to it as being the doctrine of the Church. To show that this was not the case we will now recall the known opinions of the Elizabethan bishops and divines, and let them speak for themselves. It is a comparatively easy thing to arrive at the facts, for there was a complete change in the Episcopate on the accession of Elizabeth. The men who went out were all Romanists, while the men who took their places were all pronounced Reformers. The new Act of Uniformity came into force on Midsummer Day, 1559, and, to their honour be it said, fifteen of those who had been bishops under

[1] Historical MSS. Commission—*Hatfield House MSS.* III., 754.

Mary, and were therefore papists, refused to stultify themselves by abjuring the Pope once more. The only man who faced about was Anthony Kitchin, bishop of Llandaff. As the precursor of the celebrated Vicar of Bray he contrived to continue in possession of his bishopric from 1545 to 1567, accommodating himself to all the changes introduced, and taking all the incongruous oaths required by Henry, Edward, Mary, and Elizabeth. He was the only exception, however. The rest of the Marian bishops refused to comply with the requirements of the Act of Uniformity, while others of them had died previously, so that the episcopal bench was cleared, and twenty new bishops were created in a very short time. The new men thus brought in had for the most part been exiles during the persecutions of Mary's reign, and during their residence at Frankfort, Zurich, and Geneva had come into closest relations of friendship with the German and Swiss Protestant Reformers, a friendship which was still continued in the most affectionate manner when the time of exile was over, as the *Zurich Letters* remain to testify. The men who came back and filled the offices of the Church under Elizabeth were—to give Milton's description of them— "the pastors of the saints and confessors who had suffered and died for evangelical truth. They had fled from the blood persecution, and had gathered up at length their scattered members into many congregations. These were the true Protestant divines of England, our fathers in the faith we hold."[1]

Thus, then, the question as to the opinions of the Elizabethan divines is reduced within comparatively

Elizabeth what it had been under Henry VIII., a mass of conflicting elements, Cranmer, Goodrich, Shaxton, and Latimer pulling all in the direction of Protestant reform, while Gardner, Stokesly, Tonstal, Longland, and Sherburne were working against them all they could for the papacy. Under Elizabeth the opinions of the bishops were all one way, and they were almost all of them in doctrine Zwinglian or Calvinist. The best known and most influential among them were Parker, Barlow, Cox, Grindal, Parkhurst, Scambler, Jewel, Horne, Sandy, and Pilkington. Parker was Elizabeth's first archbishop, and while a strict conformist and a rigid enforcer of conformity, he was a thorough Protestant. In his Cambridge days we find him intimately associated with a little band of students in the University who were inspired by Luther's writings, and had a large share in bringing about the Reformation in England. Among these were the martyrs, Thomas Bilney and Hugh Latimer, with whom Parker formed a permanent friendship. After he was raised to power he renewed the correspondence which Cranmer had carried on with John Calvin, as to the possibility of uniting all the Reformed Churches into one communion. During the time Martin Bucer was Regius Professor of Divinity at Cambridge Parker lived on terms of closest intimacy with him, was appointed one of his executors, and preached his funeral sermon. In July, 1559, he was made archbishop of Canterbury, and his consecration acquired exceptional importance from the fact that on that occasion for the first time the Roman ritual was not observed. Of the four bishops who took part in his consecration Barlow and Hodgkin had been consecrated according to the Sarum rite, and Scory and Coverdale according to the Ordinal of 1550. Barlow was the bishop who consecrated, the others according to use and wont, merely assisting. So that Barlow's Orders are a subject of profound interest to those ecclesiastics who lay great stress on Orders. He consecrated Parker, and a few days later Parker consecrated eleven other bishops, so that, so far as Apostolical Succession is concerned, Anglican Orders from that day to this may be said to hang by Barlow, and Barlow is a somewhat perplexing person to the ecclesiastical mind. Before the Reformation came in he held high preferment among the Austin Canons, and yet became one of the earliest advocates of Lutheran opinions in England, and wrote tracts against the Roman Church. Then, in 1531, he published an anti-Lutheran book—a dialogue on the Lutheran factions. Again, in 1535, he had become a zealous Reformer, and while he was away in Scotland, whither he had been sent on an embassy along with Lord Robert Howard, he was made bishop of St. Asaph, yet before he left Scotland he was translated to St. David's without having exercised any episcopal function. On a short visit to London his election was confirmed in Bow Church, after which he immediately returned to Scotland. The point to be noted is that there is no record of his consecration in Cranmer's registers, nor is there any in his own register at St. David's. The Roman Catholics to this day, therefore, affirm that Barlow never was consecrated,[1] and all that the Anglican can reply is, that he *was* consecrated, as is shown by the fact that he exercised episcopal functions and sat in the House of Lords; but that in troublous times the registers were carelessly kept, and so there is no entry. But this vexed question we may leave to be debated by the two contending parties, Anglican and Roman. The point which interests us in this inquiry, as bearing on the question of *intention*, is this, Did Barlow, in his Elizabethan days, believe in Apostolical Succession in the sense of conveying apostolic grace? We venture to think he did not. For these reasons: first, during the Marian exile he became the pastor of the Presbyterian Church at Embden in East Frisia, which had been founded by John à Lasco, a Presbyterian, and of which John à Lasco had been minister before him; and next, according to his own words he did not believe consecration to be necessary. In a sermon of his he says: "If the King's Grace, being supreme head of the Church of England, did choose, denominate, and elect any layman (being learned) to be a bishop, that he, so chosen (without mention being made of any Orders) should be as good a bishop as he is, or the best in England." In the same sermon he expresses the further revolutionary opinion that "wheresoever two or three simple persons, as cobblers and weavers, are in company, and elected in the name of God, there is the true Church of God."

We can only briefly glance at the opinions of the rest of the Elizabethan bishops, but it may be noted that both Scambler, bishop of Peterborough, and Bentham, bishop of Coventry and Lichfield, had been ministers of a church in London in Mary's time which had deacons to look after the poor, which kept a register of its members, met to choose its own officers, and exercised discipline within its own borders, after the manner of the Congregational Churches of to-day.

Further, both Scambler and Scory, bishop of Hereford, had during the Marian times been ministers of the Presbyterian Church at Embden, of which Barlow was at one time minister also, as we have already seen. Richard Cox, bishop of Ely, refused to minister in the Queen's Chapel because she retained the crucifix and lights. Grindal, bishop of London, and successively archbishop of York and Canterbury, had once been chaplain to Ridley the martyr, and lost his place by trying to maintain the Puritan exercises which the queen disliked. Miles Coverdale showed by his writings how strong a Puritan he was, and when he came to take part in Parker's consecration he came in a simple woollen dress. John Parkhurst, bishop of Norwich, was the man who at Merton College imbued John Jewel with his own intense Protestant beliefs, was one of the Marian exiles at Zurich, and in Elizabeth's time encouraged Nonconformist practices among his clergy and refused to suppress the Puritan prophesyings in his diocese. James Pilkington, bishop of Durham, wrote an earnest letter to the Earl of Leicester in favour of discontinuing the prescribed clerical vestments, and in 1567 carried out the injunctions for the removal of superstitious books and ornaments, and the defacing idolatrous figures from the Church plate, with great rigour. As to Bishop Jewel, it is scarcely possible to put his Protestant views too strongly. Writing to his friend Peter Martyr in 1559 he says: "Our papists oppose us most spitefully, and none more obstinately than those who have abandoned us. This it is to have once tasted of the Mass! He who drinks of it is mad. Depart from it all ye who value a sound mind: he who

"The scenic apparatus of Divine worship is now under agitation; and those very things which you and I have so often laughed at are now seriously and solemnly entertained by certain persons, as if the Christian religion could not exist without something tawdry. Our minds indeed are not sufficiently disengaged to make these fooleries of much importance." As to the sacraments, Jewel was wholly Zwinglian. In a sermon at St. Paul's Cross he plainly said that the true use of the Lord's Supper was a remembrance of Christ's death, and that all other uses are abuses. The benefits of Christ, said he, are applied to us by faith and not by the massing priest. His *Apology for the Church of England* was adopted as a statement of the Anglican position in the " Harmonia Confessionum " of 1581, and a proposal was endorsed by Parker that it should be bound with the Catechism and Articles of the Church of England, and be regarded as authoritative.[1] It may therefore be accepted as fairly representative of the Church as re-established under Elizabeth. It defines "Catholic" as that which is not shut up to one nation as the Jewish dispensation was. As to the divisions among Protestants, unity is not necessarily a sign of truth. There was perfect unity among the Israelites when they worshipped the golden calf, and among the murderers of Christ there was the greatest consent. As to those who are always laying stress upon the true Church—by the true Church "these folks" mean themselves, like those of old time who said "The temple of the Lord—the temple of the Lord," or like the Scribes and Pharisees, "which cracked that they were *Abraham's Children*. Thus with a gay and

[1] Strype's *Annals* I. i. 474.

jolly show deceive they the simple, and seek to choke us with the very name of the Church." God's grace, Jewel says, is not promised to secs and successions, but to them that fear God. In his controversy with Harding the Jesuit, referring to the scandalous lives of some of the Popes, he says, "This is M. Harding's holy Succession. Though faith fall, yet Succession must hold. For unto such Succession God hath bound the Holy Ghost. . . . But St. Paul saith, 'Faith cometh' (not by Succession, but) 'by hearing; and hearing cometh' (not of legacie or inheritance from bishop to bishop, but) 'of the Word of God.' . . . Succession you say is the chief way for any Christian man to avoid Antichrist. I grant you, if you mean Succession of Doctrine." No wonder that so pronounced a Tractarian as Hurrell Froude exclaimed, " I am weary of Jewell," and that he wrote to Keble in 1834, saying, " As to the Reformers I think worse and worse of them. Jewell was what you would call 'an irreverent Dissenter.' His Defence of the *Apology* disgusted me more than almost any work I have read."[1]

Dr. Abbott says that at a time in Newman's life when he knew extremely little about the Anglican writers, in a letter to Rickardo, he suggested the plan of "taking as a whole" their writings and finding in them "*the* English Church," and that Rickardo, who really did know them, was of opinion that "we shall employ them to most purpose by keeping them constantly in our sight and out of other people's."[2] At a later stage of Newman's progress, Abbott says that "he accused the Anglican divines (whom he had never

[1] *Remains*, iii. 407, i. 379, 1838.

seriously studied) of having 'taken him in,' and threw upon them the blame that was wholly due to himself." In 1833 he speaks of a "return," not to the Mediæval Church of England, but "to the seventeenth century." He did not quite know how far back to return. He had only made up his mind that it was to be, "not to the sixteenth century—not to the Church of the Reformation." Certainly, if Newman wished to find a belief in Apostolical Succession among the divines of the Anglican Church he was well advised in keeping clear of the sixteenth century and the Reformation Church.

IV.

In seeking further to establish the position that the doctrine of Apostolical Succession is of comparatively recent origin in the Reformed Anglican Church, let us now trace the policy of that Church in relation to foreign Protestant Churches and Presbyterian Orders.

Not merely convincing but overwhelming is the evidence that from 1552 onwards the English Church regarded herself to all intents and purposes as one with the Swiss Churches of Zurich and Geneva, and that her leaders claimed brotherhood and sympathy with the Protestant leaders in Switzerland and on the Upper Rhine. Much of this evidence has come before us already, and we now pass to that which is supplied by the case of those Foreign Churches which in times of persecution were settled in this country, and were recognised and received to protection by the ecclesiastical as well as the civil authorities. These Churches were to be found in London, Norwich, and Canterbury, also at the ports where the refugees first landed, such as Southampton, Sandwich, Rye, and Winchelsea ; at Yarmouth, where they established their fishing station ; and at Colchester, Coventry, Maidstone, Stamford, Thetford, Glastonbury, and other inland towns where they carried on their cloth manufacture. It is to be noted that these Presbyterian communities were not merely connived at, but recognised in the most formal manner. The leader of these people in the first instance was John à Lasco, or Laski, the son of Jaroslaw, Lord of the Manor of Lask, whose brother John was Archbishop of Gnesen, Cracow, and it was in the archiepiscopal residence that John à Lasco was educated. After becoming a Protestant the latter established a Presbyterian Church at Embden, and on the outbreak of persecution found his way to England. Arriving here in 1548, à Lasco was received with great favour both by the king and the archbishop. For eight months he was Cranmer's guest at Lambeth Palace, and was subsequently placed on the Commission of 1551 appointed "to peruse and make ecclesiastical laws."

In 1550 John à Lasco obtained the King's Letters Patent constituting the Dutch Church in London a *corpus corporatum et politicum ;* assigning to them the grand and effective church of the Austin Friars in the City of London ; appointing Walter Deloen and Martin Flanders as the first ministers of the Dutch or Flemish part of the congregation, and François de la Riviere and Richard François of the French, placing the whole under the care of John à Lasco as superintendent ; and further charging all mayors and aldermen, together with all other archbishops, bishops, and Churches to use and exercise their own rites and ceremonies and their own peculiar discipline without hindrance, disturbance, or interference, any statute, proclamation, or injunction to the contrary notwithstanding.[1] The number of these people increasing, a second place of worship was granted for the French-speaking part of the refugees, the church of St. Anthony's Hospital in Threadneedle Street. It is anticipating a later time, but it may here be mentioned that Archbishop Parker, with the sanction of Queen Elizabeth, granted to the exiles the free use of the Under Croft, or Crypt, of Canterbury Cathedral, which extends under the choir and high altar, and is of considerable extent. Here the "gentle and profitable strangers," as the archbishop styled them, not only celebrated their worship and taught their children, but set up their looms and carried on their several trades.[2]

Under the Marian persecution these Protestants, like others, had to flee the realm, and their Churches were broken up. When on the accession of Elizabeth they returned and asked for the Confirmation of the Charter granted by Edward VI., it was refused on political grounds. But though the queen refused to renew their Charter, she handed the church of the Austin Friars to the bishop of London for their use, and placed their various churches under the superintendency of their respective dioceses, at the same time leaving them free in the choice of their ministers, elders, and deacons, and in the use of their own forms of worship. So frank was the feeling between these people and their neigh-

[1] This document (in Latin) is printed by Burnet in his Collection of Records, but the original, on vellum, has recently been found among the archives of the London-Dutch Church.
[2] Smiles' *Huguenots and their Settlements*, 1867.

bours that there were occasions when ministers ordained in the English Church became ministers in the Dutch or French Churches, as is seen in the case of Calandrinus; and there were occasions also when these foreigners had the use of English churches when their own were under repair. As late as 1702 the bishop of Winchester instituted the minister of the congregation of Walloon strangers meeting in the quaint chapel of "God's House" in Southampton, M. Cougot, to the rectory of Millbrook in that town. To the day of his death in 1721 he was both rector of the episcopal church of Millbrook and minister of the French Presbyterian congregation meeting in "God's House."[1]

It has been said that Queen Elizabeth placed the various foreign Churches in this country under the superintendence of the bishops of their respective dioceses. This superintendence was by no means a merely nominal thing, for, as facts clearly show, many of the bishops took a very active interest in their affairs. For example, when the church of the Austin Friars had been assigned to the Walloon Church in London in 1560, Grindal, then bishop of London, joined this community in sending a request to Calvin in Geneva asking him to send them a pastor, in response to which Nicholas de Gallars was sent to undertake the office of superintendent, and received the bishop's authority. The same year also Grindal officially excommunicated Hadrian Haemstede, one of the members of this Church, for his erroneous opinions, addressing the document "to all ministers of churches in our diocese, and especially to Petrus Declen, minister of the Flemish

Church," the document running thus: "We therefore command you on our authority to excommunicate the said Adrian." The following April action was further taken against those who sympathised with Haemstede, the record being in this form: "Acted before the bishop of London, 19 April 1561, with the consent of the ministers of the Flemish and French Churches, and in the presence and with the consent of the bishop of Durham." In November 1561 again, Grindal wrote to the Senate of Frankfort, introducing to them Godfried Wing, one of the Reformed ministers, and therefore a Presbyterian, as a learned, devout man who has preached the Gospel in Flanders and whom they will find most acceptable. He also sent his own servant, Martin Van Dalen, with a letter to the London Church saying that he wished this man to be received among them as understanding English but imperfectly. He adds that an examination will show what the man knows of religion, and as to his character, he has served him creditably for about a year. Subsequently decrees were issued by Grindal, which have been preserved in the Dutch Archives, dealing with certain persons who absented themselves from the services of the London Dutch Church, and requiring them to send in their names to the ministers and elders, and declare their allegiance. They are required also to ask the Bishop's forgiveness, and express the hope that he will continue to favour their Church with his protection; to cement their concord they are to come to the Lord's Supper and take part therein with purified minds.

The active part taken in the arrangements of these Churches by Bishop Grindal was continued by his successors. In 1581, in the case of a complaint made against the superintendents of the Church by Lewes Tirrey, Aylmer, bishop of London, requests them to content the man or else make their personal appearances before him within six days. In 1611 the ministers and elders petitioned Abbot, archbishop of Canterbury, against disorderly members of their respective congregations, who, dissatisfied with their discipline, had taken the sacrament in the parish churches without being reconciled with God and the several congregations they had offended. They pray the archbishop to order that persons who voluntarily join their congregations shall submit to their orders and censures. In a similar case the bishop of London confirmed the discipline of the Dutch Churches of London and Colchester, ordering that none of their members should be received to holy communion by the minister of the parish until the bishop was satisfied they were not trying to escape ecclesiastical censure among their own people. In 1621 Archbishop Abbot gave full power " to the ministers of the Dutch Congregation in London, or any whom they may appoint, to celebrate Divine Service, preach the Word of God, and administer the Holy Sacraments (if need shall require) either in the parish church of Mortlake, or in the house of Sir Francis Crane, Knt., or in any other convenient place." As late as 1821 William Howley, then bishop of London, interposed in a quarrel between two of the ministers of the London-Dutch Church and restored harmony, for which he received the thanks of the community.[1] To these particulars may be added

[1] *Ecclesiæ Londino-Batavæ Archivvm.* Edidit Joannes Henricus Hessels, Camb., 1889. The particulars given above rest upon the authority of the original documents preserved in the archives of the London-Dutch Church. These documents have been edited with the most painstaking care by J.

the fact that a clause in the Act of Uniformity of 1662 provides "that the penalties of the Act shall not extend to the foreigners or aliens of the foreign Reformed Churches allowed or to be allowed by the King's Majesty, his heirs and successors in England." It would appear, therefore, that these Presbyterian communities were regarded as being more or less within the pale of the Anglican Church.

Let us for a moment or two turn our thoughts in another direction. In his Life of Dr. Pusey (ii. 23) Canon Liddon says that "the Channel Islands, from various causes, have been the stronghold of Puritanism for three centuries." The explanation of that fact is to be found in certain other facts deserving our careful attention, as throwing light on what was really Anglican opinion on Apostolical Succession.

The facts referred to may be found more fully set forth in a history of Jersey, published by Philip Falle in 1694,[1] but may be summed up briefly as follows. During the reign of Elizabeth great numbers of French Protestants fled for sanctuary from persecution from France to the Channel Islands, where they became possessed of the parish church of St. Heliers, where one of their number, Sieur de la Repaudiere, a French minister, preached and administered the sacrament after the manner of Geneva. After a little time a formal deputation waited on the Queen, asking leave that the other churches of the Island might be modelled after the same way. This she refused, but at the same time confirmed them in the possession of the church they

---

[1] *Channel Islands—Account of Jersey*, by Philip Falle, M.A., Rector of St. Saviour, and late Deputy from the States of the said Islands to their Majesties. London, 1694. Chapter V.—*Religion*.

already had in St. Heliers. This appears from a letter sent from the Council to the Bailly and Jurats under date August 7, 1565, which is as follows: "Knowing that you have a minister who ever since his arrival in Jarsey (*sic*) hath used the like Order of preaching and administration as in the Reformed Churches, or as it is used in the French Church at London: Her Majesty for divers respects and considerations is well pleased to admit the same Order of preaching and administration to be continued at St. Helier's as hath been hitherto accustomed by the said minister. Provided always that the residue of the parishes of the said Isle shall diligently continue there the Order of Service ordained and set forth within this realm." A similar letter was sent at the same time to Guernsey authorising the same form of service at St. Peter's which had been allowed at St. Heliers. Still, notwithstanding these letters, which were signed by seven Lords of Council, Falle tells us that all the other churches soon followed the example of St. Heliers, and the English Liturgy came to be generally disused. At this point Thomas Cartwright, the great Presbyterian leader, and Edward Snape, who took an active part in organising Presbyterianism in Northamptonshire, were sent out from England: "at whose coming a Synod of the Ministers and Elders of Jersey, Guernezey, Serk, and Alderney was convened at the town of Peter-Port in Guernezey, June 28, 1576: And there in the presence of both Governors a form of Classical Discipline was agreed on to be used from thenceforth in the four Islands; which Discipline was again confirmed in another Synod held at Guernezey Oct. 11–17, 1597." Philip Falle, who tells us all this says, "because it met and enacted Laws Ecclesiastical binding the subject without the royal authority and extending the system which was only indulged at St. Heliers in Jersey and to St. Peter-Port in Guernsey."

The Channel Islands thus became Presbyterian, not only in doctrine, but in discipline and worship, and were administered by a perfectly organised system of colloquies, consistories, and synods. These assemblies put themselves under the protection of the bishop of Winchester, whom they addressed as *their bishop*. Previously, in March, 1569, the Crown had formally transferred Guernsey and the other islands to the jurisdiction of that prelate, they having formerly been under the jurisdiction of the Roman Catholic Bishop of Coûtance in Normandy. This was done by an Order in Council. This bishop therefore subsequently received from the Presbyterian ministers a collection of all the synodical articles which they had framed for their internal ecclesiastical government.

Guernsey remained Presbyterian under James I., while Jersey, still remaining Presbyterian also, was induced to accept the Liturgy in 1623; and the office of Dean, which had been in abeyance for more than sixty years, was revived. Thus a strangely anomalous condition of things prevailed from the beginning of the seventeenth century to the early part of the nineteenth. Till the Restoration Guernsey used the Genevan form of worship, and Jersey, from 1623, the Anglican; afterwards Guernsey used the Anglican also. Still, the ministers of both islands continued to be Presbyterian as to orders and their congregations Presbyterian also; and further, all these Presbyterian ministers and Churches, by the law of the land, regarded the Episcopalian bishop of Winchester as their bishop in the same way as the London-Dutch Church regarded the bishop of London. If anything could heighten the anomaly—we had almost said the comedy—of the situation, it is the fact that these Presbyterian ministers in Presbyterian congregations administered the sacraments and pronounced absolution according to the use of the Anglican Prayer Book, and under the direction of an Episcopalian bishop, when that bishop was no other than Lancelot Andrewes, one of the most typical Anglicans of his time. Etienne de Giberd, at one time French chaplain at the Court of George III., as minister of St. Andrews in the island of Guernsey, was the last of the parish ministers who had not received episcopal ordination, and as he only died about seventy-five years ago, the system may be said to have continued till within the lifetime of men still living.

And now—to bring this part of the subject to a close—what is the plain and unmistakeable inference to be drawn from all these facts? It is that in England, from the Reformation till the time of the Stuarts, at all events, episcopacy was regarded simply as a mode of government, and not as a channel of grace. It was a national and legislative arrangement to be enforced upon Englishmen, like other laws of the realm, as the will of Crown and Parliament—enforced under penalty of fine, imprisonment, exile, and, in the case of the Congregational martyrs of 1583 and 1593, even of the scaffold. But while thus forced upon Englishmen, irrespective of their convictions, it was not regarded as at all necessary for the religious life of foreigners. It was, therefore, merely a matter of territory, a geographical expression, wide difference between episcopal jurisdiction as a convenient mode of government, though not the only mode permissible, and apostolic descent ensuring apostolic grace and personal salvation. But it certainly was episcopal jurisdiction conferred by the Crown, and not apostolic grace as an arrangement from Heaven, which was believed in by the great body of the Anglican Church from the Reformation settlement under Elizabeth till the days of Archbishop Laud.

LECTURE XI

THE ANGLICAN CHURCH FROM 1603 TO 1833

LECTURE XI

THE ANGLICAN CHURCH FROM 1603 TO 1833

AFTER the Reformation and the reign of Queen Mary the claim to Apostolical Succession was not set up in the Anglican Church till the first generation of Elizabethan bishops were all in their graves. And then only in tentative and apologetic fashion. It was started in the sixteenth century, and also revived in the nineteenth, not so much on its own merits as by way of rival claim to something else, and as a weapon of war against an opposing force. The men who advanced the stronger form of the Episcopal theory at the end of Elizabeth's reign did so by way of countermining the claim to Divine right made by the Presbyterians. As Hallam puts it: "The defenders of the established order found out that one claim of Divine right was best met by another." The Presbyterians were certain that a definite Church order stamped with Divine authority was to be found in the Scriptures, and equally certain that that order was government by presbyters. "Is it likely," asks Thomas Cartwright, "that He who appointed not only the tabernacle and the temple, but their very ornaments, would neglect the very essentials of the Church? Shall we conclude that He who remembered system of organisation for which they thus claimed the *jus divinum* they began resolutely to reduce to practical shape. Thomas Cartwright and Edward Snape, as we already know, went to the Channel Islands and organised the Churches there on the Presbyterian model, with consistories, synods, and forms of service. On the mainland a presbytery was set up at Wandsworth in 1572, and in spite of injunctions and royal prohibitions the presbyterial system was openly established in several of the Churches of Northamptonshire and Warwickshire. In 1580 Cartwright and his friend Travers published the "Book of Discipline," in which the Genevan Church system was adapted to English life, and so introduced as to come into working order in two or three years, and it is a well-known fact that a considerable section of the Puritan clergy were in sympathy with the movement. There was to be a *classis* in each given district, and these *classes* were to be consolidated into a National Assembly which was to meet in London at the same time that Parliament was in session. It was arranged that candidates for the ministry were to receive real Presbyterian Orders from the *classis*, and then apply to the bishop for the legal rite merely as a matter of form. In this way the Presbyterian system was to work under episcopal arrangements till strong enough to supersede them. The ministry, Cartwright contended, should thus be reduced to the primitive form, each Church being governed by its own minister and elders, and each minister be openly and freely chosen by the people. "To effect this reformation," he says, "every one ought to labour in his calling—the magistrate by his authority, the ministers by the Word, and all by their prayers."

This scheme for assimilating the Church of England to the Church of Scotland was felt by the episcopal party to be fraught with danger for them. They realised, too, that in carrying on the argument the Presbyterians had a distinct advantage in that they went to the Scriptures for their ecclesiastical polity, and appealed to spiritual principles; whereas the bishops seemed to derive their authority merely from the Crown and grounded their Church system on Acts of Parliament made by the State. Clearly there must be a change of front, and hence arose the doctrine of the Divine right of Episcopacy, and of an episcopal succession regularly derived from the apostles.

Richard Bancroft, an ambitious churchman and a noisy polemic, has the credit of initiating this counter-movement by the sermon he preached at St. Paul's Cross, February 9, 158⅞. It was based on the text 1 John iv. 1, setting forth the duty of trying the spirits whether they be of God. On reading the sermon it is not very obvious why so much importance should have been attached to it. It fiercely assails the Presbyterian system, but does no more than plead antiquity for Episcopacy: "There is no man living, as I suppose," he says, "able to show, where there was any Church planted ever since the apostles' time, but there the Bishops had authoritie over the rest of the ministry" (p. 69). But though Bancroft does not claim for bishops more than prescriptive authority, even this claim was resented by churchmen themselves. Sir Francis Knollys, one of the Secretaries of State, told Archbishop Whitgift that Bancroft's assertion that bishops were superior to presbyters was contrary to the command of Christ, who further: "If the bishops are not under-governors to Her Majesty of the clergy, but superior governors over their brethren by God's ordinance (i.e., *jure divino*), it will then follow that Her Majesty is not supreme governor over her clergy." Even Bancroft himself seems not to have had any extreme opinions on the necessity of episcopal ordination. Some years later, when he was archbishop of Canterbury, the question arose in reference to three Scottish ministers who were to be consecrated as bishops of Glasgow, Brechin, and Galloway, whether, since they had only received Presbyterian ordination, they ought not to be ordained by the bishop as well as consecrated. Spotswood[1] tells us that Bancroft, who was by, maintained "that thereof there was no necessity, seeing when bishops could not be had, the ordination given by presbyters must be esteemed lawful; otherwise it might be doubted if there were any lawful vocation in most of the Reformed Churches."

The question of Apostolical Succession may more truly be said to have been started by Thomas Bilson, Warden of Winchester College, whose treatise on *The Perpetual Government of Christ's Church* appeared in 1593. For Bilson not merely contended for the antiquity of Episcopacy but for Apostolical Succession as absolutely necessary to the constitution of a Church; and for bishops as a distinct order without which there can be no lawful ordaining of ministers, and by consequence no lawful administration of the Word and Sacraments. There are two things, he says, proper to bishops, but not common to presbyters—namely, singularity in succeeding and superiority in ordaining. This

---

[1] *History of the Church of Scotland*, ed. 1851, iii. 208, 209.

singularity descends from the apostles by a perpetual chain of succession and doth to this day continue.

Bilson's assertions are stronger than his arguments. The authorities on which he relies are Cyprian, Jerome, Chrysostom, Theodoret, Epiphanius, and the canons of Councils, all belonging to that later time when great changes had come over the Church since the apostles' days. And his manner of dealing with these is not always satisfactory. For example, Jerome says that bishops were superior to presbyters rather by the custom of the Church than by the truth of the Lord's ordinance, and Bilson explains that by " truth " (*veritas*) the Fathers often meant a precept from Christ's own lips, and by "custom" (*consuetudo*) an arrangement made by the apostles themselves. So again, when Jerome says that before factions arose in the Church bishop and presbyter meant one and the same office, but party spirit springing up it was decreed throughout the world that, to stop the rising of divisions, one of the presbyters should be elected and elevated above the rest, to whom the whole care of the Church should pertain ; and he was called a bishop or overseer. Bilson contends that the change which Jerome describes was brought about by the apostles themselves, and therefore they were the originators of the line of bishops. He proves it thus : Jerome does not tell us when this change was brought about from the equality of presbyters to the superiority of bishops, but he does say it was at a time when factions prevailed in the Church ; now we know from the New Testament that factions prevailed in the apostles' time, therefore the change was ordinance; a process of argumentation more facile than convincing. Moreover, Bilson, in common with nearly all Episcopalian writers, falls into the mistake of assuming that the early bishop, the pastor of a single community, and the modern diocesan bishop are one and the same thing.

Still, even after Bilson's book the theory of Apostolical Succession was not taken seriously by the great body of Churchmen, but rather regarded as a mere polemic against the Puritans. Archbishop Whitgift himself did not believe it; he said he wished he could. In his own controversy with Cartwright he plainly denied that sacraments confer grace: "You know very well," he says, "that we teach far otherwise, and that it is a certain and true doctrine of all such as do profess the Gospel, that the outward signs of the sacraments do not contain in them grace, neither yet that the grace of God is of necessity tied unto them." He held that no one system of Church government can claim exclusive Divine right. "The offices of the Church whereby this government is wrought be not namely and particularly expressed in the Scriptures, but in some points left to the discretion and liberty of the Church, to be disposed according to the state of times, places and persons" (*Works* i. 6). Even Richard Hooker, revered as the great pillar of Episcopacy, while maintaining that "the first institution of bishops was from heaven, was even of God," regards it rather as a means of stately order than as a channel of grace, and does not suppose it may never be changed, or that it is universally indispensable. "I conclude," he says, "that neither God's being Author of laws for the government of His Church, nor His committing them unto Scripture, is any reason sufficient wherefore all Churches should for ever be bound to keep them without change" (*E.P.*, iii. 10, 7). Elsewhere he says, " Whereas some do infer that no ordination can stand, but only such as is made by bishops, who have had their ordination likewise by other bishops before them till we come to the very apostles themselves . . . to this we answer that there may be sometimes very just and sufficient reason to allow ordination made without a bishop " (vii. 14, 11).

Notwithstanding the lofty tone of his argument it cannot be said that Hooker contributed much to the settlement of the question at issue. The Puritan contended for order in Church arrangements quite as much as the Episcopalian, but he maintained that the highest order was hindered, not helped, by the retention of the order and ceremonies obtaining in the Church of Rome. Order is not maintained by one form of organisation alone. The Puritan might have recalled the fact that long before Hooker used his great argument in favour of Episcopacy, Clement of Rome had used it quite as sublimely on behalf of the government of a separate community by presbyters. Clement urges the Church at Corinth to return to peaceful and orderly relations with their presbyters because order is the law of the universe. Day and night accomplish their course without hindrance. Sun and moon and dancing stars according to God's appointment circle in harmony ; the earth beareth fruit at her proper seasons ; the inscrutable depths of the abysses are constrained by the same ordinances and the basin of the boundless sea within its boundaries, even as God ordereth so it doeth. The seasons succeed each other in peace ; the winds flowing fountains created for enjoyment and health; yea, the smallest of living things come together in concord and peace. So dwell ye in harmony, says Clement to the Church of Corinth, with those presbyters of yours who have offered the gifts of the bishop's office umblameably and holily. Clement's argument thus elaborated was as sound and eloquent in favour of presbyters as Hooker's on behalf of bishops, and was put forth much nearer to the time of the apostles. So that the mere question of order, the Puritans might say, is beside the mark, and does not advance the discussion, for we are in favour of orderly government also.

Keble in his Preface to Hooker's works (1888 *ed.*) reluctantly admits that the doctrine of Apostolical Succession as he held it himself was not held by the great body of the Church in Hooker's time. He says (p. lxvii.): "It might have been expected that the defenders of the English hierarchy against the first Puritans would take the highest ground and challenge for the bishops the same unreserved submission on the same plea of exclusive apostolical prerogative, which their adversaries feared not to insist on for their elders and deacons. It is notorious, however, that such was not in general the line preferred by Jewel, Whitgift, Cooper, and others to whom the management of that controversy was entrusted during the early years of Elizabeth's reign. They do not expressly disavow, but they carefully shun that unreserved appeal to Christian antiquity in which, one would have thought, they must have discerned the very strength of their cause to lie. It is enough with them to show that the government by archbishops and bishops is ancient and allowable; they never venture to urge its *exclusive* claims, or to connect the succession with the validity of the holy sacraments; and yet it is obvious that such a course of argument alone (supposing it borne out by facts) could fully meet all the exigencies of the case." Further on in the same Preface Keble makes admissions of more than ordinary significance. He says (p. lxxxiv.): "Hooker might feel himself biassed by his respect for existing authority. For nearly up to the time when he wrote numbers had been admitted to the ministry of the Church in England and with no better than Presbyterian ordination; and it appears by Travers' supplication to the Council that the construction not uncommonly put upon the statute of 13th Elizabeth was one permitting those who had received Orders in any other form than that of the English Service Book, on giving certain securities, to exercise their calling in England. If it were really the intention of that Act to authorise other than episcopal ordination, it is but one proof more of the low, accommodating notions concerning the Church which then prevailed, and may serve to heighten our sense of the imminent risk which we were in of losing the Succession." Contrasting him with Laud, Hammond, and Leslie in the two next generations, Keble further says that Hooker "did not feel at liberty to press unreservedly and develope in all its consequences that part of the argument, which they, taught by the primitive Church, regarded as the most vital and decisive: the necessity, namely, of the apostolic commission to the derivation of sacramental grace and to our mystical communion with Christ." So that, practically, Keble gives up the great name of Hooker as well as those of the Elizabethan divines who

It was Archbishop Laud who really revived the theories of Apostolical Succession started by Bancroft and Bilson. Between Bancroft and Laud, however, came three other men who for various reasons carry weight in the history of the period to which they belong —Archbishop Abbot, Bishop Andrewes, and Richard Field, the friend of Richard Hooker. Abbot became archbishop of Canterbury on the death of Bancroft in 1611, and held the position till 1633, when he was succeeded by Laud. During Abbot's time the Puritans had some respite from the treatment they had received under Whitgift and Bancroft, and which they were to receive again under Laud—for Abbot held very moderate theories concerning the Church. In his *Treatise of the Perpetual Visibility and Succession of the True Church in all Ages* he argued that God had always, even in the darkest times, had a faithful Church, not consisting of bishops and priests, sees and successions, but of men holding the faith of Christ (p. 114). The beauty of the Church in his view consists of purity in faith, verity in doctrine, reverence in behaviour, innocency, patience, and such like spiritual qualities; whereas the external pomp of mere ceremonialists is as much despised by the Lord as it is magnified in their fleshly and carnal imaginations (p. 116).

Another representative man in the Church of England at this time was Richard Field, Dean of Gloucester, whose *Book of the Church* treats the subject with great moderation. Orders he reduces to the necessity of order. He is unwilling, he says, to condemn those worthy men who were ordained presbyters when the bishops were opposed to the truth of God. In their case ordination by presbyters was order, and therefore valid Orders. He is of opinion that there have always been bishops in the Church, but that they did not differ from presbyters; there was an orderly superiority of presbyters placed over other presbyters. He did not assent to what Bancroft and Bilson said at the Hampton Court Conference, namely, that there were special offices which were not performed by presbyters. On the contrary he held that in the primitive Church presbyters performed the offices of ordination and confirmation, and also dedicated churches.

Lancelot Andrewes holds a high place in the esteem of English Churchmen, yet as bishop of Winchester, as we have seen, he held an official relation with the Presbyterian Churches of the Channel Islands as part of his diocese. From 1618 to 1626, therefore, he either left some hundreds of the people committed to his charge without what he regarded as valid sacraments, or else he did not believe in the doctrine of Apostolic Succession. He also took part in the consecration of the three bishops for Scotland who had no other ordination than Presbyterian. He demurred, it is true, for a moment, but when Archbishop Bancroft replied that ordination given by presbyters must be esteemed lawful, otherwise it might be doubted if there were any lawful vocations in most of the Reformed Churches, his scruples were met at once, and he took part in the consecration. On another occasion, writing to Peter du Moulin, and comparing the Anglican with the French Huguenot Church, Andrewes plainly said: " Though our government be by Divine right, it follows not that there is no salvation, or that a Church cannot stand without it. He must needs be stone blind that be made of iron and hard-hearted that denies them salvation. . . . Somewhat may be wanting that is of Divine right (at least in external government), and yet salvation may be had."[1]

There is evidence sufficient to show that Andrewes was not alone in these views of his. In various dioceses French ministers who had received Presbyterian ordination were received into the ministry of the English Church without re-ordination. Charles de Beauvais was inducted to the rectory of Withyham in Sussex in 1638, and held the living for twenty-seven years; Gilbert Primrose, who was at one time Protestant minister at Bordeaux, and subsequently officiated among the French Protestants in London, was installed canon of Windsor in 1628 without re-ordination, and became chaplain in ordinary to the King; in 1662 Peter du Moulin the younger was instituted rector of Adisham and Staple in the place of Charles Nichols, one of the ejected ministers, and held the benefice for twenty-two years; Peter Allix, a native of Alençon, and for some time minister of the Reformed Church at Rouen, was in 1690 created D.D. at Cambridge and made a canon of Windsor; and John Mesnard, for sixteen years a minister at Charenton, came to England in 1688 and succeeded Isaac Vossius as a canon of Windsor, and remained King's chaplain without re-ordination. Further, it may be added that in the Treaty of Berwick, made between James and Elizabeth in 1586, the religion practised in Scotland and by the Protestant princes on the Continent is recognised without any reservation in favour of Episcopacy;[2] and the canons passed by

---

[1] *Letters*, ii. p. 24.
[2] The treaty is printed in Rymer's *Foedera*, Pt. iv. p. 185.

Convocation in 1603 and revised in 1865, by canon 55 enjoin that all preachers before their sermons "shall pray for the holy Catholic Church, that is, for the whole congregation of Christian people dispersed through the whole world; and especially for the Churches of England, *Scotland*, and Ireland," yet at that time Scotland, of course, was Presbyterian, and every minister north of the Tweed would, *ex animo*, have denounced the doctrine of Apostolical Succession. When Macaulay said that in 1604 "episcopal ordination was unknown in Scotland," Bishop Harold Browne sought to minimise the fact by saying, on the authority of Chancellor Harington, that at least a titular Episcopacy then existed in Scotland, and further that there was "a full determination to restore a regularly constituted Episcopacy." [1] As to future intentions we can, of course, say nothing, but as to present facts it appears that a *titular* bishop was so named "for want of real ecclesiastical consecration," and that titular bishops had no episcopal ordination and no episcopal character whatever.

An entry in the diary of Philip Henry, one of the ejected ministers of 1662, throws light on the real principle involved in all these cases. He says (p. 247): "All or most of the Conformity have said they could not deny us ministers, but not ministers of the Church of England. . . . Now suppose a Dutch or French Protestant minister to come into England to preach, he is not re-ordained but only licensed." That is to say that the objection then felt to Presbyterian Orders was not theological or ecclesiastical but only legal. It is therefore a geographical question, not spiritual, and it all depends on which side of the North Sea or the Tweed a man may be living as to whether supernatural grace comes through a bishop or a presbyter.

Richard Montagu (1577–1641) was the advance guard of that body of men in the seventeenth century of whom Laud is usually regarded as the leader. His one dominant idea was that of the catholicity of the English Church, and he refused to recognise the foreign Reformed Churches as lawful branches of the Church of Christ. " Non est sacerdotium nisi in ecclesia, non est ecclesia sine sacerdotio," was the short and simple way in which he summed up the question (*Orig. Eccl.*, p. 464). But while Laud's real grasp of power did not come till the accession of Charles I. he had foreshadowed his future as early as 1604. Heylyn tells us that when Laud performed his exercise for B.D. at Oxford he maintained that there could be no true Church without diocesan bishops, for which he was " shrewdly rattled " by Dr. Holland, the Regius Professor of Divinity, " as one that did endeavour to cast a bone of discord betwixt the Church of England and the Reformed Churches beyond seas." Two years later, because of a sermon he preached in St. Mary's, the University Church, " he was so openly branded for a papist, or at least very popishly inclined, that it was almost made a heresy (as I have heard from his own mouth) for any one to be seen in his company, and a misprision of heresy to give him a civil salutation as he walked the streets."[1]

In later years, with an energy untiring and an ambition for ruling men, down to the smallest details, which never wearied, Laud sought to govern England ecclesiastically as Hildebrand from the papal chair had

[1] Heylyn's *Cyprianus Anglicus*, 1671, fol., pp. 49, 50.

governed Europe before him. But there was a grandeur about Hildebrand which was wanting to Laud. If Laud was a second Hildebrand he was Hildebrand "writ small." He believed far more intensely in Episcopacy as a system for governing men and marshalling them into form, than in Episcopacy as the channel of grace and supernatural influence; and in his increasing elaboration of form and ritual he carried men with him in his schemes who were his superiors in intellect. We see this in the case of widely different men. John Cosin, afterwards bishop of Durham, from his intimacy with Laud came to be regarded with suspicion and dislike by the Puritan party. Prynne called him "Popish Master John Cosens." Two years after Laud became archbishop of Canterbury, Cosin was elected Master of Peterhouse, in the chapel of which there was a new altar set up, before which the fellows and scholars were enjoined to bow; "there were basons, candlesticks, tapers standing on it, and a great crucifix hanging over it;" there was a vessel of incense, a carved cross at the end of every seat, and "at entering and going out all made a low obeisance to the altar, being enjoined by Dr. Cosin under penalty to do it." Peterhouse chapel became one of the sights of Cambridge, scholars from other colleges coming, some out of curiosity, and others to learn and practise the popish ceremonies. The story which went the round of Cambridge circles was that none might approach to the altar in Peterhouse but in sandals, and that there was a special consecrated knife there kept upon the altar to cut the sacramental bread.[1]

The High Church Movement had now fairly set in, and then, as in our own time, men who would now be

described as of the Evangelical School were but too
ready to drift with the stream. Bishop Morton wrote
in defence of bowing before the altar, and was eagerly
quoted by the High Church party; and Davenant,
bishop of Salisbury, directed the table in the cathedral
to be placed altar-wise. More memorable still, Joseph
Hall, first bishop of Exeter, then of Norwich, lent the
sanction of his authority and learning to the extreme
views of the archbishop on the Divine right of Episcopacy. In the days when Laud was scouted in Oxford
for his popish opinions, Hall wrote an open letter inscribed to W. L., which Heylyn, Laud's biographer, says
was generally supposed to be aimed at Laud, in which
he says: " I would I knew where to find you: To-day
you are in the tents of the Romanists, to-morrow in
ours; the next day between both, against both. . . .
How long will you halt in this indifferency? Resolve
one way, and know at last what you do hold, what you
should. Cast off either your wings or your teeth, and
loathing this bat-like nature, be either a bird or a
beast." [1]

So wrote Joseph Hall in 1606, but times change and
men change with them. In 1639 Laud was archbishop
of Canterbury and Hall bishop of Exeter, and there is
somewhat of an air of mystery about their relations with
each other. On the one hand Bishop Hall in his diary
speaks bitterly of Laud, and refers to complaints which
he had to answer on his knees before the King. On the
other hand Heylyn tells us that Laud " recommended to
Hall Bp. of Exon the writing of a book in defence of the
Divine right of Episcopacy in opposition to the Scots
and their adherents. Exeter undertakes the work and

[1] Heylyn's *Life of Laud*, 1671, fol., p. 50.

sends him a rough draft or skeleton." The two main positions laid down in this preliminary sketch were: (1) That Episcopacy is a lawful, most ancient, holy and Divine institution, and where it hath obtained, cannot be departed from without a manifest violation of God's ordinance; (2) That Presbyterianism has no true footing either in Scripture or the practice of the Church in all ages, and that howsoever it may be of use in some cities or territories where episcopal government, through the iniquity of the times, cannot be had, yet to obtrude it upon a Church otherwise settled under an acknowledged monarchy is utterly incongruous and unjustifiable."

Laud having read over this outline sent it back with these pencilled notes: " You say that Episcopacy is an antient, holy and Divine institution, would it not be more full went it thus—so antient that it is of Divine institution? In your second head you grant that the Presbyterian government may be of use where Episcopacy may not be had. Is not this needless and of dangerous consequence? There is no place where Episcopacy may not be had if there be a Church more than in title only. . . . Since they challenge their Presbyterian fiction to be Christ's kingdom and ordinance, and cast out Episcopacy as opposite to it, we must not use mincing terms, but unmask them plainly, nor will I ever give way to hamper ourselves for fear of speaking plain truth, though it be against Amsterdam or Geneva." Heylyn, who as Laud's biographer was behind the scenes, tells us (p. 377): " The Bp. of Exon found good cause to correct the obliquity of his opinion according to the rules of these animadversions, agreeably name of *Episcopacy by Divine Right*," &c. But before it was published it was still further revised by authority. Farther on (p. 381) Heylyn relates: "The Bishop of Exon's book being finished and recommended by the Author to his [Laud's] last perusal before it went to the Press he took pains to read it over with care and diligence. He observed that the Bishop passed by this point, viz., whether Episcopacy be an Order or degree as not much material . . . he desired him to weigh it well and to alter it with his own pen as soon as might be." In a letter to Hall under date January 14, $16\frac{39}{40}$ Laud says: "I could not but speak with the King about it, who commanded me to write unto you that you might qualify your expressions in these particulars, and so not differ from the known judgement of his pious and learned Father. This is easily done with your own Pen." In reply Hall humbly thanks His Grace for his trouble in reading his book and for the unnecessary amount of courtesy shown in consulting him about the alterations proposed in his writings. He apologises for having given good words to the Foreign Churches, though he is really stronger against them than most people. Still "it is but a stroke of your chaplain's pen" to alter the courteous language. As to Episcopacy being a distinct Order he had advisedly left it doubtful; but now at the archbishop's bidding it was stated as he wished.[1] With a serene smile Laud concludes the narrative thus: "According to our good advice the Bishop of Exon qualified some of his expressions and deleted others to the contentment of his sovereign, the satisfaction of his metropolitan, and his own great honour."[2] As to this

---

[1] *Canterbury's Doom*, pp. 273-5.
[2] Heylyn's *Cyprianus Anglicus*, p. 381.

last point, perhaps the less said the better, and indeed the narrative as a whole does not seem to add much weight to the opinion of Anglican divines, even of the seventeenth century, as to the Divine Right of Episcopacy.

Others were not so pliant, however, as the bishop of Exeter. The "ever-memorable John Hales of Eton" wrote a tract on Schism, which was circulated from hand to hand in manuscript, "intended chiefly," says Heylyn, "for the encouragement of some of our great masters of wit and reason to despise the authority of the Church." Hale started by saying that heresy and schism were two theological scarecrows, which those who desire to uphold a party in religion make use of to frighten away all who would make inquiries. The only real schism he defined to be *unnecessary* separation from communion, and every man must be his own judge about the necessity. When separation is necessitated by the rulers of the Church the guilt of schism is theirs, and this guilt is often incurred by episcopal ambition. Hales preferred reason to authority. In a tract on the Sacrament of the Lord's Supper he denied that there was any virtue in consecration, or that it was necessary to the celebration of the Supper. It is enough, he thinks, that one thing is done by which something else is signified. His doctrine is that in the Lord's Supper there is nothing given except bread and wine, and these are signs not of something there exhibited, but of Christ's body and blood, which were given for us many centuries ago. The true use of the Lord's Supper is the commemoration of His death. It is also a witness to our union with Christ, and our communion one with another.

and that every Christian now living has this power, not only for his own use, but for the benefit of others. He knows nothing of a Church as distinct from the congregation of believers. As to the benefit of auricular confession Hales gives a quotation from Pliny, who says that when one is bitten by a scorpion, if he go and whisper it in the ear of an ass, he shall be at once relieved. Hales says he doubts not but that sin is a scorpion and that its bite is deadly. But as for the sovereign remedy of whispering it in the ear either of a priest or, what is the same thing, the animal mentioned by Pliny, he believes the one as much as the other.[1]

Laud hearing about the circulation of the tract on Schism sent for Hales. Heylyn tells the story of their talk in the garden of Lambeth Palace "till the bell rang for prayers, and after prayers till dinner was ready, and after that, too, till the coming of Lord Conway." Heylyn met them coming in, "high-coloured and almost panting for want of breath, enough to show that there had been some heats between them not then fully cooled." He says that Hales told him afterwards "that he found the Archbishop (whom he knew before for a nimble disputant) to be as well versed in books as in business; that he had been ferreted by him from one hole to another till there was none left to afford him any further shelter; that he was now resolved to be orthodox and to declare himself a true son of the Church of England both for doctrine and discipline. That to this end he had obtained leave to call himself His Grace's chaplain.[2] Dr. Rawson Gardiner is of opinion that Hales, in thus describing his interview

---

[1] Hales's *Golden Remains*, London, 1673.
[2] *Cyprianus Anglicus*, p. 340.

with the Archbishop, was simply fooling Heylyn to the top of his bent.

There was something else to be heard in those days besides the story of heated talk in Lambeth Gardens. There was the sound of the brewing storm. It was in 1640, after the book had been cut and trimmed to suit Archbishop Laud, that Bishop Hall published his *Episcopacy by Divine Right Asserted*. On the 11th of December in that same year a petition was presented in the House of Commons from 15,000 Londoners and others of His Majesty's subjects in several counties of the kingdom to the effect that "the government of Archbishops and Bishops, Deans and Archdeacons, &c., with their courts and ministration in them, have proved prejudicial and very dangerous both to the Church and Commonwealth."[1] Speaking to the question of this petition and in defence of the bishops even Lord Falkland spoke with bated breath: "I do not," he says, "believe them to be *jure divino*, nay, I believe them not to be *jure divino*; but neither do I believe them to be *injuriâ humanâ*; I neither consider them as necessary, nor as unlawful—but as convenient or inconvenient." He pleaded for reform not abolition. Time was when such a plea would have been heard, but it was now too late to stem the rising waters. The grievances complained of in the petition were ranged under various heads, one of them being the claim of the hierarchy to be a Divine institution, and the assumption on the part of the bishops of an exclusive power to ordain. When the question was raised as to the competence of Parliament to discuss these points, on a division the House voted that the "challenge of the

Divine right of Episcopacy is a question fit to be presented." This was in February, and the following May Sir Edward Dering, the member for Kent, brought in a Bill entitled "An Act for the utter abolishing and taking away of all archbishops, bishops, their chancellors, and commissaries," a short and sharp Bill which then and there went to its first reading, and not long after passed its second reading by 139 to 108.

The rest of the story belongs not to our purpose here. Suffice it to say that for years Episcopacy passed away as the ecclesiastical system of the State, giving place first to a partially organised Presbyterianism and then to Oliver Cromwell's State Church, which lasted from 1653 to 1660, and which recognised and comprised the various forms of religious conviction to be found in the nation. There was literally no Act of Uniformity. The rights of patrons were reserved, but beyond this all that was required was a certificate from some responsible persons to whom the minister presented by the patron was known, testifying that he was a worthy man and a fit person to take the cure of souls. This was all. No articles of faith were prescribed, no subscription was enforced, and no mention made by name either of Episcopacy, Presbyterianism, Congregationalism, or of the question of baptism. Beyond conserving the rights of patrons, the commissioners were limited by no statutory conditions, were guided by no creed, statute, canon, or established usage.

How this system would have stood the wear and tear of time it is difficult to say. Everything in those days depended upon the controlling force of the one strong hand of the Lord Protector, when that hand fell powerless the ecclesiastical system of the last few years fell

XI.] *The Anglican Church from* 1603 *to* 1833   421

with it. Cromwell passed away and before many months were over the King came back and the bishops with him.

At the Restoration of 1660, and after the King's Declaration from Breda of liberty to tender consciences it was sanguinely hoped by some that an era of religious freedom was about to dawn. But the proceedings of the Savoy Conference of 1661 soon dispelled this illusion. Professor Collins has recently told us that it is impossible to say that the Reformation was completed until the Savoy Conference —a century and a third after the beginning of the movement; that it was not till then that the Church defined her position as regarded Puritanism, and forbade those to preach in her name who did not believe her doctrines; it was at that Conference, he says, that for the first time the Puritans were brought face to face with the now fully-matured position of the Reformed English Church.[1] Considering that that Conference was a sham from the beginning and therefore a pre-destined failure; that it was followed by what Archdeacon Hare described as that schismatical Act of Uniformity, an Act which was meant as a scourge for Nonconformists, but which has become a yoke for the necks of Churchmen themselves—a yoke too heavy to be borne; when we further remember that the Act of Uniformity was followed by the ejectment of two thousand of the most godly ministers of the Church; by the cruel Conventicle Acts of 1664 and 1670; and by the Five Mile Act of 1665; that the story of fines and imprisonment by which during the years that followed

[1] *The Reformation and its Consequences:* A course of Lectures by the

thousands were ruined, and thousands perished for conscience' sake—when we remember all this it seems an ill-omened time for a Professor of Ecclesiastical History to point to as the time when the Puritans were first "brought face to face with the now fully-matured position of the Reformed English Church." It would be truer to say that the cruelties and tyrannies which followed the Savoy Conference brought in the Revolution of 1688 for the nation, and a century and more of spiritual deadness and worldly stagnation for the Church. Certainly it is not to this time that we are to look as the period when apostolic power and supernatural grace glorified the Episcopate most.

And this is the point with which we are still more immediately concerned. Even now, after that Conference which we are asked to accept as marking the "now fully-matured position of the Reformed English Church," that Church does not seem to have been very clear in its convictions on the subject of Apostolical Succession and the absolute indispensability of bishops to the spiritual life of the Church. One of those who took the most prominent part in the Savoy Conference on the side of the Church was Dr. Cosin. Baxter, who was his opponent, says of him that "he was excellently versed in Canons, Councils, and Fathers, which he appeared to remember very readily when there was occasion for citation."[1] Yet Dr. Cosin seems to have recognised the Orders of Presbyterians during the years of his exile in France. He was even censured for being on terms of amity and literary intercourse with Amyraldus, Dallè, Gachè, and other pastors of the Reformed French or Huguenot Church, and for being

[1] Calamy's *Abridgement of Baxter's Life and Times*, i. 172.

present at their services.[1] The Editor of the "Cosin Correspondence" for the Surtees Society, the Rev. G. Ornsby, was perplexed: "We should scarcely have expected," he says, "to have found a man like Cosin recognising the validity of the Orders of the French Protestant Ministers of Charenton, joining in their worship, and permitting his children to do the same." Further, Cosin on his return to England in 1660 was made bishop of Durham, and in the autumn of the following year, the year of the Savoy Conference, he held a synod of his clergy at Newcastle and Durham. Writing afterwards to Sancroft, his chaplain, he tells him that he has only had to silence one preacher, and that on the ground of his "having neither episcopal nor *presbiteriall* ordination." As Mr. Ornsby says, "the inference is obvious that if the latter could have been proved the bishop would not have refused to accept him as a worker in his diocese."[2] The inference is not only obvious but in accordance with what Cosin said on another occasion: "If," said he, "we are to consider the ministers of the Presbyterian Churches as unordained, we must excommunicate the Lutheran Churches, and then what will become of the Protestant party?" The bishop of Lincoln, Dr. Sanderson, who was also at the Conference, held similar views to those of the bishop of Durham. In a treatise he wrote on *Episcopacy not prejudicial to Royal Power* he explained the *jus divinum* of bishops to mean much less than it is usually supposed to mean, at most merely apostolical institution. Baxter tells us also that at his death Sanderson

[1] Smith's *Vita Cosini*, p. 19.
[2] Surtees Society Publications—*Cosin Correspondence*, vol. ii., Introduc-

made it his request that the Ejected Nonconformist Ministers might be used again in the Church.

Amongst those prominent in the ecclesiastical activities of the second half of the seventeenth century few take precedence of Edward Stillingfleet, chaplain to Charles II., and successively canon and dean of St. Paul's, and bishop of Worcester. Though his *Irenicum* was written before the Restoration, it was published after that event, and a second edition was issued after the Act of Uniformity in 1662. In it he says (p. 14) that "God by His own laws hath given men a power and liberty to determine the particular form of Church government among them. And hence it may appear that though one form of government be agreeable to the Word of God, it doth not follow that another is not; or, because one is lawful another is unlawful. Nothing is founded upon a Divine Right, nor can bind Christians as a positive law but what may be certainly known to have come from God with an intention to oblige believers to the world's end." Very much to the purpose he says that even if it can be shown that Christ by His act gave the apostles superiority of order and jurisdiction over the pastors of their time, "yet it must further be proved that it was Christ's intention that superiority should continue in their successors, or it makes nothing to the purpose." " A necessary and unalterable Divine Right," he says (p. 26), " must be founded either upon a Law of Nature or some positive Law of God sufficiently declared to be perpetually binding." " The form of Church government is left in great uncertainty in Scripture," he adds, " and when turning from Scripture we follow the scent of the Game into the wood of Antiquity it will be easier to lose ourselves therein, than to find that which we are upon the pursuit of—a *jus divinum* of any one particular form of government" (p. 294). He holds that "the Succession so much pleaded by the writers of the primitive Church was not a succession of persons in *apostolic power*, but a succession in *apostolic doctrine*." He observes "the original of the name of *Holy Orders* in the Church, not as the papists and others following them, as though it noted anything inherent by way of (I know not what) character in the person, but because the persons ordained were thereby admitted *in Ordinem* among the number of Church officers. From the Romans the use of the word came into the Church, and thence Ordination, *ex vi vocis*, imports no more than solemn admission into this order of Presbyters." These, it will be seen, are somewhat decisive utterances to be republished by a Churchman destined to be a bishop, and republished after that Savoy Conference at which "the Church defined her position as regarded Puritanism," and assumed her "now fully-matured position as the Reformed English Church." It is true that Stillingfleet was using these arguments against the claim of *jus divinum* maintained by Presbyterians, but this does not make them less true when applied to the similar claim made by Episcopalians. It is true also that as Stillingfleet grew older, like some other men, he grew more conservative, and twenty years later, as dean of St. Paul's, harked back from some of the opinions he had held and taught from his Bedfordshire rectory of Sutton. But it is possible for opinions to be still sound and good even though some men have ceased to hold them.

In 1688 came the Great Revolution and in 1689 the Act of Toleration, which, by granting liberty of worship, among the institutions of the country. Further, with the granting of Toleration came speculations about Comprehension. Happily these speculations came to nothing; at the same time they served a purpose so far as to throw light on our inquiry, inasmuch as they reveal the true inwardness of the Church leaders of the time on the question of Church Orders and Apostolical Succession. On the 13th September, 1689, a Commission was appointed by Royal Letters Patent, consisting of ten bishops and twenty divines, whose duty it should be to prepare certain matters to be considered by Convocation. About the time of passing this Commission Tillotson, then dean of St. Paul's, drew up a paper a copy of which is entered in shorthand in his commonplace book, entitled, *Concessions which will probably be made by the Church of England for the Union of Protestants; which I sent to the Earl of Portland by Dr. Stillingfleet, Sept.* 13, 1689. On this paper there are seven proposed concessions, the sixth of which is —That for the future those who have been ordained in any of the foreign Reformed Churches be not required to be re-ordained here, to render them capable of preferment in this Church. The seventh concession refers to English ministers and is to this effect: That those who have been ordained only by presbyters shall not be compelled to renounce their former ordination; but if they have any doubts as to the validity of such ordination it is sufficient if they are ordained conditionally.[1] Further, on the 11th of the following March, a Bill "for uniting their Majesties' Protestant subjects" was introduced in the House of Lords and

[1] *Life of John Tillotson, Archbishop of Canterbury*, by Thos. Birch, D.D., 2nd ed., 1753, p. 168.

that day received its first reading. On the occasion of the second reading on the 14th March, Barlowe, bishop of Lincoln, took part in the debate, saying that he considered ordination by presbyters to be good and sufficient and in order to the taking of Nonconformists into the Church, it was not necessary there should be the imposition of episcopal hands.

The Commission of Bishops and Divines, appointed September 13th, held eighteen sessions from October 3rd to November 18th, considering such alterations in the Prayer Book as might be desirable to recommend to Convocation with a view to Comprehension. No fewer than 598 changes were considered, many of them, of course, being merely verbal but others more important. The Calendar was revised and Fasts and Festivals struck out; in no fewer than fifty places *priest* was changed to *minister;* in seven others *curate* was changed to *minister;* twice the word *priests* is altered to *presbyters*, and once to *presbyters (commonly called priests)*. Where it is said in the rubric, "the Priest is to consecrate," the words are altered to, "the Minister shall use this form"; and in the Ordination Service the words "Receive the Holy Ghost for the office and work of a Priest" are proposed to be removed and a prayer for the Divine blessing upon the ordinand substituted.

The original book of Alterations was to be preserved in the Library at Lambeth; but to be kept secret and under the immediate custody of the Archbishop.[1] It was not made public till, by an Order of the House of

[1] *Copy of the Alterations in the Book of Common Prayer prepared by the*

Commons of June 2, 1854, it was eventually printed. The Commission came to no practical result, but the changes proposed by so many bishops and divines in the Book of Common Prayer show that since the revision of 1662 the leaders of 1689 had moved further away from the doctrine of Apostolic Succession and from priestly ideas and not nearer. And if this was the direction of the movements between 1662 and 1689 still more was it the case as the eighteenth century went on its way. For the question of the Divine Right of kings came to be much more urgent than that of the Divine Right of bishops. After the Revolution nine bishops and about four hundred of the clergy refused to swear allegiance to William III. Eventually the new bishops and those who remained in were on the side of the Court, while the country clergy sided with the squires. Mark Pattison says that the mass of the clergy were not in sympathy either politically or intellectually with their ecclesiastical superiors, and in confirmation points to the fact that the Tory foxhunter in the *Freeholder* (No. 22) "thinks the neighbouring shire very happy for having scarce a Presbyterian in it except the Bishop ;" while Hickes the Nonjuror "thanks God that the main body of the clergy are in their hearts Jacobites."[1] This rift in the lute as between bishops and clergy is seen by what took place in Convocation after the accession of Queen Anne. The Lower House, stung by a reflection made on the part of the bishops, as to their want of respect for the Episcopal Order, made formal declaration of their acknowledgment of that Order as superior to that of presbyters, as in fact of *Divine*, apostolical institution. The same day they presented a further

[1] *Tendencies of Religious Thought in England*, 1688-1750.

address, signifying that as they found that by their declaration just made they had given new offence, that after being accused of making too little of the Order of Bishops they were now charged with having made too much of it: they humbly besought the bishops themselves to make an authoritative deliverance on the subject, and so repress Erastian opinions. There was really more subtlety than humility in all this, for, as Perry suggests, it is probable that the majority of bishops in the Upper House at that time would have decided against the Divine Right,[1] and the Lower House knew it and were bent on getting the bishops to commit themselves. They were, however, too wary for that, knowing that any decision on the subject just then, either for or against, would only have been productive of mischief.

Succeeding bishops were equally indifferent on what is now regarded as this vital question. Archbishop Wake, who succeeded Tenison in 1715, was as fervent in his friendship with the foreign Reformed Churches as had been Cranmer or Jewel in the earlier time. He was ready to welcome a closer union with them under almost any conditions.[2] Writing, April 8, 1719, to his "very dear brothers," the pastors and professors of Geneva, after referring to the efforts he had made on behalf of the Piedmontese and Hungarian Churches, he expresses the longing desire he felt for union among the Reformed Churches. On the same subject he

[1] *History of the Church of England*, by the Rev. G. G. Perry, M.A., 1862, ii. 160-2.
[2] The *Wake Correspondence* in the Library of Christ Church, Oxford. *Cf.* also *Correspondance fraternelle de l'Église Anglicane avec les autres Églises Réformées*, par Claude Groteste de la Mothe, Ministre de l'Église

wrote letters to Professor Schürer of Berne and to Professor Turretin of Geneva; and also carried on correspondence with the Presbyterian Protestants of Nismes, Lithuania, and other countries. The archbishop of York, too, Dr. Sharp, though unwilling to discuss terms of conciliation with Nonconformists at home, was accustomed in the friendliest manner to take the communion with congregations of foreign Protestants whenever he might be travelling abroad.[1] With him Apostolic Succession was apparently a mere question of latitude and longitude, as it was with William Wall, who, good Churchman as he was, thought that members of the Church of Denmark, for instance, would have no right to separate from their fellow-members on the plea that they liked the ways even of the Church of England better.[2]

The Nonjurors, who after the Revolution still clung to the hopeless cause of the Stuarts, seem to have been the only people who kept alive anything like a belief in Apostolic Succession through the eighteenth century, and we have the extraordinary spectacle of a bishop of the Church attacking them because of this belief. After the Jacobite rising of 1715 a large mass of papers written by Dr. Hickes, the Nonjuring bishop, was seized, in portions of which he freely accused the Church of England of heresy, perjury, and schism. This led Hoadly, bishop of Bangor, to write his famous treatise, *A Preservative against the Principles and Practices of the Nonjurors in Church and State*. In this treatise Hoadly takes the general ground of denying the value of the succession of bishops altogether, rejecting the notion

---

[1] *Abbey and Overton*, i. 355, 366; Maclaine's *Mosheim*, v. 143.
[2] Wall's *History of Infant Baptism*, Pt. ii. chap. ii. 3.

of the necessity of being in communion with any particular Church, and boldly proclaiming sincerity as the only necessary requirement of a Christian profession. This brought William Law into the field, who proved a powerful antagonist on the Nonjurors' side. Still, notwithstanding the few able and conscientious men they had among them, the Nonjurors divided and dwindled and finally became extinct, and with them there seems to have passed away, too, all adherents to the doctrine of Apostolical Succession. "Would that the Nonjurors had kept up the Succession!" exclaims Hurrell Froude. The bishop of London told Newman and his friends that the belief in the Apostolic Succession had gone out with the Nonjurors. "We can count you," he said (*Apol.*, p. 94). And Dr. Arnold, writing to Dr. Pusey in 1834, after expressing his amazement at the efforts being made by him and his party to set up the idol of tradition in a Protestant Church, goes on to say that "the system pursued in Oxford seems to be leading to a revival of the Nonjurors, a party far too mischievous and too foolish ever to be revived with success. But it may be revived enough to do harm— to cause the ruin of the Church of England first—and, so far as human folly and corruption can, to obstruct the progress of the Church of Christ."[1]

The conclusion, then, to which we have thus far been led is, that with the brief exceptions of the period of Laud's ascendency in the seventeenth century and of the Nonjurors' movement in the eighteenth, it may be affirmed that till the Tractarian Movement of 1833 the doctrine of Apostolic Succession, as now understood, was *not* the doctrine of the Church of England. With

Laud it rose and with him it fell; with the Nonjurors it revived, but they were ejected from the Church, and with them it went out. Mozley, who was at first associated with the Oxford Movement, recognised the fact that the "Tracts for the Times" went straight against the whole course of the Church of England for three centuries past: they upheld what a king and a primate had lost their heads for; what the monarchy, the Church, the whole constitution, and the greater part of the gentry had been overthrown for; what afterwards bishops and clergy had been cast out for, and the Convocation suspended a century for. The doctrines advocated in these Tracts had been all but prohibited in the Church of England, as they probably would have remained to this day, he thinks, had not the revolutionary aspect of the Reformed Parliament seemed to place the Church of England in the old dilemma between the bear closing up behind and the precipice yawning in front.

During the year of the Reform Bill alarming accounts were going the round of the combination rooms at Oxford as to what was being done, said, threatened, and designed.[1] The bishops had been told to set their house in order; it was even rumoured that the Prayer Book was to be revised by Parliament and the Creeds abolished, at least in public worship. That this scare was the moving cause at the outset there is complete consensus of opinion on the part of men like Hurrell Froude, John Henry Newman, John Keble, Dean Church, and Canon Liddon. As the doctrine of Apostolical Succession was brought for-

[1] *Reminiscences chiefly of Oriel College and the Oxford Movement*, by the Rev. T. Mozley, M.A., 1882, pp. 407-8.

ward in the sixteenth century to checkmate the Presbyterians, so its revival in the nineteenth was meant as a breakwater to the rising tide of Liberalism which set in with the Repeal of the Test and Corporation Acts in 1828. Till then Newman was not a High Churchman, but in that year his Tory friend and fellow-tutor, who had rooms over his, used to come down in the evenings to talk over what he called the "shameful Repeal of Dissenters' Liabilities," and of a similar Bill soon to come on in the interests of the Romanists. When the Reform Bill of 1831 was in actual progress, Newman writes: "May the good Lord save His Church in this her hour of peril when Satan seeks to sap and corrupt where he dare not openly assault!" Writing also from Rome in 1833 he says: "We have just heard of the Irish Church Reform Bill. Well done, my blind Premier! Confiscate and rob, till, like Samson, you pull down the political structure on your own heads." In his *Apologia* he speaks of the spirit of Liberalism as characteristic of the destined Antichrist.

The case being plainly thus, we naturally ask what the changes were which carried consternation to clerical circles from 1828 to 1833, and which led to the promulgation of the doctrine of Apostolical Succession? Mozley had shared, he said, in the alarm, but though the changes had been carried out he yet lived to tell the tale—indeed, to help the doing of it; for he had to confess that some things he thought very bad then, he had come to think better of. The first of the series was the Repeal of those Test and Corporation Acts by which Nonconformists, simply for their opinions, the State. Again, till 1829 the Roman Catholics of Ireland, though a majority of the nation, saw the whole political power of the country in the hands of the Protestant minority. Excluded from every office of trust and power, they were not even permitted to send representatives of their own faith to the Imperial Parliament. The Roman Catholic Emancipation Act of 1829 removed this injustice. Till 1832 Gatton, which had five voters, and Old Sarum, which had none, each returned a member of Parliament, while Manchester, Birmingham, Leeds, Sheffield, and other large towns had no representatives at all. The majority of the House of Commons were the representatives of a few individuals or close corporations, who generally sold their right of nomination for a valuable consideration. The dreaded Reform Bill of 1832 set all this right. Till 1833 the tithes in Ireland were collected from Roman Catholics for the Protestant Church at the point of the bayonet, and were rapidly becoming uncollectable even in that way. Affrays were frequent, in which sometimes policemen were killed and sometimes peasants. It was resolved to lessen the strain by lessening the number of bishoprics, which were out of all proportion to the number of members of the Established Church. The Irish Church Bill of 1833, which was brought in by Churchmen with the view of strengthening the Church, reduced the bishoprics from twenty-two to twelve, and the archbishoprics from four to two. These were the changes that constituted, in the opinion of some, the reign of Antichrist, and against the further extension of which the standard of battle must be unfurled.

This is the chronological order: in February, 1833

the Irish Secretary brought in the Irish Church Bill for the suppression of ten dioceses; at Midsummer Hugh James Rose and his friends met in his rectory at Hadleigh for concerted action; closely following upon this meetings were held at Oriel College leading to the formation of "The Association of the Friends of the Church"; on the 14th of July Keble preached his Assize Sermon in the University pulpit on National Apostasy, and Newman says: "I have ever considered and kept the day as the start of the religious movement of 1833." Finally, on the 9th of September following, suddenly appeared the first three of the ninety "Tracts for the Times."

These first three Tracts were all written by Newman himself. In an opening address he grounds his appeal to the clergy on the political situation. "Let me," he says, come at once to the subject which leads me to address you. Should the Government and the country so far forget their God as to cast off the Church, to deprive it of its temporal honours and substance, *on what* will you rest the claim of respect and attention which you make upon your flocks? Hitherto you have been upheld by your birth, your education, your wealth, your connexions; should these secular advantages cease, on what must Christ's ministers depend? Is not this a serious practical question? . . . I fear we have neglected the real ground on which our authority is built—OUR APOSTOLICAL DESCENT. We have been born, not of blood, nor of the will of the flesh, nor of the will of man, but of God. The Lord Jesus Christ gave His Spirit to His apostles; they in their turn been handed down to our present bishops, who have appointed us as their assistants, and in some sense representatives."

Newman next makes a bold assertion. When addressing his brethren of the clergy, he says: "Now every one of us believes this. I know that some will at first deny they do; still they *do* believe it, for it is the doctrine of the Ordination Service." When we remember that it was Cranmer who drew up this Ordination Service, and that he was in closest intercourse with the Foreign Protestants at the time, this argument seems not to carry much weight. He goes on to say: "It is plain that the bishop only transmits, and that the Christian Ministry is a *succession*. And if we trace back the power of ordination from hand to hand, of course we shall come to the Apostles at last. We know we do, as a plain historical fact ; and therefore all we, who have been ordained clergy, in the very form of our ordination acknowledged the doctrine of the APOSTOLICAL SUCCESSION."

These, it will be seen, are mere assertions. For the foundations on which they rest we have to turn from this Tract No. I. to two other Tracts, both also written by Newman—to Tract No. XIX. "On arguing concerning the Apostolical Succession," and to Tract No. XLV. on "The Grounds of our Faith." Tract No. XIX. was addressed to clergy in the same perplexed condition as the bishop of whom Newman tells us, who "could not make up his mind whether he held the doctrine or not." To such as these the writer says : "Men are sometimes disappointed with the proofs offered as to the necessity of Episcopal ordination in order to constitute a minister of Christ. They consider these proofs to be not so strong as they expected, or as they think desirable. . . . Bishop Butler has convincingly shown that the faintest probabilities are strong enough to determine our *conduct* as a matter of duty. If there be but a reasonable likelihood of our pleasing Christ more by keeping than by not keeping to the fellowship of the Apostolic Ministry, this of course ought to be enough."

The Tract on "The Grounds for our Faith" is addressed not to the clergy but to such of the laity as were of doubtful mind. "When," says Newman, "a clergyman has spoken strongly in defence of Episcopacy a hearer will go away saying that there is much that is very able and forcible, but after all *there is very little about Episcopacy in Scripture.* This is the point to which a shrewd, clear-headed reasoner will resort— "after all": the doctrine is plausible, useful, generally received hitherto; granted—*but* Scripture says very little about it. Now it cannot be for a moment allowed that Scripture *contains* little on the subject of Church Government; though it may readily be granted that it *obtrudes* on the reader little about it. The doctrine is in it, not on it, not on the surface. Let us suppose *for the sake of argument* that Episcopacy is in fact not at all mentioned in Scripture : even then it would be our duty to receive it. Why? because the first Christians received it. If we wish to get at the truth, no matter how we get at it *if* we get at it. If it be a fact that the earliest Christian communities were universally Episcopal, it is a reason for our maintaining Episcopacy. Suppose we maintain, as we may well, that it *is* enjoined in Scripture. An objector will say that at all events it out by a great deal of delicate care and skill. Here comes in the operation of that principle of *faith* in opposition to *criticism:* the principle of being content with a little light, where we cannot obtain sunshine. If it is *probably* pleasing to Christ let us maintain it."

Building the whole theory of Apostolical Succession on arguments like these is like building a pyramid on its apex, and one is not much more convinced when Dr. Pusey, referring to these Early Tracts in later life, tell us "those on Apostolical Succession produced a great effect. I thought the subject dry and not likely to interest people, but it was not so. The claim had been so entirely forgotten as to be practically new. One person, a dissenter in the Isle of Wight, said she must go to Church to see these successors of the Apostles. *She went and remained.*"[1] This lady's experience seems to have made a great impression on Dr. Pusey, for he recalls it after an interval of more than forty years. The Queen of Sheba had heard the fame of King Solomon, but when she actually saw him "there was no more spirit in her." Similarly in the case referred to; at the sight of a successor of the apostles in the pulpit the lady's nonconformity all dropped from her and she remained within the fold. How long the enchantment lasted we are not told. In the case of Newman himself the effect produced by the presence of a bishop seems not to have been so permanent as we might have expected. At one time he said: "What was to me *jure divino* was the voice of my Bishop in his own person. My own Bishop was my Pope; I knew no other; the successor of the Apostles, the Vicar of Christ" (*Apol.*, 122). Again,

[1] Liddon's *Life of Pusey*, vol. i. p. 279.

writing to Dr. Pusey in 1838, and referring to his bishop, he says : "Sometimes when I have stood by as he put on his robes, I felt as if it would be such a relief if I could have fallen at his feet and kissed them." [1] But the illusion passed, and good Dr. Bagot was brought down from the pedestal of semi-deification to which his worshipper had thus exalted him. The vision divine must have long since faded into the light of common day, when on the 9th of October, 1845, at Littlemore, and at the hands of Father Dominic, the Passionist, John Henry Newman was received into the Church of Rome.

As the news of this final step passed from lip to lip in those days it carried consternation to many who had looked to him for guidance. It carries instruction now to those who have eyes to see beneath the surface. In order to obtain moral certainty Newman committed mental suicide. With all his genius, and with all his fine Christian feeling, he surrendered his mind and the control of his life to men greatly his inferiors in mental and spiritual power. He was in search of an infallible authority, and he was seeking it where it can never be found. The right attitude of the devout mind—the attitude which alone receives profit from revelation—it is true, is that of profound humility towards an infallible authority above us, but that authority is wielded by God not by man.[2] Newman was the great prophet of the sacerdotal movement of the nineteenth century, and the termination of his career may be regarded as a prophecy of its own future. He discovered that Anglican claims are built on a shifting foundation, as they certainly are. He looked up with slavish reverence to his own bishop till the discovery came that he was only an ecclesiastical phantom, destitute of reality, and therefore of authority. So he drifted to what must ever be the final goal of all who rest on mere authority. In the last resort Church authority means Roman authority. There is no halting on the Avernian steep till you reach the bottom. We must either accept human authority in its final and complete form of obstinacy against every appeal of reason; or we must set forth on the arduous but honourable path upward to truth and God for ourselves. Newman believed that the Church's infallibility was God's provision for preserving religion in the world, and for restraining freedom of thought and rescuing it from its own suicidal excesses. So far from this the assumption of infallibility has done more to foster scepticism than any other cause. When you ask men to believe too much, they usually end in believing too little. There are those who can never accept the view that the great interests of human life, all its deepest sanctities, are bound up with such questions as episcopal succession, patristic tradition, and sacerdotal grace. When, therefore, the perverse alternative comes to be—either what the Church tells you or nothing, honest men will come to think that it had better be nothing than what they know to be a lie. It will never do to put God's providence as revealed in human institutions above God's Spirit as revealed in conscience and reason. The ultimate seat of judgement to which even Divine Revelation makes its constant appeal is in the human soul itself; not in councils, popes, or bishops. We reach rest and certainty through an unswerving trust in those enduring verities which, led by the Spirit of God, our reason and the experience of life have taught us. Well said the son of Sirach : " Make the counsel of thy heart to stand ; for there is none more faithful unto thee than it. For a man's soul is sometime wont to bring him tidings, more than seven watchmen that sit on high on a watch-tower. And above all this intreat the Most High, that He may direct thy way in truth " (*Eccl.* xxxvii., 13-15).

In one important respect the sacerdotal movement of this century was a movement in advance, inasmuch as it was animated by a spiritual motive, by something higher than the old Establishment conception of the Church. The High Churchman of the Old School looked upon Dissent in all its forms as a crime against the State. To him the Church was part of the Constitution and the Prayer Book an Act of Parliament which only folly or disloyalty could quarrel with. The royal arms fixed up over the chancel arch of his parish church gave him a pleasant assurance that he was right both for this world and the next; for to be of the king's religion was the duty of every loyal Englishman. The Establishment was everything. Since Presbyterianism was the established religion in Scotland, Churchmen like Sir Robert Inglis maintained that even their own Episcopalianism, north of the Tweed, was nothing more than schismatical dissent to be frowned down and discouraged. It was a gain, therefore, a step up nearer the light, when Churchmen learnt at last the lesson Nonconformists had so long been trying to teach them, that the Church and the Establishment were not one and the same thing, and that a lion and a unicorn, as Newman

tion to a serious mind. It was a gain, too, that the clergy in many a parish underwent a transformation of character. Pluralists who built up fortunes for their families out of the Church ; country gentlemen in orders who rode to hounds, shot, danced, and farmed, not to mention other things for which not so much could be said—these gave place to men who were earnest and self-sacrificing according to their lights.

Still, when these and other concessions have all been freely made, it must yet be affirmed that sacerdotalism is a reactionary movement. It is largely a pagan revival, and it owes much of its success to the fact that it makes its appeal to men by that sensuous display in worship which satisfies people who want to have a religion without being religious. It has been said that a strong reliance on outward authority and a weak hold on inward spiritual reality is the most dangerous of all combinations. And this is the present danger of the Anglican Church. The danger is all the greater inasmuch as the Broad Church is not now the force it was, and the Evangelicals have all but effaced themselves by trimming their sails to catch the favouring breeze, and by using the passwords and following too many of the modes of a system with which in their hearts they can have but little sympathy indeed.

To those who care for the interests of spiritual religion the present outlook is not without anxiety. While sacerdotalism by its revival has awakened earnestness in many of the clergy and created a certain kind of interest in some sections of the laity, it is at the same time to be feared that, by its tawdry follies and absurd pretensions, it has alienated many sensible men from religion altogether. Further, there can be no question that it has greatly intensified sectarian bitterness by its exclusiveness; and it has created a spirit in its votaries as fierce and all-consuming as that which dwelt in the men against whom our Lord said such scathing things, the men who compassed sea and land to make one proselyte into whom they infused a spirit even worse than their own. The attitude these men assume towards all other Churches is utterly indefensible and un-Christian unless they can prove which they never have yet done, that their system, and theirs alone, is ordained of Heaven. Indeed this has been in effect admitted. Some years ago Archbishop Tait said he "could hardly imagine there were two bishops on the bench, or one clergyman in fifty, who would deny the validity of the Orders of Presbyterian clergymen, solely on account of their wanting the imposition of Episcopal hands." To this the *Church Quarterly Review* somewhat angrily, but most justly, replied: "If the episcopal hand is really unnecessary to valid ordination, the Church of England is guilty of no little tyranny—not to say schism—in her treatment of non-episcopal communities" (*Oct.*, 1885). Churchmen will be wise if they weigh these words and look into the question somewhat further.

Still, while forecasting the future with somewhat of concern, we may yet reassure ourselves of the fact that priests and sacerdotalism will never have permanent influence among the English people. The masculine mind in the Church is unfortunately too silent, but also it is unbelieving; even now there are not wanting signs of reaction, and the end is not yet.

Meantime the prevalent superstition furnishes the Free Churches with that opportunity which is their part in the national life and have no need to feel ashamed as they look back over the path they have travelled. While necessity has been laid upon them to assail abuses and to contend against wrong, their work has yet been mainly constructive. While the dominant Church has too often taken its place and used its influence on the side of wealth and privilege, Free Churchmen have been helping to carry great principles of justice and right to victory and supremacy; have taken their part in the moral and remedial legislation of the time; and have kept religion alive in places where but for their self-denying endeavours it might have died out altogether.

The work now immediately before them is not less honourable or arduous than that accomplished in the past. The thing now needing more than ever to be done is to proclaim and embody the Scripture doctrine of the Church—to realise in actual life that ecclesiastical ideal which the Epistle to the Ephesians long since placed before us, and which has only been partially realised as yet. That ideal is a community which is Christ's body, the fulness of Him that filleth all in all; a community which not only cares for the individual, but regards itself as a Divine Society intended to leaven all society; which is supernatural not because it is ruled by a Heaven-ordained priesthood, but because the Spirit of God dwells in every member of the Christian commonalty. The ideal is not that of maintaining a mere devotional worship for its own sake, but that of a process of culture and development which qualifies every saint of God for a "work of ministering;" some form of service to be rendered for others, a conscious and joyful sense of membership in the body of Christ, its dignity and responsibility, to be felt by all. And this service must not be narrowed down to the visible present but be ennobled and animated by a constant outlook towards that great time when the goal shall be reached and we "all attain unto the unity of the faith and of the knowledge of the Son of God." With all diligence we are to make our own calling and election sure; with all affection to cherish and serve the brotherhood of mankind; yet are we ever to be widening our aims and extending our vision to take in that great purpose of God which "is to sum up all things in Christ, the things in the heavens and the things upon the earth." Our mission now is "to make all men see what is the dispensation of the mystery which from all ages hath been hid in God who created all things: to the intent that now unto the principalities and powers in the heavenly places might be made known through the Church the manifold wisdom of God, according to the eternal purpose which He purposed in Christ Jesus our Lord."

APPENDIX

"A VINDICATION OF THE BULL 'APOSTOLICÆ CURÆ.'
A LETTER ON ANGLICAN ORDERS, BY THE
CARDINAL ARCHBISHOP AND BISHOPS OF THE
PROVINCE OF WESTMINSTER" (JANUARY, 1898).

WE have already seen (p. 61) that in February, 1897, the Archbishops of Canterbury and York made reply to the Papal Bull *Apostolicæ Curæ*, of the previous September, which pronounced all Anglican Orders since the Reformation to be absolutely null and utterly void. To this reply of the Archbishops, Cardinal Vaughan, and the fifteen Roman Catholic Bishops of the Province of Westminster, published a rejoinder on the 10th of January, 1898, after the present work was in type. It may be worth while in an additional page or two to show the bearing of this rejoinder on the general question at issue.

Cardinal Vaughan and his colleagues are anxious in the outset to defend the Pope from the charge of having wantonly assailed the Anglican Church by his hostile judgement on the Orders of its clergy. They plainly declare, what was pretty well known before, that the Pope's decision on the question was really

"It is matter of common knowledge," they say, "that some members of your Communion allied themselves with some members of ours in order to work for corporate reunion, and that they deemed it necessary for the success of their movement that we should cease to reject your Orders. To assist them in bringing this to pass they caused a treatise containing an effective statement of your arguments to be written in Latin, and circulated among our theologians and ecclesiastical rulers abroad. At Rome they were especially assiduous in distributing copies, and they presented one to the Holy Father himself" (p. 6).

After this preliminary statement they naturally, from their point of view, claim for the Pope the fullest right to deliver judgement with authority: "The Pope has been appointed by the Lord of all men to an office which embraces all men within its merciful scope. He must therefore be free whenever he judges it opportune, to speak out on the subject of his charge, and to address not only Catholics but others also, to whatever class or section of mankind they may belong" (p. 5). We may observe, by the way, that if the facts be as stated in the foregoing lecture on the "Development of the Papacy," this claim is simply the outgrowth of ecclesiastical ambition and is utterly destitute of Divine authority. Still, as we might expect, this is the position Cardinal Vaughan takes. Audacity, if it be audacious enough, often succeeds. He confidently asks: "If he [the Pope] be not capable of giving a final judgement on such a matter, who else in the world can be capable of giving one? And if no one can give a final judgement as to what is and what is not valid administration of a sacrament, as to what is and what is not the Christian Priesthood and Sacrifice, in what a condition of inextricable chaos has Christ left His Church! In short, to deny Leo XIII.'s competency to define the conditions of a valid sacrament, is to strike at the very roots of the sacramental system. For if there be no authority on earth capable of deciding so fundamental a point, how can we continue to attach vital importance to the sacraments, or to regard them as stable rites of Divine institution on the due observance of which the maintenance of our spiritual life depends?" (p. 3). May we not ask, Is not this way of putting the case, in effect, a tremendous argument against the whole Papal and priestly system? Is it possible to believe that deliverance from absolute chaos, the whole administration of the spiritual order of the Universe actually depends on the decision of the amiable old gentleman who happens just now to be the Master of the Vatican? To maintain this, is indeed to make an overwhelming demand on the credulity of mankind.

This pamphlet of the Cardinal makes yet more clear than ever that the whole claim of the hierarchical sacerdotal system rests upon a mere materialistic view of the sacraments, and that that materialistic view is based on the traditions of men and not on the revelations of God. "We readily allow," it says, "that Holy Scripture has left us no adequate guidance on this point"—the power of National Churches—" but the Catholic Church has never supposed that Holy Scripture to the exclusion of tradition is the sole rule of faith." . . . " Immemorial usage, whether or not it has in the course of ages incorporated superfluous accretions, must, in the estimation

Church, at least have retained whatever is necessary" (p. 42).

But, passing by this general question, the value of this Roman Catholic rejoinder consists in the fact that, as if with Ithuriel spear, it detects and exposes the vacillation, contradictory character and absolute untenableness of the present Anglican position on the matter of the consecration of the Eucharist. In the Bull which he issued the Pope did not declare Anglican Orders to be null and void because he believed the old "Nag's Head" story about Archbishop Parker's consecration, or because he doubted the genuineness of Bishop Barlow's power to consecrate. He did not even refer to these matters, but went straight to the main issue; declaring the Anglican Ordinal to be defective in matter, form, and intention, and utterly incapable of imparting "the power of consecrating and offering the true body and blood of the Lord."

When the two English Archbishops, under "a certain deep and strong emotion," made formal reply to the Pope, whom they describe as "our most venerable brother," "our revered brother in Christ," this was the one question with which they had to deal—Do you claim power to consecrate the elements of the Eucharist in the way in which it was claimed in the English Church before the Reformation? and did Cranmer and the other Reformers who drew up your formularies intend to claim that power? On these points the reply of the Archbishops was distinctly evasive. Section XI. gives their answer on this, in the sacerdotal view, vital point :—

"As regards the passages quoted by the Pope, we answer that we make provision with the greatest reverence for the consecration of the holy Eucharist, and commit it only to properly ordained priests, and to no other ministers of the Church. Further, we truly teach the doctrine of the Eucharistic sacrifice, and do not believe it to be a 'nude commemoration of the sacrifice of the Cross'—an opinion which seems to be attributed to us by the quotation made from the Council of Trent. But we think it sufficient in the Liturgy which we use in celebrating the holy Eucharist —while lifting up our hearts to the Lord, and when now consecrating the gifts already offered, that they may become to us the Body and Blood of our Lord Jesus Christ—to signify the sacrifice which is offered at that point of the service in such terms as these. We continue a perpetual memory of the precious death of Christ, who is our Advocate with the Father and the propitiation for our sins, according to His precept, until His coming again. For first we offer the sacrifice of praise and thanksgiving; then next we plead and represent before the Father the sacrifice of the Cross, and by it we confidently entreat remission of sins and all other benefits of the Lord's passion for all the whole Church; and lastly, we offer the sacrifice of ourselves to the Creator of all things, which we have already signified by the oblations of His creatures. This whole action, in which the people has necessarily to take its part with the priest, we are accustomed to call the Eucharistic sacrifice."

It is obvious that all Evangelical Nonconformists could say as much as this, which is by no means the Roman Catholic doctrine. It is the Protestant view which the Archbishops have given, but it certainly is

Cardinal Vaughan puts the Archbishops into a very serious dilemma when he says of this passage: "We have understood you to be expressing the same views as your standard writers; rejecting by implication the Real Objective Presence, the Sacrifice in which the true Body and Blood of Christ is the victim, and the Priesthood which claims to have received a specific spiritual power to offer such a sacrifice; but at the same time affirming and ascribing to your Church a sacrifice in which the thing offered is the congregation with its praise and its gifts, and claiming likewise for each individual, the layman as well as the clergyman, a metaphorical priesthood to correspond with this metaphorical sacrifice. . . . Your reminder that 'the people necessarily take part with the priest' in the offering of the sacrifice, seems to lean towards Cranmer's doctrine, that the 'difference that is between priest and layman in this matter is only in the ministration.' On the other hand you carefully abstain from affirming belief in the Real Objective Presence of the Body and Blood of Christ, and the sacrificial offering of that. . . . You no doubt tell us that 'you consecrate the gifts already offered that they may become to us the Body and Blood of our Lord Jesus Christ.' But this phrase also you seem to be using in Cranmer's sense. No doubt both these phrases might be understood in a more Catholic sense. But it appears inconceivable that, if you had really wished to ascribe to your Church belief in a Real Objective Presence you would have failed to say so with the utmost distinctness, for this is the very turning-point of the whole question.

"On the other hand, it is notorious that many members of your Communion have understood you in this passage to be affirming the doctrine of a Real Objective Presence, and of the Sacrifice founded on that, and it is this dispute about your meaning which moves us to ask you a question. It seems to us that, as the object of your letter was to make plain for all time the doctrine of your Church on the subject of Holy Orders, and this point about the Real Presence and the true Sacrifice lies at the very roots of that controversy, we are entitled to ask you to remove the doubt which has arisen in the way described, and tell us in unmistakable terms what your real meaning is.

"If, then, we have mistaken your meaning in the passage referred to, will you frankly say so?"

If the Archbishops of Canterbury and York answer this very straight question in one way they will alienate the sacerdotalists in the Anglican Church, and if they answer it in the only other possible way they will grieve, if not exasperate, the Protestants in that Communion. It seems like a modern application of an ancient controversy: "I will ask you one thing—the baptism of John, whence was it? from Heaven, or of men? And they reasoned with themselves, saying, If we shall say, From heaven, he will say unto us, Why did ye not then believe him? But if we shall say, Of men, we fear the people. And they answered and said, We cannot tell!"

INDEX

ABBEY and Overton, 430
Abbot, Archbishop, 391, 408
Abbot's *Anglican Career of Newman*, 385
Abyssinian Churches, 74
Acesius of Constantinople, 259
Acton's, Lord, *Study of History*, 15
Æneas Sylvius, 347
African province, 188
Agnellus, *Bishops of Ravenna*, 328
Akhmim, excavations at, 13
A'Lasco, John, 366, 368, 380, 387
Albigenses, the, 260, 282
Alexander II., 344
„ Peter, 366
Alexandria, Church of, 40
„ Catechetical Schools, 95, 138
Almeria, bishop of, 342
Ambervalia, the, 302
Ambrose of Milan, 102
Ammianus Marcellinus, 276, 288
Ancyra, Synod of, 315
Andrewes, Bishop, 395, 408-9
Aneas of Paris, 335
Angelo, Michel, 342, 346
Anrich's *Das antike Mysterienwesen*, 300

Anulinus, pro-consul, 274
ἀπέσταλκε and πέμπω, 46
Apostles other than the Twelve, 131
Apostles, prophets, and teachers, 129
Apostles as witnesses, 49
Apostolic Canons, 102, 105
„ Constitutions, 63, 72, 74, 102, 188, 190, 220
Apuleius, 294
Aquinas, Thomas, 59
Archbishops' *Reply to Leo XIII.*, 61
Aristides, *Apology* of, 14, 123
Armenian Church, the, 74
„ deputies, the, 59
Arnold of Brescia, 282
Arnold, Dr., 431
Articles of Religion, 368
Arsinoë, Churches of, 258
Asti, bishop of, 342
Asia Minor, Churches of, 309
Asia Proconsular, bishops of, 309
Athalaric, Bishop, 330
Athens, Church in, 213
Athos, monastery on Mount, 12
Augsburg, Confession of, 368

BAETICA, 326
Bancroft, Archbishop, 401
Baptism, lay, 19
Bardesanes, 236
Barlaam and Josaphat, 14
Barlow's Orders, 381
Barnabas, *Epistle* of, 12
Baronius, Cardinal, 336
Basilides, 235
Baur's question, 121
Benedict V., 343
,, VIII., 346
,, IX., 344, 349
Benevento, duchy of, 290
Benson's *Life of Cyprian*, 254
Bentham, Bishop, 382
Berengar of Tours, 58
Beveridge, Bishop, 44
Bilson's *Perpetual Government*, 402
Bishops and elders, 147
Bishops' Book, the, 304
Bithynia, 206
Blondel, David, 26, 339
Boehmer's *Diss. Juris Eccles.*, 142
Boniface, 127
Bonwetsch's *Die Geschichte des Montanismus*, 282
Borgias, the, 349
Bota, festival of, 291
Boudinhon, Abbé, 55, 57
Bramhall, Archbishop, 113
Bright's *Notes on the Canons*, 319
Bristol, bishop of, 63
Browne's *Exposition of the XXXIX. Articles*, 411
Brumalia, festival of, 291
Bucer, Martin, 366-7, 372
Bull, *Apostolicæ Curæ*, 6, 55
,, *Exultate Deo*, 59
,, *Satis Cognitum*, 6
Bunsen's *Hippolytus*, 122, 183, 232
Burleigh, Lord, 377
Burnet's *Hist. of the Reformation*, 362, 372
Bury's *Later Empire*, 281, 289, 293
Butler, Archer, 44
Byzantine chronicler, 286
Byzantium, 317

Caius College, Cambridge, 174
Cajetan, Cardinal, 341
Calamy's *Baxter's Life and Times*, 422
Callistus, 243, 310
Canon of New Testament, 220
Canons, Apostolic, 102, 105
Canons of Sardica, 321, 323
Cariati, bishop of, 342
Carthagena, 326
Catechetical Schools, 95, 138
Catholic Emancipation, 434
Cerularius, Michael, 335
Cesena, massacre of, 346
Chaldean Nestorians, 59
Channel Islands, 392
Chapuys' despatches, 370
Charles V., 9, 370
χειροτονήσαντες, 54, 155
Church Councils, origin of, 108
Chrysanthus of Constantinople, 259
Chrysostom, 103, 154, 171, 289
Church Quarterly Review, 20, 443
Church, R.W., *Purpose of Christian Ministry*, 227
Churches of the Gentiles, 140
,, Judea, 140
,, lesser subjected to greater, 311-315
Clarus of Mascula, 247
Claudius of Turin, 260
Clement, *Epistle* of, 13, 102, 130, 209, 212
Clement of Alexandria, *Stromata*, 95, 154 ; *Quis Divus*, 204
Clementine Homilies, 12
,, Forgeries, 334
Collins's Lectures on the Reformation, 421
Comprehension, Commission on, 426
Continuity of Anglican Church, 354
Constantinople, patriarch of, 5
,. Council of, 317
Constantine, Emperor, 270, 278
,, the Paulician, 284
Coptic deputies, 59
,, Use, 63
Corinth, Church at, 204-213
Cornelius of Rome, 249

Corsica, heathenism in, 290
Cortyna, Church at, 213
Cosin, Bishop, 413, 423
,, *Correspondence*, 421
Council of Carthage, 247
,, Chalcedon, 273, 317
,, Nicæa, 272
,, Paris, 248
,, Saragossa, 283
Coverdale, Miles, 377
Cox, Bishop, 363, 376, 383
Cranmer, Archbishop, 363
Creighton's *History of the Papacy*, 36, 347
Crescentii, the, 346
Cromwell's State Church, 420
Cureton, Canon, 12, 169, 175
Cusa, Cardinal, 336
Cyprian of Carthage, 249-258, 310
,, *De Unitate*, 252-258
,, *Epistles* of, 249, 256-7

DAILLÉ, Jean, 184
Damasus, Bishop, 273, 275, 324
Davenant, Bishop, 414
Davies' *History of Southampton*, 389
Deacon, office of, 142, 160
Decretals of Isidore, 178, 248, 335
,, Siricius, 324, 326
Demetrius, Patriarch, 40
Didaché the, 13, 76, 102, 124-8
Diocletian persecution, 312
Diognetus, *Epistle to*, 101
Dionysius of Alexandria, 258, 308
,, Corinth, 107, 178, 211, 306
,, Scythia, 337
Disciplini Arcana, 300
Döllinger, Dr., *Addresses*, 7, 86
,, *Fables respecting the Popes*, 335
Dominic, Father, 439
Dominicans, the, 226
Donation of Constantine, 334-6
Dupin, Dr., 4
Dutch Church in London, 387,

Eastern Church, reply of, 5
Ecclesia, the, and the Synagogue, 141
Echellensis, 42
Edersheim's *Life and Times of Jesus*, 142, 225
Eigg, Scuir of, 165
ἡγούμενοι, spiritual leaders, 130, 210
Elders, the, at Jerusalem, 144
Elizabeth and the XXXIX. Articles, 374
Elizabethan bishops, 378
Elias of Hadrianopolis, 292
Eleusis, temple at, 294, 301
Eleusinian Mysteries, 294, 301
Embden, Church at, 382-3, 387
Ἐπίσκοπος in the New Testament,146
,, civil significance of, 151, 215
Ephesus, Church at, 187
Epiphanius, 84, 154, 260
Epistle of Clement, 13, 102, 209
,, Polycarp, 180
Epistles to Churches, 105
,, of Dionysius, 212
Erasmus, 339
Erastian character of Anglicanism, 370
Ethiopian deputies, 59
Eucharist, the, 133, 191, 299, 301
Eugenius IV., 56, 62, 75
Eusebius, *Chronicon* of, 84, 212
,, *Ecclesiastical History*, 94, 96, 148, 149, 174, 275, 307, 308, 312, 315
Eutychius, 40, 200
Exarchs, 316-17
Expositor, the, 179, 182

FABER, Dr., 341
Fagius, Peter, 366
Fairbairn's *Christ in Modern Theology*, 31
Falkland, Lord, 419
Falle's *Account of Jersey*, 392
Fields' *Book of the Church*, 408
Firmilian of Cæsarea, 247

Florence, Council of, 59
Fonseca, John, 24
Foreign ministers in the English Church, 410
,, Protestant Churches, 386
,, ,, Refugees, 387
Formularies of the Anglican Church, 360
Fortunatus of Carthage, 249
Foucart's *Les Associations Religieuses*, 215
Franciscans, the, 226
Frankowitsch, Matthias, *Catalogue of Witnesses*, 9
Fratres Arvales, 302
Frauds and forgeries, 334
Freeman's, Professor, *Historical Essays*, 8
Free Churches, the, and sacerdotalism, 443
French Archæological Mission, 13
,, Church in Southampton, 389
Froude, Hurrell, 19, 112
Froude's *Remains*, 385

GALICIA, 326
Gallician *Use*, the, 63
Gelasius, Pope, 287
Generidus, 279
Gieseler's *Ecclesiastical History*, 274, 347
Glaber, Rudolf, 349
Gladstone's *Church Principles*, 88
Gnostics, the 235, 296-300
Goch, John of, 22
Gore's, Canon, *Ministry of the Christian Church*, 31, 39, 45, 98, 114, 188
Goths, overthrow of the, 330
Gratian, Emperor, 273, 278, 283
Greek Church, reply of, 5
,, Mysteries, the 294-6
,, schools, 137
,, *Use*, the, 63
Gregory the Great, 54, 290, 292, 294-6, 328, 331, 333
Gregory II., 274
,, VII., 335, 347

Gregory the Illuminator, 75
,, Nazianzen, 263, 313
Gregorovius, *History of Rome*, 272, 330-2
Grindal, Archbishop, 376, 383, 389
Guizot's *History of Civilisation*, 276

HADDAN, A.W., 45, 87, 111, 112, 113
Hadleigh, meeting at, 435
Hales' *Golden Remains*, 417-18
Hall's *Episcopacy by Divine Right*, 414
Harnack, A., *Present State of Research*, 15
,, *Die Chronologie des Altchristlichen Litteratur*, 180-183
,, *History of Dogma*, 94, 175, 179, 182, 192, 277
Hammond, Dr., 377
Harrington's Apostolical Succession, 44
Harris, Professor Rendel, 14, 125
Hatch, Dr., *Bampton Lecture*, 152, 188, 214, 248, 280
,, *Hibbert Lecture*, 18, 137, 282, 294
Hatfield House MSS., 378
Hauran, Inscriptions in the, 203, 215
Hefele's *History of the Councils*, 74
Hegesippus, 84, 96, 148, 150, 202, 203, 211, 239
Henning, Just, 142
Henry, Philip, 411
Hermas, *Shepherd* of, 12, 84, 130 155, 159
Hessel's *Ecclesiæ Londino-Batavæ Archivum*, 391
Heylyn's *Cyprianus Anglicus*, 412, 414, 416
Hierapolis, temple at, 301
Himerius of Tarragona, 324
Hincmar of Rheims, 57, 335
Hippolytus' *Refutation of all Heresies*, 12, 206, 237, 243-4, 299
,, Canons of, 14, 55, 63

Historical methods, 15, 17
Hoadley's *Persuasive against the Nonjurors*, 430
Hodgkin, bishop of Bedford, 380
Hodgkin's *Italy and her Invaders*, 288, 330
Holland, Dr. 414
Holy Roman Church, 35
,,   ,,   Empire, 35
Home Reunion, 4
Honorius, 279, 329
,,   II., 344
Hooker, Richard, 404
Hooper's letter to Bullinger, 360
Homeric hymn, 296
Hort's *Christian Ecclesia*, 32, 49, 73, 110, 146, 147, 231, 264
House of Commons reform, 427
Huss, John, 9
Hutton, R.H., 439
Hyginus of Cordova, 283

IBERIAN deputies, 59
Idacius of Merida, 283
Ignatius, 171
Ignatian Epistles, 165-196
Illyrian bishops, 327
Immaculate Conception, dogma of, 342
Imperial Church, 268
Indulgences, 341
Innocent IV., 336
Inquisition, 282
Institution of a Christian Man, 361
Invasions of Rome, the five, 328
Irenæus, 26, 173, 309
,,   *Adv. Hæres.*, 82, 84, 143, 237-8, 240, 299
Irish Church Bill, 434
Irving, Edward, 208
Isis, festival of, 290
Isidore of Seville, 337
,,   forged decretals of, 337-9
Isidorus, 237

JACOBITES of Syria, 59
James and the Jerusalem Church

Jerome, 21, 85, 276, 289
,,   *Epistles of*, 41
,,   *de virib. illust.*, 85
Jerusalem Conference, the, 148
Jewish priesthood, the, 86, 92
Jewel's, Bishop, *Apology*, 384
,,   opinions, 383
,,   letter to Bullinger, 375
,,   controversy with Harding, 385
John of Goch, 22
,,   the Faster, 332
,,   of Wesel, 22
,,   VIII., 347
,,   XII., 348
,,   XXII., 343
Josephus, *Antiquities*, 95, 142
Jowett's *Plato*, 17
Julius I., 319
,,   II., 346
Justin Martyr, *Apology*, 69, 77, 158

KEBLE'S *Preface to Hooker*, 406
,,   *Assize Sermon*, 435
Ken, Bishop, 10
Killen, Dr., 177
King's Book, the, 364
Kitchin, bishop of Llandaff, 379
Kittel's *History of the Hebrews*, 224
Knollys, Sir Francis, 401
Krawutzcky, Dr., 127
Kühl, *Die Gemeindeordnung*, 215

LACTANTIUS, 293
Lambeth Conference, 4
Lamb's, Dr., *Historical Account of the Articles*, 374
Langen, 125
Lares, compitalian, 290
Laud, Archbishop, 412
Lay baptism, 19
Laynez, Father, 24
Laying on of hands, 65-75
Lechler, G. von, 177
,,   *Urkundenfunde*, 15
Leighton, Archbishop, 98
Lenormant *Eleusinian Mysteries*, 291

Leo I., bishop, 273, 323, 326, 328-9
,, VIII., 343
,, XIII., *Encyclicals*, 5, 6, 27
Leonine Sacramentary, the, 55
Le Quien, 42
Liberian Catalogue, 85
Liber Pontificalis, 85, 328
Liberius, 5
Liddon, Canon, *A Father in Christ*, 19
,, *Life of Dr. Pusey*, 111., 392, 431, 438-9
Lightfoot, Dr., 16, 83, 131, 169, 171, 175, 179, 180, 186, 191
,, *Apostolic Fathers*, 16, 83, 107
,, *Commentary on Galatians*, 92, 131
,, *Essay on the Christian Ministry*, 93, 222
Lipsius, *Apokr. Apostelgg.*, 299
Liutprand, 348
Local officers of Churches, 139
Loening, Dr. Edgar, *De Gemeindeverfassung*, 25, 194, 204, 215
Lombards, the, 331
Long Parliament, 419
Lucian's *De Morte Peregrini*, 135, 186
Lupercalia festival, 287
Luther, 9, 341
Lybia, 316, 318
Lyons and Vienne, Churches of, 123, 271, 281

MACAULAY'S *Essays*, 88
Magdeburg *Centuries*, 9, 339
Mainz Pontifical, 59
Magnesia, Church of, 172, 187
Magna Mater, festival of the, 290
Makower's *Die Verfassung*, 355
Marcion, 130, 236, 212
Marcosians, 299
Maronite deputies, 59
Maronite *Use*, 63
Martyr, Peter, 366-8
Maurus, Rabanus, 57
Mead's *Pistis Sophia*, 297
Mechitarist Monks of Venice, 13

Medicean recension, 169
Meletian Schism,
Milman's *Latin Christianity*, 263
Milton, John, 21, 167, 379
Minucius Felix, 293
Mirandola, siege of, 346
Mithras worship, 286
Montagu, Richard, 412
Montanists, the, 9, 246, 281
Morinus *de sacris Ordinationibus*, 43, 59, 60
Morton, Bishop, 414
Mosheim's *Commentaries*, 110
,, *Ecclesiastical History*, 109, 142
Mozley's *Reminiscences*, 432
Muratori's *Scriptores Rerum Italicarium*, 328
Mynoides Mynas, 12
Mysteries, the Greek, 294-6

NAPLES, superstition of, 290
Necessary Doctrine and Erudition, 364
Nestorian *Use*, 63
Newman's *Tracts for the Times*, 435
,, Secession to Rome, 439
Nicæa, Council of, 315-18
Nicomedia, 124, 213
Niebuhr, 11
Nicholas of Cusa, 339
,, I., 347
,, V., 343
Nonjurors, the, 430
Novatian, 251
Novatians, the, 259-60

OCHINUS, Bernard, 366
Official grace, 89
Olympius, Master of the Offices, 279
Orders mathematically computed, 88
Ordinal, the Edwardine, 56, 365, 369
Ordinals of the Latin Church, 60
Ordinatio, 54
Ordination Prayer, 64
Ordination, various forms of, 75
Ordo, origin of Orders, 53
Origen, 171, 173, 174, 236, 301
Otto of Friesing, *Chronicle* of, 344

Index

PANTÆNUS, 95
Papal Bull *Apostolicæ Curæ*, 6, 55, 61
,, *Exultate Deo*, 59
,, *Satis Cognitum*, 6
Papal Commission, 1896, 55
Papacy, development of, 305, 350
Papias *Fragments*, 123
Parker, Archbishop, 380
πάροικοι and κάτοικοι
Parkhurst, Bishop, 383
Paschasius, 58
Passionals, Latin, 14
Pastor's *History of the Popes*, 226
Patriarchates, 272, 317
Patriarchs of Constantinople, 5, 333
Pattison's *Tendencies of Religious Thought*, 428
Paulicians, the, 283–286
Pearson, Bishop, 25, 196
Pecock, Reginald, 336
Pelagius, Pope, 331
Pella, Christians at, 203
Pentapolis, 316, 318
Perpetua and Felicitas, Acts of, 14
Perry's *History of the Church of England*, 429
Peter the Apostle, 85, 311
Peterhouse Chapel, 413
Petrarch's *Letters*, 99
Philadelphia, the Church at, 172, 176, 189–90, 193
Philippi, the Church at, 152, 154, 173
Philippopolis, 322
Piedmont, valleys of, 350
Pilkington, Bishop, 383
Pistis Sophia, the, 296
Pius II., 347
,, IX., 342
Podesti Salon, 342
Polycarp, 102, 166, 180, 184, 201
Polycrates, 309
Pontificals of Exeter, Bangor, and Sarum, 60
Porphyrius, 299
Porrectio instrumentorum, 58

Prætextus, the Roman magistrate, 275
Prayer Book of 1549, 365
,, ,, 1552, 366
Presbyterianism in the Channel Islands, 392
Priesthood of Science and Art, 93
Primitive Usage, 8
Primus of Corinth, 211
προεστῶτες, 139, 153
προϊστάμενοι, 139, 153, 200
Priscillian of Avila, 283
Priscillianism, 260
Priscus, 288
Problem for the modern Church, 7
Proconsular Asia, bishops of, 188
Procopius, 288
Prophets, New Testament, 132, 225
Prudentius, 290
Prynne's *Canterbury's Doom*, 413, 416
Pupianus, letter of, 250

QUADRATUS, 95
Queen's bearing towards the bishops, the, 376
Queen's dispensing power, the, 375
Quignon's Breviary, Cardinal, 365
Quintus of Aggya, 247

RADBERT, Paschasius, 57
Ramsay, Professor, *Church in the Roman Empire*, 186, 216
,, *Cities and Bishoprics of Phrygia*, 151, 292
,, *Encycl. Brit.*, 294
,, *St. Paul the Traveller*, 71, 155
Ratherius of Verona, 57
Ratramnus, 58
Ravenna, bishops of, 328
Reader, the office of, 68
Reformation in England, 354
Reform Bill of 1831, 433
Renan's *Hibbert Lecture*, 11
Restoration, the, 421
Richard of Capua, 344

Ritschl, *Entstehung*, &c., 144
,, 142, 144, 183
Robert Guiscard, 347
Robert of Geneva, 346
Robinson, Professor J. Armitage, *Texts and Studies*, 15
,, *The Christian Prophets*, 220
Rogation, or gang week, 302
Roger of Sicily, 346
Rogers, Henry, *Essays*, 89
Roman decretals, 324
Romans, Epistle to the, 306
Roman (Leonine) *Use*, 63
,, Succession, 81
,, Sacramentary, 62
Rome, the Church in, 306-310
,, as the *Ecclesia principalis*, 311
Romulus Augustulus, 329
Rothe, Richard, 148
Routh's *Reliquiæ Sacræ*, 247
Rufinus' *Hist. Eccl. s.*, 318
Rufus, 181
Rushworth's *Historical Collections*, 419
Rymer's *Fœdera*, 410
Sabinianus, 332
St. Barbatus, 290
St. Sophia, Church of, 286
Sage's *Reasonableness of Toleration*, 87
Samothrace, Temple at, 301
San Clemente, Church of, 286
Sanderson, Bishop, 423
Saragossa, Council of, 283
Sardica, Council of, 321
Sardinia, 244, 290
Sarpi, Paolo, *History of the Council of Trent*, 23, 43
Sarum Missal, 365
Savoy Conference, 421
Scambler, Bishop, 382
Schism, the Great, 36, 343
Scottish Bishops, 402
Scythia, Churches in, 260
Secundinus of Carpi, 247
Selden, John, 42

Sergius the Paulician, 284
Seven of Acts vi., the, 142
Sharp, Archbishop, 430
Sibylline Books, 292
Simplicianus, 288
Siricius, 324-7, 337
Six Articles, the, 372
Smalkaldic League, 25
Smile's *Huguenots and their Settlements*, 388
Smith's *Vita Cosini*, 423
Smyrna, Church of, 172
Snape, Edward, 393
Socrates, *Hist. Eccl.*, 259
Sohm's *Kirchenrecht*, 311-12, 314, 321, 323
Soter of Rome, 212, 307, 310
Southampton, "God's House" in, 389
Southern Gaul, 326
Sozomen, *Hist. Eccl.*, 259
Sparta, Church at, 213
Spotswood's *History of the Church of Scotland*, 402
Stanley's *Christian Institutions*, 97
Stephen of Rome, 247, 308
Stillingfleet MSS., 392
,, *Irenicum*, 424
Strabo, 203
Strype's *Life of Cranmer*, 364, 366
Submission of the clergy, 373
Suburbicarian Churches, 318
Supremacy, Act of, 370
Surtees Society Publications, 423
Sylvester, Bishop of Rome, 319, 323, 336
Symeon, the son of Clopas, 146, 149, 203
Synagogue, place of, in Jewish life, 141
Syracuse, archbishop of, 342
Syriac Version of *Ignatian Epistles*, 12

TACITUS, 307
Tait, Archbishop, 443
Tarragona, 326
Tatian's *Diatessaron*, 13, 15

Index 463

Tattam, Archdeacon, 175
Taylor, Dr., 125
Teachers, 137
Temple, the, and the Christian Church, 202
Temporal Power, the, 331
Ten Articles of 1536, 360
Tertullian, *Adv. Marcion*, 130
,, *Apologia*, 159, 206, 232, 234
,, *De exhort Cast*, 53
,, *De Jejuniis*, 108
,, *De Præscriptione*, 241
,, *De Pudicitia*, 246
Test and Corporation Acts, 433
Tetzel, 341
Texte und Untersuchungen, 14
Theodosius I., 278, 324
Theophilus of Alexandria, 338
Thessalonians, Church of, 200
Tillotson, Archbishop, 4
Tischendorf, 12
Timothy's ordination, 67
Tolomeo of Lucca, 336
Tongues, Gift of, 208
Tracts for the Times, 19, 432, 435
Tractarian Movement, 431
Tralles, Church of, 172, 187, 189
Traver's *Supplication*, 407
Trajan, forum of, 289
Treaty of Berwick, 410
Trede's *Das Heidentum*, 342
Trent, Council of, 23, 43
Tubingen School, 122
Tuning the pulpits, 373
Tusculum, Counts of, 346, 348

Uncovenanted mercies, 114
Uniformity, Act of 1559, 378
Urban VI., 343
Ursicinus, 275
Ussher, Archbishop, 25, 174, 183

VALENS, Emperor, 278
Valens of Philippi, 102, 185
Valentine I., 278
Valentinian, 273, 299
,, III., 326-7

Valentinus, 235
Valerian persecution, 312
Valla, Lorenzo, 336
Vatican Gallery, 342
Vicarii, or Vice-præfects, 272
Vicarius Urbis, 318
Victor of Rome, 16, 179, 245, 309, 338,
Victor III., 349
Vigilius, 6
Villemain, M., 12
Virgin, worship of the, 341
Vitringa, *De Synag. Vet.*, 142
Völter, *De ignat. Briefe*, 171
Voss, Isaac, 175, 183
Vossian Recension, 169

WADDINGTON's *Syrian Inscriptions*, 152, 203, 215
Wake's, Archbishop, *Correspondence*, 429
Wakeman's *History of the Church of England*, 365-6
Waldenses, the, 260, 282
Walloon Church in London, the, 389
Wall's *Infant Baptism*, 430
Weizäcker's *Apostolic Age*, 111
Wesel, John of, 22
Westcott's, Bishop, *Gospel of St. John*, 46
Whitgift, Archbishop, 401. 404
Wickliff, John, 9, 174
Wideford, William de, 174
Wieseler, 179
Wiseman's *Lectures*, Cardinal, 340

XYSTUS of Rome, 16

YORK, Archbishop of, *Sermon in Westminster Abbey*, 268

ZAHN, 125, 182
Zephyrinus, 242-4, 310
Zosimus, 6, 181, 322
,, *History of the Roman Emperors*, 279, 288
Zurich Letters, 360, 375, 379, 383

Congregational Union of England & Wales.

THE CONGREGATIONAL UNION LECTURE.

THE INSPIRATION OF THE OLD TESTAMENT INDUC-
TIVELY CONSIDERED. By ALFRED CAVE, B.A., D.D., Principal of Hackney
College. Being the Seventh Congregational Union Lecture. Demy 8vo 10s. 6d.
Second Edition. Crown 8vo, 4s. net.

JOHN THE BAPTIST: a Contribution to Christian Evidences.
By HENRY ROBERT REYNOLDS, D.D., President of Cheshunt College. Third
Edition. Crown 8vo, 4s. net.

BICENTENARY OF 1688. Bicentenary Lectures. In connection
with the Congregational Union of England and Wales. Contributors: Principal
Fairbairn, M.A., D.D., J. Guinness Rogers, B.A., D.D., J. Carvell Williams, M.P.,
Alex. Mackennal, B.A., D.D., Chas. A. Berry, D.D. Crown 8vo, 3s. 9d. net. cloth.

THE ATONEMENT. By R. W. DALE, M.A., LL.D., Birmingham.
Nineteenth Edition. Crown 8vo, 4s. net.

PRIESTHOOD, IN THE LIGHT OF THE NEW TESTA-
MENT. By the late E. E. MELLOR, D.D., Halifax. Demy 8vo, 5s. net ; Third
Edition, Crown 8vo, 3s. net.

THE BASIS OF FAITH. By the late E. R. CONDER, M.A., D.D.,
Leeds. Second Edition. Crown 8vo, cloth, 3s. net.

CHURCH SYSTEMS OF ENGLAND IN THE NINE-
TEENTH CENTURY. By J. GUINNESS ROGERS, B.A., D.D. Demy 8vo, cloth,
5s. net. Second Edition, Crown 8vo, 4s. net.

JUBILEE LECTURES. An Historical Series delivered on the
occasion of the Jubilee of the Congregational Union of England and Wales. With
an Introductory Chapter by Principal A. M. Fairbairn, D.D. CHEAP EDITION,
Two Vols. in one, 8vo, cloth, 3s. net. Contributors : R. W. Dale, M.A., LL.D., H.
Allon, D.D., J. Stoughton, D.D., E. R. Conder, D.D., J. Kennedy, D.D., S. Pearson,
M.A., J. Baldwin Brown, B.A., A. Mackennal, B.A., D.D., E. White, J. Guinness
Rogers, B.A., D.D., H. Richard, M.P.

THE CONGREGATIONAL HANDBOOK, being a Guide to
the Administration of a Congregational Church. By J. BAINTON. Cloth, 2s.

MANUAL OF CONGREGATIONAL CHURCH PRINCI-
PLES. By R. W. DALE, M.A., LL.D. Seventh Edition. Crown 8vo, cloth, 1s. 6d.

CONGREGATIONAL CHURCH POLITY. By R. W. DALE,
M.A., LL.D. Crown 8vo, cloth, 1s. 3d.

THE REVOLUTION OF 1688 IN ITS BEARINGS ON
PROTESTANT NONCONFORMITY. By J. Stoughton, D.D. Paper wrapper,
6d., cloth, 8d.

HANDBOOK TO GUILDS. By F. HERBERT STEAD, M.A., F'cap
8vo, limp cloth, 8d. post free.

HISTORY OF CONGREGATIONALISM. By J. KNAGGS.
Part I.—From the Apostolic Age to the Present Times. Crown 8vo, 64 pp., 4d. net.
Part II. From the Formation of the Congregational Union to 1862. Crown 8vo,
72 pp., 4d. net.

A PRIMER OF CONGREGATIONALISM. By ALBERT
GOODRICH, D.D. Price 6d. net. Postage, 1½d. extra.

PROTESTANTISM, ITS ULTIMATE PRINCIPLE. By R.
W. DALE, M.A., LL.D. Price 6d. net. Postage 1d. extra.

CHRISTIAN BAPTISM, as usually practised in Congregational
Churches. An Exposition and Defence. Introductory Note by G. S. BARRETT,
D.D. Demy 16mo, 112 pp. Price 6d. net. Postage, 1d. extra.

THE PILGRIM FATHERS OF NEW ENGLAND, and their
Puritan Successors. Second Edition, complete with all original Illustrations by
Charles Whymper. 5s. By Jno. Brown, D.D.

THE EARLY CHRISTIANS. The Story of Christianity during
the first three centuries. By WALTER F. ADENEY, M.A. (In preparation.)

All orders and inquiries sent by post will receive prompt attention.

www.ingramcontent.com/pod-product-compliance
Lightning Source LLC
Chambersburg PA
CBHW051852300426
44117CB00006B/365